LETTERS ON A LIFE OF VIRTUE

A MODERN ADAPTATION OF SENECA'S LETTERS TO LUCILIUS

LUCIUS ANNAEUS SENECA

Translated by
FILIBOOKS TRANSLATION

FILIBOOKS.COM

Cover by: Filibooks Covers

Published by: Filibooks Classics

Filibooks ApS

info@filibooks.com

CVR: 37100161

~

©Filibooks 2024

Original work by Seneca is in the public domain

Paperback ISBN: 978-87-94559-29-4
Ebook ISBN: 978-87-94559-30-0

CONTENTS

FOREWORD

Seneca's "Letters to Lucilius" stands as a seminal work in the canon of Stoic philosophy, offering a profound and enduring exploration of the human condition. This modern adaptation, aptly titled "Letters on a Life of Virtue," not only breathes new life into Seneca's timeless wisdom but also underscores the critical importance of engaging with classical texts in our contemporary era.

The structure of this adaptation, with each letter carefully titled to reflect its central theme, provides a compelling framework for navigating the complexities of Seneca's thought. By illuminating the core ideas that underpin each epistle, this approach allows readers to grasp the essential teachings of Stoicism with unparalleled clarity and coherence.

At its heart, Seneca's philosophy is concerned with the perennial questions that have haunted humanity since the dawn of civilization: What constitutes a life well-lived? How can we attain true happiness and fulfillment? What is the role of virtue in human flourishing? Through his correspondence with Lucilius, Seneca grapples with these questions, offering insights that are at once deeply personal and universally resonant.

One of the most striking aspects of Seneca's thought is his

emphasis on the practical application of philosophical principles. Far from being an abstract intellectual exercise, Stoicism, as articulated in these letters, is a way of life, a framework for navigating the challenges and vicissitudes of human existence. By grounding his insights in concrete examples and lived experience, Seneca demonstrates the transformative power of philosophy to shape our attitudes, actions, and ultimately, our destinies.

The relevance of Seneca's teachings to our modern age cannot be overstated. In a world marked by rapid change, uncertainty, and moral ambiguity, the Stoic virtues of resilience, integrity, and self-mastery offer a powerful antidote to the ennui and despair that so often characterize contemporary life. By engaging with Seneca's ideas, we are challenged to examine our own lives with unflinching honesty, to confront our fears and limitations, and to cultivate the inner strength and clarity of purpose that are essential for navigating the complexities of the human experience.

For scholars of classical philosophy, this adaptation represents a significant contribution to the field, shedding new light on the enduring relevance of Stoic thought. By presenting Seneca's ideas in a fresh and accessible format, "Letters on a Life of Virtue" opens up new avenues for exploration and interpretation, inviting readers to engage with the text on a deeper level and to consider its implications for our understanding of the human condition.

At the same time, the impact of this work extends far beyond the realm of academia. By distilling the essence of Seneca's wisdom and presenting it in a language that speaks directly to the concerns and aspirations of modern readers, this adaptation serves as a powerful tool for personal growth and transformation. Whether one is seeking to cultivate greater resilience in the face of adversity, to find meaning and purpose in a world that often seems chaotic and uncertain, or simply to live a life of greater authenticity and integrity, Seneca's teachings offer a roadmap for the journey ahead.

Ultimately, "Letters on a Life of Virtue" is a testament to the enduring power of philosophical reflection to illuminate the human experience. By engaging with Seneca's ideas, we are invited to participate in a timeless conversation about what it means to live a life of purpose and fulfillment, to grapple with the fundamental questions that have preoccupied humanity for millennia, and to emerge with a deeper understanding of ourselves and our place in the world.

As we embark on this journey of self-discovery and transformation, let us draw strength and inspiration from the wisdom of the ancients, and let us embrace the challenge of living a life that is truly meaningful, authentic, and whole. In doing so, we will not only honor the enduring legacy of Seneca and the Stoic tradition but also contribute to the ongoing quest for wisdom and understanding that lies at the heart of the human experience.

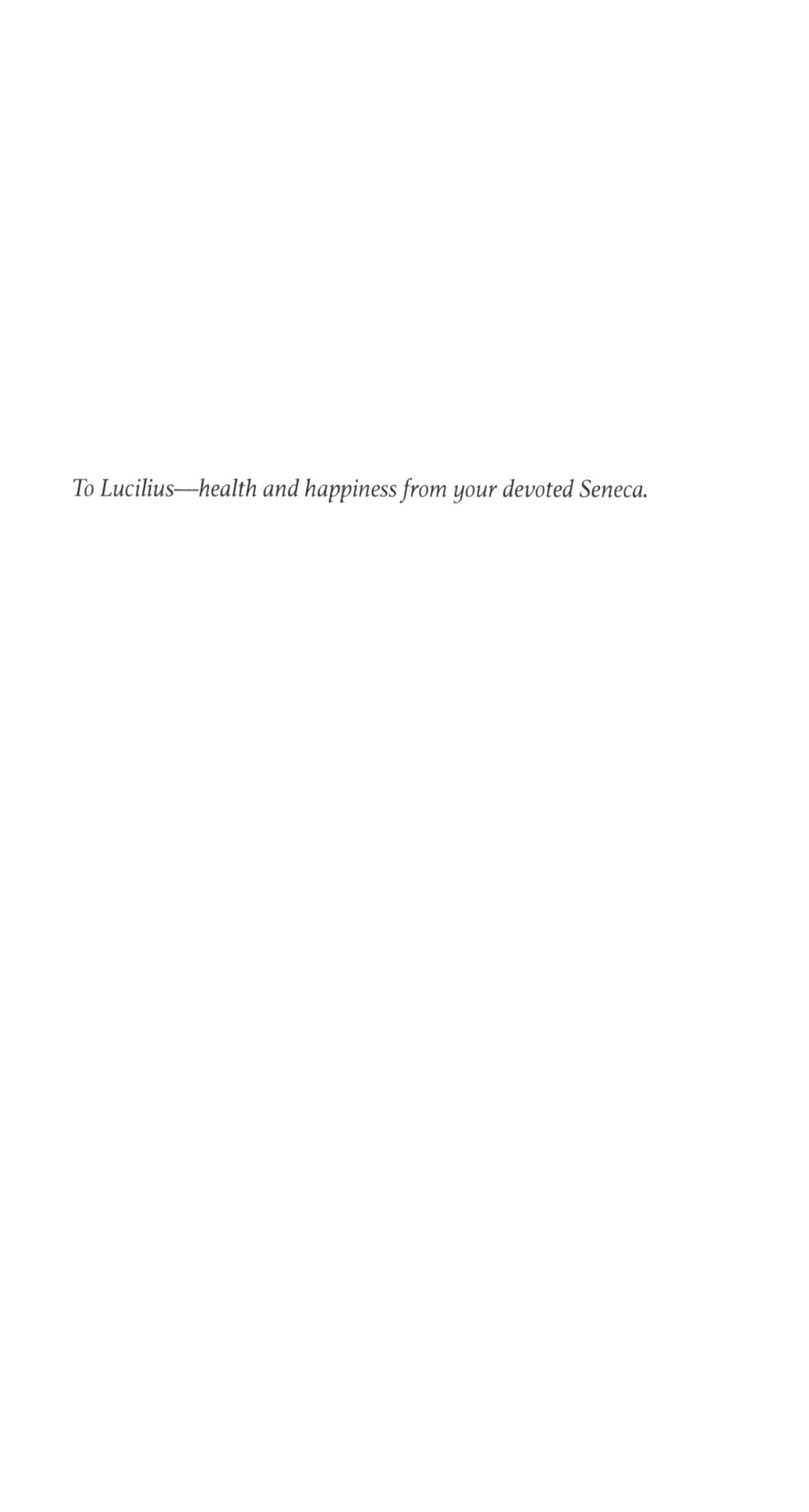

To Lucilius—health and happiness from your devoted Seneca.

LETTER 1

ON SAVING TIME AND VALUING LIFE'S FLEETING NATURE

[1] MY DEAR LUCILIUS, YOU MUST CLAIM YOURSELF FOR YOURSELF. Gather up and save all the time that until now has been either taken from you, stolen away, or has simply slipped through your fingers. Convince yourself that what I write is true: certain moments are torn from us, some gently pulled away, and others glide beyond our reach. The most disgraceful loss, though, is that due to carelessness. If you pay close attention, you'll see that the largest portion of life escapes those who do evil, a great portion those who do nothing, and a lifetime those who do anything other than what they should.

[2] Who can you show me that places any value on their time, that reckons the worth of each day, that understands that they are dying daily? We are deceived because we look ahead to death; a large part of death has already passed. All the years behind us now belong to death.

Therefore, my dear Lucilius, do as you write that you are doing: embrace all your hours. In doing so, you will depend less upon tomorrow if you seize hold of today. While we procrastinate, life speeds by.

[3] Lucilius, all things are foreign to us; time alone is ours. Nature has granted us ownership of this single, fleeting, slippery thing, from

which anyone who wishes can oust us. The folly of mortals is so great that they allow the smallest, most worthless things - certainly replaceable things - to be charged to their accounts after they have acquired them; yet no one thinks they owe anything for time that they have received. This is the one loan that even a grateful recipient cannot repay.

[4] You may wonder, perhaps, what I do, who preach these things to you. I will honestly confess: as happens with a spendthrift but diligent person, I keep a record of my expenditures. I cannot claim that I lose nothing, but I can tell you what I lose, why, and how - I will give an account of the causes of my poverty. But it happens to me as to many who have been reduced to destitution through no fault of their own: everyone forgives but no one comes to their aid.

[5] What then is the case? I do not consider poor the person who, however little they have, finds it sufficient. Nevertheless, I would prefer that you keep what is yours, and begin in good time. For, as our ancestors believed, it is too late to spare when you reach the dregs of the cask. Of that which remains at the bottom, not only is there little, but it is also of inferior quality. Farewell.

LETTER 2

THE DANGERS OF ASSOCIATION WITH THE CROWD AND FOCUSING THE MIND

[1] FROM WHAT YOU WRITE TO ME, AND FROM WHAT I HEAR, I AM forming a good opinion of you. You do not wander about nor are you unsettled by changing your abode. Such unsteadiness is symptomatic of a disordered spirit. The first proof of a well-ordered mind, I believe, is the ability to remain in one place and linger with oneself.

[2] Be careful, however, that your habit of reading many authors and books of every sort does not possess a certain wandering and unstable quality. You should linger over and dwell upon selected intellects if you wish to derive something that will reliably settle in your mind. Nowhere is he who is everywhere. This mishap occurs to those who pass their life in foreign travel - they have many lodgings, but no friendships. The same must necessarily happen to those who do not intimately attach themselves to the intellect of any one great man, but let everything pass them by in a rush and a hurry.

[3] Food does no good and is not assimilated into the body if it is immediately expelled after being consumed. Nothing hinders good health so much as frequent changes of treatment. No wound will heal if various salves are tried on it. No plant grows strong if it is often transplanted. Nothing is so efficacious that it can be helpful in passing. A multitude of books distracts the mind.

[4] Therefore, since you cannot read all the books you possess, it is enough to possess only as many as you can read. "But," you reply, "I would rather unroll this book now, now that one." It is a fastidious stomach that tastes many dishes, which, when various and diverse, do not nourish but cloy. So you should always read tested authors, and when you desire to turn to others, return to those you have read before. Each day acquire something to fortify you against poverty, against death, and against other misfortunes. And after you have surveyed many thoughts, select one to digest that day.

[5] This is my own custom. From the many things I have read, I claim some one part for myself. The thought I acquired today was this, which I discovered in Epicurus - for I am in the habit of crossing even into the enemy's camp, not as a deserter, but as a scout.

[6] "Cheerful poverty," he says, "is an honorable state." Indeed, that is not poverty at all if it is cheerful. It is not the man who has little, but the man who craves more, that is poor. What does it matter how much lies in a man's safe or in his barns, how many head of stock he grazes or how much capital he puts out at interest, if he is always coveting his neighbor's property, reckoning not his past gains but his hopes for gaining more? Do you ask what is the proper limit to wealth? It is, first, to have what is necessary, and second, to have what is enough. Farewell.

LETTER 3

TRUE FRIENDSHIP AND SHARING ALL WITH A FRIEND

[1] YOU ENTRUSTED THE LETTERS MEANT FOR ME TO YOUR FRIEND, AS you write, and then you warn me not to share everything pertaining to you with him, because you say you do not usually do so yourself. Thus, in the same letter you have both called him a friend and denied it. So if you have used that word in a general sense, as one does in public, and have called him a friend in the way we call all candidates "good men" or the way we greet anyone we meet as "sir" if their name does not come readily to mind, then let it pass.

[2] But if you consider someone a true friend, to whom you do not entrust as much as you do to yourself, you are gravely mistaken and do not sufficiently understand the power of genuine friendship. In truth, you should share all your deliberations with a friend, but first deliberate about the friend himself. After establishing the friendship, there must be trust; before the friendship, there must be judgment. Those who mix up these duties put the cart before the horse, judging a person after they have grown fond of them, contrary to the teachings of Theophrastus[1], and not growing fond only after they have judged them. Ponder for a long time whether you should admit someone into your friendship. When you have decided to do so,

welcome him with all your heart, and speak as boldly with him as you would with yourself.

[3] As for you, live your life in such a way that you trust yourself with nothing which you could not entrust even to your enemy. But since certain matters arise that convention has caused to be considered secrets, share all your worries and thoughts with your friend. If you consider him faithful, you will make him so. For some have taught men to deceive by fearing to be deceived, and have given them the right to do wrong by suspecting them. Why should I hold back any words in the presence of my friend? Why should I not feel alone when in his company?

[4] Some people tell casual acquaintances what should only be confided to friends, unburdening whatever troubles them into any ears they find. Others, in turn, dread even the knowledge of their dearest friends, and if possible, would not trust even themselves, pushing every secret deep inside. Neither course should be followed. For both are faults—to trust everyone and to trust no one. But the former I would call a more honorable fault, the latter a safer one. So you may blame both—those who are always uneasy and those who are always at rest.

[5] The former state, forever delighting in commotion, is not industriousness but the restlessness of a disturbed mind. The latter is not true tranquility that judges every motion a nuisance, but rather a lazy languor.

[6] Therefore, take to heart this maxim which I found in Pomponius[2]: "Some have retreated so far into obscurity that they see everything in the light of day as suspicious." These two qualities must be blended—the man at leisure must act and the man of action must take repose. Consult nature; she will tell you that she created both day and night. Farewell.

---

1. Theophrastus was a Greek philosopher and successor to Aristotle as head of the Lyceum
2. Pomponius Secundus was a Roman historian, public official, and dramatist.

LETTER 4

PHILOSOPHIZING IN PREPARATION FOR DEATH

[1] STAY THE COURSE YOU HAVE BEGUN, MY DEAR LUCILIUS, AND HASTEN forward with all your might, so that you may delight in your renewed and composed mind for longer. Even now as you refine and arrange yourself you are finding enjoyment; yet a different pleasure entirely is felt when contemplating a mind cleansed of every blemish and radiating splendor.

[2] Surely you remember the immense joy you felt when, setting aside the bordered toga [of youth], you donned the toga virilis and were escorted to the forum. Anticipate an even greater joy when you cast off your childish spirit and philosophy enrolls you among men. For it is not childhood that still clings to us, but something worse - childishness. And the problem is compounded by our having the authority of the elderly while retaining the faults of the young - no, not even of youths, but of infants. The young fear trifles, infants fear illusions; we fear both.

[3] Just make progress, and you will understand that some things are less to be dreaded precisely because they terrify us greatly. No evil is great which is the last evil. Death approaches you; it would be fearsome if it could remain with you, but it must either not arrive or else pass on.

[4] "It is difficult," you say, "to bring the mind to a point where it can scorn life." But do you not see how life is scorned for the most trivial reasons? One man hangs himself before his mistress' door; another hurls himself from the roof that he may no longer endure his master's harangues; a third, to escape being brought back to bondage, plunges a blade into his gut. Do you doubt that virtue will be as efficacious as excessive fear? No one can enjoy a peaceful life who thinks too much about prolonging it, counting many consulships among life's great blessings.

[5] Meditate daily on leaving life behind with contentment - a life that many cling to and cling to as men caught in a rushing torrent grasp at brambles and sharp rocks. Most poor wretches vacillate between the fear of death and the hardships of life; they are unwilling to live, yet do not know how to die.

[6] So make your life joyous by laying aside all worry over it. No good thing benefits its possessor unless his mind is prepared to relinquish it; and nothing is easier to relinquish than that which, once lost, cannot be missed. Therefore, steel and harden yourself against those blows of fate that can strike even the mightiest among us.

[7] A ward and a eunuch pronounced sentence on Pompey's head; a cruel and insolent Parthian passed judgment on Crassus. Gaius Caesar ordered Lepidus to offer his neck to the Tribune Dexter - and then offered his own neck to Chaerea. No one has been so exalted by Fortune that she did not threaten him as greatly as she had previously indulged him. Do not trust tranquility; in a moment the sea turns rough. On the very day that ships have frolicked, they are swallowed up.

[8] Consider this: a robber or an enemy could put a sword to your throat. Even if a greater power is absent, any slave holds the power of life and death over you. Let me tell you this: whoever has contempt for their own life is master of yours. Recall the examples of those who perished by domestic treachery, either by open violence or deceit; you will realize that no fewer have fallen by the wrath of slaves than by that of kings. So what does it matter how powerful the one you fear is, when the very thing you fear is something anyone can do?

[9] But if by chance you fall into the hands of the enemy, the victor will command you to be led away—to that place, no doubt, where you are already being led. Why do you deceive yourself and only now understand what you have long endured? I tell you this: from the moment you were born, you are being led away. These and similar thoughts must be pondered if we wish to await that final hour peacefully, the fear of which makes all other hours troubled.

[10] But to conclude this letter, hear what pleased me today. This too is taken from another's garden: "Great riches are poverty composed by the law of nature." But do you know what limits that law of nature sets for us? Not to hunger, not to thirst, not to be cold. To banish hunger and thirst, there is no need to sit at the doorsteps of the haughty, nor to endure a heavy brow and insulting benevolence. There is no need to dare the perils of the sea or follow the camp; what nature requires is easily obtained and close at hand.

[11] It is for superfluities that we sweat. These are the things that wear out the toga, that compel us to grow old in a tent, that dash us upon foreign shores. What suffices is readily available. He with whom poverty is on good terms is rich. Farewell.

LETTER 5

AVOIDING THE CROWD AND DEVOTING ONESELF TO STUDY

[1] Your persistent studies and single-minded dedication to daily self-improvement win my approval and delight. I not only urge you to continue, but implore you to do so. However, I must warn you: don't be like those who crave recognition rather than progress, doing things that call attention to your appearance or way of life.

[2] Avoid a harsh demeanor, unkempt hair, a carelessly groomed beard, a conspicuous disdain for silver, sleeping on the ground, and any other misguided means of pursuing ambition[1]. The very name of philosophy, even if practiced modestly, is off-putting enough. What if we start to withdraw from the customs of society? Let our interior be different, but our exterior align with the crowd.

[3] Our togas needn't glitter, but they shouldn't be filthy either. We may forgo silver engraved with solid gold, but lacking gold and silver is no proof of frugality. Let us strive to live better than the masses, not in opposition to them; otherwise we repel and alienate the very people we wish to reform. We also cause our followers to shun imitation, fearing they must imitate us in everything.

[4] Philosophy's foremost promise is a sense of fellowship, humanity, and community. Obvious deviation separates us from this profession. Beware lest the means by which we seek admiration

become ridiculous and loathsome. Our goal is to live according to nature; it's unnatural to torment one's body, abhor basic hygiene, court squalor, and eat food that's not just cheap but foul and unappetizing.

[5] Craving luxuries is decadent, but shunning the commonplace and affordable is madness. Philosophy demands frugality, not penance; frugality need not mean shabbiness. Here is the standard I propose: let our lives be a balance between good morals and social norms. Let everyone respect our way of life, but recognize it as well.

[6] "What then?" you ask. "Shall we act like everyone else? Will nothing distinguish us from them?" A great deal. The discerning observer will know we are different. Let visitors marvel more at us than at our furnishings. The person who uses earthenware like silver is great; no less great is the one who uses silver like earthenware. Inability to tolerate wealth betrays a weak spirit.

[7] But to share with you the small profit of this day as well, I discovered in our friend Hecato that the end of desires also serves as a remedy for fears. "You will cease to fear," he says, "if you cease to hope." You may wonder, "How can things so different go together?" But indeed, my dear Lucilius, though they seem to be at odds, they are in fact linked. Just as the same chain binds both the prison guard and the soldier, so these emotions, though quite dissimilar, march in unison; fear follows hope. I am not surprised that they proceed in this way; both belong to a mind in suspense, both are troubled by the anticipation of the future.

[8] The main cause of both is that we do not adapt ourselves to the present, but instead send our thoughts far ahead. Thus foresight, the greatest blessing of the human condition, has been turned into a curse.

[9] Wild beasts flee from the dangers they see, and once they have escaped, they are free from care; but we are tormented both by the future and the past. Many of our blessings bring us harm, for memory recalls the agony of fear, while foresight anticipates it. No one is wretched only in the present moment. Farewell.

---

1. The manuscripts have "ambitionem perversa" but Gertz emends to "ambitio nempe perversa".

LETTER 6
RETIRING INTO PHILOSOPHY AND SHUNNING AMBITION

[1] Lucilius, I understand that I am not merely being reformed, but transformed. Yet I do not promise or hope that no flaws remain to be changed in me. Undoubtedly many things in myself still need to be restrained, reduced, or elevated. Indeed, the very fact that I now perceive faults in myself which I was previously ignorant of is proof that my soul has changed for the better. For certain sick people, the mere recognition of their illness is cause for congratulation.

[2] How I wish, then, that I could share with you this sudden transformation in myself. Then I would begin to have more certain confidence in our friendship—that true kind which no hope, no fear, no concern for personal gain can sever; the kind with which men die and for which men die.

[3] I will give you many examples of those who lost not a friend, but friendship itself. This cannot happen when an equal willingness to pursue virtue draws souls into fellowship. Why should it not be possible? For they know that they hold all things in common, especially adversities.

You cannot conceive what progress I see myself making each day. [4] "Share with us," you say, "these precepts you have found so effectual." Indeed, I desire nothing more than to transfer every lesson to you, and I rejoice to learn in part so that I may teach. No knowledge will delight me, however excellent and beneficial, if I must keep it to myself. If wisdom were offered to me on the condition that I keep it shut away and not divulge it, I would refuse. There is no enjoying the possession of anything valuable unless one has someone to share it with.

[5] Therefore, I will send you the books themselves. To spare you scouring through them for the useful parts, I will mark the passages so you can turn at once to those which I approve and admire. Yet conversing in person will benefit you more than reading. You really must visit me to experience the lessons firsthand. Firstly, because people trust their eyes more than their ears. Secondly, because the road is long if traveled by precepts but short and effectual if by example.

[6] Cleanthes would not have so perfectly embodied Zeno if he had merely heard his lectures. He shared in his life, examined his hidden thoughts, and watched to see if Zeno lived according to his own principles. Plato, Aristotle, and the whole throng of sages destined to follow divergent paths drew more from Socrates' conduct than from his words. It was not the school of Epicurus, but living together with him, that made great men of Metrodorus, Hermarchus, and Polyaenus. So I summon you not merely to benefit yourself, but to benefit me. We shall be of the utmost assistance to each other.

[7] Meanwhile, since I owe you your daily allowance [of wisdom], let me share with you what delighted me today in Hecato. "You ask," he says, "what progress I have made? I have begun to be a friend to myself." He has indeed made great progress; he will never be alone. Know that such a person is a friend to all. Farewell.

LETTER 7

ON CROWDS, EXILE, AND
THE STOIC IDEAL

[1] You ask what I believe you should especially avoid? The crowd. You are not yet ready to trust yourself to them safely. I will certainly confess my own weakness: I never bring home the same character that I took out with me. Something of what I have put in order within myself becomes disturbed; some of the things I have banished return. The same thing happens to those who are recovering from a long illness and have been affected by it to the point that they can go nowhere without discomfort. This is what happens to us, whose souls are recovering from a long sickness.

[2] Associating with the crowd is harmful, for there is no one who does not stamp some fault upon us, or impart one to us, or taint us unconsciously. Certainly, the larger the crowd with which we mingle, the greater the danger.

But nothing is so damaging to good character as sitting idly at some spectacle. For then, vices more easily steal upon one through the avenue of pleasure.

[3] What do you think I am saying? That I come home greedier, more ambitious, more self-indulgent - even crueler and more inhumane - because I have been among humans. By chance, I turned into the midday spectacle, expecting games and wit and some relaxation

to rest men's eyes from the sight of human blood. But it was quite the contrary. Whatever fights had come before were acts of mercy in comparison. Now, setting frivolities aside, it is pure murder. The men have no protection; their entire bodies are exposed to the blows; no stroke falls in vain.

[4] Many spectators prefer this to the ordinary pairings and special matches. Of course they do - no helmet or shield repels the blade. What is the need for armor? What use is skill? All these merely postpone death. In the morning, men are thrown to lions and bears; at midday, to the spectators. The killers are ordered to kill those who will kill them; and the victor is detained for another slaughter. The outcome for the combatants is death; the fight is waged with sword and fire. This goes on while the arena is empty.

[5] "But he was a criminal, and had killed a man!" What of it? Granted that he deserved to suffer this punishment, what crime have you committed, poor fellow, that you should deserve to watch it? "Kill him! Beat him! Burn him! Why does he run upon the blade so timidly? Why does he not kill more boldly? Why does he not die more readily? Let him be driven by blows into wounds, to receive the mutual thrusts with bared and opposing breasts." The show is interrupted: "Meanwhile, let men be butchered, so that nothing is left undone."

Well now, do you not even understand this - that such evil examples rebound upon those who set them? Give thanks to the immortal gods that you are teaching cruelty to a man who cannot learn to be cruel.

[6] The young character, which cannot hold fast to righteousness, must be rescued from the mob; it is too easy to go over to the majority. Even a Socrates, a Cato or a Laelius might have had their principles shaken by a crowd that was unlike them; so true it is that none of us, even as we perfect our character, can endure the onslaught of vices when they come with such a mighty retinue.

[7] A single example of excess or greed does much harm; a luxurious companion gradually weakens and softens you, a wealthy neighbor provokes envy, a malicious comrade rubs his own rust onto

even the most pure and simple. What then do you think happens to one's character when assaulted by the public at large? You must either imitate or loathe them.

[8] But both must be avoided; do not become like the wicked because they are many, nor be hostile to the many because they are unlike you. Withdraw into yourself, as much as you can. Associate with those who will make you a better man. Welcome those whom you yourself can improve. These things are mutually beneficial, for men learn while they teach.

[9] There is no need for the desire to publicize your talents to draw you out before the crowd, to make you want to give readings or engage in debates—which I would encourage if you had goods suited for that mob. But there is no one there who can understand you. Perhaps one or two individuals will come your way, and even they will need to be molded and trained by you to comprehend your meaning. "For whom, then, did I learn all this?" Don't worry that you've wasted your efforts; it was for yourself that you learned.

[10] But so that I do not learn solely for myself today, I will share with you three excellently expressed ideas I encountered that bear on our theme. One this letter will discharge as a debt; the other two accept as an advance. Democritus says: "One man means to me as much as a multitude, and a multitude only as much as one man."

[11] Admirable also was the reply of the man (whose identity is debated) who, when asked why he devoted so much diligence to an art that would reach very few, said: "A few are enough for me; one is enough; none is enough." Most excellently put was this third remark by Epicurus, writing to one of his fellow scholars: "I write this not for the many, but for you; for each of us is audience enough for the other."

[12] Engrave these things in your mind, Lucilius, that you may scorn the pleasure that comes from the applause of the majority. Many men praise you. But have you really any reason for being pleased with yourself, if you are a person whom the many can understand? Let your good qualities face inward. Farewell.

LETTER 8

THE EQUANIMITY OF
THE SAGE

[1] "You tell me," you say, "to avoid the crowd, to withdraw and be content with my own conscience? Where are those precepts of yours that command us to die in action?" Well, what I now urge upon you is precisely this—I have secluded myself and shut the door, so that I may be of greater service to more people. Not a single day passes for me in idleness. I claim a portion of the nights for my studies. I do not yield myself to sleep, but rather succumb to it, struggling to keep my weary, drooping eyes at their task.

[2] I have withdrawn not only from men, but from affairs, especially from my own affairs. I am working for later generations, writing down some ideas that may be of assistance to them. I am committing to writing healthful admonitions, like a useful prescription of medicines, having found them effective in ministering to my own sores, which, if not wholly healed, have at least ceased to spread.

[3] I point out to others the right path, which I have found late in life, when wearied with wandering. I cry out to them: "Avoid whatever pleases the throng! Avoid the gifts of Chance! Halt before every good which Chance brings to you, in a spirit of doubt and fear; for it is the dumb animals and fish that are deceived by tempting hopes. Do you think these are the real goods, the things Fortune bestows? They

are snares. And none of you who desire to live a life of safety will ever fall for them—as we clutch at them and think we have them in our grasp, we are caught.

[4] That track leads us to precipices; the end of such a rising career is a fall. Moreover, we cannot even stand up against prosperity when it begins to drive us to leeward; nor can we go down, either, 'with the ship at least on her course,' or once for all; Fortune does not capsize us, but merely tosses us about and bumps us.

[5] So hold fast, then, to this sound and wholesome way of life; indulge the body just so far as suffices for good health. It needs to be treated somewhat strictly, to prevent it from being disobedient to the mind. Let your food appease your hunger, your drink quench your thirst, your clothing keep out the cold, your house be a protection against inclement weather. It makes no difference whether it is built of turf or of variegated marble imported from another country; what you have to understand is that thatch makes a person just as good a roof as gold. Despise everything that useless toil creates as an ornament and a decoration. Reflect that nothing except the soul is worthy of admiration, for to the soul, if it be great, naught is great."

[6] When I commune with myself in such terms, and with future generations, do you not think that I am doing more good than when I appear as counsel in court, or stamp my seal upon a will, or lend my assistance in the senate, by word or action, to a candidate? Believe me, those who seem to be busied with nothing are busied with the greater tasks; they are dealing at the same time with things mortal and things immortal.

[7] But now I must bring this letter to a close and, as is my custom, pay out something in return for it. This will not come from my own pocket; I am still unrolling Epicurus, from whom I read this saying today: "You must be a slave to philosophy in order to attain true freedom." There is no postponement for one who subjects and surrenders himself to her; he is emancipated on the spot. For the very service of philosophy is freedom.

[8] You may wonder why I quote so many fine sayings from Epicurus rather than from our own school. But why should you

regard them as sayings of Epicurus and not common property? How many poets say things which have been said, or ought to be said, by philosophers! Not to mention the tragedians or our native comedy[1]— for these also have a serious element and stand halfway between comedy and tragedy. What a quantity of highly eloquent verses are buried in the mime! How many of Publilius'[2] lines are worthy of being spoken not by barefooted comic actors, but by tragedians in their buskins!

[9] I shall quote one of his verses which concerns philosophy and the part of it which we were just discussing, wherein he says that the gifts of chance are not to be regarded as part of our possessions:

Whatever comes by chance is foreign to us.

[10] I recall that you yourself expressed this thought far better and more concisely:

What Fortune has made yours is not your own.

And I shall not omit another fine saying of yours, even better than the last:

The good that could be given can be removed.

I am not charging this up to my account; I have given you back what was yours.

---

1. The "fabula togata" or "togata" was a genre of Latin comedy that dealt with Roman subject matter and featured Roman characters, in contrast to the "fabula palliata" which was adapted from Greek New Comedy.
2. Publilius Syrus was a Latin writer of mimes, celebrated for his sententious maxims.

LETTER 9

ON PHILOSOPHY AND FRIENDSHIP

[1] You desire to know whether Epicurus is right to criticize, in one of his letters, those who say that the wise man is content with himself and therefore does not need a friend. This criticism is leveled by Epicurus against Stilbo and those who believe the highest good is a soul immune to feeling.

[2] We will fall into ambiguity if we try to express the Greek term ἀπάθειαν too hastily with the single word "impassivity." The opposite of what we wish to convey may then be understood. We want to describe a man who rejects all sensation of evil, but it could be taken to mean one who can endure no evil. Consider, therefore, whether it may be better to say either "a soul invulnerable" or "a soul positioned beyond all endurance."

[3] The difference between us [Stoics] and them [Epicureans] is this: Our wise man overcomes all misfortune, but he does feel it. Theirs does not even feel it. Yet we and they share this in common - the wise man is content with himself. Nevertheless, he still desires to have a friend, a neighbor, and a companion, even though he is sufficient unto himself.

[4] See how self-content he is; sometimes he is content with only a part of himself. If a hand, a disease, or an enemy should cut off his

hand, if some accident should pluck out one or both eyes, what remains of him will be satisfactory. He will be just as cheerful with a diminished and maimed body as he was when whole. But while he does not long for what is missing, he prefers that they not be missing.

[5] Thus the wise man is self-content, not in the sense that he wants to be without a friend, but that he can be. And when I say "can be", I mean that he bears the loss of a friend with equanimity.

But he will never be without a friend. He has it in his own power how quickly he will make another. Just as, if Phidias should lose a statue, he will immediately make another, so this master craftsman of friendship will substitute another in place of the one lost.

[6] If you ask how he can make a friend so quickly, I will tell you - but only if we strike a deal, that I may at once pay my debt to you and square our accounts for this letter. Hecato says: "I will show you a love potion without drugs, herbs, or any witch's spell: If you want to be loved, love." There is great enjoyment not only in maintaining an old and established friendship, but also in beginning and building a new one.

[7] The difference between a farmer who is planting and one who is harvesting is the same as between a man who has gained a friend and one who is gaining one. The philosopher Attalus used to say that it is more pleasant to make a friend than to have one, just as an artist derives more pleasure from painting than from having painted. That absorbing preoccupation with his work carries with it an immense satisfaction in the work itself. He does not enjoy it as much when he has lifted his hand from the finished piece. Then he is already reaping the fruits of his art; but it was the art itself he enjoyed while he was painting. The adolescence of our children is more fruitful, but their infancy is sweeter.

[8] Now let us return to our subject. The wise man, even if he is content with himself, still desires to have a friend, if for no other reason than to practice friendship and ensure that such a noble virtue does not lie dormant. Not for the purpose Epicurus advocated in this same letter: "to have someone to sit by his bedside when he is ill or come to his aid when he is thrown into prison or falls into

poverty." Rather, the wise man needs a friend so that he himself may sit at his friend's bedside when sick, and rescue him from the encirclement of the enemy's guard. Whoever considers only himself and enters into friendship for this reason has miscalculated. As he began, so he will end; he has made a friend who would bring assistance against bondage, but as soon as the chains clatter, the friend will desert him.

[9] These are what people call "fair-weather friendships." He who is adopted as a friend for the sake of utility will only be pleasing as long as he is useful. It is prosperity that attracts a crowd of these friends; but adversity leaves a man in solitude, and it is then that they flee, when their loyalty is put to the test. That is how all those shameful instances arise of friends abandoning or betraying each other out of fear. The beginning and the end must necessarily align. The man who begins to be your friend because it pays will also cease to be your friend because it pays[1]. Some compensation will be preferred over friendship, if any is valued more highly than friendship itself.

[10] For what purpose, then, do I gain a friend? So that I may have someone for whom I can die, someone whom I can accompany into exile, someone whose death I can oppose [and on whom I can stake my own life]. What you describe is a business transaction, not a friendship – something that looks to what profit it can derive, that seeks to gain some external reward.

[11] Without doubt, the affection of lovers has some similarity to friendship; you might even say it is a kind of crazy friendship. Does anyone, then, love for the sake of gain, or promotion, or renown? Pure love, heedless of all other considerations, kindles the soul with desire for the beautiful form, not without hope of a loving return. What then? Can this shameful emotion arise from a nobler cause?"

[12] "But," you say, "the question at hand is not whether friendship should be sought for its own sake." On the contrary, nothing deserves more to be examined. For if friendship is to be desired in and of itself, then one who is content with himself can attain it. "How, then, does he attain it?" In the same way one approaches anything of great

beauty - not lured by profit nor deterred by the fickleness of fortune. The majesty of friendship is diminished by the one who seeks it only for favorable circumstances.

[13] The wise man is content with himself. Most people, my dear Lucilius, wrongly interpret this sentiment. They isolate the sage on all sides and confine him to his own skin. But we must distinguish the meaning and extent of this maxim. The wise man is self-sufficient for the purpose of living happily, not merely for the purpose of living. For the latter, he needs many things, but for the former, he requires only a sound and upright mind that disdains fortune.

[14] I wish to share with you a distinction made by Chrysippus. He says the wise man lacks nothing, yet still needs many things. "On the other hand, the fool needs nothing, for he does not know how to use anything, but he lacks everything." The sage needs hands, eyes, and many necessities for daily use, but he lacks nothing. For to lack is a matter of necessity, and nothing is necessary to the wise man.

[15] Therefore, although the sage is content with himself, he needs friends. He desires to have as many as possible, not for the sake of living happily - for he will live happily even without friends. The highest good seeks no external instruments. It is cultivated at home and arises entirely from itself. If the sage seeks any part of himself from without, he begins to be subject to fortune.

[16] "But what will the life of the sage be like if he is left without friends, thrown into prison, abandoned among strange people, detained on a long sea voyage, or cast upon a deserted shore?" It will be like that of Jupiter who, when the universe dissolves and the gods merge into one, when nature ceases for a time, reposes in himself, absorbed in his own thoughts. The sage does something similar. He retires into himself and is his own companion.

[17] As long as he is permitted to arrange his affairs according to his own judgment, he is content with himself. He marries; content with himself, he raises children; content with himself, yet he would not live if he had to live without human society. It is not any personal advantage that leads him to friendship, but a natural instinct. For just as we have an innate fondness for other things, so it is with friend-

ship. Just as there is a hatred of solitude and a desire for society, just as nature unites one person to another, so there is also in friendship a stimulus that makes us seek it out.

[18] Nevertheless, though he is the most loving of friends, though he compares them to himself and often puts them ahead of himself, the wise man will confine all his good within himself and say what Stilbo said, the Stilbo whom Epicurus' letter attacks. For when his homeland was captured, his children lost, and his wife carried off, as he emerged from the general conflagration alone and yet happy, Demetrius, whose cognomen was Poliorcetes [the Besieger] from his destruction of cities, asked him if he had lost anything. "All my goods," he replied, "are with me."

[19] Behold a strong and vigorous man! He was victorious over his enemy's victory itself. "I have lost nothing," he said, compelling Demetrius to doubt whether he had actually conquered. "All my goods^2 are with me — that is, to consider nothing that can be taken away as good."

We marvel at certain animals that can pass unharmed through the midst of flames. How much more marvelous is a man who comes out unscathed and unharmed through fire and sword and ruin! You see how much easier it is to conquer a whole people than one man? The words of Stilbo are the same as those of the Stoic. He too bears his untouched goods through burned cities. For he is content with himself. This is how he defines his own happiness.

[20] Do not think that we alone utter noble words; Epicurus himself, the critic of Stilbo, uttered a similar sentiment, which I ask you to consider fairly, even if I have already settled my account for today. "If anyone," he says, "does not regard what he has as most ample wealth, even if he is master of the whole world, he is still unhappy." Or, if you think the following sounds better—for we must try to express the meaning and not just use the actual words—"A man is wretched if he does not consider himself supremely blessed, even if he commands the world."

[21] To show that these sentiments are universal, as nature indeed dictates, you will find in a comic poet:

The man who does not think himself blessed is not blessed.

For what does your condition matter if it seems bad to you?

[22] "What then," you say, "if yonder man, shamefully rich and master of many but slave of more, calls himself happy, will he be so in his own opinion?" It matters not what he says, but what he feels, and not what he feels on one particular day, but what he feels consistently. But there is no reason for you to fear that so great a privilege will fall into unworthy hands. Only the wise man is pleased with what is his own. All folly suffers from weariness of itself. Farewell.

---

1. amicitiam, si ullum in illa placet praeter ipsam
2. Justice, virtue, prudence etc.

LETTER 10

THE FOLLY OF ASSOCIATING WITH THE CROWD

[1] My view remains unchanged: avoid the crowd, avoid the few, avoid even the individual. I have no one to whom I would entrust you. And see the opinion I have of you—I dare to trust you with yourself. Crates, the disciple of Stilbo (whom I mentioned in a previous letter), saw a young man walking by himself and asked what he was doing all alone. "I am communing with myself," replied the youth. "Pray be careful then," said Crates, "and take good heed; you are communing with a bad man!"

[2] When a person is in mourning or fearful, we tend to keep watch over them lest they use their solitude unwisely. No foolish person ought to be left alone; for at such times they hatch wicked schemes, plotting future dangers for themselves or others. They arrange their unscrupulous desires, and whatever their mind concealed out of fear or shame, it now lays bare. Solitude rouses their recklessness, inflames their lust, and incites their anger. In short, the one advantage solitude offers—to confide in no one and fear no informer—the fool loses, betraying himself.

Consider, therefore, what I hope for you—nay, what I promise myself (for hope suggests an uncertain good): I would prefer you to be with no other companion than yourself.

[3] I recall the noble spirit with which you cast forth certain words, so full of strength. At once I congratulated myself and said: "These utterances did not come from the edge of the lips; they have a solid foundation. This man is not one of the crowd; he has regard for his real welfare."

[4] Speak and live in this way; see to it that nothing keeps you down. As for your former prayers, you may dispense the gods from answering them; offer new ones instead. Pray for a sound mind and good health, first of soul and then of body. Why not make such prayers often? Ask boldly of God; you will be asking for nothing that belongs to another.

[5] But let me share a little gift with this letter, as is my custom. It is a true saying which I found in Athenodorus: "Know that you are freed from all desires when you have reached the point that you ask God for nothing except what you can ask openly." How mad are men now! They whisper the basest of prayers to the gods, but if anyone listens, they fall silent. What they are unwilling to have men know, they communicate to God. Therefore, consider whether this advice may be wisely given: live among men as if God beheld you; speak with God as if men were listening. Farewell.

LETTER 11
THE QUALITIES OF A TRUE FRIEND

[1] I HAD A CONVERSATION WITH YOUR GOOD-NATURED FRIEND, WHOSE great intellect, talent, and progress were evident from our very first exchange. He gave me a taste of what to expect from him going forward. His words were not rehearsed, but rather the result of being caught off guard. As he collected himself, he could barely shake off his modesty, a good sign in a young man; a deep blush spread over his face. This modesty, I suspect, will stay with him even as he grows in confidence and sheds all his faults on the path to wisdom. For no amount of wisdom can eliminate the natural imperfections of the body and mind[1]. Whatever is deeply rooted and inborn can be mitigated with skill, but never fully overcome.

[2] Even the most self-assured individuals sometimes break out in a sweat when in the public eye, just as those who are tired and overheated often do. Some people's knees tremble when they are about to speak, others' teeth chatter, their tongue falters, their lips quiver. Neither training nor experience can ever completely eliminate these traits; nature exerts its power and uses these "flaws" to remind even the strongest among us of our humanity[2].

[3] I know that blushing is one of these traits, which can suddenly overtake even the most serious of men. It is certainly more noticeable

in young people, who have more heat in them and tender faces, but it affects veterans and the elderly too. Some are never more to be feared than when they have blushed, as if they have poured out all their modesty.

[4] Sulla was at his most violent when the blood had rushed to his face. No one had a gentler countenance than Pompey, yet he always blushed in front of a crowd, especially when giving speeches. I remember Fabianus blushing when he was brought in as a witness before the Senate, and this modesty was wonderfully becoming on him.

[5] This does not happen because of a weak mind, but because of the novelty of the situation, which stirs up even the inexperienced, if not rattling them, due to a natural bodily tendency toward this reaction. For just as some people have good blood, others have blood that is easily stirred up, quick to rush to the face.

[6] As I said, no wisdom can drive these traits away; otherwise, it would have power over nature itself if it could root out all imperfections. Whatever one's natural-born condition and bodily constitution have bestowed will persist, even after the mind has composed itself over a long time. None of these traits can be forbidden, any more than they can be summoned at will.

[7] Actors on the stage who imitate emotions—portraying fear, anxiety, and sadness—use this tell to mimic modesty: they cast their eyes down, lower their voices, and fix their gaze on the ground. But they cannot produce an actual blush; it can neither be prevented nor induced. Wisdom makes no promises against these things and has no effect; they have a will of their own, coming and going unbidden.

[8] The letter now demands a closing thought. Take this, a useful and wholesome one, which I wish for you to affix in your mind: "We ought to choose some good man, and always keep him before our eyes, so that we may live as if he were watching, and do all things as if he saw what we were doing."

[9] This, my dear Lucilius, is what Epicurus prescribed. He has given us a guardian and a teacher, and not without reason. A great portion of sins is removed if a witness stands by the would-be sinners.

The soul should have someone whom it can respect, by whose example it can make its inner sanctum more inviolable. Happy is the man who can so revere another as to compose and order his thoughts by the mere memory of him! One who can so revere another, will soon be himself worthy of reverence.

[10] Choose therefore a Cato[3]. If he seems too rigid for you, choose a man of a more relaxed spirit, a Laelius[4]. Choose one whose way of life and manner of speech are pleasing to you, and picture to yourself his mind and countenance; then always keep him before you either as a guardian or as a model. For we must indeed have someone according to whom we may regulate our characters; you can never straighten that which is crooked unless you use a ruler. Farewell.

---

1. Madvig suggests deleting "aut animi" after "corporis".
2. Schweighäuser suggests "illo" instead of "illos" in the manuscripts.
3. Cato the Younger, a Roman statesman renowned for his moral integrity.
4. Gaius Laelius Sapiens, a Roman statesman known for his friendship with Scipio Aemilianus.

LETTER 12

THE CYCLES OF LIFE AND HOW TO FACE DEATH

[1] EVERYWHERE I TURN, I SEE SIGNS OF MY OLD AGE. I HAD COME TO MY suburban villa and was lamenting the expenses of a crumbling building. My steward told me it was not the fault of his negligence; he was doing everything, but the villa was old. This villa grew up under my very hands; what will become of me, if the stones of my lifetime are so decayed?

[2] Angry, I seized upon the next occasion to vent my spleen. "It's clear," I said, "that these plane-trees are neglected; they have no leaves. How gnarled and withered the branches are, how sad and squalid the trunks! This would not happen if someone dug around them and watered them." He swore by my guardian spirit that he was doing everything, neglecting nothing in his care, but those trees were old crones. Between you and me, I had planted them, I had seen their first leaf.

[3] Turning to the door, I asked, "Who is that decrepit man, rightly placed at the entrance? For he faces outward. Where did you find him? What pleasure did it give you to take up some other man's dead?" But he replied, "Don't you recognize me? I am Felicio, to whom you used to bring little gifts. I am the son of Philositus the steward, your little darling." "He's perfectly off his rocker," I said. "Has even my

little pet become a pupil[1]? It's entirely possible; his teeth are just now falling out."

[4] I owe it to my suburban villa, that wherever I turned my attention, my old age appeared before me. Let us embrace it and love it; it is full of pleasure, if you know how to use it. Fruits are most pleasing when their time is fleeting; boyhood has its greatest charm just as it slips away; devotees of drink take the greatest delight in the last draught that submerges them, that puts the final touch on their drunkenness.

[5] Every pleasure puts off its most exquisite delights until the very end. The age most ripe for enjoyment is the one already sloping downhill, but not yet in headlong descent. And I deem that even the final stage has its pleasures, or else this very thing takes their place -- the need for none. How sweet it is to have exhausted one's appetites and left them behind!

[6] "It is bothersome," you say, "to have death before your eyes." This, in the first place, should be before the eyes of an old man as much as a youth, for we are not summoned according to our census roll. Moreover, no one is so old that it would be improper for him to hope for one more day. Yet one day is a rung on life's ladder.

Our whole life is made of parts, consisting of circles revolving within larger circles. There is one circle that embraces and encircles them all, stretching from birth to our final day. Another encloses the years of youth. Another encompasses the entirety of childhood within its orbit. Then there is the year itself, containing within it all the seasons by whose cyclic repetition life is woven together. The month is girdled by a narrower ring. The day describes the tightest circuit, but even this proceeds from dawn to dusk, from rising to setting.

[7] Thus Heraclitus, whose obscure teachings earned him the nickname "The Riddler," said: "One day is equal to every day." Different people interpreted this differently. Some say he meant that the hours of every day are equal, and in this he was not mistaken. For if a day is a twenty-four hour period, then all days must be equal to each other, since the night claims what the day loses. Another says

one day is equal to all days through resemblance, for even the longest span of time possesses nothing that you cannot find in a single day: light and darkness. Though a day makes these alternations more frequently, some being shorter, some longer[2].

[8] Therefore, each and every day should be arranged as if it draws up the rear, as if it rounds out and completes our life.

Pacuvius, who by habit made Syria his own, would hold a banquet for himself with wine and a funeral feast, after which he was carried from the dinner table to his bedroom while the applause of his male lovers resounded and they sang in accompaniment: "He has lived, he has lived!"

[9] Not a day passed by that he did not conduct his own funeral procession. Let us do from a healthy state of mind what he used to do from a sick one. As we retire to bed, let us say with joy and good cheer:

> *I have lived; I have finished the course that fortune set*
> *for me.*

If God grants us tomorrow, let us welcome it with glad hearts. The most blessed and secure possessor of himself is he who awaits tomorrow without anxiety. Whoever has said, "I have lived," rises daily to reap anew.

[10] But now, I must bring this letter to a close. "What's this," you ask, "will it come to me without any little gift attached?" Fear not, for it carries something with it. Why did I say "something"? It carries much! For what could be more glorious than this saying, which I entrust to the letter to convey to you? "It is bad to live under constraint; but no constraint compels you to live under constraint." Why, indeed, should it not be possible to escape constraint? On all sides, many short and simple paths to freedom lie open. Let us thank God that no one can be kept in life against their will. We may spurn the very constraints themselves.

[11] "But," you say, "that was Epicurus who said this. What business do you have with someone else's words?" Whatever is true, I consider

my own. I shall persist in foisting Epicurus upon you, so that these people who swear by the words of another, without considering the merit of what is said, may understand that the best ideas are common property. Farewell.

---

1. A pun on the similarity of pupulus ("little boy") and pupillus ("ward").
2. The text is uncertain here and the meaning unclear. This represents a best guess based on the surviving manuscripts.

LETTER 13

OVERCOMING GROUNDLESS FEARS

[1] I KNOW THE STRENGTH OF YOUR SPIRIT, LUCILIUS. EVEN BEFORE YOU armed yourself with the life-giving precepts that overcome hardships, you held your own against Fortune's assaults. And your confidence has only grown since you wrestled with her directly and tested your own powers. True mettle can never be assured until it has faced down many difficulties from all sides, and even allowed them to draw near. Only the spirit that will not surrender to another's will is thus proven.

[2] This is the touchstone of courage: no athlete can enter the fray with great enthusiasm if he has never been bloodied. The one who has seen his own blood, who has felt his teeth rattle under his opponent's fist, who has been tripped and crushed under the full weight of his foe, yet has not let his spirit falter even as he falls—the one who rises each time he is knocked down, ever more defiant—he enters the fight brimming with hope.

[3] And so, to belabor the comparison, Fortune has often gotten the upper hand on you, yet you have never yielded. You have leapt back to your feet and faced her with still greater determination. For virtue, when challenged, only adds to its own strength. But let me offer you some reinforcements to fortify your defenses, if you're open to it.

[4] We are more often frightened than hurt, Lucilius, and we suffer more in imagination than in reality. I won't address you in the Stoic manner, but in plainer terms. For while we Stoics may argue that all those things that elicit wails and groans are trivial and beneath our notice—and rightly so, by the gods—let us set aside the lofty words for now. My advice to you is this: don't be miserable before it's warranted. Those things you dread as imminent may never come to pass at all; certainly, they have not done so yet.

[5] Some things torment us more than they should, some torment us before they should, and some torment us when they should not torment us at all. We either exaggerate our pain, invent it, or anticipate it.

That first category I mentioned—whether such pains truly deserve the weight we give them—is controversial, so let us postpone that topic for now, as the case is still pending. I may call something trivial that you deem excruciating. I know that some can laugh in the face of flogging, while others whimper at a slap. We'll examine later whether these things owe their power to their own strength or to our weakness.

[6] For now, I ask you this: whenever you find yourself surrounded by those who would convince you of your own misery, ignore their words and focus on your own feelings. Reflect carefully and ask yourself, as one who knows his own mind best: "Why do they weep for me? Why do they tremble and fear to touch me, as if misfortune were contagious? Is there truly some evil in my state, or is my condition more disreputable than dire?" Question yourself: "Am I tormenting myself for no reason, making something a source of grief and sorrow that is not, in fact, a true ill?"

[7] "But how," you ask, "can I discern whether the things that trouble me are true or false?" Here is a rule for doing so: we are tormented either by things in the present or things to come—or both. It is easy to judge the present; if your body is free and healthy, and you feel no pain from injury, we shall see what the future holds.

[8] Today, there is no trouble at hand. "But surely," you say, "it will come." First, consider whether there are sure signs of approaching

evil. For we often suffer from mere suspicions, and that rumor which usually initiates war deceives us—but how much more does it undo individuals! It is true, my dear Lucilius; we are quick to lend credence to opinion. We do not refute those things that lead us into fear, nor do we examine them. Instead, we tremble and turn our backs, just as those who have been driven from their camp by the dust stirred up from a stampeding herd, or those who have been terrified by some unauthenticated rumor.

[9] Somehow, the more insubstantial our fears, the more they disturb us. For real dangers have their limits, but whatever springs from uncertainty is left to guesswork and the license of a frightened mind. No fears are so ruinous and inescapable as those of a panic-stricken person, for while others are irrational, these lack sense altogether.

[10] Let us, therefore, diligently inquire into the matter at hand. It is probable that some misfortune will befall us, but that does not make it a certainty. How many unexpected things have come to pass! How many expected things have never materialized! Even if it is to be, what good does it do to run out and meet your suffering? You will suffer soon enough when it arrives; in the meantime, expect better things.

[11] What shall you gain by doing this? Time. Many things may intervene, whereby a danger that is near at hand or on the very verge of happening may halt, cease, or pass on to another. A way of escape has opened up amidst a fire; sometimes a gentle collapse of a ruin has safely deposited its victims; sometimes the very sword has been pulled back even from the neck; some have survived their own executioners. Even misfortune is fickle. Perhaps it will come, perhaps not; in the meantime, it is not. Propose better things for yourself.

[12] Sometimes, with no apparent signs foretelling anything bad, the mind fashions false impressions for itself. It either twists some word of doubtful meaning into a worse sense or imagines a greater affront than actually exists, not considering how angry the other person is but how much he might do in his anger. But there is no reason for living and no limit to our miseries if we let our fears sway

us as much as they can. Here let prudence help you, and contemn fear with a resolute spirit even when it is in plain sight. If you cannot do this, counter one weakness with another and temper your fear with hope. There is nothing so certain among those things we fear that it is not more certain still that things we dread sink into nothing and that things we hope for mock us.

[13] Therefore, weigh hope and fear, and whenever all is uncertain, favor yourself; believe what you prefer. If fear holds more sway, nonetheless incline towards this side and cease troubling yourself. Continually turn this thought in your mind: the greater part of mortals, though no evil befalls them nor any assuredly will, seethe in anxiety and rush about. For no one resists themselves once they start to be driven, nor do they reduce their fear to truth. No one says, "The author is unreliable, he either invented these things or believed them falsely." We give ourselves over to be carried by the breeze[1].

[14] We dread uncertainties as certainties. We do not keep things in proportion. The slightest qualm at once turns to fear[2].

I am ashamed to speak with you in such plaintive terms[3] and to coddle you with such gentle remedies. Someone else may say, "Perhaps it will not come to pass." You should say, "And what if it does? Let us see which prevails. Perhaps it comes for my benefit, and that death will dignify my life." The hemlock made Socrates great[4]. Wrest from Cato the sword, freedom's champion - you will have stripped away a large part of his glory.

[15] I have exhorted you for too long, when you are more in need of reminding than encouragement. We are not leading you contrary to your nature; you were born for the principles we are discussing. All the more, then, amplify and adorn your good qualities.

[16] But now I will close this letter, if I may stamp it with my seal - that is, entrust to you some striking phrase to ponder. "Among its other ills, folly has this too: it always begins to live." Consider, Lucilius, best of men, what this saying signifies, and you will understand how base is the fickleness of those who daily lay new foundations for their lives, who begin new hopes even at the point of death.

[17] Look around at individuals with me; you will come across old

men who at the very moment are preparing themselves for pursuing office, for travel, for commerce. What indeed is baser than an old man just beginning to live? I would not add the author's name to this saying, were it not rather obscure and not among Epicurus' popular sayings - which I have allowed myself to praise and adopt. Farewell.

---

1. "aurae ferendos" in the original, which Buecheler amended from "referendis" in the manuscripts
2. "vertit" (turns) is Haase's emendation; the manuscripts have "venit" (comes).
3. Capps suggests "et triste" (and plaintively) for the manuscripts' unclear "ibi sic".
4. The manuscripts have "confecit" (finished off), but Hense suggests this may be a corruption of "effecit" (made).

LETTER 14
HOW PHILOSOPHY HELPS US
MINIMIZE DANGER

[1] I confess that we have an innate affection for our body; I admit that we are its guardians. I do not deny that we should be indulgent towards it, but I deny that we should be its slaves. For he who serves the body, who fears excessively for it, who refers everything to it, will be enslaved to many masters.

[2] We ought to conduct ourselves not as if we should live for the body, but as if we cannot live without it. An excessive love for the body disturbs us with fears, burdens us with worries, and exposes us to insults. To one who cherishes the body too much, honor becomes worthless. Let us attend to it with the utmost care, yet in such a way that, when reason, dignity, or loyalty requires it, we are prepared to cast it into the flames.

[3] Nevertheless, let us avoid discomforts as much as possible, not just dangers, and withdraw ourselves to safety, continually devising ways to ward off fearsome things. There are, if I am not mistaken, three kinds of fears: poverty, diseases, and the violence inflicted by the more powerful.

[4] Of all these, nothing shakes us more than what hangs over us from another's power, for it comes with great clamor and tumult. The natural evils I have mentioned, poverty and disease, approach

silently, striking neither eyes nor ears with any terror. But the display of the other evil is enormous, bearing swords, fires, chains, and a horde of wild beasts to unleash upon human flesh.

[5] Picture here the prison, the crosses, the racks, the hook, the stake driven through a man and emerging from his mouth, limbs torn apart by chariots driven in opposite directions, the tunic smeared and interwoven with flammable materials, and whatever else cruelty has devised beyond these torments.

[6] It is no wonder, then, that the fear of this evil is greatest, as its variety is vast and its preparation terrifying. For just as the torturer achieves more the more instruments of pain he displays (since those who would have resisted with fortitude are conquered by the spectacle), so too, of the afflictions that subdue and dominate our minds, those which have something to exhibit are the most effective. Those other plagues—I mean hunger, thirst, the festering of the organs, and the fever that scorches the very vitals—are no less severe, but they are hidden, having nothing to brandish or parade. But these, like great wars, have conquered by their appearance and equipment.

[7] Let us strive, therefore, to avoid giving offense. Sometimes it is the people whom we should fear; sometimes, if the state is governed in such a way that most affairs are transacted through the senate, it is the influential men there; sometimes it is individuals to whom the people's power over the people has been entrusted. To have all of these as friends is laborious; it is enough not to have them as enemies. Thus, the wise man will never provoke the wrath of the powerful; rather, he will turn from it, just as one turns from a storm while sailing[1].

[8] When you crossed over to Sicily, you braved the strait. Your reckless helmsman scorned the threats of the south wind, which whips the Sicilian sea into a maelstrom, and he sought not the left bank but the nearer course where Charybdis churns the waters. A more cautious sailor asks those familiar with the area about the tides and storm-warning signs and steers clear of that region notorious for its whirlpools. The wise man does the same. He avoids harmful power, taking care firstly not to seem to be avoiding it. For part of

being secure is not openly seeking security, since condemning what one flees.

[9] We must therefore look to how we can protect ourselves from the masses. Firstly, let us not covet the same things, for quarrels arise between competitors. Next, let us not possess anything that might be snatched away by a plotting thief to his great profit. Keep the spoils on your person to a minimum. Few if any come after a man's blood just for the sake of it; more count the cost than hate the victim. A bandit lets a naked man pass by; even on a besieged road, a pauper goes in peace.

[10] Further, we must follow the old precept of shunning three things: hatred, envy, and scorn. How to do this, only wisdom will show. It is a difficult balance, and we must beware lest the fear of envy deliver us into scorn, lest in being unwilling to trample, we seem able to be trampled. The ability to be feared has given many cause for fear. Let us draw back on all sides; being despised hurts no less than being suspected.

[11] Therefore, take refuge in philosophy. These letters, I do not say among the good but among the only moderately bad, take the place of sacred fillets [offering protection]. For forensic eloquence and all other arts that stir the crowd meet with opposition. This quiet pursuit of one's own business cannot be despised; even among the worst men, all other arts honor it. Wickedness will never grow so strong, nor will there ever be such a conspiracy against virtue, that the name of philosophy shall cease to be venerable and sacred.

But philosophy itself must be practiced with calm and modesty. [12] "What then?" you say, "Does it seem to you that Marcus Cato philosophized modestly, he who tried to stem the civil war with his voice? Who intervened between the weapons of raging leaders? Who provoked both Pompey and Caesar at once, while others were busy offending one or the other?"

[13] One could argue whether it was right for a wise man to enter public life in those days. "What are you thinking, Marcus Cato? The fight is no longer about liberty - that was destroyed long ago. The question is whether Caesar or Pompey will control the republic.

What do you have to do with that feud? You have no stake in it; they merely vie to be master. What does it matter to you which of them wins? The better man may prevail, but whoever triumphs will undoubtedly be the worse for it." I have touched on Cato's final years, but even his earlier days were hardly conducive for a wise man to be swept up in the plundering of the state. What else did Cato accomplish beyond shouting himself hoarse and voicing futile protests as he was hoisted up by the hands of the rabble, drenched in spit, and dragged out of the forum to be deported[2], or led from the Senate to prison?

[14] But we shall examine later whether a wise man should devote his efforts to statecraft. For now, I summon you to these Stoics who, shut out from public affairs, withdrew to cultivate their personal lives and establish laws for the human race without offending those in power. The sage will not upend societal norms or turn the masses against himself through an unconventional lifestyle.

[15] "What then? Will one really be safe in pursuing this course?" I can no more promise you that than I can assure sound health in a temperate person, yet temperance does promote good health. The occasional ship sinks in port, but what do you think happens in the middle of the ocean? How much greater would the danger be to someone perpetually toiling away at endless tasks, for whom even leisure is unsafe? Sometimes the innocent perish - who would deny it? But the guilty far more often. The man slain amid his finery has at least mastered his craft.

[16] In the end, the wise man considers the intent behind all things, not their outcome. Beginnings are within our power; fortune judges the results, and I grant her no say over me. "But she will bring some vexation, some adversity," you say. The highwayman does not pass sentence when he slays.

[17] Now you reach out your hand for your daily alms. I shall fill it with golden coins, and since gold has been mentioned, hear how you can delight more in its use and enjoyment: "He most relishes riches who has least need for riches." "Name the author," you demand. To

show how generous I am, I've made it my mission to praise the words of others. It comes from Epicurus, Metrodorus, or one of that school.

[18] And what difference does it make who said it? They spoke to all. Those who crave wealth live in fear for their possessions. No one can truly enjoy a blessing that breeds anxiety; they're always striving to add more. While fixated on increasing their fortune, they forget how to use it. They pore over accounts, wear down the courts, and flip through their calendars, morphing from master to mere manager. Farewell.

---

1. "Declinabit" (he will turn away) is the preferred reading, while "nec declinabit" would negate the idea.
2. As suggested by Pincianus; the manuscripts read "and carried."

LETTER 15

THE PRIMACY OF THE MIND
OVER THE BODY

[1] The ancients had a custom, maintained even into my lifetime, of adding to the opening words of a letter: "If you are well, it is well; I am well." We would do better to say: "If you are studying philosophy, it is well." For this is what it means to be truly well. Without philosophy, the mind is sickly, and the body too, for all its strength, is no more sound than that of a madman or lunatic.

[2] Therefore, attend especially to that primary wellness of the mind, and only secondarily to mere bodily health, which will cost you little if your real desire is to be well. Surely it is foolish, my dear Lucilius, and hardly fitting for an educated man to work at developing the muscles, broadening the neck and chest. Even if you succeed in bulking up, you will never match the strength or weight of a prize ox. Besides, an overgrown body crushes the soul and renders it less agile. So limit the body's dimensions as much as you can and make plenty of room for the spirit.

[3] Many disadvantages attend those who devote themselves to such bodily concerns. First, the exertions drain the breath and make one less fit for intense study and reflection. Second, heavy eating impairs mental acuity. Worse still, we put ourselves under the tutelage of the vilest sort of slaves--men steeped in oil and wine, whose

idea of a good day is to have sweated profusely and then to replace their lost fluids by drinking deeper than ever on an empty stomach[1]. To drink and sweat--that is the life of a heart patient!

[4] There are exercises that are quick and easy, tiring the body without undue delay and stealing little time, which is a commodity always to be guarded most carefully. Running is one such exercise, as are weight-lifting and various kinds of jumping--either the sort that lifts the body straight up, or that propels it forward, or the "priest's dance" as I call it (or if an even more disdainful term is called for, the "fuller's jump"[2]). Choose any of these for your untrained, unpracticed body.

[5] But whatever you do, come back quickly from body to mind. Exercise the mind night and day--it is nourished by moderate labor. And this form of exercise will not be hampered by cold or heat or even old age. Cultivate that good which improves with the years.

[6] Of course, I am not ordering you to be constantly hunched over book or writing tablet. The mind must be given some relief, but in a way that reinvigorates rather than relaxes it. A carriage ride shakes up the body without interfering with mental activity--you can read, dictate, converse, or listen, none of which are impossible even while walking.

[7] Do not disregard the modulation of your voice, which I recommend you raise through fixed steps and measures, and then lower again. What if you wished to learn how to walk? Allow in those teachers whom hunger has taught new skills; there will be someone to regulate your steps, watch your mouth as you speak, and lead you on as far as your patience and credulity allow his impudence to go. Well then, will your voice launch straight into shouting at the highest pitch? It is natural to build up gradually to such an extent that even those in a dispute begin with speaking and transition to yelling. Nobody immediately [8] calls for aid from the Roman citizens.

Therefore, however your spirit moves you, deliver your reproach more vehemently at times, more gently at others, as your voice also prompts you to do. When you rein it back in and call it back, let it descend in a controlled manner, not collapse. Let it proceed from the middle range of your mouth[3], not raging wildly in an untrained, rustic fashion. For we are not practicing so that the voice may be exercised, but so that it may exercise us.

[9] I have relieved you of no small trouble; to these benefits will be added the reward of a single Greek maxim. Here is a notable precept: "The life of folly is thankless and fearful; it is utterly fixated on the future." "Who says this," you ask? The same author as above. Which life do you now think is being called foolish? That of Baba and Isio? No, it refers to us, whom blind desire hurls towards harmful things that certainly never satisfy - we who, if anything could be enough, would have had enough already - we who fail to realize how pleasant it is to ask for nothing, how magnificent to be content and not depend on Fortune.

[10] And so, Lucilius, reflect often on how much you have achieved. When you see how many are ahead of you, consider how many are behind you. If you wish to be thankful to the gods and to your own life, think of how many you have surpassed. What business do you have with the rest? You have surpassed your former self.

[11] Establish a limit for yourself, one that you are unwilling to cross even if you could, and one that you cannot cross even if you wished to[4]. Let these treacherous goods that promise more to those who hope for them than to those who have attained them depart at last. If there were anything substantial in them, they would eventually satisfy; as it is, they only provoke a thirst that must be quenched.

Cast aside these showy trappings. Why should I beg Fortune to give me what the uncertain lot of the future may bring, rather than asking myself not to desire it? And why should I even desire it? Shall I, forgetful of human frailty, amass more and more? For what shall I toil? Behold, this day is my last. Even if it is not, it is near the last. Farewell.

---

1. The text is uncertain here. An alternative translation might be: "drinking deeply while still fasting."
2. The precise meaning of these terms is debated, but they likely refer to jumping

straight upward, broad jumping, ritual leaping, and jumping up and down in place as fullers did to clean cloth.

3. Translating Madvig and Buecheler's emendation "media oris via abeat."
4. The original Latin text has "ne possis quidem si velis" ("you cannot even if you wish to") before "si possis" ("if you could"), but the order has been corrected by Gertz for clarity.

LETTER 16

PERSEVERANCE IN PHILOSOPHIZING

[1] I KNOW, MY DEAR LUCILIUS, THAT YOU ARE WELL AWARE NO ONE CAN live happily, or even tolerably, without the pursuit of wisdom, and that the perfection of wisdom is what makes the happy life, although even the beginnings of wisdom make life tolerable. Yet this conviction, clear as it is, must be strengthened and deepened by daily reflection. We must work to maintain our good resolutions and make them into lasting habits of mind. There is more work needed in guarding what you have proposed than in the initial proposing of honorable aims. We must persevere and reinforce our resolve with constant application, until the will to good becomes a disposition to good.

[2] Therefore, in proving this to you, I don't need to belabor the point or resort to long-winded arguments. I understand you have made great progress. I know the source of what you write to me; these are no figments or empty flourishes. Yet I will tell you what I think: I have hopes for you, but not yet full confidence. I would have you adopt the same attitude towards yourself. There is no reason to quickly and easily trust in oneself. Examine yourself, scrutinize your mind from various angles; but above all consider whether you have advanced in philosophy or merely in your manner of living.

[3] Philosophy is no common mechanic art, put on display for

show. It does not reside in words, but in deeds. It is not employed to help pass the day with some delight, as a balm against boredom. It molds and builds the mind, orders our life, guides our actions, shows what we should do and not do. It sits at the rudder and directs our course as we waver amid uncertainties. Without it, no one can live free from fear or worry. Countless things happen every hour that require advice, and this we must seek from philosophy.

[4] Someone may say: "What good is philosophy to me, if Fate exists? What good, if God governs the universe? What good, if Chance reigns supreme? For the certainties cannot be altered, and no preparation can be made to face uncertainties. Either God has anticipated my plans and decided what I am to do, or Fortune permits my plans no say."

[5] Whichever of these is true, Lucilius, or even if all of them are true, we must still practice philosophy. Whether the Fates bind us with an inexorable law, or whether God as arbiter of the universe has arranged all things, or whether Chance drives and tosses human affairs without method, philosophy must be our defense. She will encourage us to obey God with gladness, but Fortune with defiance. She will teach us to follow God and endure Chance.

[6] But this is not the time to be drawn into a debate about what degree of free will we possess, if Providence rules, or if we are at the mercy of a sequence of binding fates, or if sudden and unexpected forces hold sway. I return now to my original aim of warning and exhorting you not to let your mental energies falter and cool. Hold fast to your mind and establish it, so that what is now a resolution may turn into an abiding disposition.

[7] If I know you well, my friend, you are already eagerly examining this letter to discover what little gift it has brought you. Go ahead and shake it out, and you shall find it. My generosity should come as no surprise; for the time being, I am still spending another's coin. But why do I say "another's"? Every truth uttered by anyone belongs to me. Here is another gem from Epicurus: "If you live according to nature, you will never be poor; if you live according to opinion, you will never be rich."

[8] Nature's needs are slight; the demands of opinion are boundless. Imagine that the possessions of many a wealthy man were heaped upon you. Picture Fortune carrying you beyond the limits of a private citizen's wealth, decking you in gold, arraying you in royal purple, and transporting you to such heights of luxury and riches that you can bury the earth under your marble floors. Envision not merely having these things, but trampling them underfoot. Add to this statues, paintings, and all that art has devised for the sake of luxury; you will only learn from such things to crave still greater.

[9] Natural desires are limited; those which spring from false opinion have nowhere to stop, for falsehood has no point of termination. When you walk on a road, there is an end to it somewhere; but wandering is interminable. Therefore, draw back from idle fancies, and when you would know whether the desires you pursue are natural or imaginary, consider whether they can come to rest at any definite point. If you find, after having traveled far, that there is always a longer journey ahead, you may be sure that this is not a natural desire. Farewell.

LETTER 17
THE BENEFITS OF VOLUNTARY POVERTY

[1] IF YOU ARE WISE, CAST AWAY ALL THOSE THINGS THAT HINDER YOU—indeed, to be wise, strain with all your might and at full speed towards good sense. If anything holds you back, either disentangle yourself or cut it away. "But," you protest, "my family affairs detain me; I wish to arrange them in such a way that they may suffice without my active attention, so that neither poverty may be a burden to me, nor I to others."

[2] When you say this, you do not seem to fully grasp the power and potency of the good you have in mind. You perceive the essence of the matter—how much philosophy may benefit you—but you do not yet discern the details with enough clarity. You do not yet realize how much it aids us in every situation, how it brings succor [to use Cicero's word] in the greatest matters and stoops to help even in the smallest. Believe me, call philosophy into counsel; it will advise you not to sit down to your ledgers.

[3] Surely this is what you seek and wish to obtain by this delay: that you may not have to fear poverty. But what if poverty is something to be sought? Riches have hindered many from pursuing philosophy; poverty is unencumbered, free from care. When the

battle trumpet sounds, the poor man knows he is not the target; when the cry of "fire!" goes up, his only concern is how to get out, not what to carry with him. If he must set sail, the harbor does not echo with an uproar, nor are the shores abuzz with the retinue of just one passenger. A throng of servants does not mill about him, their upkeep requiring the fertility of lands beyond the sea[1].

[4] It is easy to feed a few stomachs that are well-disciplined and crave nothing more than to be filled. Hunger is cheap, but squeamishness costs dearly. Poverty is content to satisfy pressing needs.

So why, then, would you reject poverty as a roommate, when a sensible rich man strives to imitate poverty's ways? If you wish to be free in mind, you must either be poor or resemble the poor.

[5] Devotion to study cannot come to fruition without a commitment to frugal living—and frugality is simply voluntary poverty. So away with those excuses: "I do not yet have enough; when I obtain a certain sum, then I will devote myself wholly to philosophy." Yet this is the very thing that must be secured first, the thing that you keep putting off and seeking after other things. "I wish to acquire a means of living," you say. At the same time, learn as you acquire; for if something is preventing you from living well, nothing prevents you from dying well[2].

[6] Let not poverty, nor even destitution, deter us from the pursuit of philosophy. For those who make haste towards it must bear even hunger, as men have endured during sieges. And what other reward for their endurance did they obtain than not falling under the conqueror's power? How much greater is the promise here: perpetual liberty, to fear neither man nor god! One would surely come to this, even if starving.

[7] Armies have endured scarcity of all things, subsisting on roots and, shockingly, even bearing hunger. All this they suffered for a kingdom—more surprisingly, someone else's kingdom. Will any man hesitate to endure poverty so that he may liberate his mind from madness?

Therefore one need not acquire riches first; one may come to philosophy even without provisions. [8] Is this so? When you have obtained all things, then you will wish to obtain wisdom as well? Shall philosophy be the last equipment for life and, as it were, its extra? Whether you have anything or nothing, philosophize now—for how do you know if you already have too much? If you have nothing, seek wisdom before anything else.

[9] "But," you say, "necessities will be lacking." First, they cannot be lacking, because nature demands little, and the wise man adapts himself to nature. Should extreme necessity befall, he will promptly depart from life and cease to be troublesome to himself. But if his means are meager and scanty for sustaining life, he will make the best of it, not unduly anxious about necessities beyond securing food and shelter. He will render unto his belly and shoulders their due, while serenely and cheerfully laughing at the preoccupations of the rich and those hustling after wealth. He will say, "Why do you defer your own happiness?

[10] Will you wait for some profit on your investments, some lucrative trade, or the will of a wealthy old man, when you can be instantly rich? Wisdom offers riches in ready money, having rendered them superfluous to all to whom she has granted them." This concerns other men; you are closer to the wealthy class. Change the age in which you live, and you have too much. But what is enough is the same in every age.

[11] Here I could have ended my epistle, except that I have spoiled you. One cannot greet the Parthian kings without a gift; you cannot bid me farewell for nothing. What then? I shall borrow from Epicurus: "The acquisition of riches has been for many men not an end, but merely a change, of troubles."

[12] This does not surprise me. For the fault lies not in circumstances, but in the mind itself. The same trait that made poverty a burden to us has also made wealth onerous. Just as it makes no difference whether you place a sick person on a wooden bed or a golden one—wherever you move them, they will bring their sickness with them—so too it matters not whether a diseased mind is beset by

riches or by poverty. Its own malady follows it wherever it goes. Farewell.

---

1. Gertz and Buecheler read "aqua conclamata" ("when 'water!' is shouted") while the MSS have "aliqua conclamata" ("when something is shouted").
2. Madvig suggests "para et" ("acquire and"), while the MSS have "parare" ("to acquire"); Haase proposes "et te parare" ("and that you acquire").

LETTER 18
THE GODLIKE NATURE OF DESPISING WEALTH

[1] December, that month when the city especially loves to sweat and sprawl in luxury's excess, has arrived. The whole place resounds with colossal preparations, as if there were any real difference between the Saturnalia and a regular workday. Indeed, the difference has become so negligible that the witticism seems quite apt: December used to be a month; now it's a whole year.

[2] If I had you here with me, I'd happily discuss what you think should be done. Should we change nothing in our daily routine? Or should we dine a bit more festively and doff the toga, lest we seem out of step with popular custom? After all, we change our clothes for pleasure's sake on holidays, though it's usually done only in times of civil unrest or crisis.

[3] If I know you well, you would have us play the part of impartial judges. You'd want us neither identical to the cap-wearing rabble in all respects, nor entirely different. Unless, perhaps, it's precisely at times like these that we should command our spirits to abstain from pleasures in solitude, while the whole mob is sprawling in them. For resisting temptations that beckon us to indulgence provides the surest proof of our resolve's firmness.

[4] It takes far greater strength to remain dry and sober when the

people are drunk and vomiting. The more temperate path is to not set oneself apart conspicuously, yet not blend in with the masses either —to do the same things, but in a different way. For one can celebrate a holiday without going to excess.

[5] In fact, testing your soul's steadfastness pleases me so much that I shall prescribe for you what great men have prescribed: interpose a few days where you are content with the barest minimum of the cheapest food, wearing coarse and rough clothing, and say to yourself: "Is this what I used to dread?"

[6] Let the mind prepare itself for hardships during times of ease and fortify itself against Fortune's injuries while experiencing her favors. The soldier practices maneuvres in peacetime, building ramparts against an absent enemy and tiring himself with needless toil so he might manage the unavoidable. If you don't want someone panicking during the real ordeal, train them before it arrives. Those who followed this practice imitated poverty for short stints every month, nearly reaching a state of indigence, so that they might never dread what they had often rehearsed.

[7] Don't imagine that I'm speaking now of Timon's dinners[1], the hovels of the destitute, or any other forms of mockery by which luxurious living makes sport of ennui at being wealthy. Let the cot be a true one, the cloak truly coarse, the bread hard and grimy. Endure this for three or four days at a time, occasionally for longer, so it's not a game but a test. Then, believe me, Lucilius, you will leap for joy when filled for just two coins and understand that to gain peace of mind, Fortune is unnecessary. For she provides what suffices for our basic needs even when raging in anger.

[8] However, you should not think that you are doing anything extraordinary. You will merely be doing what many thousands of slaves and poor people do. Take pride in yourself for this reason— that you will do it without being forced, and that it will always be as easy for you to endure as it is to make the attempt. Let us train ourselves against difficulties, and let poverty become familiar to us, so that fortune may not catch us unprepared. We will be wealthy with more peace of mind if we know how minor a burden it is to be poor.

[9] Epicurus, that teacher of pleasure, used to set aside certain days on which he would sparingly satisfy his hunger, to see whether anything was lacking from full and complete pleasure, how much was lacking, and whether it was worth spending great effort to fill the gap. Indeed, he boasts in these very letters, which he wrote to Polyaenus during the tenure of Charinus the magistrate, that he himself lived on less than a penny, while Metrodorus, who had not yet made such progress, required a whole penny.

[10] Do you think mere satiety is found in such a diet? No—there is pleasure in it. Not the fickle, fleeting kind that needs constant renewal, but a stable and sure pleasure. For it is not the water, the barley porridge, or the crust of barley bread that is inherently pleasant, but the supreme pleasure lies in being able to derive joy even from these things, and in having reduced oneself to a state that no harshness of fortune can snatch away.

[11] The fare of a prison is more generous; one with a death sentence is fed less sparingly by the executioner. What greatness of spirit it shows to willingly descend to a level which even those facing the ultimate punishment need not fear! This is truly to blunt the weapons of fortune in advance.

[12] So begin, my dear Lucilius, to follow the custom of these men; set aside some days when you withdraw from your business affairs and make yourself at home with the scantiest fare. Start to have dealings with poverty:

> *Dare, my friend, to scorn wealth, and mold yourself too,*
> *To be worthy of God.*

[13] No one is worthy of God except the one who has scorned riches. I am not barring you from possessing them, but I want to ensure that you possess them without tremors; and this you will only achieve in one way, by convincing yourself that you can live happily without them, and by always regarding them as something on the verge of vanishing.

[14] But let us now start folding up this letter. "First," you say, "pay

up what you owe." I will refer you to Epicurus for the reckoning; he will make the payment: "Unbridled anger begets madness." You must know how true this is, since you have had both a slave and an enemy.

[15] This passionate sentiment blazes forth towards all persons; it arises as much from love as from hatred, and emerges no less amidst serious affairs than during play and jest. What matters is not the magnitude of the cause from which it springs, but the quality of the mind into which it enters. Just as it is of no consequence how great a fire is, but rather what it falls upon—for solid objects have repelled even the greatest flames, while dry and easily inflammable substances nourish a mere spark into a conflagration—so it is, my dear Lucilius, that the outcome of a mighty anger is madness, and thus anger should be avoided, not merely for the sake of moderation, but for the sake of sanity. Farewell.

---

1. Timon of Athens was a notorious misanthrope of Hellenistic Greece who lived a life of self-imposed isolation and deprivation.

LETTER 19
BREAKING FREE FROM FORTUNE'S YOKE

[1] I REJOICE WHENEVER I RECEIVE YOUR LETTERS, FOR THEY FILL ME with high hopes—no longer mere promises about you, but solemn pledges. I entreat and implore you, continue on this path! For what better request could I make of a friend than that which I would make on his own behalf? If possible, extricate yourself from those occupations of yours; if not, tear yourself away. We have squandered enough of our time already; let us begin gathering our baggage in preparation for old age.

[2] Is this an invidious proposal? We have lived amid the waves; let us die in harbor. Not that I would advise you to seek renown through retirement—a thing you should neither advertise nor conceal. For I will never banish you to such a degree, having condemned the madness of humankind, that I would wish for you to be prepared a hiding place, to be forgotten. Rather, manage that your repose be not conspicuous, but visible.

[3] Then let those whose plans are as yet unfixed and in their infancy decide whether they wish to pass their life in obscurity; you have no free choice. Your intellectual vigor, the elegance of your writings, illustrious and noble friendships have thrust you into the public

eye. Even if you plunge into the depths and hide yourself completely, your former brilliance will still betray you.

[4] You cannot shroud yourself in darkness now; much of your prior luster will follow you wherever you flee.

You can lay claim to peace without incurring hatred, without longing or any pang of regret. For what will you leave behind that you could not bear to remember leaving? Your dependents? None of them cares for you yourself, only for what they can get from you. Friendship was once sought, but now plunder; the wills of forsaken old men will be altered, the morning caller migrate to another doorstep. A great matter cannot be purchased at a trifling cost; consider whether it is better to leave your own self or something of your possessions.

[5] Would that you had been able to grow old within the bounds of your birth, and that Fortune had not lifted you to such heights! That swift-rising felicity bore you far from the sight of a wholesome life—the province, the procuratorship, and all that is promised by such things; then still greater offices will seize you, one after another.

[6] What will the end be? For what do you wait, until you cease to have desires? That time will never come. Just as we describe a chain of causes from which fate is woven, so it is with our wants; one springs from the end of another. You have been plunged into a life which will itself never put an end to your miseries and servitude. Withdraw your neck from the yoke it has worn for so long; better to have it cut once than be forever bowed.

[7] If you turn your attention to private matters, everything will seem lesser, but it will be more than enough to satisfy you. As things stand now, abundance from all sides fails to satiate you. Which would you prefer—contentment from scarcity or hunger amid plenty? Happiness is both greedy and exposed to the greed of others. As long as nothing is enough for you, you yourself will not be enough for others.

[8] "How then," you ask, "shall I escape my current state?" In whatever way you can. Consider how many things you have rashly attempted for money, how many hardships you have endured for the sake of reputation. For the sake of leisure, too, something must be

ventured. Otherwise, you will grow old amid the bustle of your many duties, forever beset by new waves of turmoil from which no moderation or tranquility of life can deliver you. What does it matter if you wish to be at peace? Your fortune does not wish it. What if you allow it to grow even greater? The more success you attain, the more you will have to fear.

[9] Here I wish to relate to you a saying of Maecenas, uttered when he stood at the very pinnacle[1]: "It is the height itself that stuns the mind." If you ask in which of his works he said this, it is in the one entitled Prometheus. What he meant is that lofty positions leave one thunderstruck. Is any power so valuable that you would put up with such drunken speech? Maecenas was a man of talent who might have provided a great example of Roman eloquence, had prosperity not enervated him—or rather, unmanned him. This same end awaits you unless you trim your sails now and, as Maecenas wished to do too late, hug the shore.

[10] I could square my accounts with you using this judgment of Maecenas. But you will raise an objection, knowing you as I do, and you will be unwilling to accept from a disagreeable and uncompromising source what I owe you. As matters stand, I must borrow from Epicurus: "First," he says, "consider with whom you eat and drink, rather than what you eat and drink. For dining without a friend is the life of a lion or a wolf."

[11] This will not happen to you unless you withdraw from society. Otherwise, you will have dinner guests sorted out by your secretary from the crowd of your acquaintances paying their respects. But he errs who seeks a friend in the atrium and tests him at the dinner table. The busy man obsessed with his own possessions has no greater affliction than mistaking for friends those to whom he himself is no friend. He judges his favors effective in winning friends, though some who owe him the most hate him the more for it. A small debt makes a man your debtor; a large one makes him your enemy.

[12] What then? Do favors not secure friendships? They do, if you were able to choose suitable recipients, if they were well placed rather than scattered at random.

Therefore, as you begin to become your own master, make use of this maxim of the wise in the meantime: consider the person who received your favor to matter more than the favor itself. Farewell.

---

1. The manuscripts read "in ipso eculeo" ("on the rack itself"), but the scholar Capps emends this to "in ipso culmine" ("at the very summit").

LETTER 20

LIVING IN HARMONY WITH ONESELF AND PRACTICING POVERTY

[1] IF YOU ARE WELL AND CONSIDER YOURSELF WORTHY OF ONE DAY being your own master, I rejoice. For it will be to my glory if I can pull you out from those waters where you are tossed about with no hope of escape. But this, my dear Lucilius, is what I ask and urge you to do: let philosophy sink deep into your heart, and gauge your progress not by mere speech or writings, but by stoutness of mind and decrease of desire. Prove your words by your deeds.

[2] Declaimers seeking the crowd's applause have one purpose, while those who with shifting and glib arguments entrance the ears of young idlers have another. Philosophy teaches us to act, not merely to speak. She demands that each of us live according to her laws, that our life not contradict our words, and that our inner life be of one hue and not out of harmony with our outward actions. This is the highest duty and proof of wisdom: that our deeds match our words, that a person be consistent and the same in every respect. "Who can achieve this?" you ask. Few, but some can. It is a hard task, nor do I claim the sage will always walk with the selfsame gait, only that he will follow the selfsame path.

[3] Therefore, scrutinize yourself: see whether your clothes and lodging are discordant, whether you are lavish with yourself but

stingy with your family, whether you dine frugally but build extravagantly. Pick one definite standard to live by and align your entire life with it. Some restrict themselves at home but strut abroad with pompous airs; such inconsistency is a fault, a sign of a wavering mind that has not yet found its proper bearings.

[4] Let me tell you the source of this fickleness and variability of plans and decisions: it is because no one resolves upon what he truly wants, and even if he does, he does not persist but leaps aside and not only changes course but circles back, returning to what he once abandoned and condemned.

[5] To forsake the ancient definitions of wisdom and embrace the whole scope of human life, I could be satisfied with this: What is wisdom? Always desiring and always refusing the same things. Though you need not add the proviso that what you desire must be right, for nothing can always satisfy a person unless it is right.

[6] People do not really know what they want, then, except at the actual moment of wanting it. No one is absolutely committed to desiring or rejecting anything. Opinions shift daily and veer the opposite way, and for most people life is but a game. So press on as you have begun, and perhaps you will be led to the summit, or to that height which to you alone is still not the summit.

[7] "But what," you ask, "will become of that crowd of servants without the means to support them?" When they cease to be fed by you, that crowd will feed itself. Through the blessing of poverty, you will come to understand what your wealth could not teach you. Poverty will keep your true and certain friends; whoever followed you for gain rather than for you will depart. And is this not reason enough to love poverty - that it will reveal those who truly love you? Oh, when will the day come when no one lies to honor you!

[8] Therefore, let your thoughts incline in this direction. Care for this, wish for this, disregarding all other prayers to God - that you may be content with your own self and the good that is born from within you. What nearer happiness can there be? Reduce yourself to little, from which you cannot fall. To encourage you in this, I shall at once pay out my contribution for this letter.

[9] Though you may envy me, even now Epicurus gladly pays out on my behalf: "Believe me, your discourse will seem more magnificent when given from a pallet and in rags. For then your words will not merely be spoken, but proven true." I certainly hear the words of our Demetrius differently when I see him lying naked, on something even less than straw. He is not a teacher of truth, but a witness to it.

[10] "What then?" you say. "Is one not allowed to despise riches even when they rest in one's bosom?" And why not? Even one of great spirit, after marveling long at riches poured around him, laughs that they came to him, and hears more than he feels that they are his. It is a great thing not to be corrupted by the companionship of riches. Mighty is the person who is poor amidst wealth.

[11] "I don't know," you say, "how your poor man would bear poverty, should he fall into it." Nor do I know, Epicurus, whether that poor man of yours would despise riches, should he happen upon them. Therefore, in either case, we must judge the mind and examine whether the one indulges in poverty, or the other does not indulge in riches. Otherwise, a pallet or rags are a feeble proof of good intent, unless it is clear that one suffers them not out of necessity, but by choice.

[12] Besides, it is the mark of a great nature not to hasten towards such things as being better, but to be prepared for them as being easy. And they are easy, Lucilius. When you approach them after much prior meditation, they are even pleasant. For they contain that without which nothing is pleasant - peace of mind.

[13] Therefore, I deem it necessary to do what I have written to you that great men have often done: to set aside some days during which we may train ourselves in imaginary poverty for the real thing. This must be done all the more because we have been steeped in luxury and regard all things that are hard and difficult as unbearable. Rather, the mind must be roused from sleep and pinched awake, and reminded that nature has ordained very little for us. No one is born rich. Whoever comes into the light is commanded to be content with milk and swaddling clothes; from these beginnings, kingdoms cannot contain us. Farewell.

LETTER 21

THE RADIANCE OF THE
PHILOSOPHICAL LIFE

[I] YOU BELIEVE YOU HAVE TROUBLES WITH THOSE YOU WROTE TO ME
about? Your greatest trouble is with yourself; you are your own source
of disturbance. You do not know what you want; you approve of
moral rectitude more than you practice it; you see where happiness
lies, yet you dare not venture there. But I shall tell you what it is that
hinders you, since you discern it too little yourself.

You regard the things you are about to leave behind as significant,
and although you have set your sights on the peace of mind to which
you will cross over, the glitter of this life, from which you are to
depart, holds you back as if you were to fall into squalor and
obscurity.

[2] You are mistaken, Lucilius; one ascends from this life to that.
The difference between that resplendent destination and our present
light is this: our light has a definite source and shines by its own
power, while the glitter here is struck by a brilliance coming from
without, and anyone standing in its way will instantly cast a thick
shadow over it. But that life is illuminated by its own radiance.

It is your studies that will make you illustrious and noble.

[3] I shall cite the example of Epicurus. When he was writing to
Idomeneus, seeking to call him back from a life of ostentatious

service to a steadfast and genuine glory - for Idomeneus was then a minister of a rigid[1] power, occupied with weighty matters - Epicurus said: "If fame is what you seek, my letters will make you more renowned than all those things which you cherish and for which you are cherished."

[4] Was he wrong? Who would have known of Idomeneus, had not Epicurus etched his name in his correspondence? All those governors, satraps, and even the king himself, from whom Idomeneus derived his title, have been suppressed by deep oblivion. Cicero's letters do not allow the name of Atticus to perish. It would have profited Atticus nothing to have Agrippa for a son-in-law, Tiberius for a grandson-in-law, and Drusus Caesar for a great-grandson; amid these illustrious names he would find no mention, had not Cicero allied him with his own.

[5] The deep abyss of time will engulf us; a few great minds will raise their heads, destined to resist oblivion for a while before eventually subsiding into the same silence. What Epicurus could promise his friend, I promise you, Lucilius. I shall find favor with posterity; I have the power to bring forth names that will endure with my own. Our Virgil promised an eternal remembrance to two men, and he keeps his word:

> *Blessed pair! If aught my verse avail,*
> *No day shall ever blot you from the scroll*
> *Of memory, while yet the Capitol*
> *Stands fast, and Roman Father rules the world.*

[6] All those whom Fortune has brought into the limelight, who have served as limbs and organs of another's power - their influence flourished and their houses were thronged only so long as they themselves stood tall. Once they fell, all remembrance of them soon faded. But the prestige of great minds only grows after their passing. Honor is paid not just to the geniuses themselves, but to all that clings to their memory.

[7] (Lest Idomeneus appear in my letter without paying his way,

he shall compensate us from his own purse.) It was to Idomeneus that Epicurus addressed his famous maxim urging him to make Pythocles rich not by the well-trod path that the masses take, but by a road less traveled. "If you wish," he says, "to make Pythocles wealthy, don't add to his money but subtract from his desires."

[8] This dictum is too clear to require interpretation and too eloquent to require elaboration. But let me offer you this one reminder: don't think that this advice applies only to riches. Wherever you apply it, the same holds true. If you wish to make Pythocles honorable, add not to his honors but subtract from his cravings. If you wish Pythocles to have enduring pleasure, heap not more pleasures upon him but diminish his desires. If you wish Pythocles to be an old man and live his life to the fullest, add not to his years but take away from his passions.

[9] There's no reason for you to suppose these sayings belong to Epicurus alone - they are common property. In philosophy, I think we should do as is often done in the Senate: when someone offers an opinion that I agree with in part, I ask him to divide the question[2] and I follow what I approve. That's why I am all the more glad to quote Epicurus's noble utterances, to prove to those who flee to him under the wrong impression, hoping to find a cover for their own vices, that whatever direction they take, they must live uprightly.

[10] When you visit his little garden and read the inscription there "Stranger, here you will live well; here pleasure is the highest good", the custodian of that abode will be ready to receive you. He is a kindly, hospitable fellow and will graciously welcome you with barley-meal and ample supplies of water, saying "Have you not been well entertained? These little gardens do not whet hunger but quench it, nor do they increase thirst with the very drinks they provide, but slay it with a natural, cost-free cure. In this pleasure I have grown old."

[11] I am speaking to you about those desires which do not admit of consolation, which must be given something so that they will cease. For regarding those extraordinary desires which can be postponed, chastised and suppressed, I will give you this one reminder:

that pleasure is natural but not necessary. You owe nothing to it; if you expend anything on it, it is of your own free will.

The stomach does not listen to precepts; it makes demands, it importunes. Yet it is not a troublesome creditor; it is dismissed at small cost if you only give it what you owe, not what you are able. Farewell.

----

1. Lipsius proposed reading "regiae" (like that of a king) instead of "rigidae" (rigid), which may be correct.
2. In the Roman Senate, this procedure allowed a motion to be split into parts to be voted on separately.

LETTER 22

ON RETIRING FROM
WORLDLY AFFAIRS

[1] You now understand that you must extricate yourself from these specious yet pernicious occupations. But how, you ask, can this be accomplished? Some things can only be demonstrated in person. A doctor cannot select the proper times for eating or bathing by letter; the pulse must be felt. As the old proverb goes, a gladiator takes counsel in the arena; the demeanor of his opponent, the motion of his hand, the very tilt of his body offers guidance to the attentive observer.

[2] What is customary and what is proper can be outlined and communicated in general terms, both to those absent and to posterity. But no one can advise from afar when something should be done, or how; these deliberations must be made in the moment, with the matters at hand.

[3] It takes not just presence, but vigilance to seize the fleeting opportunity. So be circumspect, and when you spot it, grasp it and pursue it with all your might and main, that you may free yourself from those duties that ensnare you.

And mark well the opinion I shall now impart. I believe you must either quit that life, or life altogether. But I also hold that you should depart by a gentle path, untangling rather than abruptly severing your badly-formed attachments - unless no other means of extrication remains. No one is so timid as to prefer perpetual suspension to a single fall.

[4] In the meantime, as your first step, do not hinder yourself. Be content with the affairs you have descended into, or rather, as you prefer to have it seem, fallen into. Do not strive for more, lest you lose your excuse and reveal your complicity. The common refrains - "I could not do otherwise," "But what if I refused?" "It was necessary" - ring hollow. No one must pursue happiness at a sprint; even if one does not resist, one can yet halt and refuse to hasten after fortune's lead.

[5] I hope you will not take offense if I offer counsel, and even summon those wiser than myself, whom I customarily consult when deliberating. Read Epicurus' letter on this matter, the one addressed to Idomeneus[1], in which he urges him to flee with all speed, before some greater force intervenes and steals away his liberty to retire.

[6] Yet Epicurus also adds that nothing should be attempted except when it can be attempted suitably and seasonably. But when that long-awaited moment arrives, he declares one must leap. He forbids us to slumber when contemplating escape, and holds out hope for a saving egress even from the most difficult straits - if we neither hurry before the time nor dawdle when the time comes.

[7] I suppose you're now asking about the Stoic view as well. There's no need for anyone to accuse them of rashness in your presence; they are more cautious than courageous. Perhaps you're expecting them to say things like: "It is disgraceful to yield under a burden. Wrestle with the duty you have taken on. The person who flees from labor, unless his spirit grows with the very difficulty of his affairs, is not a brave and vigorous person."

[8] Such things will be said to you if perseverance is worthwhile, if nothing unworthy of a good person must be done or endured. Otherwise, he will not wear himself out with demeaning and insulting labor, nor be occupied with business for business' sake. He won't even do what you think he will - remain perpetually entangled in ambitious pursuits, bearing their turmoil. But when he sees that the things

in which he was embroiled are burdensome, uncertain, and perilous, he will step back - not turn his back, but gradually withdraw to safety.

[9] It is easy, my dear Lucilius, to escape occupations if you disdain the rewards of those occupations. These are the things that delay and detain us: "What then? Am I to abandon such great hopes? Am I to depart when the harvest itself is at hand? Will my entourage be stripped, my litter unattended, my hall empty?" It is from these things that people withdraw reluctantly, loving the wages of their miseries even while cursing the miseries themselves.

[10] Thus they complain about ambition as they do about a mistress; that is, if you examine their true feelings, they do not hate these things but quarrel with them. Scrutinize those who lament what they have desired and talk about fleeing from things they cannot do without - you will see that they linger willingly in what they themselves claim to bear painfully and wretchedly.

[11] So it is, Lucilius; servitude holds few, but many hold fast to servitude. However, if your intention is to lay aside servitude, and freedom has genuinely found favor with you, and for this one purpose you seek counsel - that you may manage to do this without perpetual anxiety - why would not the whole chorus of Stoics applaud you? All the Zenos and Chrysippuses will urge moderate, honorable, and fitting counsel.

[12] But if you keep turning back so that you may see how much you are carrying with you and with how great a sum you are furnishing your retirement, you will never find a way out. No one escapes while carrying baggage. Emerge to a better life with the gods' favor - but not in the way the gods favor those on whom, with generous and kindly countenance, they bestow outrageous fortunes, excused in this alone: that what burns and torments them is given to those who pray for it.

[13] I was just about to seal this letter, but I am compelled to break the seal, so that it may come to you with a small customary gift bearing some magnificent saying. And lo, one occurs to me, though I am not sure whether it is more true or more eloquent. "Whose is it?"

you ask. It is Epicurus' - for I am still asserting the baggage of others. "Everyone leaves life just as if they had but lately entered it."

[14] Seize anyone you please - young, old, or middle-aged - you will find them equally afraid of death and equally ignorant of life. No one has anything finished, for we have put off all our undertakings to the future. Nothing delights me more in that saying than that childishness is ascribed to the elderly.

[15] "No one," he says, "leaves life differently than one who has just been born." That is false - we die worse than we are born. The fault is ours, not Nature's. She ought to bring a complaint against us, saying: "What is this? I brought you into the world without desires, without fears, without superstition, without treachery and the other plagues; leave as you entered!"

[16] If anyone dies as free from care as he is born, he has gained wisdom. But as it is, we are all a-tremble when danger draws near; our spirit and color do not remain steady; useless tears flow. What is more shameful than to be troubled just when one has reached the very threshold of security?

[17] The reason for this, however, is that we are destitute of all goods; we fret over the loss of life. For no part of it remains with us - it has all passed by and flowed away. No one is concerned with living well, but only with living long, although it is within everyone's grasp to live well, but within no one's power to live long. Farewell.

---

1. The letter Seneca refers to does not survive among Epicurus' known writings.

LETTER 23

TRUE JOY SPRINGS FROM WITHIN

[1] You may expect me to write about how mildly the winter has treated us, being both brief and moderate, or about how dismal and unseasonably cold the spring is, or other such inanities that people grasping for words write about. But no, I will write something that may be of use to both you and me. And what could that be, if not an exhortation towards a sound mind? You ask what the foundation of a sound mind is? It is this: do not rejoice in vanities. This, I say, is the foundation; the pinnacle is to have reached the point where you find joy in the right things.

[2] The person who knows what to rejoice in, who does not stake their happiness on things outside their control, has reached the heights [of wisdom]. But one who is tantalized by some hope, even if it is close at hand, even if it is not hard to attain, even if their hopes have never deceived them before, remains anxious and uncertain of themselves.

[3] Above all else, my dear Lucilius, learn how to rejoice in the right way. You may think I am depriving you of many pleasures by discouraging reliance on chance and by judging hopes, those sweetest of delights, as things to be avoided. On the contrary, I do not ever want you to be without joy. I want joy to be born in your own

home; and it is born there, as long as it originates within yourself. Other kinds of gaiety do not fill the heart; they merely smooth the brow. They are shallow—unless perhaps you consider a person who laughs to be joyful. No, the mind must be cheerful, confident, and above all, elevated.

[4] Believe me, true joy is a serious thing. Or do you imagine that anyone with a carefree expression and a perpetual (as those dandies call it) little smile, can scorn death, open their door to poverty, rein in their desires, and contemplate enduring pain? The person turning these things over in their mind experiences a great joy, but not a giddy one. I want you to possess this kind of joy. It will never fail you once you have found its source.

[5] The fruits of shallow ore deposits lie on the surface; the richest veins are those whose bounty lies deep and will yield all the more, the more deeply they are mined. The delights that enthrall the masses provide a thin and fleeting pleasure, and any imported joy lacks a solid foundation. But this joy I speak of, that I am trying to guide you towards, is substantial and reveals more the further in you go.

[6] My dearest Lucilius, I implore you to do the one thing that can bring true happiness: cast aside and trample underfoot those things that outwardly glitter, those things promised to you by another or from another. Instead, look to the true good and rejoice in what is yours. And what is meant by "yours"? Your very self and the best part of you. Even though nothing can be accomplished without it, consider the body as more of a necessity than a great thing; it suggests vain pleasures, short-lived and regrettable, which, unless tempered with great moderation, will turn to their opposite. This I assert: pleasure teeters on the precipice of pain if it does not keep measure.

Maintaining measure is difficult in that which you have come to believe is good. The desire for true good, however, is safe.

[7] You ask what this true good is and whence it comes? I will tell you: from a good conscience, from honorable plans, from right actions, from a contempt of the vagaries of chance, from a peaceful

life of unwavering course, treading a single path. For those who leap from one purpose to another, or rather do not leap but are carried over by some happenstance, how can they possess anything certain or lasting, suspended and wandering as they are?

[8] Few are those who order themselves and their affairs by deliberate plan; the rest, like objects floating on rivers, do not go but are carried along. Some are held back by a gentler wave and transported more smoothly; others are seized by a more vehement current. Some, as the flow languishes near the bank, are deposited there, while others are cast into the sea by the torrent's impetus. Therefore, we must decide what we wish and persevere in it.

[9] Here is the place to pay off my debt. For I can give you back the words of your beloved Epicurus and thus absolve this letter: "It is irksome always to be beginning life." Or, if this sentiment can be better expressed: "They live badly who are always beginning to live."

[10] "Why?" you ask, for this saying demands an explanation. Because for them, life is always incomplete. One who is just beginning to live cannot be ready for death. We must strive to have lived enough. No one thinks this who is just now beginning life in earnest.

[11] Do not think that these are but few; almost all are in this state. Some indeed begin just when they ought to be ending. If you find this strange, I will add something that you will find more surprising: some have left off living before they have begun. Farewell.

LETTER 24

FACING TRIALS AND MISFORTUNES WITH COURAGE

[1] You write that you are worried about the outcome of a trial, as your raging enemy is threatening you with one. You think I will advise you to set your sights on a more positive outcome and take comfort in optimistic hopes. But what is the point of borrowing trouble - of suffering prematurely what will come soon enough, and squandering the present moment in fear of the future? It is undoubtedly foolish to make yourself miserable now just because you may be miserable at some point. Let me guide you to peace of mind by a different path:

[2] If you wish to shed all anxiety, envision that whatever you dread will indeed come to pass. Take the measure of that misfortune, whatever it may be, and put a price on your fear. You will surely realize that what you dread is either not that bad or will not last that long.

[3] One need not search long for examples to boost your confidence; every age has produced them. No matter where you direct your thoughts in the annals of domestic or foreign affairs, you will find instances of remarkable advancement, ambition, or genius.

If you are condemned, can anything worse befall you than being exiled or thrown in prison? Is there anything beyond that for anyone to fear, other than being burned or killed? Consider each of these fates and summon up those who have faced them with disdain - and there are many to choose from, not just seek out.

[4] Rutilius bore his own condemnation as if the only thing that troubled him was that the verdict was unjust. Metellus endured exile bravely, Rutilius even gladly. The former made a deal with the state to secure his return; the latter refused to return even when Sulla, who was never refused anything in those days, offered it. Socrates continued his philosophical discourses in prison and declined an opportunity to escape when some promised to arrange it. He remained where he was to relieve mankind's twin fears of death and imprisonment.

[5] Mucius thrust his hand into the flames. It is painful to be burned - how much more so to submit to it willingly! Here we see a man, unschooled and armed with no maxims against death and suffering, equipped only with the grit of a soldier, exacting a penalty from himself for a foiled attempt. He stood watching his own right hand drip and sizzle on the enemy's brazier, never pulling back the charring appendage until his foe removed the fire. He could have accomplished something more successful in that camp, but nothing more courageous. See how much more eager valor is to court danger than cruelty is to inflict it: Porsenna more readily forgave Mucius for wanting to kill him than Mucius forgave himself for failing to do so.

[6] "These stories," you say, "have been droned to death in all the schools; now, when it comes to despising death, you're going to tell me about Cato." And why shouldn't I recount how, on that last night, he read Plato's book with his sword placed by his head? He had provided himself with these two instruments in this time of crisis - one that he might will to die, the other that he might be able to do so. So, having put his affairs in order (as well as one can put in order that which is ruined and near its end), he thought it his duty to see to it that no one should have the power either to slay Cato or to save him.

[7] Drawing the sword which he had kept unstained from all bloodshed up to that day, he cried: "Fortune, you have accomplished nothing by resisting all my endeavors. I have fought, till now, for my

country's freedom, and not for my own, I did not strive with such obstinacy to be free, but only to live among the free. Now, since the affairs of mankind are beyond hope, let Cato be withdrawn to safety."

[8] So saying, he inflicted a mortal wound upon his body. After the physicians had bound it up, Cato had less blood and less strength, but no less courage. Angered now not only at Caesar but also at himself, he thrust his naked hands into the wound, and with a soul that scorned all earthly power, he expelled, rather than dismissed, that noble spirit which had been consecrated to freedom.

[9] I am not now heaping up these illustrations for the purpose of exercising my wit, but for the purpose of encouraging you to face that which is thought to be most terrible. And I shall encourage you all the more easily by showing that not only resolute men have despised that moment when the soul breathes its last, but that even men who were craven in some respects have equalled in this regard the courage of the bravest. Take, for example, Scipio, the father-in-law of Gnaeus Pompeius: he was driven back upon the African coast by a head-wind and saw his ship in the power of the enemy. He therefore pierced his body with a sword; and when they asked where the commander was, he replied: "All is well with the commander."

[10] This remark placed him on a level with his ancestors and suffered not the glory which fate gave to the Scipios in Africa to lose its continuity. It was a great deed to conquer Carthage, but a greater deed to conquer death. "All is well with the commander!" Ought a general to die otherwise, especially one of Cato's generals?

[11] I shall not refer you to history or collect examples of those men who throughout the ages have despised death (for they are very many). Consider these times of ours, of whose enervation and over-refinement we complain; they nevertheless will include men of every rank, of every lot in life, and of every age, who have cut short their misfortunes by death.

Believe me, Lucius, death is so little to be feared that through its good offices nothing is to be feared[1]. Therefore, listen fearlessly to the threats of your enemies.

[12] Even if your conscience gives you confidence, remember that

many factors outside the case itself can influence the outcome. Hope for the fairest result, but prepare yourself for the most unjust. Above all, keep this in mind: remove the turmoil from events and see each thing for what it really is. You will realize there is nothing terrible in them except fear itself.

[13] What you see happen to children also happens to us, those slightly older children. When they see the masks of those they love, are used to, and play with, they are terrified. We must strip away the mask, not only from people but from things, and restore their true face.

[14] Why do you show me swords, fires, and a crowd of executioners raging around you? Take away the pageantry under which you hide and terrify fools! You are death, recently scorned by my slave, by my maidservant. Why again do you elaborately unfold for me whips and racks? Why the machines fitted to each joint to wrench them apart, and the thousand other instruments for flaying a person piece by piece? Set aside these things that stupefy us. Silence the groans, shouts, and bitter cries of voices torn from mutilated bodies! You are pain, which that gout-sufferer despises, which that dyspeptic endures in the midst of his delicacies, which that young woman undergoes in childbirth. You are trivial if I can bear you, brief if I cannot.

[15] Turn over in your mind the things you have often heard and often said. But prove by your actions whether you have truly heard and truly said them. This is the most shameful charge leveled against us - that we treat philosophy as words rather than deeds.

You learned just now that death threatens you, that exile and pain loom? You were born for these things. Let us consider as likely to happen whatever can happen.

[16] I know you have already done what I urge you to do. Now I advise you not to submerge your spirit in anxiety over this matter. Your mind will be dulled and have less vigor when it is time to rise up. Turn it from your private troubles to the common condition. Say that you have a mortal, fragile body which can have pain declared against it not just from injury or the force of someone stronger. Plea-

sures themselves turn into torments - feasts bring indigestion, drunkenness brings torpor and trembling of the nerves, lust brings distortions of the feet, hands, and every joint.

[17] I may become poor; I will be among many then. I may be exiled; I will consider myself born wherever I am sent. I may be imprisoned—but am I free now? Nature has bound me to this burdensome body. I will die; you mean to say I will no longer be able to be sick, to be imprisoned, to die.

[18] I am not so foolish as to discuss here the Epicurean doctrine and claim that the fears of the underworld are empty—that Ixion is not spun on a wheel, that Sisyphus does not struggle to push his boulder uphill, that no one's entrails can be devoured and regrow daily to be feasted on again. No one is so childish as to fear Cerberus, the darkness, and the ghostly appearance of skeletons. Death either consumes us or strips us bare. If we are released, the better part remains when the burden has been removed; if we are consumed, nothing remains at all—blessings and curses alike are taken away.

[19] Allow me here to quote your own verse—but let me first remind you that you composed it not only for others, but for yourself as well. It is shameful to say one thing but think another; how much worse to write one thing and think another! I recall you once discussed how we do not suddenly fall into death, but advance toward it gradually; we die daily.

[20] For each day, a portion of our life is taken, and even as we grow, our life is diminishing. We lose our infancy, then our childhood, then our youth. Up through yesterday, whatever time has passed is lost; this very day we share with death. Just as a water clock is not drained by the last drop, but by all that has flowed out before, so the final hour when we cease to exist does not itself bring death— it merely completes the process. We reach death at that moment, but we have been journeying toward it all along.

[21] Having expressed these thoughts in your customary manner —always grand, but never more impassioned than when you lend your words to the truth—you said:

> *Death does not come once, but the one that seizes us is the*
> *final death.*

[2]I would prefer you read your own words again than my letter. For it will make clear to you that this death we fear is the last, but not the only one.

[22] I see where you are looking; you are asking what pithy saying or useful precept I have sprinkled into this letter. Something will be sent from the very matter we have been handling. Epicurus rebukes equally those who crave death and those who fear it, saying: "It is absurd to run toward death out of weariness with life, when it is your manner of life that has made you run toward death."

[23] Likewise, in another passage he says: "What could be more absurd than to seek death when you have made your life troubled through fear of death?" To these you may add another remark of the same purport—that the foolishness, nay madness, of humans is so great that some are driven to death by the fear of death.

[24] Whichever of these matters you grapple with, you will fortify your spirit to withstand either death or life. For we must be counseled and bolstered in two directions: neither to love life too much nor to hate it in excess. Even when reason persuades one to end their life, the impulse must not be adopted rashly nor with haste.

[25] The brave and wise man should not flee from life, but take his leave of it. And above all, one must avoid that sentiment which has seized many: a lust for dying. For there exists, my dear Lucilius, an ill-considered propensity of the mind toward death, just as toward other things—one that often grips men of noble and most zealous nature, and often the craven and feeble. The former spurn life; the latter find it burdensome.

[26] Some are overtaken by a satiety of doing and seeing the same things, and not a hatred of life but a weariness with it, into which we slip with philosophy itself impelling us, while we say: "How long the same things? To be sure, I will wake, I will sleep, I will be hungry, I will be full[3], I will be cold, I will be hot. There is no end to anything, but all things are linked in a cycle; they flee and they follow.

Night presses upon day, day upon night; summer passes into autumn, winter threatens after autumn, which is constrained by spring. All things pass so that they may return. I do nothing new, I see nothing new; eventually one feels nausea even at this."

There are many who judge living not bitter, but superfluous. Farewell.

---

1. An alternative reading: "death is so little to be feared that nothing is to be preferred to its good offices".
2. The original text has "ultima" (last) instead of "una" (one), according to Muretus' emendation.
3. Hense adds fastidiam ("I will be full").

LETTER 25

THE WISE MAN'S APPROACH
TO CROWDS AND SOLITUDE

[1] WHEN IT COMES TO OUR TWO FRIENDS, DIFFERENT APPROACHES ARE needed; the faults of one must be corrected, those of the other stamped out. I will be perfectly frank. I care not for a man if I cannot offend him. "What then?" you say, "Do you imagine you can keep a forty-year-old ward under your tutelage? Consider his age, already tough and intractable.

[2] He cannot be reshaped; only the tender are malleable." Whether I will make progress, I know not. But I would rather lack success than lack faith. Do not despair that even chronic invalids can be cured, if only you stand firm against their intemperance, if you compel them, reluctant as they are, to do and submit to many things. As for the other friend, I lack sufficient confidence, except in this - that so far he still blushes to do wrong. This modesty must be nurtured, for as long as it endures in his soul, there is good hope. With this hardened veteran, I think we must deal more carefully, lest he fall into despair over himself.

[3] There has been no better time to approach him than now, while he is resting, while he resembles one reformed. Others are deceived by this interval of his; not I. I await the return of his vices with heavy interest, those which I know now lie dormant, not dead. I

will devote some days to this matter and test whether progress can or cannot be made.

[4] As for you, show yourself strong to me, as you do, and lighten your burdens. None of what we possess is necessary. Let us return to the law of nature; riches await us there. What we need is either free or cheap; nature craves only bread and water. No one is poor in regard to these, and whoever has confined his desire within these bounds can rival Jupiter himself for happiness, as Epicurus says, a sentiment of whose I will enfold in this letter.

[5] "Act thus," he says, "as if Epicurus were watching." It undoubtedly aids us to set a guardian over ourselves, and to have someone whom you regard as a witness to your thoughts. Yet how much grander it is to live as though under the gaze of some good man, always present. But for now, I am content that you act, whatever you do, as if someone were watching; solitude persuades us to all evils.

[6] When you have advanced so far that you have respect even for yourself, you may dispense with your tutor; in the meantime, protect yourself by the authority of others. Let it be Cato, or Scipio, or Laelius, or one whose mere presence would suppress the sins even of the dissolute, while you shape yourself into one with whom you would not dare transgress. Once achieved, once a certain dignity has taken hold within you, I will begin to permit you that which Epicurus also advises: "Retire especially into yourself when you are forced to be in a crowd."

[7] You must become different from the masses. As long as it is unsafe for you to withdraw into yourself, scrutinize those around you; there is no one for whom it is not better to be with anyone else than with themselves. "It is especially then that you should retreat into yourself, when you are compelled to be in a crowd," if you are a good person, calm and self-controlled. Otherwise, you must flee from yourself into the crowd; when in your own company, you are closer to an evil man. Farewell.

LETTER 26

REFLECTIONS ON AGING AND THE APPROACH OF DEATH

[1] I WAS JUST REMARKING HOW OLD AGE WAS IN SIGHT FOR ME; BUT NOW I fear I have left even that behind. At my stage of life, this body of mine deserves a different name altogether. For old age is a term for weariness, not decrepitude; count me among the feeble, one foot in the grave.

[2] Yet I thank you, for my spirit feels no ravages of time, though my body surely does. Only my vices and their accessories have aged; my mind remains vigorous, delighting that so little binds it to the body. It has shed a great burden, exulting as it disputes with me the question of old age. This, it claims, is the mind's time to flower.

[3] Let us trust it then, and let it use its boon. It bids me ponder and examine how much of this tranquility and restraint of character I owe to wisdom, and how much to my time of life. Let me scrupulously sift out what I can no longer do and what I no longer wish to do[1]. For what ground is there for complaint, what hardship, if whatever was bound to end has ended?

[4] "But," you say, "the supreme hardship is to be diminished, to waste away and, bluntly put, to dissolve. For it is not a sudden blow that topples us; we are worn down incrementally, each day chips away at our powers." Yet what better way is there to meet one's end

than to glide towards it by nature's dissolution? Not that there is anything inherently bad about a sudden blow[2] that abruptly rips us from life, but this gradual ebbing is a gentle path. I at least, as if that day of reckoning were near, when judgment will be passed on all my years, keep watch over myself and say:

[5] "Nothing that I have put forth, in deed or word, amounts to anything yet. These are but shallow, deceitful tokens of the spirit, veiled with many blandishments. I will entrust the appraisal of my progress to death. Thus, I am composing myself for that day, not timidly but intently, when, artifice and veneer stripped away, I will judge whether my brave utterances arise from conviction or pretense, whether all my defiant speeches flung at Fortune were genuine or mere act."

[6] Disregard the opinions of men, for they are always uncertain and divided. Disregard the pursuits that have consumed your entire life, for death will pass judgment on you. I tell you this: learned discussions, erudite conversations, collections of wise sayings, and scholarly speeches do not reveal true strength of character. Even the most timid can be bold in speech. Your true nature will be revealed when you breathe your last. I accept this condition and do not fear the judgment.

[7] I say these things to myself, but consider that I have said them to you as well. You are younger, but what does it matter? Years are not counted. It is uncertain where death awaits you, so you must await it everywhere.

[8] I wished to conclude here, and my hand was reaching for the closing, but sacred rites must be performed and this letter must be given provisions for its journey. Suppose I do not say from where I will borrow the funds—you know whose coffers I will use. Wait for me a moment, and the sum will be paid from my own house. In the meantime, Epicurus will lend to us, he who says: "*Meditare mortem*" (Ponder upon death), or if it sounds better, "Cross over to the gods."

[9] The meaning here is clear: it is an excellent thing to learn how to die. Perhaps you think it superfluous to learn something that will

only be used once. This is precisely why we ought to study it—we must always be learning that which we cannot prove we know until we face it.

[10] "Ponder upon death"—he who says this urges us to ponder upon freedom. He who has learned to die has unlearned slavery; he is above all power, certainly beyond it. What to him are prison, guards, and bars? He has a free door. The one chain that binds us is the love of life, which, though it need not be cast aside, should be lessened so that when circumstances demand, nothing may hinder or hold us back from being prepared to do at once what we must do at some time. Farewell.

---

1. This passage is severely corrupted, making a precise translation difficult. However, based on the context and flow of the argument, Seneca seems to be conveying the following idea: It is equally advantageous for me to be unable to do what I do not want to do, as it is to be able to do what brings me joy.
2. aliquid mali ictus pL; est, found in a few less important MSS., is inserted by Hense.

LETTER 27
THE IMPORTANCE OF SELF-EXAMINATION AND REPROACH

[1] "So, you presume to admonish me?" you ask. "Have you already admonished and corrected yourself, that you now have leisure to reform others?" I am not so shameless as to take up the art of healing when I myself am sick. But, as though lying in the same hospital, I am discussing with you the illness we share and dividing the remedies. So listen to me as if I were speaking to myself. I am admitting you to my inmost thoughts, and summoning you to examine me in your presence.

[2] I cry out to myself: "Count your years, and you will blush to desire and strive for the same things you desired when a boy. As death looms nearer, ensure that your vices at least die before you. Forsake those turbulent pleasures that must be atoned for at great cost - they harm not only those to come but those past. Just as crimes, even if undetected when committed, still cause anxiety after the fact, so with base pleasures there remains regret even after they are experienced. They are not solid nor trustworthy; even if not harmful, they are fleeting.

[3] Rather seek out some lasting good. But there is none except what the mind discovers for itself within itself. Virtue alone offers perpetual and secure joy; even if some obstacle intervenes, it is but a

passing cloud, drifting below and never prevailing over the light of day."

[4] When will it be your lot to attain this joy? Your effort does not slacken yet, but let it hasten. Much work remains which you yourself must devote your waking hours and toil to accomplish, if you desire success. This matter does not allow for delegation.

[5] Other types of literary pursuits admit of outside help. There was in my time a certain wealthy man named Calvisius Sabinus; he had the fortune of a freedman and the temperament to match. I have never seen a man whose good fortune was a greater misfit. His memory was so faulty that he would forget now the name of Ulysses, now of Achilles, now of Priam - men as well known to us as our own attendants. No aged nomenclator[1], who in lieu of remembering names makes them up, ever saluted the tribes so incorrectly as he did the Trojans and Achaeans. Yet he desired to appear learned.

[6] So he devised this shortcut: for a vast sum he purchased slaves, one to know Homer by heart and another Hesiod; he also assigned nine to the nine lyric poets. You need not wonder that he paid high prices - if he did not find slaves on the market, he had them made to order. After assembling this retinue, he began to make life miserable for his guests. He would keep these slaves at the foot of his couch, and ask them from time to time for verses to recite - but he often stumbled in the middle of a word.

[7] Satellius Quadratus, a flatterer of foolish rich men, and moreover a sycophant and mocker, suggested that Sabinus acquire grammarians as his literary valets. When Sabinus mentioned that each of his slaves cost him a hundred thousand sesterces, Satellius quipped, "You could have bought just as many book-boxes for less!" Sabinus, however, held the opinion that he knew everything any member of his household knew.

[8] This same Satellius began urging the sickly, pale, and thin Sabinus to take up wrestling. When Sabinus replied, "How can I possibly do that? I barely have the strength to live," Satellius retorted, "I beg you, don't say such things! Don't you see how many robust slaves you have?" A sound mind can neither be lent nor bought. And I

imagine that if it were put up for sale, it would find no buyer. But a corrupt mind is purchased daily.

[9] Now, accept what I owe you and farewell. "Poverty, when regulated according to the law of nature, is great wealth." Epicurus expresses this thought in various ways, but it can never be repeated too often, for it is never learned thoroughly enough. To some, remedies must be shown; to others, they must be diligently applied. Farewell.

---

1. One who announces visitors' names.

LETTER 28

WE CANNOT ESCAPE
OURSELVES BY TRAVELING

[1] Do you imagine, my dear Lucilius, that this predicament is yours alone? Do you marvel as if at some novelty that even after journeying so far and through such a diversity of places, you have not shaken off the gloom and heaviness of your mind? It is your soul you must change, not your sky. Though you may cross vast seas, though, as our Virgil says,

"Lands and cities are left astern,"

your faults will follow you whithersoever you travel.

[2] When a certain person made this same complaint to Socrates, he replied: "Why do you wonder that globe-trotting does not help you, seeing that you always take yourself with you? The reason which set you wandering is ever at your heels." What pleasure can seeing new lands or surveying famous cities and sites afford you? All that hurrying from place to place is useless. Do you ask why such flight does not help you? It is because you flee along with yourself. You must lay aside the burdens of the mind; until you do this, no place will satisfy you.

[3] Reflect that your present behavior is like that of the prophetess

whom Virgil describes, panting and raging as if under the influence of some powerful spirit beyond her control:

> *"The Sibyl raves, if haply she may shake*
> *The mighty god from off her breast."*

You wander hither and yon, to rid yourself of the burden that rests upon you, though it becomes more troublesome by reason of your very restlessness, just as in a ship the cargo when stationary makes no trouble, but when it shifts to this side or that, it causes the vessel to heel more quickly in the direction where it has settled. Anything you do tells against you, and you hurt yourself by your very unrest; for you are shaking up a sick man.

[4] That trouble once removed, all change of scene will become pleasant; though you may be banished to the ends of the earth, in whatever corner of a savage land you may find yourself, that place, however forbidding, will be to you a hospitable abode. The person you are matters more than the place to which you go; for that reason we should not make the mind a bondsman to any one place. We must live with this conviction: "I am not born for any one corner of the universe; this whole world is my country."

[5] If you saw this fact clearly, you would not be surprised at getting no benefit from the fresh scenes to which you roam each time through weariness of the old scenes. For the first would have pleased you in each case, had you believed it wholly yours. As it is, instead of travelling, you are rambling and drifting, exchanging one place for another when the thing you are seeking, the good life, is found everywhere.

[6] Can there be any spot so full of confusion as the Forum? Yet even there, if need be, you can live in peace. Of course, if one were allowed to make one's own arrangements, I should flee far from the very sight and neighborhood of the Forum. For just as pestilential places assail even the strongest constitution, so there are some places which are also unwholesome for a healthy mind which is not yet quite sound, though recovering from its ailment.

[7] I disagree with those who plunge into the midst of life's turbulent waters and, welcoming a tumultuous existence, wrestle daily against hardships with great courage. The wise man will endure such trials, not seek them out, and will prefer peace to battle. There is little benefit in casting off one's own vices only to quarrel with those of others.

[8] "Thirty tyrants besieged Socrates," [Epicurus] said, "yet they could not break his spirit." What does it matter how many masters one has? Slavery is but one condition. The person who has learned to scorn it remains free, however large the throng of overlords.

[9] It is time to conclude, but first I must pay the fare. "The beginning of salvation is the recognition of sin." A striking sentiment from Epicurus, it seems to me. For the person who does not know he is doing wrong has no desire to be set right. You must catch yourself in the act before you can reform yourself.

[10] Some folks take pride in their vices. Do you think someone who counts his flaws as virtues spares a thought for remedies? Therefore, reproach yourself as much as you can. Interrogate yourself. First, take on the role of prosecutor, then of judge, and finally of intercessor. And sometimes, give yourself offense. Farewell.

LETTER 29
THE RISKS OF ASSOCIATING
WITH THE CROWD

[1] You ask about our friend Marcellinus and want to know how he's doing. He rarely comes to visit us, for no other reason than that he fears hearing the truth—a danger he is now safely removed from. For one should only speak to those willing to listen. This is why there's often debate whether Diogenes and the other Cynics, who made free use of their outspokenness and admonished whoever they met, should have acted as they did.

[2] After all, what's the point in rebuking the deaf or those mute by nature or disease? "Why," you ask, "should I spare my words? They cost nothing. I can't be sure whether my advice will benefit the person I'm advising, but I do know that if I advise many, I'm bound to benefit someone. I must scatter the seeds widely. It's impossible that success won't come sometimes when one tries often."

[3] This approach, my dear Lucilius, I don't think becoming for a great man. His authority gets diluted and lacks sufficient weight with those he could set straight before his reputation fades. An archer shouldn't just hit the mark sometimes, but miss only sometimes. An art that reaches its aim by chance is no art at all. But wisdom is an art —it should choose a sure target, select those it can improve, and turn

away from those it deems hopeless. Yet it shouldn't give up on them too quickly, but try extreme remedies even in the midst of despair.

[4] Our Marcellinus I have not yet despaired of. He can still be saved, but only if a helping hand reaches him quickly. There is a risk, no doubt, that he may drag down the one extending it. His natural talent is powerful but already inclining towards vice. Nevertheless, I will brave this danger and dare to show him his faults.

[5] He'll do what he usually does—summon those witticisms that can elicit laughter from mourners and joke first about himself, then about us. He'll anticipate everything I plan to say. He'll skewer our philosophic schools and reproach philosophers for their stipends, mistresses, and gluttony. He'll point out to me one philosopher caught in adultery, another in the tavern, another in the halls of power.

[6] He'll point out to me Marcus Lepidus' philosopher friend Aristo, who held forth during a pleasure ride—for that's when he found time to produce his literary works. When people asked about Aristo's philosophical sect, Scaurus quipped: "He's certainly no Peripatetic![1]" When Julius Graecinus, an excellent man, was asked his opinion of Aristo, he replied: "I can't tell you, for I don't know what he does when he dismounts"—as if asked about a chariot gladiator!

[7] These charlatans who would have more honorably neglected philosophy than peddled it, he will thrust in my face. Yet I have resolved to endure their insults; that man may move me to laughter, but I will perhaps move him to tears. Or if he persists in laughing, I will rejoice as though in misfortune that he has been afflicted with that cheerful sort of insanity. But such mirth does not last long. Watch closely; you will see the same people laughing bitterly and raging bitterly within a short span of time.

[8] My purpose is to confront him and show how much more valuable he was when he seemed of less worth to the masses. Even if I do not cut out his vices, I will check them; they will not cease but will be suspended. Perhaps they will even cease if they form the habit of being interrupted. This in itself is not to be disdained, since for the gravely afflicted, a favorable remission takes the place of health.

[9] While I prepare myself for him, you in the meantime, who are able, who understand from where and to what point you have progressed, and from that infer how far you will advance, discipline your character, elevate your mind, stand firm against the things you dread. Do not count those who cause you fear. Would a man not seem foolish if he feared a multitude in a place through which they pass one by one? Equally, the way to your death is not open to many, though many may threaten it. Nature has arranged it thus: the breath of life will be snatched from you by one, just as by one it was bestowed.

[10] If you had any shame, you would have remitted my final payment. But I will not conduct myself basely in ending my debt and will thrust upon you what I owe. "I have never wished to please the crowd. For what I know, the public does not approve; what the public approves, I do not know.[2]"

[11] "Who said this?" you ask, as if you did not know whose command I follow. It is Epicurus. But the same message will be shouted to you from every philosophical school - Peripatetics, Academics, Stoics, Cynics. For who can please the crowd if he is pleasing to virtue? Popular favor is sought by evil arts. You must make yourself similar to them; they will not approve unless they recognize themselves in you. It is far more relevant how you seem to yourself than how you seem to others. The love of base people cannot be won except by base means.

[12] What, then, will that lauded philosophy, preferable to all other arts and pursuits, bestow upon you? It will undoubtedly grant you the ability to please yourself rather than the masses, to weigh judgments instead of merely counting them, to live without fear of gods or men, and to either conquer misfortunes or put an end to them.

However, if I see you becoming renowned and praised by the fickle voices of the crowd, if shouts, applause, and the trappings of pantomime resound as you enter, if women and boys throughout the entire city extol you—how could I not pity you, knowing the path that leads to such fleeting favor? Farewell.

1. A pun, since the Peripatetics were known for walking around while teaching.
2. imperem and imperim in the manuscripts; imputem is Rossbach's conjecture. Buecheler suggests: nescias, aes cui imperem, "you did not know the man upon whom I am levying for a loan."

LETTER 30
ON FACING DEATH WITH EQUANIMITY

[1] I RECENTLY SAW BASSUS AUFIDIUS, AN EXCELLENT MAN, STRUGGLING against the assaults of age. But the burden now weighs on him more heavily than he can bear; old age has settled upon him with its full force. You know that he was always of a frail and feeble constitution. For a long time he managed to hold it together, or rather, hold it up. But now, suddenly, he collapses.

[2] It is like on a ship that springs a leak - at first you can counter a crack here or there, but when it starts breaking apart in many places, the gaping hull cannot be saved. So too in an elderly body, weakness can be propped up to a point. But when every joint starts pulling apart as in a crumbling building, and while one part is being repaired another is splitting open, it's time to look for a way out.

[3] Yet our friend Bassus remains spirited. This is what philosophy grants us - cheerfulness in the face of death, courage and joy in any state of the body, never failing even as we fail. A great pilot still sails on with torn sheets, and even if stripped bare, still steers the remnants of his ship. This is what our Bassus does, regarding his own end with a spirit and countenance that you'd think almost too unconcerned if he were watching another man's.

[4] It is a great feat, Lucilius, one long in the learning, to depart

with equanimity when that inevitable hour arrives. Other forms of death are mixed with hope - an illness ends, a fire is put out, a collapse spares those it seemed about to crush. The sea casts back unharmed those it had swallowed, with the same force that engulfed them. The soldier pulls back his sword from the very neck of his soon-to-be victim. But he whom old age leads to death has nothing to hope for. This alone cannot be held back. Yet in no way do men die more gently, though also no more slowly.

[5] Our Bassus seemed to me to be attending his own funeral, putting his affairs in order, and living as one who has survived himself, bearing the loss of himself with wisdom. For he speaks much about death, and takes pains to persuade us that if there is anything troubling or fearful in this business, it is the fault of the dying person, not of death - that there is no more distress in death itself than there is after it.

[6] But it is as foolish to fear what you will not feel, as to fear what you will not experience. Or does anyone believe that that through which nothing is felt, might yet be felt? "Therefore," he says, "death is so completely beyond all evil that it is even beyond the fear of all evils."

[7] I know these things have been said often and will need to be said often again, but they did not benefit me as much when I merely read them or heard them from those who claimed there was nothing to fear in what they themselves feared. No, it was this man, speaking about his own imminent death, who had the greatest impact on me.

[8] For I will tell you what I think: a man in the very grip of death is braver than one for whom death is near. When death is upon us, even the inexperienced find the courage not to avoid the inevitable. Thus the most timid gladiator, throughout the entire fight, offers his throat to his opponent and guides the wavering blade to himself. But that steady firmness of mind, required for facing an approaching yet still distant death, is rarer and can only be displayed by the wise.

[9] And so I listened to him with the utmost pleasure, as if he were pronouncing judgment on death and indicating its nature from a closer vantage point. You would probably have more confidence,

more respect, for someone who had died and come back to life to report that there is nothing bad in death. But as for the distress caused by the approach of death, those who have stood in its presence, who have seen it coming and welcomed it, are the best ones to describe it to you.

[10] Among these you may count Bassus, who did not wish to deceive us. He says that fearing death is as foolish as fearing old age. For just as old age follows youth, so death follows old age. The man who does not wish to die does not wish to live. For life is granted to us with the stipulation of death; to death we are bound to go. Therefore, it is the act of a madman to fear it, because while the certain is merely expected, it is the uncertain that is feared!

[11] Death imposes a necessity that is impartial and inescapable. Who can complain of being in a condition shared by all of mankind? Indeed, the first principle of fairness is equality.

But there is no need now to plead the case of Nature, who has willed that our law should be the same as her own; whatever she has put together, she takes apart, and whatever she has taken apart, she puts together again.

[12] Indeed, if anyone has had the good fortune of being gently released by old age, not suddenly torn from life but gradually withdrawn, oh how he should give thanks to all the gods that, having had his fill, he has been brought to that rest so necessary for a human being, so welcome to the weary. You see certain people wishing for death, and in fact more intensely than life is usually begged for. I do not know which I should judge as showing greater courage: those who summon death, or those who await it cheerfully and calmly. The former attitude sometimes arises from madness and a sudden fit of rage, while the latter is a tranquility born of firm judgment. An angry man may rush to meet his death, but no one except a man who has long prepared himself for it can greet approaching death with cheerfulness.

[13] I confess that I visited this dear friend of mine more frequently for many reasons - to see if I would find him the same each time, and to observe whether his mental vigor was diminishing along

with his bodily strength. On the contrary, his mind was growing just as the joy of charioteers becomes more evident when they are approaching the palm branch in the final lap.

[14] Indeed, following the precepts of Epicurus, he said that he hoped there would be no pain in that final gasp; but if there was, it would be somewhat consoled by its very brevity. For no great pain lasts long. Moreover, he said it would aid him, even in the very separation of mind and body, if it happened with torment - after that pain, he could feel pain no more. He had no doubt that an aged soul resides just on the lips and would not require great force to be detached from the body. "A fire that has seized readily combustible material must be extinguished by water or sometimes by the collapse of the building; but one that lacks fuel dies out on its own."

[15] I enjoy hearing these things, my dear Lucilius, not as if they were novel, but as if I had been brought face to face with the event. Indeed, have I not seen many people break off their lives? I have truly seen it, but those who come to death without hatred of life and accept it rather than pull it towards them have more impact on me.

[16] He also said that we feel that torture is of our own doing, because we become agitated when we believe death is near. But for whom is it not near, ready in all places and at all times? "But let us consider," he said, "when some apparent cause of dying seems to approach, how many other causes are nearer which are not feared." An enemy threatened someone with death - but indigestion overtook him first.

[17] If we wished to distinguish the causes of our fear, we would find that some exist and others only seem to. We do not fear death, but the thought of death. For we are always just as far from death itself. So if death is to be feared, it is to be feared always. For what time is exempt from death?

[18] But I should be wary that you may dislike letters as long as these even worse than death. So I will end here. However, so that you may never fear death, always think on it. Farewell.

LETTER 31

THE SOUL'S ASCENT TO FREEDOM AND WISDOM

[1] I RECOGNIZE MY FRIEND LUCILIUS; HE IS BEGINNING TO EXHIBIT THE man he promised to be. Follow that impulse of your soul, by which you were proceeding towards all the best things, trampling under foot the common goods. I do not desire you to become greater and better than you were striving to be. Your foundations have already occupied much ground; now accomplish as much as you have endeavored, and deal with those plans which you have pondered in your mind.

[2] In short, you will be wise if you close your ears, which are scarcely sufficiently stopped up with wax; a firmer density is necessary than what they say Ulysses used on his comrades. That voice which was feared was alluring, yet not public; but this voice which is to be dreaded does not resound from a single rock, but from every corner of the world. Sail past, therefore, not only that one place suspected for its treacherous pleasure, but all cities. Be deaf to those who love you most; with good intentions, they wish evil upon you. And if you wish to be happy, pray to the gods that none of these things which are desired for you may come to pass.

[3] Those things which these people wish to be heaped upon you are not good; there is only one good, which is the cause and support

of a happy life—to trust in oneself. But this cannot happen unless toil is despised and counted among those things which are neither good nor bad. For it is impossible that a single thing can at one time be bad, at another time good; at one time light and to be endured, at another time to be dreaded.

[4] Toil is not a good. What, then, is good? Contempt for toil. Therefore, I should blame those who toil to no purpose. On the other hand, I shall approve of those striving towards honorable things, the more they have leaned in and the less they have allowed themselves to be overcome and to slacken[1], and I shall exclaim: "By so much better, rise up and breathe deeply, and surmount that hill, if you can, in one breath!"

[5] Toil nourishes noble minds. There is no reason, therefore, for you to choose from that old vow of your parents what you wish to befall you, what you desire; and for a man already in all respects driven through the greatest affairs, it is shameful even now to weary the gods. What need is there for vows? Make yourself happy. More-over, you will do this if you understand that those things are good to which virtue has been added, and shameful to which wickedness has been conjoined. Just as without the admixture of light nothing is bright, nothing is dark unless it contains shadows or has drawn some-thing of obscurity into itself; just as without the aid of fire nothing is hot, nothing is cold without air; so the alliance of virtue and wicked-ness makes things honorable and base.

[6] What then is good? Knowledge of things. What is evil? Lack of knowledge of things. The wise and skillful man will, according to the occasion, repel or choose each thing. But he neither fears what he repels, nor admires what he chooses, if only his spirit is great and unconquered. I forbid you to be cast down and depressed. It is not enough to merely not refuse toil; demand it!

[7] "What then?" you say, "Is toil that is frivolous, superfluous, and called forth by humble causes not an evil?" No more than that which is spent on noble pursuits, since it is the very endurance of the mind that urges itself to hard and rough tasks and says: "Why do you hesi-tate? It is unfit for a man to fear sweat."

[8] To this let it be added that, for virtue to be perfect, there must be consistency and an even tenor of life that is thoroughly in harmony with itself. This cannot be achieved unless knowledge of things is attained and the art by which things human and divine are known. This is the supreme good. If you seize it, you begin to be an associate of the gods, not a suppliant.

[9] "How," you ask, "does one arrive at that goal?" You need not cross the Pennine or Graian mountains, or traverse the wastelands of Candavia, or face the Syrtes, Scylla, or Charybdis [legendary dangers], all of which you have nevertheless braved for the reward of a petty office. The journey is safe and pleasant, for which nature has equipped you. She has given you the means, which if you do not forsake, you will rise equal to god.

[10] But money will not make you equal to god; god has nothing. The purple robe will not do it; god is naked. Fame will not do it, nor the parading of yourself and the publicity of your name among the peoples; no one knows god, many think ill of him, and do so with impunity. Nor will a crowd of slaves bearing your litter through city streets and on journeys abroad; that greatest and most powerful god himself bears all things. Not even beauty and strength can make you blessed; none of these withstands old age.

[11] We must seek that which does not deteriorate day by day, that which cannot be obstructed. What is this? It is the soul—but the soul that is upright, good, and great. What else could you call such a soul but a god dwelling as a guest in a human body? This soul may descend into a Roman knight just as easily as into a freedman or a slave. For what is a "Roman knight," a "freedman," or a "slave"? They are mere titles, born from ambition or injustice. One may leap up to heaven from any corner of the earth. So rise up and make yourself worthy of God.

But you cannot mold yourself from gold or silver; no likeness of God can be fashioned from such materials. Remember, even when the gods were propitious, their images were made of clay. Farewell.

———————————————

1. Haase's emendation "adprobabo" is adopted here in place of the manuscript reading "adprobator" or "admirabor."

LETTER 32

LIVE AS IF UNDER THE GAZE
OF A DISTINGUISHED MAN

[1] I INQUIRE ABOUT YOU AND ASK ALL WHO COME FROM YOUR REGION how you are doing, where and with whom you are living. You cannot deceive me; I am with you. Live as though I would hear what you are doing, nay, as though I would see it. Do you ask what delights me most from what I hear about you? That I hear nothing, that most of those I ask do not know what you are doing.

[2] It is salutary not to associate with those dissimilar to us and desiring different things. Indeed, I am confident you cannot be swayed and will remain steadfast in your purpose, even if a crowd of tempters surrounds you. What, then, is it? I do not fear they will change you, but that they will hinder you. Even one who merely delays you does much harm, especially in a life so short, which we make shorter still by inconsistency, by repeatedly making a new beginning of it. We tear it into pieces and mangle it.

[3] So make haste, my dearest Lucilius, and consider how much speed you would add if an enemy were pressing from behind, if you suspected cavalry was approaching and trampling the footprints of the fleeing. This is happening; you are hard pressed. Hurry and escape, conveying yourself to safety. Continually reflect on what a beautiful thing it is to complete your life before death, then to await

the remaining portion of your time secure, with nothing left for yourself, resting in possession of the happy life, which doesn't become happier if made longer.

[4] Oh, when will you see that time when you will know time no longer pertains to you, when you will be tranquil and serene, indifferent to tomorrow, utterly content with yourself! Do you want to know what makes people so greedy for the future? No one has fully attained themselves. And so your parents wished other things for you, but I, contrary to them all, wish for you a contempt of the very things they wished for you in abundance. Their wishes rob many to enrich you. Whatever is transferred to you must be taken from another.

[5] I wish for you self-possession, so that your mind, agitated by wandering thoughts, may at last resist and be resolute, content with itself and, having understood the true goods which are possessed the moment they are understood, not requiring the addition of years[1]. Only one who has surmounted necessities and been discharged from service is truly free - one who lives with life completed. Farewell.

---

1. Erasmus's correction of "veris" for "verbis" is accepted here.

LETTER 33

THE UNITY AND CONSISTENCY OF THE STOIC TEACHINGS

[1] IN THESE EPISTLES, JUST AS IN EARLIER ONES, YOU DESIRE THAT I include some sayings from our great men. They were not occupied with mere ornamental flourishes; their entire discourse is robust and manly. Know that where certain passages stand out, there is bound to be unevenness. A single tree is not remarkable where the whole forest has risen to the same height.

[2] Verses are full of such expressions, as are histories. Therefore, I would not have you think these utterances belong to Epicurus alone; they are common property and quintessentially ours. But in his works they are more noticeable because they appear infrequently and unexpectedly. It is surprising to hear something brave from a man who professed softness—for so most people judge him. To me, Epicurus is indeed a brave man, even though he may wear long sleeves. Courage, energy, and a mind ready for combat can fall to the lot of Persians as well as Romans.

[3] So you must not insist on extracts and repetitions. Among our Stoic philosophers, whatever is extracted forms a continuous whole. We do not have those dainty morsels, nor do we deceive the buyer, who will find nothing when he enters the shop except those goods

which are displayed in the window. We allow them to take their samples from anywhere they wish.

[4] Suppose we did want to sort out separate maxims from the throng; to whom shall we attribute them? To Zeno, Cleanthes, Chrysippus, Panaetius, or Posidonius? We Stoics are not subjects of a despot; each of us lays claim to his own freedom. With the Epicureans, on the contrary, whatever Hermarchus said, or Metrodorus, is ascribed to one source. In that brotherhood, everything that any man utters is spoken under the leadership and command of one alone. We cannot, I maintain, no matter how we try, pick out anything from so great a multitude of equally good sayings. Only a poor man counts his flock. Wherever you direct your gaze, you will meet with something that might stand out, if the context in which you read it were not equally notable.

[5] So give up hoping that you can skim, by means of epitomes, the wisdom of distinguished men. Look into their wisdom as a whole, study it as a whole. They are working out a plan and weaving together, line upon line, a masterpiece, from which nothing can be taken away without injury to the whole. Examine the separate parts, if you like, provided you examine them as parts of the man himself. She is not a beautiful woman whose ankle or arm is praised, but she whose general appearance makes you forget to admire her single attributes.

[6] If, however, you insist, I shall not be niggardly with you, but lavish; for there is a huge multitude of these sayings. They are scattered about, not gathered deliberately. They do not drip forth, but flow continuously. They are closely connected and are woven together. No doubt these utterances will be of much benefit to those who are still novices and worshipping outside the shrine; for single maxims sink in more easily when they are marked off and bounded like a line of verse.

[7] This is why we have children memorize maxims and what the Greeks call "chrias" [concise statements of general truths], because a child's mind can grasp these, having no capacity yet for more. But for

a grown man to hunt after choice flowers of speech and prop himself up with well-known and tiny scraps, relying on his memory, is shameful. Let him instead stand on his own feet. Let him voice ideas, not simply hold onto them. It's disgraceful for an old man or one nearing old age to have wisdom that comes from a notebook. "Zeno said this." But what have you yourself said? "Cleanthes said that." But what have you said? How long will you be compelled by the claims of another? Take command and utter something that may be handed down to posterity.

[8] Produce something from your own resources. This is why I think none of those men, who are never their own masters but always lurk in someone else's shadow, have any noble qualities, since they have never dared to do even once what they have spent so long learning. They have exercised their memories on other men's material. It is one thing to remember, another to know. To remember is to safeguard something entrusted to your memory, whereas to know is to make it your own, and not depend on some original and be always looking back to your teacher.

[9] "Zeno said this, and Cleanthes that!" Let there be a difference between yourself and your book. How long are you going to be a student? From now on be a teacher as well. "Why," men say, "should I listen to what I can read for myself?" "The living voice," one replies, "counts for a great deal." Not when it is just acting as a proxy, conveying someone else's words.

[10] Moreover, those who never attain self-reliance are, in the first place, following the views of predecessors in matters where everyone has abandoned the previous authority. Secondly, they are following them in a field which is still under investigation. But the truth will never be discovered if we rest contented with discoveries already made. Besides, a man who follows someone else follows nothing, discovers nothing, nay, is not even investigating.

[11] What then? Shall I not follow in the footsteps of my predecessors? I shall indeed use the old road, but if I find one that makes a shorter cut and is smoother to travel, I shall open the new road. Men

who have made these discoveries before us are not our masters, but our guides. Truth lies open for all; it has not yet been monopolized. And there is plenty of it left even for posterity to discover. Farewell.

LETTER 34
SENECA REJOICES IN LUCILIUS' PHILOSOPHIC PROGRESS

[1] I GROW ELATED AND REJOICE, SHAKING OFF MY OLD AGE AND growing warm again, whenever I understand from your actions and your writings how far you have risen above yourself—for you long ago left the crowd behind. If a farmer delights in a tree that has been brought to bear fruit, if a shepherd takes pleasure from the offspring of his flock, if no one looks upon his ward in any other way than to judge the youth as his own, what do you believe happens to those who have nourished young minds and suddenly see them grown to maturity, having carefully shaped them when they were tender?

[2] I claim you for myself; you are my handiwork. When I saw your natural ability, I laid my hand upon you, I spurred you on, I applied the lash and did not allow you to proceed slowly, but urged you on continually. And now I do the same, but by this time I am cheering on one who is in full career and who in turn cheers me on.

[3] "What else do I want?" you ask. "I want more still." This is the greatest part: it is not like how they say that the beginning is half of the whole work. In this case, it is the mind that counts. Therefore, a large part of goodness is the desire to become good. Do you know whom I call good? One who is perfect and complete, whom no force or necessity can render bad.

[4] I see you becoming this person, if you persevere, apply yourself, and strive that all your actions and words harmonize and correspond with each other and are stamped in the same mold. The mind of one whose deeds are at variance is not right. Farewell.

LETTER 35

CULTIVATING GENUINE FRIENDSHIP THROUGH SHARED DEVOTION TO WISDOM

[1] WHEN I ENTREAT YOU SO EARNESTLY TO DEVOTE YOURSELF TO STUDY, I am promoting my own interests. I want you to be my friend, which cannot happen unless you continue to cultivate your mind as you have begun to do. For at present, you love me but are not yet my friend. "What?" you say, "Are these things distinct?" Indeed, they are different. One who is a friend loves, but one who loves is not necessarily a friend. And so friendship always benefits, while love sometimes even harms. If nothing else, strive to learn how to love.

[2] Hurry then, while you can still gain ground with me, lest you learn this lesson for another's benefit. I am already reaping the harvest when I imagine us two sharing one spirit, and that whatever vigor has departed from my years will return to me from your youth, though there is no great difference between us.

[3] But I want to rejoice in the actual reality as well. Joy comes to us from those we love even when they are absent, but that joy is fleeting and quick to vanish. The sight, the presence, the conversation of one we love holds a lively pleasure, especially if we see them not only as we wish but as we wish them to be. So bring yourself to me—that is a great gift. And to spur you on, consider that you are mortal and I am old.

[4] Hasten to me, but to yourself first. Make progress, and above all else, strive to be consistent. Whenever you want to test whether you have accomplished anything, observe whether you want the same things today that you wanted yesterday. A shifting of the will indicates that the mind is adrift, appearing now here, now there, according to the direction of the wind. What is firmly rooted does not wander. This state is achieved by the perfected sage; the progressing, advancing student attains it to some degree. What, then, is the difference? The latter wavers but does not change his ground; the sage does not waver at all. Farewell.

LETTER 36

REMAINING STEADFAST AMIDST WORLDLY DISTRACTIONS AND CHANGE

[1] Encourage your friend to view with great contempt those who reproach him for seeking solitude and leisure, for abandoning his post, and for preferring tranquility over all else despite his potential for greater attainment. Let him demonstrate to them daily how profitably he spends his time. Those who are envied will not cease to march past; some will be crushed, others will fall. Prosperity is a restless thing; it torments itself. It stirs the brain in more ways than one; it goads people in different directions, some toward power, some toward decadence. It puffs up some, while others it softens and utterly enervates.

[2] "But someone carries prosperity well," you say. Yes, just as he carries wine. So don't let those folks convince you that he is content who is besieged by the crowd; they flock to him as to a lake which they drain and muddy. "They call him trifling and lazy." You know that some speak perversely and mean the opposite of what they say.

[3] They used to call him happy; what then? Was he? I do not concern myself even with this—that to some he seems too grim and stern. Aristo used to say that he preferred a youth who was serious rather than one who was cheerful and agreeable to the crowd. For good wine, he said, becomes more pleasing with age, though when

new it seemed harsh and rough; but that which delights in the cask does not endure. Let them call him stern and hostile to their pursuits; this very sternness will serve him well as it ages, provided he continues to cultivate virtue and imbibe liberal studies—not those with which it is sufficient to be sprinkled, but those in which the mind should be thoroughly steeped.

[4] Now is the time to learn. "What then?" you ask, "Is there any time when one should not learn?" By no means. But just as it is honorable to study at all ages, it is not honorable to be instructed at all ages. It is a disgraceful and absurd thing to be an old man just learning his ABC's; a youth must store up, an old man must use. Therefore, you will be doing yourself a great service if you make your friend as good a man as possible. These, they say, are the sort of benefits that are worth seeking and bestowing—those that profit the giver no less than the receiver.

[5] In short, your friend no longer has complete freedom; he has given his word. It is less disgraceful to be insolvent to a creditor than to disappoint a promising hope. To pay off that other kind of debt [that of worldly obligations], the merchant needs favorable winds, the farmer needs rich harvests and the favor of the skies; but your friend can fulfill his obligation through will alone.

[6] Fortune has no jurisdiction over character. Let her regulate outward circumstances as she pleases, but let her not tamper with that inward spirit which must come, in perfect serenity, to its full maturity—the spirit that feels neither loss nor gain, but remains in one unchanging posture, however events may fall out. Whether the ordinary blessings of life are heaped upon it, it rises above its goods; or if chance robs it of some or all of them, it is not impoverished.

[7] If a man were born in Parthia, he would be early taught to bend the bow; in Germany, he would at once be brandishing his slender javelin; if he had lived in the times of our forefathers, he would have learned to ride a horse and smite his enemy hand to hand. These are the occupations which the system of each race recommends to the individual.

[8] And to what, then, shall this one be trained? To that which is

the most essential defense against all weapons, against every foe—contempt of death. Life holds no terrors for him who has thoroughly understood that not to live is no evil. Though there is something instinctively repugnant about death which offends even minds molded by nature to love it, still, training would not be needed to urge us toward a goal to which we are drawn by a certain voluntary instinct, as all men are impelled to self-preservation.

[9] No one learns how to lie comfortably on a bed of roses if need be; rather, men steel themselves to keep their faith inviolate even under torture— to stand on guard, if necessary, wounded, sleepless, and leaning on a spear, for sleep easily creeps over those who lean on any support. Death brings no inconvenience, for that which experiences the inconvenience must itself exist.

[10] But if you are possessed by such a keen desire for a longer life, reflect that none of the things which vanish from our gaze and are re-absorbed into the universe from whence they came, and into which they will soon pass again, is really lost: such things merely end, they do not perish. And death, which we so fear and shun, merely interrupts life, it does not steal it away. The day will come again which will return us to the light—a day which many would refuse, were they not brought back forgetful of the past.

[11] But I will show you later, with more care, that everything which seems to perish merely changes. He who is to return, then, ought to depart with equanimity. Observe the round of the universe which incessantly repeats itself; you will see that in this world nothing is extinguished, but only alternates between descent and ascent. Summer has gone, but another year will bring it again; winter lies low, but will be restored by its own proper months; night obscures the sun, but day will soon rout the night. The procession of the stars revisits whatever it has left behind; a part of the sky is rising unceasingly, a part is sinking.

[12] In conclusion, I will end with this one final thought: it is most shameful that neither infants, children, nor the mentally impaired fear death, yet reason fails to provide us with the peace of mind that foolishness grants them. Farewell.

LETTER 37
VIRTUE REQUIRES DEDICATION AND SACRIFICE

[1] YOU HAVE PROMISED TO BE A GOOD MAN; YOU HAVE ENLISTED UNDER oath. Anyone who tells you this is an easy and gentle military service is trying to fool you. I won't have you deceived. The words which bind you to this most honorable and that most disgraceful of callings are the same:

[2] "To be burned, imprisoned, and slain by the sword." Those who hire out their strength for the arena, who eat and drink what they must pay for with their blood, are forced to suffer such trials. From you, obedience must be willing, even eager. They are permitted to lower their weapons and implore the crowd's mercy, but you will neither lower yours nor beg for life. You must die erect and unyielding. What good does it do to gain a few days or years? We are born into service without discharge.

[3] "How then," you ask, "shall I free myself?" You cannot escape necessities, but you can overcome them.

By force a way is made[1].

And philosophy will provide you this way. Commit to it if you wish to be safe, secure, blessed—in a word, free. This cannot be achieved otherwise.

[4] Folly is base, abject, sordid, servile, beholden to many of the cruelest passions. Cast off these oppressive masters, which sometimes rule by turns, other times together, with wisdom, which alone is liberty. The one path to it, a straight one, is offered by philosophy; you will not go astray. Proceed with steady steps. If you wish to have all things under your command, put yourself under the command of reason. You will rule many if reason rules you. From philosophy you will learn what and how you should undertake; you will not blunder into things.

[5] You cannot show me anyone who knows how he began to desire what he desires. He was led to that state not deliberately, but by chance impulse. Fortune attacks us as often as we attack Fortune. It is shameful to be carried rather than to walk, and to be surprised, in the midst of the whirlwind of events, to ask in a daze: "How did I get here?" Farewell.

---

1. This line is quoted from Vergil. Its source was omitted in Seneca's original text.

LETTER 38

THE POWER OF PHILOSOPHIC PRECEPTS TO TRANSFORM THE MIND

[1] You are right to insist that we should maintain a frequent exchange of letters. Conversation is immensely beneficial, as it gradually seeps into the soul. Meticulously prepared disputations, delivered before a listening crowd, may be more dazzling, but they offer less intimacy. Philosophy is good counsel, and no one gives counsel at the top of their lungs. At times, we must also make use of those grand orations, so to speak, where the doubter must be swayed. But when the goal is not to inspire the will to learn, but to impart knowledge itself, we must turn to humbler words. They enter more easily and linger longer, for it is not an abundance of words that is needed, but effective ones.

[2] Ideas must be scattered like seeds. However small a seed may be, when it lands in a suitable place, it unfurls its strength and grows from the tiniest thing into the mightiest. Reason works the same way; it may not seem impressive at first glance, but it grows in application. The teachings may be few, but if the mind receives them well, they gain vigor and flourish. The nature of precepts, I say, is the same as that of seeds; they yield a great harvest from a small beginning. The mind need only be receptive and draw the teachings into itself. In

turn, the mind will generate many new ideas of its own and will give back more than it received. Farewell.

LETTER 39

THE PERILS OF EXCESS AND
THE VALUE OF MODERATION

[1] I WILL INDEED COMPILE FOR YOU THE WELL-ORGANIZED AND CONCISE commentaries that you request. But consider whether a standard approach might be more beneficial for you than what is nowadays commonly called a "breviary" and was once known as a "summary" back when people still spoke proper Latin. The former method is more necessary for the learner, the latter for the knowledgeable. One teaches, the other reminds. But I will provide you with both. You need not request this or that author from me, for someone who directs you to a noteworthy writer remains unknown themselves.

[2] Therefore, I will write what you wish, but in my own style. In the meantime, you have many authors whose writings may or may not be sufficiently systematic. Pick up a catalog of the philosophers— the very act will spur you to wake up when you see how many have labored for your benefit. You too will desire to be counted as one of them. For an noble mind has this excellent quality: it is roused to honorable acts.

No man of lofty talent is satisfied with the base and sordid. The sight of great endeavors beckons him and lifts him up. [3] Just as a flame rises straight upward, unable to lie down or be suppressed any more than it can rest, so too our soul is always in motion—the more vigorous its action, the more dynamic its mobility. But happy is he who has directed this impulse toward better ends! He will place himself beyond the jurisdiction and authority of Fortune. He will moderate favorable circumstances and diminish adversities, looking down upon what others admire.

[4] It is the mark of a great soul to despise greatness and to prefer moderation over excess. For the moderate is beneficial and life-sustaining, while the superfluous causes harm by its very excess. Thus, overabundance lays low the crop, branches break under too heavy a load, and excessive fertility prevents ripening. The same thing happens to the soul, which unchecked prosperity shatters, prompting men to misuse it not only to others' detriment but even to their own.

[5] What enemy has ever been as insolent toward another as the self-indulgent are to themselves? One could almost forgive their incontinence and mad desires for this reason alone—that they suffer the consequences of their own actions. It is no wonder such madness plagues them, for unrestrained greed that overleaps natural limits must inevitably run to extremes. Natural desires have their boundary, but those arising from false cravings know no limit.

[6] Utility measures what is necessary; so where do you relegate the superfluous? They immerse themselves in pleasures which, once made habitual, they can't do without. Thus they are most wretched, having reached the point where the superfluous has become necessary. They are slaves to their pleasures, not enjoying them, and they love their own vices—the ultimate of evils.

The height of unhappiness is reached when the shameful not only delights but pleases, and there ceases to be any room for remedy once vices have become habits. Farewell.

LETTER 40

THE MARKS OF A PROPER PHILOSOPHIC DISCOURSE

[1] I thank you for writing to me so frequently. It is the only way you can show yourself to me. Never do I receive a letter from you without our being together instantly. If portraits of absent friends are pleasing to us, renewing our memories of them and relieving the pain of absence with a false and empty consolation, how much more pleasing are letters which carry genuine traces of an absent friend, real evidence of their presence? For that which is sweetest when we meet face to face is afforded by the imprint of a friend's hand upon his letter - the sense of recognition.

[2] You write that you heard the philosopher Serapion when he dropped anchor here, and that "he is accustomed to wrench forth his words with great momentum, pouring them forth not singly but all in a rush and onslaught, for more crowd in than one voice can handle." I do not approve of this in a philosopher, whose speech, like his life, ought to be composed; nothing that is rushed and hurried is well-ordered. This is why in Homer that rapid and unceasing speech, falling like snow, is assigned to the younger orator, while from the old man's lips it flows gently, sweeter than honey.

[3] So hold fast to this principle - that such a rapid and abundant power of speaking is more suited to a mountebank than to a man who

is discussing and teaching an important and serious subject. I would as little have him drip words as race through them; he should neither stretch our ears on the rack nor bury them under his masses of words. For that poverty-stricken and thin-spun style also keeps the attention from being roused, because the audience is wearied by the annoying halts and delays; nevertheless, the word which has been long awaited sinks in more easily than the word which flits past us on the wing. Finally, people are said to hand down precepts to their pupils; but one cannot hand down that which eludes the grasp.

[4] Besides, speech that aims at truth should be unadorned and plain. This popular style has nothing to do with truth; its aim is to impress the crowd and carry away the untrained listener with its rapid flow, but it does not allow itself to be examined and is like something carried off by the wind. But how can that speech govern others which cannot itself be governed? Indeed, this sort of speech which is employed for the cure of sick minds - ought it not to sink into us? Remedies do not avail unless they remain in the system.

[5] There is also a great deal of emptiness and vanity in such speech; it has more sound than power. My terrors need soothing, my irritations need restraining, my illusions need shaking off, my indulgences need to be reined in, my greed needs to be rebuked. And which of these can be done in a hurry? What physician can heal his patient on a flying visit? Furthermore, such clatter of words without discrimination brings not even any pleasure.

[6] Just as it is sufficient to have learned about most things that you would not believe possible, it is more than enough to have heard those word-twisters once. For what could one wish to learn or imitate from them? What judgment can be made about the mental state of those whose speech is disordered, unrestrained, and impossible to rein in?

[7] It is like those running headlong down a steep slope—they cannot stop their pace where they wish, but their body's momentum carries them forward and they are borne further than intended. In the same way, that rapid manner of speaking is not under their control and lacks the dignity befitting philosophy, which ought to

place its words deliberately, not hurl them out, and advance step by step.

[8] "What then," you ask, "will philosophy never rise to the attack?" Of course it will, but while maintaining the dignity of its character, which this violent and excessive force strips away. Let philosophy have great strength, but moderated; let its stream be steady, not a torrent. I would scarcely allow even an orator such an irrevocable velocity of speech that charges on without restraint. For how can the judge, who is sometimes inexperienced and unlearned, follow along? Even then, when either showmanship or uncontrolled passion has carried the orator away, he should only hasten and heap on as much as the ears can endure.

[9] You will do well, then, to avoid those who are concerned with how much they say rather than how they say it. You would do better to speak, if necessary, as Publius Vinicius[1] does—haltingly. When Publius Vinicius' manner of speaking was under discussion, Asellius remarked, "Slowly drawn out." Indeed, Geminus Varius said, "I don't know how you can call him eloquent; he can't string three words together." Why would you not prefer to speak like Vinicius?

[10] Should someone so foolish interject, as one did to Vinicius while he was carefully considering each word, as if dictating rather than speaking: "Say, do you have something to say?" As for Quintus Haterius[2], the most celebrated orator of his day, I would have his manner far removed from a sane man's; he never paused, never hesitated; he would begin once and end once.

[11] I do think, however, that certain styles are more or less suitable to certain nations. You might tolerate this unrestrained manner in the Greeks; but we Romans have grown accustomed to taking breaks even when we write. Our own Cicero, from whom Roman eloquence sprang forth, was a steady pacer. The Roman style is more circumspect, weighing itself and allowing itself to be weighed.

[12] Fabianus, a man of outstanding character, knowledge, and, not least of all, eloquence, used to discourse with ease rather than intensity. One might say his speech possessed facility, not rapidity. This steady pace I allow in a wise man; I do not demand it. I prefer

that his speech advance without hindrance, though I would rather it be deliberately put forth than pour out in a torrent.

[13] All the more do I warn you against this affliction, because it can only befall you if you have lost all sense of shame. You must scour your brow clean of blushes and stop listening to your own self-criticism. For that unrestrained rush of words will carry along many things you would wish to reproach. This failing cannot, I tell you, come upon you while your modesty remains intact. Moreover, it requires daily practice, and your devotion must be transferred from the subject matter to the words themselves.

[14] But even if you possess such skill and can speak with effortless fluency, you must still rein it in. For just as a more modest gait befits the wise man, so too does compressed speech rather than bold bluster. The sum total of my advice, therefore, is this: I bid you become a deliberate speaker. Farewell.

---

1. A Roman orator known for his deliberate style]
2. An orator known for his rapid, flowing style.

LETTER 41

THE DIVINE SPIRIT
WITHIN US

[1] You ARE DOING AN EXCELLENT AND SELF-BENEFITING THING, IF, AS you write, you persevere in pursuing a sound mind. How foolish it is to wish for this, when you can obtain it from yourself! There is no need to raise our hands to heaven or to beg the temple keeper to allow us near the idol's ear, as if we could be heard better there; god is near you, with you, within you.

[2] Yes, Lucilius, a sacred spirit dwells within us, observing and guarding our good and evil deeds. As we treat this spirit, so are we treated by it. Indeed, no one can be a good person without god; can anyone rise above fortune unless aided by the divine? The divine gives us lofty and upright counsel. In every good person,

"What god is there is uncertain; a god dwells there.[1]"

[3] If you come across a grove thick with ancient trees that have grown far beyond their usual height, their interlacing branches shutting out the sight of the sky, that towering forest canopy, the seclusion of the spot, and your wonder at the unbroken shade in open daylight will make you feel the presence of the divine. If a cave, hollowed out deep into the rocks—not by human hands, but by natural forces—

holds up a mountain, your soul will be struck with a sense of religious awe. We revere the sources of mighty rivers; we erect altars where a great stream bursts suddenly from hidden sources; we worship hot springs, and certain pools have been sacred due to their dark waters or immeasurable depth. If you see a person undaunted by dangers, untouched by desires, happy in adversity, peaceful amid the storm, viewing humanity from a higher plane, and the gods as equals—will you not feel veneration for such a one?

[4] Will you not say: "This being is too grand and lofty to be regarded as of the same substance as the puny body it inhabits"? A divine power has descended there.

[5] A soul that is preeminent, well-regulated, passing by all things as if they were beneath it, smiling at what we fear and desire—a heavenly power impels such a soul. So great a thing cannot stand without the support of the divine. Thus, the greater part of it is situated whence it came down. Just as the rays of the sun touch the earth, but reside at the source from which they emanate, so too does a great and sacred soul, sent here to reveal divinity more closely to us, associate with us, but cleaves to its origin. The soul depends on and gazes toward the source, and joins us as one more noble than ourselves.

[6] What then is this mind? One that shines with no good but its own. For what is more foolish than to praise a man for qualities not his own? What is more insane than to admire things that can be transferred to another in a moment? A golden bit does not make a better horse. A lion with gilded mane, having endured handling and decoration, compelled to weariness, differs from an untamed lion of unbroken spirit—fierce in strength, as nature intended—magnificent in wildness, whose beauty inspires fearful admiration. The latter is surely preferable to one enfeebled by golden trinkets.

[7] No man should glory except in that which is his own. We praise a vine if its branches are laden with fruit, if by their weight it pulls down the poles supporting the fruit it has produced. Would anyone prefer instead a vine with gold grapes and gold leaves dangling from it? The proper virtue of the vine is fertility; in man also, that which is his own is to be praised. He has a beautiful house-

hold, a handsome house, he sows much, he lends much; yet none of these are in the man himself, but are things around him.

[8] Praise in him what can be neither taken away nor given, what is peculiar to the man. Do you ask what this is? It is soul, and reason brought to perfection in the soul. For man is a rational animal. Man's good is attained if he has fulfilled the good for which nature designed him at birth.

[9] And what is it that this reason demands of him? The easiest thing in the world—to live according to his own nature. But this is turned into a hard task by the general madness of mankind; we push one another into vice. And how can people be recalled to salvation, when no one restrains them, and the people urge them on? Farewell.

----

1. A quote from Virgil's Aeneid (VIII.352), referring to the divine spirit within good people.

LETTER 42
PHILOSOPHY AS A REFUGE FROM WORLDLY DISTRACTIONS

[1] Has that man already convinced you that he is a good man? But a good man cannot be made nor understood so quickly. Do you know who I would now call a good man? One of second rank. For perhaps that other sort, like the phoenix, is born only once every five hundred years. Nor is it surprising that greatness emerges at intervals; fortune often produces the mediocre and those born for the crowd, but she distinguishes the exceptional by their very rarity.

[2] But that man is still far from what he professes. Even if he knew what a good man was, he would not yet believe himself to be one, and perhaps he would despair of even being able to become one. "But he thinks ill of bad men." Even bad men do this, and there is no greater punishment for wickedness than to be displeasing to oneself and one's own kind.

[3] "But he hates those who use sudden and great power without restraint." He will do the same when he is able. The vices of many are hidden because they are weak, but they will dare no less when their strengths please them than those vices which prosperity has already laid bare.

[4] They lack the means to unfold their wickedness. Thus even a poisonous snake can be handled safely while it is stiff with cold; its

venom is not lacking then, but is dormant. The cruelty, ambition, and luxury of many fall short of daring the worst only by the favor of fortune. You will soon recognize that they wish for the same things, if you give them the power to do as much as they wish.

[5] Do you remember when you declared that a certain man was in your power, and I told you that he was flighty and fickle, and that you were grasping not his foot but a feather? Was I mistaken? He was held by a feather, which he released before flying away. You know what sport he has made of you since, how many things he has attempted that were sure to fall back upon his own head. He did not see that through the dangers of others he was rushing into his own. He did not consider how burdensome the things he sought would be, even if they were not superfluous.

[6] Therefore, in those things which we desire and strive for with great effort, we ought to examine whether there is no advantage in them or more disadvantage. Some things are superfluous, some are not worth so much. But we do not see this through, and things seem free to us which cost us most dearly.

[7] The extent of our folly is laid bare when we imagine that we purchase only those things for which money changes hands, while those things for which we spend our very selves we consider free. We would be unwilling to buy certain things if the price was our home, a pleasant and fruitful estate—yet to acquire these same things, we are most ready to sacrifice our peace of mind, our freedom, our integrity, and our time. Nothing, it seems, is cheaper to any man than himself.

[8] Therefore, in all our deliberations and dealings, let us apply the same principle we habitually employ whenever we approach a merchant to inquire about his wares. Let us examine what it is we so desire and ascertain the asking price, for often the cost is highest where no money is paid at all. I could point out to you many things which, once obtained and accepted, wrest away our liberty. We would belong to ourselves, if those possessions did not belong to us.

[9] So I bid you, ponder these matters, not only when it is a question of gain, but also of loss. You say, "This will be lost." But remember, it was an extra to begin with. You will live just as easily without it

as you did before. If you possessed it for a long time, then you lose it after having had your fill. If not for long, then you lose it before growing accustomed to it. "You will have less money." Yes, and also less trouble. "Less influence." Yes, and also less envy.

[10] Survey all these things that drive us to distraction, that we lose with so many tears, and you will realize it is not the loss that troubles us, but the idea of loss. No one feels that those things are lost, but merely thinks it. The person who owns himself has lost nothing. But how rare it is for anyone to truly own himself! Farewell.

LETTER 43

ON QUELLING THE FEAR OF RUMORS AND OPINIONS

[1] You ask how the rumor reached me, who told me that you were thinking something you had told no one? It was that most knowledgeable source—rumor itself. "What then?" you say, "Am I so great that I can stir up rumors?" Don't judge yourself by looking here, at the renowned sender; look instead to the place where you dwell.

[2] Anything that stands out among its neighbors is great in that context. After all, greatness has no fixed measure; comparison either raises or lowers it. A ship that looms large in a river seems tiny on the ocean. A rudder that is massive for one vessel is puny for another.

[3] In your province, though you may despise yourself, you are important. People ask what you are doing, how you dine, how you sleep—they want to know. Therefore you must live all the more diligently. But consider yourself truly happy when you can live openly, when your walls shelter you but do not hide you. Too often we surround ourselves with walls, thinking they will let us live more securely, when in fact they merely let us sin more secretly.

[4] I'll tell you something that reveals the state of our morals: you will scarcely find anyone who can live with their door wide open. It is our conscience, not our pride, that has posted doormen at our entrances. We live our lives hoping not to be caught suddenly

exposed. But what is the point of secluding oneself and shunning the eyes and ears of others?

[5] A clear conscience invites the crowd, while a guilty one is anxious and worried even in isolation. If your deeds are honorable, let everyone know. If they are shameful, what does it matter if no one else knows, since you yourself are aware? How wretched you are if you despise such a witness! Farewell.

LETTER 44

THE EQUALITY OF ALL IN PHILOSOPHY

[1] Once again, you disparage yourself as insignificant, claiming that Nature has treated you poorly, and Fortune worse—and yet, you have the power to rise above the masses and ascend to the highest pinnacle of human happiness. If philosophy offers any boon, it is this: it pays no heed to pedigree. Trace back every person's lineage far enough, and you will find it stems from the gods.

[2] You are a Roman knight, having attained this rank through your own industriousness. But I swear, the "fourteen rows[1]" are closed off to many; not everyone is admitted into the Senate; even the army, in selecting recruits to face toil and danger, is discriminating. Yet a sound mind is open to all—in this regard, we are all noble. Philosophy neither rejects nor selects anyone; its light shines for all.

[3] Socrates was no patrician. Cleanthes drew water and hired out his hands to irrigate gardens. Philosophy did not find Plato already noble; it made him so. What reason have you to despair that you cannot match these men? They are all your ancestors, if you conduct yourself worthy of them—and you will, if you convince yourself at once that no one surpasses you in true nobility.

[4] We all have the same number of forebears; no one's origin lies beyond the reach of memory. Plato said that every king springs from

slaves, and every slave has kings in his lineage. The long march of time has jumbled all such things together, fortune turning them upside down.

[5] Who, then, is well-born? The one whose natural disposition is well-suited for virtue. That is the one thing to consider; otherwise, if you hark back to antiquity, everyone traces their origin to a time before which there was nothing. From the earliest beginnings of the universe to the present day, we have been led forward by an alternating sequence of distinguished and shameful ancestries. A hall full of smoke-stained ancestor masks does not make one noble. No one has lived for our glory, nor is anything that existed before us ours to claim. It is the soul that ennobles us, a soul that—whatever the circumstances—can rise above fortune's caprice.

[6] Imagine, then, that you are not a Roman knight, but a freedman. You have it in your power to be the only free person amid a throng of the well-born. "How?" you ask. By distinguishing good from bad based on its own merits, not popular opinion. We must consider not the source of things, but their destination. If there is anything that can create a happy life, it is a good in its own right.

[7] For it is not possible for it to be corrupted into evil. What, then, is the mistake made when all people desire a happy life? They treat the means of obtaining it as if they were the thing itself, and while seeking it, they flee from it. For although the essence of a supremely happy life is complete security and unshakable confidence in this security, people accumulate causes for worry. And along the treacherous journey of life, they not only carry burdens but drag them along, thereby constantly moving further away from the result they seek. The more effort they expend, the more they hinder themselves and are carried backward. The same thing happens to those hurrying in a labyrinth; their very speed entangles them. Farewell.

---

1. Referring to the first fourteen rows in the theater reserved for the Roman equestrian order.

LETTER 45

THE TRUE PURPOSE OF PHILOSOPHICAL DEBATE

[1] You lament the scarcity of books where you are. But what matters is not how many books you have, but how good they are. Reading that is focused benefits the mind; reading that is scattered merely entertains. The person who wants to arrive at their destination must follow a single road, not wander off on many side paths. What you are doing is not traveling, but merely wandering astray.

[2] "I wish," you say, "that you would give me advice rather than books[1]." But I am ready to send you all the books I have, to shake out my whole storehouse. I would even transfer myself to be with you, if I could. And if I did not hope that you would soon obtain leave from your official duties, I would have imposed upon myself this expedition in my old age; not even Charybdis, Scylla or the legendary dangers of that strait could have deterred me. I would have swum across, not merely sailed through, if only I could embrace you and witness in person how much your mind has grown.

[3] As for your desire to have my books sent to you, this does not make me think myself more eloquent, any more than I would think myself handsome if you asked for my portrait. I know this is a matter of your kind indulgence, not your critical judgment—though if it is in fact your judgment, kindness has biased it in my favor.

[4] But whatever their quality, I want you to read my works as if I were still seeking the truth, not claiming to know it, obstinately questioning everything. For I have not enslaved myself to anyone; I bear no master's name. I give great weight to the judgments of eminent men, but I also claim something for my own. They too have left us not certainties to accept, but questions to ponder. Perhaps they would have discovered the essential truth, if they had not also pursued the trivial and superfluous.

[5] Quibbling about words has stolen much of their time—those captious arguments that pointlessly exercise the intellect. We tie knots and entangle meaning in words, only to untie them again. Do we have so much free time? Do we already know how to live, how to die? We must press on with our whole mind to the place where we have to ensure that it is realities, not words, that guide us.

[6] Why do you ask me to untangle verbal resemblances by which no one is ever deceived except in the course of disputation? Things are what lead us astray; it is things you must learn to distinguish. We embrace evil instead of good; we pray for the opposite of what we have prayed for. Our prayers clash with our prayers, our plans with our plans.

[7] How similar flattery is to friendship! It not only imitates friendship, but outdoes it and passes it by. It is received with open and welcoming ears and descends into the innermost heart, and it is most pleasing precisely where it does the most harm. Teach me how I can discern the one from the other. The flatterer comes to me in the guise of a friend, an enemy disguised as a well-wisher. Vices creep up on us under the name of virtues: rashness lurks under the title of courage, moderation is called laziness, the coward is regarded as prudent. In this the danger of delusion is very great. Stamp these things with distinctive marks for me.

[8] Besides, a person who is asked whether he has horns is not so foolish as to feel his forehead, nor again so silly or dull-witted as not to know that you have persuaded him of this through the most subtle line of reasoning. Your argumentation may have convinced him he has horns, though he knows deep down this cannot actually be true.

These deceptions are harmless, just like the cups and pebbles of the magicians, in which the very trickery delights me. Show me how the trick is done, and I have lost interest. I say the same about these word-traps - for what better name is there for sophisms? They neither harm the ignorant nor aid the wise.

[9] If you really wish to untangle the ambiguities of language, teach us this: that the happy man is not the one hailed as such by the crowd, into whose coffers great wealth flows, but rather he who has all good things within his soul - upright, lofty, and trampling upon the vicissitudes of chance; who looks up to no one with envy; who judges a person only by their humanity; who heeds Nature as his guide, conforming to her laws and living as she ordains; whose blessings no force can snatch away; who transforms evils into goods, sure in judgment, unshaken, undaunted; who may be moved by some force but is disturbed by none; whom Fortune, having hurled her most hurtful weapon with all her might, may graze but cannot wound - and even that rarely. For Fortune's other missiles, with which she vanquishes humankind, shatter like hailstones which, having battered the roof, crack and dissolve without harm to the occupant within.

[10] Why do you detain me with that which you yourself call a pseudomenos [fallacy], about which so many books have been compiled? Behold, my entire life is a lie; refute it, reduce it to truth, if you are sharp. It judges as necessary things which are largely superfluous. Even what is not superfluous carries no weight in making one fortunate and happy. For a thing is not automatically good just because it is necessary; else we debase the good if we grant that label to bread, porridge, and other items without which life cannot be sustained.

[11] What is good is certainly necessary; but what is necessary is not always good, since some necessary things are rather common. No one is so ignorant of the dignity of the good as to degrade it to the level of these quotidian utilities.

[12] Why not redirect your attention to demonstrating to all that so many of life's superfluities are acquired at a great expense of time,

and that many have passed through life while merely gathering the instruments of living? Examine individuals, consider mankind as a whole—you'll see that nearly every life looks toward tomorrow.

[13] And what, you ask, is so wrong with this? The harm is boundless. For in doing so, they are not truly living, but merely planning to live. They postpone everything to the future. Even if we paid strict attention, life would still outpace us; but as it stands, hesitating as if life belonged to another, it passes us by and is ended on that final day, perishing entirely at the very moment of our death.

But let me not exceed the proper length of a letter, which ought not spill over into the reader's other hand[2]. I will postpone until another day this quarrel with those oversubtle dialecticians who concern themselves only with such arguments and not also with how to live. Farewell.

––––––––––––––––––––

1. Hense suggests that from the context, we should expect Lucilius to say "I would not wish" (nollem) rather than "I would wish" (vellem).
2. Referring to letters written on papyrus rolls that had to be unrolled with both hands to be read.

LETTER 46
PRAISE FOR LUCILIUS' BOOK

[1] I RECEIVED YOUR BOOK, AS YOU PROMISED, AND EAGERLY OPENED IT, intending only to take a taste. But its charm drew me in and enticed me to read further. You can tell how eloquent it was from this: though neither lengthy in papyrus nor content, at first glance it could be mistaken for the work of Livy or Epicurus. It held me captivated with such sweetness that I consumed it entirely without delay. The sun beckoned, hunger called, clouds threatened—yet I devoured it all.

[2] I was not merely delighted, but overjoyed. What wit, what spirit it displayed! I would praise its forcefulness, had it paused to catch its breath and risen again after an interlude[1]. But this was no mere impulse; it was a sustained, manly, and majestic flow. Yet a certain sweetness intervened, gentle and well-placed. You have achieved grandeur and dignity; maintain this, march on in this way. The subject matter played a role, thus one must choose a fertile field that seizes the intellect and spurs it on.

[3] I will write more about the book once I have revisited it; for now, my judgment is unsettled, as if I heard the words spoken rather than read them. Allow me to investigate further. You need not fear; you will hear the truth. How fortunate you are to have no reason for

anyone to tell you such a lengthy lie! Except that now, even when motive is absent, we lie out of habit. Farewell.

---

1. As Madvig suggests, "if after an interval."

LETTER 47

THE PROPER TREATMENT OF SLAVES

[1] I WAS DELIGHTED TO LEARN FROM THOSE WHO CAME FROM YOU THAT you live on friendly terms with your slaves. This befits your wisdom and your education. "They are slaves," people declare. No, rather they are human beings. "They are slaves." No, rather they are comrades. "They are slaves." No, rather they are humble friends. "They are slaves." No, rather they are fellow slaves, if you consider that Fortune has as much power over slaves as over free men.

[2] That is why I laugh at those who think it degrading to dine with their slave. For what reason is this, except that arrogant custom surrounds a dining master with a crowd of standing slaves? The master eats more than he can hold and overloads his distended belly with immense greed, so his stomach, having lost the habit of its proper function, requires greater effort to discharge all that he has crammed into it. But the poor slaves are not permitted even to move their lips, let alone speak.

[3] Every murmur is repressed with the rod, and not even accidental noises are exempt from the lash - a cough, a sneeze, a hiccup. The slaves incur heavy punishment if silence is interrupted by a single sound. Throughout the night they stand hungry and mute.

[4] And so it happens that the slaves talk about their master,

although they are not allowed to talk in front of him. But those who conversed not only in the presence of their masters but with them, whose mouths were not stitched shut, were ready to risk their necks for their master, to divert onto their own heads any danger that threatened him; they spoke at dinner parties, but kept silent under torture.

[5] It is also a symptom of this same arrogance that we hear the proverb: "As many enemies as you have slaves." They are not enemies to us when we acquire them; we make them so.

I pass over other cruel and inhuman acts, such as the way we abuse them, not as if they were human beings, but as if they were beasts of burden. When we recline at a banquet, one slave wipes up the spittle; another, situated beneath the table, collects the leavings of the drunks.

[6] Another carves the expensive birds, expertly drawing his practiced hand through breast and rump, eliciting choice morsels. Wretched fellow, to live for the single purpose of carving fattened poultry in the correct style - unless his teacher is even more miserable, training this skill for pleasure's sake rather than out of necessity.

[7] Another slave, adorned like a woman, wrestles against his years. He cannot escape his boyhood; he is dragged back to it. Though he has already assumed the military garb, he remains hairless, either by shaving or plucking out each individual hair. He passes the entire night awake, dividing his time between his master's drunkenness and his lust. In the bedchamber he is a man; at the feast he is a boy.

[8] Another unfortunate soul, entrusted with organizing the banquet seating, persists in his duties, waiting to see which guests flattery, intemperance of the stomach or of the tongue might entice to return again tomorrow. Consider too the professional tasters, with their refined knowledge of their master's palate, who know precisely which flavors will excite his appetite, which presentations will delight his eyes, which novelties might rouse him from his nauseous stupor, which dishes he now spurns out of sheer satiety, and what he craves to eat that day. The master cannot bear to dine with such slaves,

considering it beneath his dignity to sit at the same table as his servant. The gods have mercy!

[9] How many masters are subservient to these slaves! I myself witnessed Callistus' master standing before his threshold, shut out while others entered—the same master who had bestowed on Callistus his current status, who had paraded him among the junk goods at the slave market. That slave, now elevated to the foremost ranks where the auctioneer tests his voice, repaid his former master in kind, rejecting him in turn, judging him unworthy of his house. The master once sold Callistus, but now how much Callistus controls his master!

[10] Can you not grasp that this person you call your slave was born from the same seeds, enjoys the same sky, breathes the same air, lives and dies just as you do? You can no more see him as a freeborn man than he can see you as a slave. By the disaster at the river Mariu, many of the most illustrious birth, just commencing a senatorial career in the military, were laid low by fortune; she made one into a shepherd, another a humble hut-keeper. So go ahead, scorn now a man of the same fortune into which you yourself, even as you scorn it, may descend.

[11] I have no wish to launch into a major discourse debating the treatment of slaves, towards whom we are excessively arrogant, cruel, and abusive. However, the essence of my advice is this: live with your inferior as you would wish your superior to live with you. Whenever it occurs to you how much power you have over your slave, let it also come to mind how much power your master has over you.

[12] "But," you protest, "I have no master." How fortunate for you; perhaps you will have one someday. Do you not know at what age Hecuba began to be a slave, or Croesus, or the mother of Darius, or Plato, or Diogenes?

[13] Interact with your slave with compassion, engage him in conversation, include him in your deliberations and communal life. At this point, the entire assembly of the privileged will cry out against me: "Nothing is more demeaning, more disgraceful than this!" Yet

these are the same people I catch kissing the hands of other people's slaves.

[14] Do you not see how our ancestors removed all odium from masters and all insult from slaves? They called the master the "father of the household," and the slaves "members of the household," a term still used even in mimes today. They instituted a holiday on which masters dined together with slaves—not as the only day for this, but as the day it must happen. They permitted slaves to attain honors in the household, to pronounce judgment, and they considered the home a miniature republic.

[15] "What then?" you say. "Shall I seat all my slaves at my table?" No more than you would all free men. You are mistaken if you think I would bar certain slaves as if their work is too sordid, like the muleteer or the herdsman. I will judge them not by their duties, but by their character. Each person creates their own character; circumstance assigns their duties. Let some dine with you because they are worthy, and some so that they may become worthy. For if there is anything slavish in them from their lowly associations, interaction with their betters will shake it off.

[16] You need not only seek a friend in the forum or the Senate House, my dear Lucilius. If you pay close attention, you may find one even at home. Good material often goes to waste without an artist to shape it. Test it, and see[1]. As foolish as one who intends to buy a horse but inspects only its saddle and bridle, even more foolish is the person who judges another by their clothing, or by their social rank, which is only a kind of garment draped around us.

[17] You say, "But he is a slave." Yet perhaps he is free in spirit. "But he is a slave." Will this harm him? Show me who is not. One person is a slave to lust, another to greed, another to ambition, all to fear. I will show you a former consul enslaved to an old woman, a rich man enslaved to a serving-maid. I will show you noble youths who are the property of actors! No slavery is more disgraceful than that which is self-imposed.

So do not let those snobbish critics deter you from showing yourself cheerful to your slaves, or from being their superior without arrogance. Let them respect you rather than fear you.

[18] Someone will now claim that I am inviting slaves to don the cap of freedom and toppling masters from their high perch, because I said "Let them respect rather than fear their master." He will say, "Yes, let them respect him just like clients and morning greeters do!" One who says this forgets that what is enough for a god is not too little for a master. The revered are also loved—love cannot be mixed with fear.

[19] I judge that you act most rightly in not wishing to be feared by your slaves and in disciplining them with verbal reproofs; dumb animals are admonished with lashes. It is not everything that offends or injures us. But our excessive self-indulgence drives us to rage, so that whenever anything fails to answer to our will, we provoke anger.

[20] We have assumed the dispositions of kings. For they too, forgetful of their own strength and the weakness of others, blaze up and rage as if they had received an injury, though their lofty station shields them utterly from such risk. They are not unaware of this, but they seek excuses to inflict harm; they accept an injury so that they may do one in return.

[21] I do not wish to detain you longer, for you do not require exhortation. Among their other good qualities, righteous characters have this: they are self-contented and steadfast. Vice is fickle, often changing, not for the better, but into some other form. Farewell.

---

1. Some manuscripts read "test and see," others "test it, and you will see."

LETTER 48

THE UNSUITABILITY OF SYLLOGISMS FOR PHILOSOPHICAL INQUIRY

[1] I will respond later to the letter you sent me from your journey, which was as long as the journey itself. I need to spend time alone and carefully consider what advice to give you. After all, you too pondered at length whether you should seek my counsel in the first place. How much more, then, should I do the same, since more time is needed to solve your dilemma than to propose it? Especially since what benefits you may not benefit me. Am I speaking like an Epicurean again?

[2] No, truly, what benefits you also benefits me. I am no friend at all if I do not consider whatever concerns you to be my own concern as well. Friendship makes all things common between us. Nothing good or bad happens to one that does not happen to the other; we live a shared life. No one can live happily who looks only to himself and turns everything to his own advantage. You should live for another if you wish to live for yourself.

[3] This partnership, when diligently and scrupulously observed, which mingles us humans with one another and judges there to be a certain common law of the human race, is of the greatest benefit also for fostering that inner fellowship of friendship of which I was speak-

ing. For he who holds many things in common with a fellow human will hold all things in common with a friend.

[4] I prefer to be taught by those subtle thinkers, my excellent Lucilius, what duties I owe to a friend and to a fellow man, rather than in how many senses the word "friend" or "man" is spoken. Behold how wisdom and folly diverge in opposite directions. Which do I choose? Which side do you bid me to take? To the one, a man passes for a friend; to the other, a friend does not pass for a man. The one makes a friend for himself, the other makes himself for a friend. You quibble over words and arrange syllables for me.

[5] Of course, unless I construct the most cunning interrogations and bind the falsehood born of a true premise with my conclusion, I will not be able to separate what to seek from what to avoid. I am ashamed; we old men amuse ourselves with such serious matters.

[6] "Mouse is a syllable. But a mouse gnaws cheese; therefore, a syllable gnaws cheese." Suppose I were unable to resolve this. What danger threatens me from that ignorance? What harm? No doubt I must fear lest I someday trap syllables in a mousetrap or lest a book eat my cheese if I am too careless. Unless perhaps this sharper reasoning applies: "Mouse is a syllable. But a syllable does not gnaw cheese; therefore, a mouse does not gnaw cheese."

[7] Oh, what childish absurdities! Is this why we have furrowed our brows and grown long beards? Is this what we teach with such grim and pallid faces?

Do you want to know what philosophy promises to humanity? Counsel. Death calls one man, poverty gnaws at another, while riches torture a third—whether they belong to others or to himself. This one dreads misfortune, that one longs to escape his own prosperity. Humankind treats one harshly, the gods another.

[8] Why do you contrive these frivolous little syllogisms? Now is not the time for jesting; you have been summoned to aid the wretched. You have promised to bring assistance to the shipwrecked, the imprisoned, the sick, the needy, to those holding their heads beneath a drawn sword. Where are you wandering off to? What are you doing?

This man with whom you are playing word games is stricken with terror; go help him, snapping the ropes of whatever dread leaves him dangling[1]. From all sides they stretch out their hands to you, these ruined and soon-to-perish lives, begging for some aid; in you rest their hopes and resources. They implore you to extract them from this vortex, to show a bright light of truth to the scattered and wandering.

[9] Tell them what nature has made necessary and what superfluous, how uncomplicated are the laws she has laid down, how pleasant and unimpeded life is for those who follow them, but how bitter and convoluted it becomes for those who have placed more trust in opinion than in nature.

As for alleviating their troubles, I would think your frivolous word games could only be effective if you first taught to what degree they can mitigate any of them[2]. Which of those desires do they remove? Which do they moderate? Would that they merely did no good! They do harm. I will make this utterly clear to you whenever you wish—a noble nature is shattered and crippled when subjected to these petty quibblings.

[10] It is shameful to say what weapons they proffer to those who would do battle against Fortune, how they equip them. Is this the path to the highest good? Is it through these "if there is snow" sophisms[3], and dishonorable quibbles that bring infamy even on those who sit as judges? For what else are you doing, when you knowingly lead the person you are questioning into a trap, than making it appear he has lost on a technicality? But just as the praetor restores people to their full rights, so does philosophy.

[11] Why do you turn away from those lofty promises, abandoning your grand discourse? You claimed you would steel my eyes so that the glint of gold dazzles no more than the flash of a sword, that with towering constancy I would trample what all men crave and what all men fear. Yet now you descend to the rudiments of grammarians? What's this you say -

Thus one journeys to the stars?[4]

This is what philosophy promises me - to make me equal to a god! To this I was summoned, for this I came. Keep your word!

[12] Therefore, my dear Lucilius, as much as you can, draw yourself back from these quibbles and hair-splitting of the philosophers. Openness and simplicity befit goodness. Even if a great span of life remained, it would need to be parceled out frugally to suffice for necessities. In such poverty of time, what folly it is now to learn superfluous things! Farewell.

---

1. The original Latin passage here is corrupt, but this translation captures the general sense. The scholar Buecheler suggests the Latin should read: "succurre, quidquid laqueist timore pendenti rumpens", which would translate to "go help, snapping whatever rope of fear he hangs by."
2. This sentence was added by the scholar Hense as supplying the needed connection in thought.
3. Some manuscripts read "philosophiae" (of philosophy) here, but the scholar Page emends it to the more sensible "philosophia" (philosophy), as translated.
4. Quote from Virgil, Aeneid 9.641

LETTER 49
THE SWIFT PASSAGE OF TIME

[1] TRULY, MY DEAR LUCILIUS, A MAN IS LETHARGIC AND NEGLECTFUL IF he is prompted to remember a friend only when reminded by some location. Yet at times, familiar places call forth the longing stored in our hearts. They do not revive an extinguished memory but rather stir one that has grown still, just as a dear servant's name, a garment, or a house renews a mourner's grief, even if it has been softened by time.

Behold, Campania, and especially the sight of Naples and your beloved Pompeii—it is incredible how they have rekindled my fresh desire for you. You are entirely before my eyes. I feel I have only just parted from you. I see you swallowing back tears and not fully resisting the emotions that slip out despite your restraint. I feel as if I lost you only a moment ago.

[2] For what is not "a moment ago" if you stop to remember? A moment ago I sat as a boy at the philosopher Sotion's feet; a moment ago I began to plead cases; a moment ago I lost the desire to plead them; a moment ago I lost the ability. Time's swiftness is infinite, a fact that is more apparent to those looking back. For it deceives those intent on the present; so gentle is the passing of its headlong flight.

[3] Do you ask the reason for this? All time that passes lies in the

same place; it is seen as one and lies together. Everything falls into the same abyss. Besides, there can be no long intervals in a thing that is altogether brief. The point we live is just that—a point, and even less than a point. But even this tiny point nature has mocked with a semblance of a longer span, making one part infancy, another childhood, another youth, another a slope from youth to old age, another old age itself. How few the steps she has placed on such a narrow platform!

[4] A moment ago I escorted you, and yet this "moment" is a good portion of our lives, whose brevity we should contemplate, as it will one day run out. Time did not used to seem so swift to me; now its incredible passage is apparent, whether because I sense the finish line being moved closer or because I have begun to pay heed and reckon my losses.

[5] All the more, then, I resent that some squander the greater part of this time—which cannot suffice even for necessary things, however diligently guarded—on superfluities. Cicero claims that even if his lifespan were doubled, he would not have time to read the lyric poets. Put the dialecticians in the same category—they are gloomier time-wasters. The former are avowedly frivolous; the latter fancy themselves to be accomplishing something.

[6] I do not deny that such matters should be studied, but only studied, and greeted from the doorstep, for this sole purpose: lest we be deceived by them and judge them to contain some great and secret good. Why do you torment and exhaust yourself with a question which it is more subtle to despise than to resolve? When an enemy presses from behind and the soldier has been ordered to move, necessity shakes off whatever baggage peacetime leisure had accumulated; likewise, a person secure in their convictions and departing life at their own convenience can afford to quibble over minutiae.

[7] I do not have time to chase after ambiguously falling words and test my cleverness on them. "Behold the peoples assembling, the walls where at closed gates they sharpen the sword[1]." With great spirit must I listen to the din of war resounding all around me.

[8] I would rightly seem mad to everyone, if, while old men and

women were heaping stones to fortify the walls, while the armed youth within the gates awaited or demanded the signal to sally forth, while enemy spears quivered in the gates and the very ground trembled with mines and tunnels, I sat idle, propounding petty questions like this: "What you have not lost, you have. But you have not lost horns. Therefore, you have horns!" And other tricks fashioned after the likeness of this sort of fatuous hairsplitting.

[9] And yet, you would think me equally crazy if I spent my energy on those things, besieged as I am now. In that other situation[2], at least the danger threatening me would be external, with a wall separating me from the enemy. Now, deadly perils are inside with me. I have no time for such foolishness; a monumental undertaking is at hand. What should I do? Death pursues me, life flees away. Teach me something to counter this.

[10] Enable me to stop fleeing from death, and to stop life from fleeing me. Exhort me to face difficulties; instill in me equanimity in the face of the inevitable. Expand the cramped quarters of my time. Teach me that the good in life lies not in life's length, but in the use we make of it; that it is possible, indeed often the case, that one who has lived long has lived little. Tell me when I am about to sleep: "You may not wake again." Tell me when I have woken: "You may not go to sleep again." Tell me when I go out: "You may not return." Tell me when I return: "You may not go out again."

[11] You are mistaken if you think that only at sea is the gap between life and death so narrow; in every place, the interval is equally slender. Death does not always show itself so near, yet everywhere it looms just as close.

Dispel these shadows, and you will more easily convey the lessons for which I am prepared. Nature has made us teachable, endowing us with reason that is imperfect but capable of being perfected. [12] Discuss with me justice, piety, frugality, and both forms of chastity— the one that abstains from another's body, and the other that takes care of its own. If you do not wish to lead me along roundabout paths, I will more easily reach my destination. For, as the tragic poet says, "The language of truth is simple.[3]" Therefore, it should not be made complicated; indeed, nothing is less fitting for souls striving for great things than that sort of crafty cleverness. Farewell.

---

1. Lines from an unknown tragedy.
2. Described in section 8.
3. A quote from Seneca's tragedy, Thyestes.

LETTER 50

RECOGNIZING AND TREATING THE MALADIES OF THE MIND

[1] MONTHS AFTER YOU SENT IT, I FINALLY RECEIVED YOUR LETTER. IT seemed pointless to ask the courier how you were doing - he must have an impressive memory indeed if he can still recall! But I hope that your life has become such that wherever you may be, I know how you are living. For what else should you be doing but striving each day to improve yourself, to shed some of your misconceptions, to recognize that the flaws you attribute to circumstances are in fact your own? We often blame our surroundings and the times, but those faults will follow us wherever we may go.

[2] You know that Harpaste, my wife's fool, has remained in my house as an inherited burden. I myself am utterly averse to such monstrosities; if I ever wish to be amused by a fool, I need not look far - I laugh at myself. This foolish woman has suddenly gone blind. It sounds unbelievable, I know, but it's true: she does not realize that she is blind. She keeps asking her attendant to take her elsewhere, claiming that the house is too dark.

[3] Let me make it clear to you that what we laugh at in her case applies to us all. No one recognizes their own greed or avarice. The blind at least seek out a guide, while we wander astray without one, saying, "I am not ambitious, but one cannot live any other way in

Rome. I am not extravagant, but city life demands great expenditure. It is not my fault that I am quick to anger, that I have not yet settled on a definite way of life; it is due to my youth."

[4] Why do we deceive ourselves? Our ills do not come from without; they reside within us, in our very core. That is why we have such difficulty regaining our health - we do not even know that we are sick.

If we were to begin treatment, when would we shake off the overwhelming power of so many diseases[1]? As it stands, we do not even seek a physician. He would have less work to do if called in at the first sign of illness. Tender, unshaped minds would follow one pointing the way to righteousness.

[5] No one finds it hard to return to nature, except for those who have deserted her. We blush to learn the way to a sound mind. But I swear, if it is shameful to seek a teacher for this, then we must despair of ever stumbling upon such a great good by chance alone.

We must put in the work. And to speak frankly, it is not even a great labor, if only we begin to shape and correct our minds before our crooked ways become hardened, as I have said. But even when hardened, I do not consider them beyond hope.

[6] There is nothing that persistent effort, attentive and diligent care cannot conquer. You can straighten even the sturdiest oak trees, however bent they may be. Heat unbends curved beams, and wood that grew in a different shape can be molded to the form our purpose requires. How much more easily, then, does the mind yield to shaping, being more pliant and yielding than any liquid! For what else is the mind if not spirit in a certain state? And you see that spirit is more easily altered than any other substance, in as much as it is more rarefied.

[7] My dear Lucilius, there is no reason for you to despair about our chances for improvement, even though wickedness already has us in its grasp and has long been in possession of us. No one becomes good until after being bad—we are all preoccupied with wrongdoing. Learning virtue means unlearning vice.

[8] We should approach our own reformation with all the more energy because, once we are committed to goodness, it will be ours

forever. Virtue, once learned, is never forgotten. For qualities foreign to us cling only superficially and thus can be stripped away and expelled, but those that take their proper place abide faithfully. Virtue is in accordance with nature; vices are hostile and inimical to it.

[9] But just as virtues, once acquired, cannot depart, and are easy to safeguard, so the initial steps toward virtues are arduous, because it is characteristic of a weak and sickly mind to fear the unfamiliar. The mind must, therefore, be forced to make a start; from then on, the medicine is not bitter. For while it is curing, it gives delight at the same time. The pleasure of other remedies comes after health is restored, but philosophy is both restorative and pleasurable at the same time. Farewell.

---

1. Reading "morborum tantas vires" with Gertz instead of "morbos tantas ve res".

LETTER 51

THE WISE MAN'S APPROACH
TO RETIREMENT AND
SOLITUDE

[1] My dear Lucilius, we must each make do as best we can! There in Sicily, you have mighty Aetna, that most renowned of mountains. I cannot determine why either Messala or Valgius called it "unparalleled" (for I have read this in both their works), since there are many places that spew forth flames, not only in high mountains, which is more common since fire rises to the greatest heights, but also in low-lying areas. Here in Baiae, I am content with what I have, though I left the day after arriving, deeming it a place to be avoided. For while it has certain natural charms, it has been claimed by luxury as its own celebratory haven.

[2] "What then?" you ask, "Should one despise any place?" Not at all. But just as certain garments are more suited to the wise and upright man than others - and while he abhors no color, he considers some less fitting for one who professes frugality - so too there are regions that a wise man, or one aiming at wisdom, will shun as incompatible with good character.

[3] Therefore, in considering a retreat, the sage will never choose Canopus, even though nothing prevents one from being respectable in Canopus, nor even Baiae, which has become a resort of vice.

There, luxury allows itself the most indulgence; there, as if the place itself grants some license, it runs even more riot.

[4] We ought to pick a location that is salubrious not only for the body but for the morals too. Just as I would refuse to live among torture chambers, so too I would avoid residing amidst cookshops. What need is there to witness drunkards staggering along the beach, the boating parties with their blaring orchestras, the lakes resounding with song, and all the other ways in which luxury, as if released from legal constraints, not only sins but flaunts its sins in public?

[5] We should strive to flee as far as possible from provocations to vice. The mind must be toughened and withdrawn far from the enticements of pleasure. A single winter in quarters unraveled Hannibal; the luxuries of Campania conquered the man unconquered by Alpine snows. He won with weapons, but was vanquished by vices.

[6] We too have a battle to wage, a type of campaign in which there is never any respite, never a truce. Pleasures are the first foes that must be conquered; as you see, they have carried off even fierce natures. If one proposes to realize the magnitude of the undertaking, he will know that nothing can be done casually or delicately. What business have I with those hot baths? With steam rooms where dry heat to drain the body is trapped within? Let every drop of sweat be wrung by toil!

[7] If we were to do as Hannibal did - suspend active operations and neglect the war in order to pamper our bodies - everyone would rightly rebuke such untimely sloth as a danger to victory already won, much more to hopes of winning. We have less license than those who followed Punic banners; more dangers remain if we slacken, more work even if we persevere.

[8] Fortune wages war against me, but I will not be commanded. I refuse the yoke - no, with even greater courage, I cast it off. The spirit must not be softened. If I yield to pleasure, I must also yield to pain, to toil, to poverty. Ambition and anger will claim that same right over

me. Amidst so many passions, I would be torn asunder - nay, ripped to pieces.

[9] Freedom is held out before me; it is the reward for this struggle. And what is freedom, you ask? It is owing servitude to nothing - no necessity, no chance events; it is putting fortune on level ground. On the day I come to understand that fortune has greater power, it will have no power at all. Shall I endure fortune, when I have death in my own hands?

[10] In pondering such thoughts, one ought to choose serious and sacred places. Excessive comfort weakens the spirit, and there's no doubt that one's surroundings can have a corrupting influence on one's resolve. Pack animals can endure any road when their hooves are hardened by rough terrain, but when fattened on soft, marshy pastures, they quickly break down. The strongest soldier comes from harsh lands; the fashionable city dweller is lazy. No task is refused by hands that go from plow to weapon; but the perfumed dandy fails at the first cloud of dust.

[11] The strict discipline of a place strengthens the mind and prepares it for great endeavors. Scipio's exile was more honorable at Liternum than at Baiae[1]; one should not make his ruin too comfortable. Even those men - Gaius Marius, Gnaeus Pompey, and Caesar - to whom the fortune of the Roman people first passed the public riches, built villas in the Baian region, but placed them atop the mountain ridges. This seemed more soldierly, to gaze from on high upon the lands spread out below. Observe what positions they chose, in what places and in what manner they raised their abodes, and you will see they were not villas, but military camps.

[12] Do you think Cato would ever have lived in a pleasure-palace, to count the adulterous women sailing by, the many kinds of boats painted in various colors, the roses floating on the whole lake, to hear the nocturnal quarrels of serenading lovers? Would he not have preferred to remain within the rampart that he himself had built with his own hands for a single night's encampment? Surely any true man would prefer to have his sleep broken by the call of the bugle rather than by a symphony.

[13] But we have quarreled with Baiae long enough, though never long enough with our vices. I implore you, Lucilius, to relentlessly pursue them without restraint or end, for they too know no bounds or measure. Cast away everything that tears at your heart; if there were no other way to extract them, your heart itself would have to be plucked out along with them. Above all, drive out pleasures and regard them as your greatest foes. Like the bandits the Egyptians call "Philetae," they embrace us only to strangle us in the end. Farewell.

---

1. Reading "morborum tantas vires" with Gertz instead of "morbos tantas ve res".

LETTER 52

THE PROPER MANNER OF PHILOSOPHICAL DISCOURSE

[1] What is this force, Lucilius, that drags us in one direction when we aim for another, urging us toward the very thing we long to retreat from? What wrestles against our spirit, preventing us from willing anything once and for all? We vacillate between competing plans. Our will is not free, not absolute, not constantly fixed on anything.

[2] "It is folly," you say, "that is inconsistent, that finds nothing pleasing for long." But how and when shall we tear ourselves free from its grip? No one is strong enough to emerge by their own efforts; someone must extend a hand, someone must lead us out.

[3] Epicurus says that certain people have made their way to the truth without anyone's assistance, carving their own path. He holds in greatest esteem those who impelled themselves forward, who took themselves to the fore. But certain others, he says, require outside help—they won't make progress unless someone guides them, but they will follow well. Metrodorus is of this second type, according to Epicurus: still an impressive mind, but of the second rank. We are not numbered among that first group; we will be treated well if we are accepted into the second. And do not look down upon a person who

can attain salvation with the help of another—wanting to be saved is itself an important step.

[4] In addition to these, you will find a third type of person, also not to be disdained: those who can be compelled and driven to righteousness, who require not just a guide but a helper and, so to speak, an enforcer. This is the third color [rank]. If you seek an example of this type too, Epicurus says that Hermarchus was such a person. Thus he congratulates the one type more, but admires the other more—for although both reached the same destination, it is a greater credit to have brought about the same result with more difficult raw material.

[5] Imagine two buildings have been erected, equally tall and magnificent but built on different foundations from the ground up. One received clear ground on which the structure could immediately rise. The other's foundation was exhausted by having been sunk in soft, soggy soil, and much labor was expended to reach solid ground. Looking at both, all the work of the first is visible, but the second's great and difficult labor is largely hidden.

[6] Some talents are easy, adaptable, quick to learn. But some must be worked by hand, as they say, absorbed in building their own foundations. Therefore, I would call the first type more fortunate, encountering no resistance within themselves. But the second has earned a better triumph over themselves, for they have conquered the malignancy of their own nature, not merely escorting themselves to wisdom but dragging themselves there.

[7] Though you may recognize that this challenging and demanding character has been granted to us, we still press on through the obstacles in our way. Let us therefore fight, and call upon the help of others. "Whom," you ask, "shall I call upon, this man or that one?" But I urge you, turn also to those who came before, who are free to help; it is not only the living who can aid us, but also those who have passed.

[8] From the living, however, let us choose not those who toss out words at great speed, rehashing commonplaces and performing for their private circles, but rather those who teach by their lives. They prove their words through action, exemplifying what must be done

and never being caught in the very things they denounce. Choose as your helper one whom you admire more in person than in speech.

[9] This is not to say I would forbid you from also hearing those who make a practice of admitting the crowd and declaiming, if their purpose in appearing publicly is to better themselves and their listeners, rather than out of ambition. For what could be more disgraceful than a philosopher courting applause? Does a sick man praise the surgeon as he operates?

[10] Be silent, pay heed, and offer yourselves up to the cure. Even if you should cry out, I will listen as if you were groaning at the touch upon your vices. Do you wish to testify that you are attentive and moved by the grandeur of the subject? By all means, I will allow it, so that you may judge and cast your vote for the better course. Did not Pythagoras' disciples keep silent for five years? Do you therefore think they were immediately permitted to speak and offer praise?

[11] How mad then is the speaker who leaves the lecture hall delighted by the shouts of the ignorant! Why rejoice at being praised by those whom you yourself cannot praise? Fabianus used to discourse before the people, but he was heard with restraint. Occasionally a great clamor of praise would burst forth, but one called out by the magnitude of his words, not by the sound of a speech gliding by without giving offense, aimed at pleasing the ear.

[12] There should be a difference between the clamor of the theater and that of the school; there is a certain decorum even in praise[1]. All things reveal signs of their true nature if observed, and one can glean proof of character even from the smallest details: a shameless man is exposed by his gait, by the movement of his hand, sometimes by a single response, by a finger brought to the head, by a glance of the eyes. A laugh betrays the scoundrel, his face and bearing the madman. For such traits emerge into the open through external signs; you will know a person's true nature if you observe how he gives and receives praise.

[13] The philosopher's listeners thrust their hands toward him from all sides, and a crowd of admirers gathers around his very head. If you understand, he is not merely praised now, but acclaimed. Let

us leave such voices to those arts which aim to please the crowd; philosophy should be revered.

[14] Sometimes, the young must be permitted to follow the impulse of their spirit—but only when they act from this impulse, when they cannot command themselves to be silent. Such praise brings some encouragement to the listeners themselves and stimulates the minds of youth. Let them be moved by substance, not by polished words; otherwise, eloquence harms them if it creates a desire not for the subject matter, but for itself.

[15] I shall postpone this for now, for it requires its own lengthy discussion: how one should discourse to the people, what one should allow oneself before the people, and what the people should permit in one's presence. There will be no doubt that philosophy has suffered a loss, now that she has prostituted herself. But she can still be displayed in her sanctuary, if only she has found a steward and not a peddler. Farewell.

---

1. Koch suggests "decentia" (decorum) for the manuscript reading "licentia" (license), which Hense retains; other manuscripts have "scientia" (knowledge). Gertz conjectures "diligentia" (discernment).

LETTER 53

THE FREEDOM AND PEACE OF WISDOM

[1] WHAT COULD I NOT BE PERSUADED TO DO, HAVING BEEN PERSUADED to set sail? I put out to sea when it was listless. Undoubtedly, the sky was heavy with foul clouds, which generally dissolve into either rain or wind. But I thought that the few miles from your dear Parthenope to Puteoli could be stolen, even with a doubtful and threatening sky. And so, to make my escape more swiftly, I set my course straight across the deep to

[2] Nesis, intending to cut off all the bays. When I had already advanced to the point that it made no difference to me whether I proceeded or turned back, first that calmness, which had seduced me, disappeared. It was not yet a tempest, but the swell of the sea and the increasingly frequent waves had begun. I started asking the helmsman to set me down on some shore. He said that the shores were rough and harborless and that there was nothing he feared as much in a storm as land.

[3] But I was too distressed for danger to come to my aid. For a sluggish and inescapable seasickness tormented me, which stirs the bile but does not expel it. And so I insisted and compelled the helmsman, whether he wished it or not, to make for shore. As we neared

the vicinity of land, without waiting for anything to happen from Virgil's precepts—

"They turn their prows seaward"

"The anchor is cast from the prow"

—mindful of my old practices as a devotee of cold water, wrapped in my cloak, I threw myself into the sea, as befits a cold-water enthusiast.

[4] Can you imagine what I endured, as I clambered over the rough ground, as I searched out a path, as I made my way? I understood that sailors have good reason to fear the land. What I suffered is incredible, when I could not even bear myself[1]. Know this, that Ulysses was not born under such an angry sea that he was shipwrecked everywhere; he was prone to seasickness. And I, wherever I will need to sail, will arrive in my twentieth year.

[5] As soon as I had collected my stomach (which you know does not escape seasickness along with the sea), as I had refreshed my body with an anointing, I began to ponder how great an oblivion of our vices would follow us—even of the bodily ones, which repeatedly remind us of themselves, let alone of those which lie more hidden the greater they are.

[6] A slight shiver deceives one; but when it has grown and true fever has blazed up, it elicits confession even from the hardy and long-suffering. The feet ache, the joints feel needle-pricks; so far we dissemble and say that we have either sprained an ankle or strained something in some exercise. In a doubtful and beginning illness a name is sought; when it has begun to stretch even the ankles[2] and has made both right feet[3], one must confess to gout.

[7] The opposite happens with the diseases that afflict the mind: the worse a person's condition, the less he perceives it. You need not wonder at this, my dearest Lucilius. For one who sleeps lightly still glimpses visions in his dreams, and sometimes while dreaming he is aware that he is asleep; but deep slumber obliterates even dreams

and immerses the mind too deeply for it to have any consciousness of itself.

Why does no one confess his own vices? Because he is still mired in them; only one who is awake can recount his dream, and to confess one's vices is a sign of health.

[8] Let us awaken, then, so that we may rebuke our own errors. Philosophy alone will rouse us, she alone will shake off our heavy slumber. Devote yourself wholly to her. You are worthy of her, and she of you; embrace one another unreservedly. Resolutely and openly deny yourself to all other pursuits. You need not plead for the chance to practice philosophy.

[9] If you were ill, you would neglect your household duties and legal affairs would fall by the wayside. Nor would you deem any client so important that you would attend to his case during your convalescence. Your whole aim would be to free yourself from the disease as soon as possible. Well then, will you not do the same now? Cast aside all obstacles and make room for a sound mind; no one who is distracted can attain it.

Philosophy wields her own authority; she bestows time rather than receiving it. She is no part-time matter but a full-time occupation; she is the mistress, and she bids us attend on her.

[10] When a certain state promised Alexander a portion of its lands and half of all its possessions, he replied, "I invaded Asia with the intention not of accepting what you might give, but of leaving you in possession of what I might leave behind." Philosophy gives the same answer to all other preoccupations: "I will not accept the time you have left over, but you shall have what I reject."

[11] Turn your full attention to philosophy; sit at her feet, cherish her—a vast gap will then open between yourself and other mortals. You will far outpace all men, and even the gods will not outpace you by much. Do you ask what the difference will be between yourself and the gods? They will live longer. But truly, it is the hallmark of a great artist to have captured the whole in a small space. The wise man's life spans as wide a range as does God's, though there is one

point in which the wise man can surpass God: God is fearless by the bounty of nature, the wise man by his own bounty.

[12] Behold, it is a great thing to possess the frailty of a human being, yet the security of a god. The power of philosophy to repel all random forces is truly incredible. No weapon can lodge itself in philosophy's body; it is fortified and solid. Some assaults philosophy wearies out, evading them as if they were light darts, with a loose and yielding fold of its gown. Other attacks it shakes off and hurls back at the sender. Farewell.

---

1. Reading 'possem' with Erasmus instead of 'possim'.
2. Reading 'etiam talaria' with Hense instead of 'ut talaria'.
3. Hense suspects 'dextros', for which Toup conjectured 'distortos', comparing Ep. lxvii. 3.

LETTER 54

FACING DEATH WITH
REASON AND COURAGE

[1] MY ILL HEALTH HAD GRANTED ME A LONG FURLOUGH, BUT NOW IT has abruptly attacked me again. "What kind of illness?" you ask. You are right to inquire, for no sickness is unknown to me. Yet I am as if assigned to one particular ailment, which I do not know why I should call by its Greek name, for it can aptly enough be described as a "gasping." Its onslaught is very brief and like a storm; it usually subsides within an hour.

[2] For who could gasp for long? All bodily discomforts and dangers have passed through me; none seems more troublesome than this. Why? Because anything else is merely being sick, while this is drawing out the soul. Thus physicians call it the "meditation of death." For someday that breath will succeed in doing what it has so often essayed.

[3] Do you think I write these words to you cheerfully because I have escaped? I would be as ridiculous if I took delight in such a reprieve as in good health, as would a defendant who thinks he has won his case when he has postponed his trial. Even in the midst of suffocation, I did not cease to find comfort in joyous and brave thoughts.

[4] "What is this?" I say. "So often does death test me? Let it do so; I

myself have for a long time tested death." "When?" you ask. Before I was born. Death is non-existence, and I already know what that means. What was before me will be after me. If there is any torment in this state, there must also have been such before we entered the light of day; yet we felt no distress then.

[5] I ask you, would you not say that one was the greatest of fools who believed that a lamp was worse off when it was extinguished than before it was lighted? We mortals also are lighted and extinguished; we suffer somewhat in the interval, but at either end there is deep security. For, unless I am mistaken, my dear Lucilius, we go astray in thinking that death follows, when it has both preceded and will follow us. Whatever condition existed before our birth, is death. For what does it matter whether you do not begin at all, or whether you leave off, inasmuch as the result of both these states is non-existence?

[6] With these and similar reflections, silent of course—for there was no opportunity for words—I did not cease to encourage myself. Then little by little this gasping, which had already begun to be the panting of my final breaths, came at longer intervals and subsided. Even now, although it has ceased, my breathing does not flow naturally; I feel a sort of hesitation and delay in it. Let it be as it will, provided I do not gasp from the soul!

Take this pledge from me: I shall not tremble at the end, for I am now prepared. I give no thought to how much time remains in the day.

[7] Praise and emulate the man who does not regret dying, though he delights in living. For what virtue is there in departing when you are driven out? Ah, but herein lies virtue indeed; I may be driven out, but I go forth as if by my own will.

And thus the wise man is never ejected, for to be ejected is to be expelled from a place you are loath to depart. The sage does nothing unwillingly; he escapes necessity because he wills what would be forced upon him. Farewell.

LETTER 55

PLACES INCOMPATIBLE
WITH THE PHILOSOPHIC LIFE

[1] I HAVE JUST RETURNED FROM A RIDE, NO LESS FATIGUED THAN IF I had walked as far as I sat. For it is laborious to be carried for a long time, and perhaps all the more so because it is contrary to nature, which gave us feet to walk on our own and eyes to see for ourselves. Luxuries have inflicted weakness upon us, and we have ceased to be able to do that which we have long refused to do.

[2] Nevertheless, it was necessary for me to shake up my body, so that if any bile had settled in my throat, it might be shaken out, or if my breath had become too thick for some reason, the jostling—which I felt did me good—might thin it out. Therefore, I persevered in riding for a long time, enticed by the very shore itself, which curves between Cumae and Servilius Vatia's villa and is enclosed by the sea on one side and the lake on the other, like a narrow path. For it was dense from the recent storm. As you know, the waves, when frequent and agitated, smooth it out, but a longer period of tranquility loosens it when the moisture that binds the sand has receded.

[3] Out of my habit, however, I began to look around to see if I might find something there that could be of benefit to me, and I directed[1] my eyes to the villa which once belonged to Vatia. In it, that

wealthy ex-praetor, known for nothing else but his leisure, grew old and was considered happy for this reason alone. For whenever Asinius Gallus' friendship or Sejanus' hatred and later his favor had sunk some men—for it was equally dangerous to have offended him or to have loved him—people would exclaim: "O Vatia, you alone know how to live!"

[4] But he knew how to hide, not how to live. There is a great difference between your life being at leisure or being indolent. I never passed by this villa while Vatia was alive without saying, "Here lies Vatia."

But, my dear Lucilius, philosophy is something so sacred and venerable that even if there is anything similar to it, it pleases us by the very illusion. For the common crowd considers a retired man to be both carefree and self-contented, living for himself—none of which can befall anyone except the wise man.

[5] Does that man who is anxious know how to live for himself[2]? Indeed, does he even know how to live at all, which is the first thing? For the man who shuns people and affairs, whom the wretchedness of his own desires has banished, who cannot bear to see others happier, who like a timid, inert creature has grown numb with fear - that man does not live for himself. Instead, most disgracefully, he lives for his belly, his sleep, his lust. The man who lives for no one does not automatically live for himself. Yet consistency and persever- ance in one's purpose are such great things that even stubbornness in idleness carries some authority.

[6] About the villa itself I can write you nothing definite. I am only acquainted with its façade and the parts exposed to view, which are apparent even to passers-by. There are two artificial caves of impressive workmanship, as large as the most spacious reception halls, one of which never admits the sun, while the other retains it until it sets. A plane-tree-lined stream, suitable for raising fish even if constantly drawn upon, divides the grounds in the manner of a canal, taking in water from both the sea and Lake Acherusian. But the supply is spared when the sea is open; when storms give the fish-

ermen a holiday, a ready supply for the table is available. However, the most convenient thing about this villa is that it has Baiae right over the wall - you enjoy its pleasures while escaping its nuisances.

[7] I know these praises of the villa from my own experience; I believe it is delightful all year round. For it faces the west wind which it intercepts so completely that it is denied to Baiae. It seems Vatia was no fool in selecting this place to which to consign the leisure of his indolent old age.

[8] But it is not so much the place that brings tranquility; it is the mind, which can make all things acceptable to itself. I have seen gloomy people in a cheerful, charming villa; I have seen people in the depths of a solitude acting as if they were in a metropolis. So there is no reason for you to think that your own lack of composure is due to not being in Campania. But why aren't you there? Extend the range of your thoughts this far.

[9] One can converse with absent friends - indeed, as often as you wish and for as long as you wish. This pleasure, which is the greatest of all, is more fully enjoyed when we are absent from one another. For being together spoils us; and because sometimes we talk, walk, and sit together, when we are separated we give no thought to those whom we have just seen.

[10] And so, we ought to bear the absence of our loved ones with a calm mind, for no one is truly absent from those they hold dear for long, even when they are present. Consider first the nights spent apart, then the differing occupations that consume our days, the private studies we pursue, and the journeys we take to the outskirts of the city; you will see that it is not much that a sojourn abroad can take from us.

[11] A friend must be held in the heart; there, they are never absent. Whenever one desires, they can see their friend each day.

Therefore, my dear Lucilius, study with me, dine with me, walk with me. We would live in narrow confines indeed if anything were closed off from our thoughts. I see you, my Lucilius; even now, I hear your voice. So much am I with you that I question whether I should begin writing to you not letters, but notes [as if we were in the same room]. Farewell.

---

1. The manuscripts have "direxi," but Hense suggests "derexi."
2. The text here is uncertain. Some manuscripts read "solus" (alone) instead of "sollicitus" (anxious).

LETTER 56

REMAINING STEADFAST AMIDST NOISE AND DISTRACTIONS

[1] I'll be damned if silence is as necessary as it seems for a person sequestered in study. Behold, a cacophony of various noises rings out all around me. I live right above the baths. Just imagine every type of sound that can assault and offend the ears: The grunts of strong men exercising and heaving lead weights, some straining, others imitating the strained, the sharp hissing when they release their pent-up breath. When I chance upon some lazy fellow content with a plebeian massage, I hear the crack of hand on shoulder, the sound changing depending on whether it lands flat or cupped. And heaven help me if the ball-players arrive and begin tallying their throws—then it's all over.

[2] Add to this the brawler, the caught thief, and the man who loves the sound of his own voice in the baths. Add those who leap into the pool with a huge splash of displaced water. Besides these voices, which are at least natural, picture the hair-plucker with his thin, piercing cry (the better to draw attention) that he never ceases except when he's ripping out armpit hair and making his victim yell instead. Then there are the various shouts of the cake-seller, the sausage-man, the confectioner, and all the food-hawkers peddling their wares, each with his own distinctive intonation.

[3] "You must be made of iron or stone deaf," you say, "to keep your wits about you amidst so many noises, so varied and discordant, when our friend Chrysippus is driven to his death bed by the incessant greetings of his pupils!" But I swear, this hubbub bothers me no more than the sound of waves or falling water—though I'm told of a certain tribe that found the din of the Nile cataracts reason enough to move their whole city.

[4] To my mind, voices are more distracting than mere noises. Voices command the attention of the mind, while noises merely fill and batter the ears. The sounds that clamor around me without diverting my focus, I lump together—the passing carriages, the handyman in my apartment, the carpenter next door, or the fellow at the Sweating Statue who tests his flutes and pipes and doesn't so much play them as screech.

[5] An intermittent noise still annoys me more than a steady one. But by now I've so steeled myself against all such provocations that I could endure even a coxswain with a ghastly voice giving stroke to his crew. For I force my mind to concentrate within itself and not be distracted by external things. Let everything resound outside, as long as there's no commotion within, as long as desire and fear aren't at odds, as long as meanness and extravagance aren't at each other's throats, one harassing the other. For what good is the silence of the whole region if the emotions are in an uproar?

[6] "All things were settled in the still silence of night." This is false. There is no tranquility except that which reason has composed. Night may alter our troubles but it does not remove them; it merely shifts our anxieties. Even the dreams of those who slumber are as tumultuous as their days. True peace is that into which the rational mind can unfold itself.

[7] Picture the man who seeks sleep in the stillness of a spacious house, who demands that no sound disturb his ears. His whole crowd of servants is hushed; those approaching walk on tiptoe. And yet, he tosses this way and that, snatching only fitful rest amid his anguish. He complains of hearing noises that never happened. What do you suppose is the cause? His mind is in uproar. This is what must be

quieted, this inner tumult must be suppressed. Do not assume that the mind is tranquil just because the body lies still. Sometimes inactivity is restless.

[8] And so we must rouse ourselves to action and occupy ourselves with worthy pursuits whenever we are ill-content with our own company and impatient with idleness. Great commanders, seeing their soldiers becoming unruly, constrain them with toil and keep them busy with expeditions. Those who are never idle have no time for mischief, and there is no surer truth than that the vices of leisure are dispelled by activity.

[9] We often appear to have withdrawn out of weariness with worldly affairs and regret for our unhappy and thankless position. Yet in that retreat where fear and exhaustion have driven us, ambition sometimes revives. For it is not eliminated when tired out or even when embittered by lack of success[1].

[10] I say the same of luxury, which seems at times to have retreated. Then it pesters those who have professed frugality, and in the midst of thrift seeks out pleasures—not condemned but only set aside for a time—and with all the more intensity for being concealed. For all vices are less serious when in the open; diseases too are then beginning to be cured when they break forth from hiding and reveal their power. So too with greed, ambition, and the other evils of the human mind—you may be sure that they are most pernicious when they subside under a pretense of sanity.

[11] We may seem at leisure, but we are not. For if we are acting in good faith, if we have sounded the retreat, if we scorn outward show, as I was just saying, nothing will distract us. No chorus of men or birds will interrupt our wholesome meditations, which are by now solid and sure.

[12] That is a feeble mind which has not yet withdrawn into itself, which is aroused by voices and happenings. It harbors some inner anxiety, some trace of lurking dread, which makes it curious and fearful, as our own Virgil says:

"And as for me, whom once no spears could move

Nor Greeks swarming in hostile ranks—
Now every breeze affrights me, every sound disturbs
My anxious mind, trembling alike for its charge and itself."

[13] The wise man is the one who is not terrified by quivering spears, nor by the clashing arms of the dense battle line, nor by the din of a city under siege. The other, the inexperienced man, fears for his possessions, startling at every clatter, thrown off balance by any cry taken for the roar of an attacking horde, paralyzed by the slightest disturbance; his very baggage makes him timid.

[14] Choose any of those men deemed fortunate as they haul and carry their many burdens, and you will see one "fearing for his companion and his load."

So know that you are truly composed when no clamor can shake you, when no voice can jolt you out of yourself—not cajoling flattery, not menacing threats, not the vain din making an empty racket all around.

[15] "What then?" you ask. "Is it not sometimes more pleasant to be free from vexation?" I admit it. And for that reason, I will depart from this place. I wished to test and train myself. What need is there to be tormented any longer, when Ulysses devised so easy a remedy for his companions even against the Sirens? Farewell.

----

1. Gemoll's emendation qua ("by which") is preferable to the manuscript reading quam in this sentence.

LETTER 57

THE TRIALS OF THE ROAD
TO PHILOSOPHY

[1] When I had to return to Naples from Baiae, I readily believed there was a storm brewing, to avoid getting on a boat again; and there was so much mud the whole way that I might as well have been at sea anyway. I had to endure the full fate of an athlete that day; from the wrestling ring I was received by a vapor-bath in the grotto at Naples.

[2] Nothing is longer than that dungeon passage, nothing dimmer than those torches, which allow us not to see through the darkness, but to see the darkness itself. Even if the place did have light, the dust would take it away—an oppressive and annoying thing even in the open air. How much worse there, where it rolls back on itself, and with no ventilation, falls back on those by whom it was stirred up in the first place? We suffered two opposing discomforts at the same time: on the same road, on the same day, we struggled with both mud and dust.

[3] Yet that darkness gave me something to ponder. I felt a certain blow to my spirit and a change, without fear, which the strangeness and foulness of this unusual thing had produced. I am not talking about myself with you now—I who am far from being an endurable

man, let alone a perfect one—but about a man over whom fortune has lost her rights. Even his spirit will be struck, his color will change.

[4] For there are certain things, my dear Lucilius, that no virtue can escape; nature reminds it of its own mortality. And so it will draw the face into sadness, shudder at sudden things, and grow dizzy if, standing on the edge of a cliff, it looks down into the vast depths below. This is not fear, but a natural feeling that reason cannot conquer.

[5] Thus brave men, most ready to shed their own blood, cannot bear to see another's. Some faint and lose consciousness at treating and examining a fresh wound, others at an old and festering one. Some receive a sword more readily than they look at one.

[6] So I felt, as I said, not a disturbance exactly, but a change. Then, at the first sight of returning light, my cheerfulness returned unbidden and unasked for. I then began to reflect how foolishly we fear some things more or less than others, when the end of all is the same. For what difference does it make whether a watchtower or a mountain falls on someone? You will find none. Yet there will be those who fear the latter ruin more, although each is equally deadly —showing that fear regards not the effect, but the cause of the effect.

[7] Do you think I'm talking about the Stoics now, who believe the soul of a man crushed by a great weight cannot endure and is immediately dispersed, because its exit was not free? I truly do not. Those who say this seem to me to be mistaken.

[8] Just as a flame cannot be smothered, for it will escape around the edges of whatever is pressed upon it, and just as air cannot be harmed or even cut by blows and strikes, but rather flows back around the object that tried to displace it, so too the mind, which is made of the finest stuff, cannot be caught or crushed within the body. By virtue of its subtlety, it bursts forth through the very things that attempt to constrain it. Consider how lightning, even when it has struck and flashed most widely, finds its way back through a tiny opening. In the same way, the mind, which is even more tenuous than fire, has means of escape through every part of the body.

[9] Therefore, we must inquire whether the mind can be immortal. Of this much you can be certain: if the mind outlasts the body, it cannot be harmed by the thing that destroys the body, because no immortality comes with exceptions, and nothing can harm that which is eternal. Farewell.

LETTER 58

THE PLATONIC CLASSIFICATION OF EXISTENCES

[1] Never before today have I understood the extent of our poverty of language, indeed our utter lack of words. A thousand things came up, as we happened to be speaking of Plato, which required names but had none, and certain others which, though once possessed, have been lost through our disdain.

[2] But who can tolerate disdain in the midst of poverty? That creature which the Greeks call "oestrus", which drives cattle mad and scatters them through all the groves, was called "asilus" by our countrymen. You may trust Virgil on this:

> *Near Silarus' groves and the green holm-oaks flits*
> *In throngs Alburnus' fly, to Romans "asilus",*
> *But "oestrus" in the Greek tongue's turning phrase,*
> *Fierce, with harsh hum, at which whole herds in terror*
> *Scatter through the woods.*

[3] I believe this word has disappeared. Not to lead you too far afield, certain simple words were in common use, as when they said "to decern with the sword amongst themselves." The same Virgil will prove this to you:

> *Giants born in opposite regions of the world*
> *Clashed amongst themselves and decerned with the sword.*

What we now call "to decide" [decernere]. The use of that simple word [cernere] has been lost.

[4] The ancients used to say "si iusso," that is, "if I shall have ordered." I don't want you to just believe me, but again our Virgil[1]:

> *Let the rest of the troop, as I shall have ordered, join me in*
> *bearing arms.*

[5] My purpose now with this diligence is not to show how much time I have wasted with the grammarian, but that you may understand from this how great a decay of words had taken possession of Ennius and Accius, when even in this poet, who is daily thumbed, some words have been filched from us.

[6] "What," you ask, "is the point of this preamble? What are you driving at?" I will not conceal it from you; I desire, if it can be done, to say "essentia" with your kind indulgence; if not, I will say it even against your anger. I have Cicero as authority for this word, and I deem him an ample authority. If you seek one more recent, I have Fabianus, a learned and elegant man, of a style polished even to our tastes. For what will happen, my Lucilius? How will οὐσία[2], that necessary thing, that nature which is the foundation of all, be named? I ask therefore that you permit me to use this word. Nevertheless I will exert myself to exercise the right you have granted most sparingly; perhaps I will be content with the mere permission.

[7] What good will your facilitas be to me, when there is absolutely no way I can express this idea in Latin—the very reason I criticized our language in the first place? You will condemn the poverty of the Roman tongue even more when you realize that what I cannot translate is a mere syllable. What is this syllable, you ask? τὸ ὄν. You must think me a bit dense not to translate this simply as "quod est.[3]" But I assure you, there is a vast difference. I am forced to render a single word with a complete phrase.

[8] But if I must, I will translate it as "quod est." Our most learned friend was saying just today that Plato expressed this concept in six different ways. I will lay them all out for you, but first let me explain that there is such a thing as genus and species. For now, we are seeking that original genus on which all the other species depend, from which every division arises, and in which all things are encompassed. We will discover it if we trace each thing back, step by step, for this will lead us to the very first.

[9] Man is a species, as Aristotle says; horse is a species; dog is a species. Therefore, we must find some common bond between them, which embraces them and holds them under itself. What is it? Animal. And so, "animal" has become the genus of all those I just mentioned: man, horse, and dog.

[10] However, there are certain things that have a soul [anima] but are not animals [animalia]. For it is quite agreeable to believe that trees and plants also possess a soul. Thus, we say that they live and die. Consequently, "living things" [animantia] will occupy a higher place, because both animals and plants fall under this category. But there are some things that lack a soul, like rocks. Therefore, there will be something even more primordial than living things—namely, body [corpus]. I will divide it like this, and say that all bodies are either living or inanimate.

[11] There is still something superior to body. For we say that certain things are corporeal, and others incorporeal. What, then, will be the term from which these are derived? That to which we just now gave the rather unfitting name, "quod est." For this will be divided into species such that we can say: "quod est" is either corporeal or incorporeal.

[12] This, then, is the first and most ancient genus, the broadest classification, if you will. The other genera certainly exist, but they are more specific. For instance, man is a genus, as it contains within itself the species of nations: Greeks, Romans, Parthians. Of colors: white, black, yellow. It comprises individuals: Cato, Cicero, Lucretius. Thus, insofar as it contains many things, it falls into the category of genus; insofar as it is subordinate to another, it is a species. That most

general genus, "quod est," has nothing above it. It is the beginning of things. All else falls beneath it.

[13] The Stoics wish to place above this classification an even more primary type of being, about which I will speak presently, if I can first demonstrate that this classification I have discussed is justly put first, since it encompasses all things.

[14] I divide "that which is" into these categories: corporeal or incorporeal - there is no third option. How do I subdivide the corporeal? By stating: they are either animate or inanimate. Again, how do I subdivide the animate? By stating: some have mind, while others have only life. Or put another way: some have impulse, they move about and go from place to place, while others are fixed in place by their roots, nourished and growing. Once more, into what categories do I divide animals? They are either mortal or immortal.

[15] To certain Stoics, the primary classification seems to be "something". I will explain their rationale. They say, "In the nature of things, some things exist, some do not. But even these things that do not exist are encompassed by the nature of things. They arise in the mind, like Centaurs, Giants, and whatever else, formed by false thought, begins to take on some shape, although lacking substance."

[16] Now I return to what I promised you - how Plato divides all existing things into six types. The first is that which cannot be grasped by sight, touch or any sense; it is only thinkable. That which exists in general, like the general concept of Man, does not come before our eyes, but a specific man does, like Cicero or Cato. The animal is not seen but thought; yet its species, like the horse and dog, are seen.

[17] In the second type of existence Plato puts that which stands out and surpasses all else. He says this exists by way of excellence. Just as "poet" is a common term for all writers of verse, but among the Greeks it has become the mark of a single man - when you hear "the poet", understand Homer. So what is this surpassing existence? God, naturally - greater and more powerful than all things.

[18] The third type is of those things which exist in the proper sense; these are innumerable but lie outside our view. What are they,

you ask? Plato's special conception - he calls them Ideas, from which all things we see come to be, and after which all things are formed.

[19] These [ideal forms] are immortal, immutable, inviolable. Hear what an idea is—that is, what Plato believes it to be: "An idea is the eternal archetype of things that arise in nature." Let me add an explanation to the definition to make the matter clearer to you. Suppose I want to make a portrait of you. I have you as the model for my painting, from which our mind derives a certain impression that it can impose upon its work. In this way, the face that instructs and guides me, from which the imitation is sought, is the idea. Nature thus has an infinite number of such archetypes—of men, fish, trees—according to which everything that must be created by her is modeled.

[20] The idos will take fourth place [in the hierarchy of reality]. You must pay close attention to what this idos is, and attribute this difficulty of concepts to Plato, not to me. For there is no subtlety without difficulty. A moment ago I was using the analogy of a painter. When he wanted to render Virgil in color, he gazed upon the man himself. The idea was the appearance of Virgil, the archetype for the future work. What the artist derives from this [idea] and imposes upon his work is the idos.

[21] What is the difference, you ask? One is the model, the other the form taken from the model and imposed upon the work. The artist imitates the one, and creates the other. The statue has a certain appearance—this is the idos. The model itself, which the craftsman looked at while shaping the statue, also has a certain appearance—this is the idea. If you desire another distinction, the idos is in the work, the idea is outside the work—and not only outside the work, but prior to it.

[22] The fifth class is of those things that exist in a general sense; these begin to pertain to us. Here we find everything—men, animals, things. The sixth class is of those things that "subsist"—like the void, like time.

Plato does not count among true existences the things we see or touch. For they are in flux, constantly diminishing and increasing.

None of us is the same in old age as he was in youth; none of us is the same in the morning as he was the day before. Our bodies are swept along like rivers. Everything you see runs along with time. Nothing that we see remains. Even I myself, as I comment on these changes, have changed.

[23] This is what Heraclitus means when he says, "We step and do not step into the same rivers; we are and are not." For the name of the river remains the same, but the water has flowed on. This is more evident in a river than in a human being, but we too are carried past by no less swift a course. And so I marvel at our madness in cleaving so tightly to this most fleeting thing, the body, and in fearing lest we die someday, when every instant is the death of a previous state. Will you really not fear something happening once that happens every day!

[24] I have spoken of man, a substance that is fluid and perishable, exposed to every influence that can affect it. The universe too, eternal and indestructible as it is, changes and never remains the same. For though it possesses all that it has ever possessed, it possesses it in a different way from that in which it once possessed it; [25] it keeps changing its arrangement.

"How," you ask, "will these subtle speculations benefit me?" If you must know, I reply that they will be of no benefit at all. But just as the engraver rests and refreshes his eyes when they have long been under strain, turning them away and, as the saying is, feeding them, so we at times should slacken our minds and refresh them with some sort of entertainment. But let the entertainment itself be work. From such speculations, if you keep a watchful eye, you will cull much that may be applied to the healing of the spirit.

[26] This, my dear Lucilius, is what I usually do: I try to extract and render useful some element from every notion, even if it be one very remote from philosophy. What teaching could be farther removed from reforming morals than the words we have just been discussing? How can the Platonic Ideas make me a better man? What can I draw from them to curb my passions? Perhaps just this - Plato

teaches that those things which appeal to the senses, which enflame and excite us, do not belong among the things that really exist[4].

[27] Therefore, such things are imaginings and present a mere appearance that is short-lived; none of them is stable or substantial. Yet we crave them as if they would last forever or as if we would possess them forever. We are weak, watery beings standing in the midst of unrealities; so let us turn our minds to the things that are everlasting. Let us look up to the ideal outlines of all things, flitting about on high, and to the god who moves among them and plans how he may defend from death what he could not make imperishable because its substance forbade, and so by reason may overcome the defects of the body.

[28] For all things abide, not because they are eternal, but because they are protected by the watchful care of the ruler; things imperishable would need no guardian. The Creator, by his virtue, overcomes the frailness of matter. Let us despise everything that is so little valued that it is dubious whether it exists at all.

[29] Let us at the same time reflect on this thought: if providence rescues the world itself, no less mortal than we ourselves, from its perils, then to some extent our own providence can prolong the life of this frail body of ours, provided we can control and restrain the pleasures by which the greater portion of mankind perishes.

[30] Plato himself, through diligent care, prolonged his life to old age. He was indeed blessed with a strong and robust body, and his broad chest had given him his name. However, his voyages and perils had greatly diminished his strength; yet, through frugality, moderation in things that provoke desire, and careful self-care, he reached old age despite many hindering factors.

[31] For you know, I believe, that it was due to Plato's diligent care that he passed away on his birthday, having completed his eighty-first year without any diminution. Therefore, the magi who happened to be in Athens made offerings to the deceased, deeming him to have possessed a lot greater than that of mere mortals, because he had consummated the most perfect number, which is composed of nine

multiplied by nine. I do not doubt that he would have been prepared to relinquish even a few days from that sum and the sacrifice[5].

[32] Frugality can prolong old age, which, though I do not think it should be eagerly desired, yet it should not be refused either. It is pleasant to be with oneself for as long as possible, when one has made oneself worthy of such enjoyment. Thus, we shall pass judgment on this matter, whether one should disdain the extremities of old age and not await the end, but bring it about by one's own hand. He who sluggishly awaits fate is not far from being a coward, just as he who is excessively devoted to wine is one who drains the amphora and gulps down even the dregs.

[33] However, we shall inquire about this: whether the final part of life is dregs or something most liquid and pure, provided that the mind is unimpaired and the senses, still intact, aid the spirit, and the body is not worn out and prematurely dead. For it matters greatly whether one is prolonging life or death.

[34] But if the body is useless for service, why should it not be right to release the troubled soul? And perhaps it should be done a little before it must, lest when it must be done, you may not be able to do it. And since there is greater risk in living badly than in dying quickly, he is a fool who does not, for a small price in time, buy off the hazard of a great misfortune.

Extreme old age has brought few to death without impairment; for many, an idle life has lain stagnant without any use of itself. How much more cruel, then, do you judge it to have lost something of life than the right of ending it[6]?

[35] Do not listen to me unwillingly, as if this sentiment now pertains to you, and consider what I say: I will not forsake old age, if it preserves me whole for myself, and whole in that better part of me. But if it begins to shake my mind, to tear away its faculties, if it leaves me not life, but mere breath, I shall leap from this putrid and tottering edifice.

[36] I will not flee disease by means of death, so long as the disease is curable and does not impede my soul. I will not lay violent hands upon myself on account of pain; to die thus is to be conquered.

Yet, if I know that I must suffer with this pain perpetually, I will depart, not because of the pain itself, but because it will be a hindrance to me in all the purposes for which I live. He who dies because of pain is a weakling and a coward; but he is a fool who lives merely for the sake of enduring pain.

[37] But I digress too long. Besides, there is matter here that could occupy a day. And how can one who cannot put an end to a letter put an end to his own life? So farewell—a word you will read with more pleasure than all my moralizing. Farewell!

---

1. Some manuscripts give "fidem" instead of specifying Virgil again.
2. "ousia" is a fundamental concept that refers to the true nature or essence of something. It is often associated with the idea of unchanging, eternal reality as opposed to the transient, mutable world of appearances.
3. The Greek phrase "τὸ ὄν" means "that which is" or "being". Seneca is grappling with how to translate this fundamental ontological concept into Latin.
4. Seneca is referring to Plato's Theory of Forms or Ideas, which posits that the material world is an imperfect reflection of a perfect realm of abstract and unchanging Forms.
5. The reading paratus sit et is nearest to Madvig's paratus sis et; par laus sit Buecheler; parat auset p, parat ausisset L; parata xusset V ɪ; paratus esset O; parat auisset b. Haupt conj. paratus et
6. quam ius Madvig; quamius p; quamvis LVPb.

LETTER 59

THE DIFFERENCE BETWEEN TRUE JOY AND FALSE PLEASURE

[1] Your letter brought me great delight—allow me to use a common expression without ascribing to it the Stoic meaning. We believe that pleasure is a vice. Let it be so; nevertheless, we are accustomed to using the word to signify a cheerful state of mind.

[2] I am aware that pleasure, if we are to be precise in our language[1], is an infamous thing, and that joy is reserved for the wise alone. For it is an elation of the spirit, confident in its own true blessings. However, in everyday speech, we often say that we have derived great joy from someone's consulship, marriage, or the birth of a child —events which are so far from being joys that they are often the beginnings of future sorrows. True joy, on the other hand, never ceases nor turns into its opposite.

[3] Thus, when our Virgil says, "And the mind's evil joys," he speaks eloquently, yet not quite accurately. For no joy is evil. He has applied this name to pleasures and expressed what he intended. He meant that people take delight in their own misfortunes.

[4] Nevertheless, I was not wrong in saying that I had derived great pleasure from your letter; for although an inexperienced person may rejoice for an honorable reason, I still call their unrestrained emotion, which is prone to suddenly veer in the opposite direction,

pleasure—a feeling stirred by the impression of a false good, immoderate and excessive.

But to return to my point, hear what delighted me in your letter: you have mastery over your words. Your language does not carry you away or lead you further than you intended.

[5] Many writers are lured by the charm of a pleasing word to write something they had not planned, but this does not happen to you; your words are precise and suited to the subject. You say as much as you wish and imply more than you say. This is a sign of a greater matter; it is evident that your mind, too, has nothing superfluous or inflated.

[6] However, I do find metaphors that, while not reckless, have taken risks. I find similes, and if anyone forbids us to use them, deeming them the sole province of poets, it seems to me they have not read the ancients, whose speech was not yet aimed at soliciting applause. Those who spoke plainly and for the purpose of making a point are full of comparisons, which I consider necessary, not for the same reason as poets, but as aids to our weakness, to bring both speaker and listener face to face with the subject at hand.

[7] At this very moment, I am reading Sextius, a keen man who philosophizes using Greek words but with Roman values. An analogy he presents struck me: an army marches in square formation when the enemy is suspected on all sides, ready for battle. "The wise man," he says, "should do the same; he should deploy all his virtues on every side so that wherever trouble rears its head, his defenses are ready and respond to the commander's signal without confusion." We see this happen in those armies marshaled by great generals, where all the troops simultaneously sense the leader's command, arrayed such that an order given by one man passes through the infantry and cavalry alike. This, he claims, is even more vital for us.

[8] For soldiers often fear the enemy without cause, and the path they regard as most perilous is in fact the safest. But folly grants no peace. It dreads dangers from above as much as from below. Both flanks are aquiver. Perils follow it and rush to meet it. It quails at everything, unprepared, and is undone by the very defenses meant to

aid it. The wise man, however, is fortified against every assault, on guard, and will not retreat whether poverty, grief, disgrace, or pain launch their attack. Fearless, he will march out to face them, and through their midst.

[9] Many things bind us, many things sap our strength. We have lain too long in these vices; it is difficult to wash clean. For we are not merely sullied, but stained through and through. But let me not flit from one metaphor to the next. I shall ask this, a question I often ponder: why does folly grip us so stubbornly? Firstly, because we do not stoutly push it away, nor strive for our salvation with all our might. Secondly, because we do not place sufficient faith in what wise men have discovered, nor drink it in with open hearts, and we set about so great a task too lightly.

[10] But how can anyone learn enough to combat vices when what he learns depends on how free he is from those very vices? None of us delves deep within. We merely pluck at surfaces, and for those with no shortage of duties, devoting even a little time to philosophy seemed more than enough.

[11] What hinders us above all is that we are too easily pleased with ourselves. If we meet someone who calls us good, sensible, or upright, we recognize it as our due. We are not content with modest praise; whatever flattery showers upon us shamelessly, we seize as our rightful claim. When others affirm that we are the best and wisest, we agree, knowing full well how often they lie. We indulge ourselves so much that we wish to be praised for the very things we do the opposite of[2]. In the midst of tortures, a man hears himself called most merciful; in the midst of plundering, most generous; in the midst of drunkenness and lust, most temperate. And so it follows that we refuse to change precisely because we believe ourselves to be the best already.

[12] As Alexander wandered through India, ravaging tribes scarcely known even to their neighbors, he found himself laying siege to a certain city. While circling the walls in search of the weakest points in the fortifications, he was struck by an arrow. For a long time, he persevered, remaining at his post and carrying on with his tasks.

But as the bleeding stopped, the pain of the dry wound increased, and his leg, hanging stiffly from his horse, gradually grew numb. Forced to dismount, he said, "All swear that I am the son of Jupiter, but this wound proclaims me a mere mortal."

[13] Let us do the same. Flattery infatuates each of us according to our share. Let us say, "You indeed call me wise, but I see how many useless things I desire and how many harmful things I wish for. I do not even understand what satiety teaches the animals—what should be the measure of my food and drink. I still do not know how much I should consume."

[14] Now I will teach you how to understand that you are not wise. The wise man is full of joy, cheerful and at peace, unshakable; he lives as an equal with the gods. Now, consult yourself: if you are never sad, if no hope agitates your mind with anticipation of the future, if day and night your mind maintains an equal, uplifted tenor, pleased with itself—you have attained the pinnacle of human happiness. But if you seek pleasures from all quarters and of all kinds, know that you are as far from wisdom as you are from joy. You wish to reach that state, but you are mistaken if you hope to arrive there amid riches and honors—that is, you seek joy amid worries. The very things you seek as if they will bring happiness and pleasure are in fact the causes of grief.

[15] All those people, I say, strive for joy, but they do not know where to find a joy that is steadfast and great. One seeks it in feasts and luxury, another in ambition and the throng of clients surrounding him, another in a mistress, and still another in the vain display of liberal studies and literature that heals nothing. All of these are deceived by false and fleeting pleasures, like drunkenness, which purchases one hour of cheerful madness at the cost of a long period of disgust, or like the applause and favor of a flattering crowd, which is gained and atoned for with great anxiety.

[16] Therefore, consider this: the effect of wisdom is evenness of joy. The mind of the wise man is like the world above the moon; there, it is always serene[3]. Thus, you have reason to wish to be wise, if

the wise man is never without joy. This joy arises only from the awareness of the virtues.

[17] Only the strong, the just, and the temperate can experience true joy. "What then?" you may ask, "Do the foolish and the wicked not rejoice?" No more than lions who have seized their prey. When they have exhausted themselves with wine and lust, when the night has failed them amid their vices, when their narrow bodies have begun to fester from pleasures ingested beyond capacity, then these wretched souls cry out that Virgilian verse:

"For well you know how we spent that final night
Amidst false joys.[4]*"*

[18] The self-indulgent spend every night amidst false joys, as if it were their last; but the joy that follows the gods and those who emulate them is uninterrupted and unceasing. It would cease if it were derived from elsewhere. Because it is not the gift of another, it is not subject to the whim of another. What fortune has not given, fortune cannot take away. Farewell.

---

1. Referring to the distinction between the common usage of "album" and the Stoic interpretation.
2. The text here originally included the phrase "et in," which was deleted by Mentel.
3. Seneca refers to the common ancient belief that the celestial realm beyond the moon was perfect and unchanging, in contrast to the ever-shifting sublunary sphere.
4. Virgil, Aeneid, 6.513-514

LETTER 60

THE FOLLY OF INSATIABLE
GREED AND AMBITION

[1] I PROTEST, I QUARREL, I GROW ANGRY. DO YOU STILL DESIRE WHAT your nurse, your guardian, or your mother wished for you? Do you not yet understand how much evil they desired? Oh, how hostile to us are the wishes of our loved ones! All the more hostile, the more successfully they are fulfilled. I no longer marvel that every evil has attended us from our earliest childhood; we have grown up amid the curses of our parents. Let the gods hear this cry of ours too, a cry uttered freely on our own behalf.

[2] How long shall we go on demanding something from the gods as if we were not yet able to support ourselves? How long will we fill the fields of great cities with our crops? How long will the people harvest for us? How long will many ships convey the furnishings for a single table, and from more than one sea at that? A bull is satisfied by grazing in a few acres; a single forest suffices for many elephants. Man feeds himself from both earth and sea.

[3] What then? Has nature given us bellies so insatiable, though she has given us such puny bodies, that we should surpass the greed of the vastest and most voracious animals? Not at all. How little it is that nature demands! She is content with little. It is not the hunger of our belly that costs us dear, but our ambition.

[4] Therefore, as Sallust says, let us count these "slaves of the belly" as animals, not men—and some of them not even as animals, but as dead men. He lives who is of use to many; he lives who makes use of himself. But those who hide away and grow torpid are in their house as if it were a tomb. You may inscribe their name on the very threshold in marble; they have already held their own funeral before their death. Farewell.

LETTER 61
PERSEVERING IN
PREPARATION FOR DEATH

[1] Let us cease to want what we once wished for. I, at least, am laboring at this task: as an old man, I have stopped desiring the same things I wanted as a boy. My days and nights are spent on this alone; it is my work, my thought: to put an end to my chronic ills. I strive to make each day a microcosm of my entire life. And I swear, I do not snatch at it as if it were my last, but I regard it as if it could be my final day.

[2] It is in this spirit that I write this letter to you, as if death might call me away at any moment, even as I write. I am ready to depart, and thus I will enjoy life, because I am not greatly anxious about how long this state of readiness may continue.

Before old age, I took care to live well; in old age, I take care to die well. But dying well means dying willingly. Endeavor never to do anything unwillingly.

[3] Whatever must come to pass despite our struggle ceases to be a necessity if we accept it willingly. What I mean is this: he who willingly accepts commands escapes the bitterest part of slavery—doing what one does not want to do. The person who does something because he is ordered is not miserable; it is the one who does it against his will. Therefore, let us so compose our minds that we

desire whatever the situation demands, and above all, that we contemplate our end without sadness.

[4] We must be prepared for death before we are prepared for life. Life is well enough furnished, but we are too greedy for its trappings; something always seems to be missing, and always will. It is not years or days that make us have lived enough, but our minds. I have lived, my dearest Lucilius, as much as was sufficient; I await death with contentment. Farewell.

LETTER 62

THE WISE MAN'S RETREAT
INTO PHILOSOPHY

[1] THOSE WHO CLAIM THAT THE WHIRLWIND OF THEIR AFFAIRS prevents them from studying the liberal arts are deceiving themselves. They feign busyness, exaggerate it, and occupy themselves needlessly. I am at leisure, Lucilius, true leisure, and wherever I am, I am my own master. For I do not surrender myself to my affairs, but merely lend myself to them, and I do not go out of my way to waste time. Wherever I find myself, I exercise my thoughts and turn over some edifying reflection in my mind.

[2] When I give myself to my friends, I do not take myself away from myself, nor do I linger with those whom some chance occasion or civic duty has brought into my company. Instead, I commune with the best of men. To them I direct my thoughts, in whatever place, in whatever age they lived.

[3] I carry about with me Demetrius, that best of men, and, forsaking those clad in purple, I talk with him in his semi-nakedness. I admire him. And why should I not? I have seen that he lacks nothing. Anyone can despise all things, but no one can possess all things. The shortest path to riches is through contempt of riches. Our Demetrius lives not as one who has despised all things, but as one who has left their possession to others. Farewell.

LETTER 63

CONSOLATION AGAINST GRIEF AND MOURNING

[1] I AM DEEPLY SADDENED BY THE PASSING OF YOUR FRIEND FLACCUS, but I do not wish for you to grieve beyond what is fitting. It would be too bold of me to demand that you not feel sorrow at all, and I know there is a better way. But who can attain such strength of spirit, unless they have already risen far above the whims of fortune? Even such a person will be stung by this loss, though only stung. We, however, can be forgiven for shedding tears, as long as they do not flow too abundantly and we rein them in ourselves. When a friend is lost, our eyes should not remain dry, nor should they overflow. Tears are warranted, but wailing is not.

[2] You may think I lay down a harsh rule, considering that the greatest of the Greek poets[1] granted the right to weep for one full day, and even said that Niobe[2] thought of food in her grief. You may ask, whence come these lamentations, these excessive tears? We seek proof of our anguish through weeping, putting our pain on display rather than simply experiencing it. No one is mournful merely for their own sake. What unhappy foolishness! Even grief can be a source of pride.

[3] "What then?" you ask, "Am I to forget my friend?" You promise him but a brief remembrance if it must coexist with sorrow. Soon

enough, some chance occurrence will redirect that furrowed brow to laughter. I do not postpone this shift to a distant time when all yearning is soothed and even the sharpest agonies subside. As soon as you cease to observe yourself, this façade of sadness will fade. Even now, you are the guardian of your own grief, but it slips away even under a guardian's watch, and all the more swiftly the more intense it burns.

[4] Let us strive to make our remembrance of lost loved ones a pleasant exercise. No one willingly revisits thoughts that must be endured with anguish. It is inevitable that the names of those dear to us whom we have lost will occur to us with a certain pang. Yet even this pang holds a pleasure of its own.

[5] For, as our friend Attalus used to say, "The memory of departed friends is sweet, just as certain fruits have a tart sweetness, or as in well-aged wine we savor the very bitterness. But after a time, all that pained us is extinguished, leaving us with pure delight."

[6] If we trust Attalus: "To contemplate living friends is to enjoy honey and fine cakes. To recall those who have passed, however, carries a bittersweetness that nevertheless pleases. And who could deny that bitter flavors also stimulate the palate?"

[7] I do not feel the same. For me, reflecting on departed friends is a sweet and soothing experience. I had them as if I would lose them; I have lost them as if I still have them.

Therefore, my dear Lucilius, do as befits your sense of justice. Cease to construe Fortune's gift in a negative light. She has taken away, but first she gave.

[8] Therefore, let us eagerly enjoy our friends, for it is uncertain how long this opportunity will be granted to us. Let us consider how often we have left them behind when setting out on some long journey, how frequently we failed to see them though staying in the same place; we will realize that we have lost more time while they lived.

[9] Can you tolerate those who treat their friends with utmost neglect, then mourn them most pitifully, not loving anyone unless they have lost them? And so they grieve more excessively then,

because they fear it may be doubted whether they loved at all; they seek belated proofs of their affection.

[10] If we have other friends, we do them an injustice in both thought and deed, deeming them inadequate to console us in the loss of one. If we do not, the greater injury we have done to ourselves exceeds what fortune inflicted; she took away one, but we deprived ourselves of any we failed to make.

[11] Furthermore, he who could not love more than one never truly loved even that one. If a man, stripped of his only tunic, chose to bewail his loss rather than look about for a way to escape the cold and find something to cover his shoulders, would you not think him utterly foolish?

You have buried the one you loved; seek another to love.

[12] It is better to replace a friend than to weep for him. I know the following thought is trite, yet I will not omit it because it has been voiced by all: even he who could not resolve his grief through reason finds it ended by time. But it is most shameful for a wise man to have weariness of mourning as the remedy for sorrow. I would rather you abandon grief than it abandon you - cease this as soon as possible, which you could not long continue even if you desired.

[13] Our ancestors set a year as the mourning period for women, not so that they should grieve that long, but no longer; for men there is no prescribed time, because none is honorable. Yet what woman could you show me, scarcely pulled back from the pyre and torn from the corpse, whose tears lasted an entire month? Nothing becomes loathsome more quickly than grief, which in its freshness finds comforters and attracts some to itself, but when chronic is derided, and deservedly so - for it is either feigned or foolish.

[14] I who write this to you wept so excessively for my dearest friend Annaeus Serenus that, much against my will, I must be counted among examples of those whom sorrow has overcome. But today I condemn my behavior and understand that my greatest reason for such mourning was that I had never considered he might die before me. This alone occurred to me, that he was younger by far, as if the fates observed our order of birth.

[15] Therefore, let us continually meditate on our own mortality and that of all whom we hold dear. At that time, I should have said: "My beloved Serenus is younger than I; what does it matter? He ought to die after me, but he may well die before me." Because I did not do this, Fortune has caught me off guard with a sudden blow. Now, consider that all things are not only mortal but subject to mortality's uncertain law. Today, anything that can ever happen, can happen.

[16] Let us therefore reflect, my dearest Lucilius, that we will soon arrive at that place where we mourn that he [Serenus] has gone. And perhaps, if only the renown of the wise is true and some place welcomes us, the one whom we think has perished has merely been sent ahead. Farewell.

---

1. Referring to Homer.
2. In Greek mythology, Niobe was a queen who lost all her children and was turned to stone while weeping.

TRUE ADMIRATION FOR THE WISE AND THEIR TEACHINGS

[1] YOU WERE HERE WITH US YESTERDAY. YOU CAN COMPLAIN ONLY IF IT was just yesterday, so I added "with us". For you are always with me. Some friends had dropped by, occasioning a bit more smoke than usual - not the kind that typically billows from the kitchens of the extravagant and alarms the night watchmen, but the modest sort that signals the arrival of guests.

[2] Our conversation meandered, as happens at dinner parties, never delving deeply into any one matter but leaping from one subject to the next. We then read a book by Quintus Sextius the Elder, a great man, believe you me, and a Stoic, though he denies it.

[3] Ye gods, what vigor, what spirit there is in him! You will not find this in all philosophers; the writings of some renowned figures are lifeless things. They lecture, they argue, they quibble; they do not enflame the spirit because they have none themselves. But when you read Sextius, you will say: "He is alive, he is strong, he is free, he is more than a man; he sends me away brimming with immense confidence."

[4] I will confess to you my state of mind when I read him: I am ready to brave any hazard, I long to cry: "Why do you hold back, Fortune? Enter the fray; you see I am prepared." I put on the spirit of

one who seeks a test to prove himself, a chance to demonstrate his virtue:

> *Amid the slothful herds, he prays some foaming boar*
> *Or tawny lion will descend the mountain slopes.*

[5] I crave something to conquer, some hardship by which to exercise my endurance. For this too is Sextius' remarkable quality: he shows you the grandeur of the happy life while not making you despair of attaining it. You will recognize that it dwells on high, yet is accessible to him who has the will.

[6] Virtue herself will grant you the same realization - that you venerate her and yet have hope of reaching her. The contemplation of wisdom often consumes much of my time; I gaze upon her, awestruck, as I sometimes do upon the universe itself, which I frequently behold as though I were seeing it for the first time.

[7] Therefore, I revere the discoveries of wisdom and those who discovered them; I delight in approaching this inheritance of many as if it were my own. These things were gained for me, toiled for on my behalf. But let us act as a good head of household; let us increase what we have inherited. May this legacy pass from me to my descendants still greater than before. Much work remains and much will always remain; even someone born a thousand ages hence will not be barred from adding something further.

[8] But even if the ancients discovered all, this will always remain new: the application, understanding, and arrangement of what others have invented. Suppose, for instance, that the ancients bequeathed to us medicines to heal the eyes. I need not seek out different remedies, yet I must still adapt these to the particular diseases and circumstances. This salve alleviates irritation of the eyes; that reduces swelling of the eyelids; this diverts a sudden afflux of humor[1]; this sharpens vision. You must grind these ingredients, choose the right time, and apply the proper amount to each case.

[9] The ancients discovered remedies for the soul, but it remains for us to determine how and when to apply them. They accom-

plished much, those who came before us, but they did not finish the task. Still, we must look up to them and venerate them as gods. Why should I not keep images of great men as spurs to my spirit and celebrate their birthdays? Why should I not call upon them always, in reverence? The same awe I owe my own teachers I owe to those universal teachers of humanity from whom the beginnings of such great good have flowed.

[10] If I see a consul or a praetor, I will do everything customary to show them respect: dismount my horse, uncover my head, yield the road. What then? Shall I welcome into my soul, without the deepest appreciation, the two Catos and Laelius the Wise, and Socrates with Plato, and Zeno and Cleanthes? Indeed, I venerate them and always rise to salute such great names. Farewell.

---

1. Some manuscripts have "sudden fear" instead of "sudden afflux of humor."

LETTER 65

THE EQUALITY OF ALL
GOODS AND VIRTUES

[1] YESTERDAY I DIVIDED MY TIME WITH ILLNESS; THE MORNING IT claimed for itself, but the afternoon it yielded to me. And so I first tested my mind with reading. Then, when it had accepted this, I dared to impose more upon it - nay, to allow it more; I wrote something, and indeed with more intensity than I usually do, while I struggled with difficult subject matter and refused to be overcome, until friends arrived who would do me violence and subdue me like an unruly patient.

[2] Conversation took the place of writing, and from that I will relate to you the part which is in dispute - for we have appointed you as the arbitrator. You have more business on your hands than you realize; the case is threefold.

Our Stoics say, as you know, that there are two things in nature from which all things come to be: cause and matter. Matter lies inert, a substance ready for anything, destined to remain idle if no one sets it in motion. Cause, however, by which I mean reason, molds matter and turns it wherever it will, producing various works from it. There must, therefore, be that from which something is made, and then that by which it is made. The latter is the cause, the former the matter.

[3] Every art is an imitation of nature. And so apply what I was

saying about the universe to the things which are to be made by man. A statue had both the matter which was to submit to the craftsman, and the craftsman who was to give form to the matter. Thus, in the case of the statue, the material was bronze, the cause was the workman. And so it is with all things - they consist of that which is made and of that which makes.

[4] The Stoics believe that there is one cause - that which makes. Aristotle thinks that "cause" is used in three ways. "The first cause," he says, "is the actual matter, without which nothing can be created. The second is the workman. The third is the form, which is impressed upon every work as it is upon a statue"; for this, Aristotle calls the idos. "There is also a fourth," he says, "the purpose of the whole work."

[5] I shall explain what this means. The primary cause of a statue is the bronze, for it never would have been made unless there had been something from which it could be cast and shaped. The second cause is the sculptor, for the bronze could not have been shaped to the contour of the statue without the artist's trained hands. The third cause is the form, for the statue would not be called "The Spear-Bearer" or "The Boy Binding His Hair" were not this shape impressed upon it. The fourth cause is the purpose of making it, for if this had not been present, the statue would not have been made.

[6] What, then, is the purpose [of a work of art]? It is that which invited the artisan, which he pursued in his creation—whether money, if he fabricated it to sell; or glory, if he labored for renown; or religion, if he prepared it as an offering for a temple. This, therefore, is also the cause for which it is made. Or do you not think that among the causes of a work's creation should be numbered that, without which, it would not have been made?

[7] To these four, Plato adds a fifth: the exemplar, which he himself calls the "idea". For this is that to which the artisan, looking to it, fashioned what he had purposed. It matters not whether he has the exemplar outside, to which he may direct his eyes, or inside, which he himself conceived and placed there [in his mind]. These exemplars of all things, god has within himself, and the numbers and measures of all that is to be done, he has embraced in his mind. He is

filled with these figures, which Plato calls "ideas"—immortal, unchanging, untiring. And so, indeed, individual men perish, but mankind itself, after which man is fashioned, endures. Though men labor and die, mankind suffers nothing.

[8] There are, therefore, five causes, as Plato says: that from which, that by which, that in which, that in reference to which, and that on account of which. Lastly, that which results from these. So in a statue (since we began by speaking of this), that from which [it is made] is the bronze; that by which [it is made] is the artisan; that in which [it is made] is the form which is adapted to it; that in reference to which [it is made] is the exemplar imitated by him who makes it; that on account of which [it is made] is the purpose of the maker. That which results from these is the statue itself.

[9] The universe also has all these [causes], as Plato says: a maker (this is god); that from which it is made (this is matter); form (this is the shape and order of the universe which we see); an exemplar, evidently, in reference to which god made the magnificence of this most beautiful work; and a purpose, on account of which he made it.

[10] You ask, what was god's purpose? Goodness. Thus indeed Plato says: "What cause had god for making the world? He is good, and in the good there is no envy of any good thing. Therefore he made it the best he could." So pronounce your judgment, and declare who seems to you to speak most truly—not who speaks the absolute truth. For that is as far above us as truth itself.

[11] This multitude of causes laid out by Aristotle and Plato either encompasses too much or too little. For if they judge a cause to be that which, when removed, prevents an effect from occurring, then they have named too few. Let them count time among the causes, for nothing can happen without time. Let them count place, for if there is nowhere for something to occur, it will not happen at all. Let them count motion, for without it, nothing either happens or perishes. No art, no change exists without motion.

[12] But we are now seeking the first and general cause, which must be simple, just as matter is simple. We ask, what is the cause? Evidently, it is the creative reason—in other words, God[1]. For those

things you have listed are not many separate causes but depend on one—on that which will create.

[13] Do you say that form is the cause? The artisan imposes this upon his work; it is part of the cause, not the cause itself. Nor is the pattern the cause, but a necessary tool of the cause. The pattern is as necessary to the artisan as the chisel or the file; without these, art cannot proceed. Yet these are not parts of the art nor its causes.

[14] "The artisan's purpose," one objects, "the reason why he undertakes to make something, is the cause." Even if we grant this as a cause, it is not the efficient cause but a subsequent one. But such causes are innumerable, while we seek the general cause. And to say that the whole world and the completed work are the cause, as they have, does not show their customary subtlety. For there is a great difference between the work and the cause of the work.

[15] Either make a definitive judgment or, as is easier in such matters, admit you are not certain and bid us return to the question. "Why," you ask, "do you delight in wasting time on these matters which relieve you of no passion, drive away no desire?" I, indeed, grapple with and ponder these more important issues by which the mind is pacified. I first examine myself, then this world.

[16] Even now, I am not wasting time, as you suppose. For all these studies, if not chopped up and fragmented into such useless minutiae, elevate and uplift the mind, which, burdened by a heavy load, yearns to be unshackled and return to the things to which it once belonged. For this body is a weight upon the soul and its penance; as the soul is oppressed by it, it is shackled, unless philosophy has come to its aid, bidding it take fresh courage from the contemplation of nature and directing it onward from earthly to divine things. This is the soul's liberty, this its escape; meanwhile, it withdraws from the prison in which it is bound and is refreshed by the sky.

[17] Just as artisans of intricate crafts that strain the eyes with intense focus venture out in public and delight their eyes with the free light in some place dedicated to the leisure of the people when they have poor and fickle lighting, so too does the mind, hemmed in

within this gloomy and dim dwelling, seek the open air whenever possible and find rest in contemplation of the natural world.

[18] The wise man, a devotee of wisdom, remains attached to his body, yet is absent in his best part, directing his thoughts to lofty matters. Bound by a sacred oath, he considers this life he lives a form of military service. He is so disposed as to have neither love nor hatred for life, enduring mortal affairs while knowing greater things await beyond.

[19] Do you forbid me from examining the nature of things, dragging me back when I had retreated from the part to the whole? Shall I not inquire what are the origins of the universe? Who is the shaper of things? Who separated all that was immersed in one and entwined in inert matter? Shall I not seek out who is the architect of this world? By what plan such vastness fell into law and order? Who gathered the scattered, distinguished the entangled, divided a countenance among things lying in shapeless disarray? From where is such abundant light poured forth? Is it fire, or something more luminous than fire?

[20] Shall I not ponder these questions? Shall I remain ignorant of whence I have descended? Are these things to be beheld only once, or must I be born many times? Where shall I go when I depart from here? What abode awaits the soul released from the laws of human servitude? You forbid me to contemplate the heavens, in other words you bid me live with head bowed low?

[21] I am greater and born for greater things than to be a slave to my body, which I regard as nothing other than a shackle fastened around my liberty. This, therefore, I set against fortune as a bulwark to withstand her, allowing no wound to pass through it to me. This is all that can suffer injury in me. In this vulnerable dwelling resides a free soul.

[22] Never shall this flesh compel me to fear, never to an unworthy pretense ill-befitting a good man; never shall I lie for the sake of this pitiful body. When it seems right, I shall dissolve my partnership with it. And yet, for now, while we remain joined, we shall not be partners on equal terms; the mind shall claim all authority for itself. Disdain for one's body is a sure freedom.

[23] But to return to my point, this freedom I speak of will be greatly served by the contemplation we just discussed. For indeed, all things consist of both matter and God. God tempers these things, which, having been set in motion, follow their guide and ruler. That which acts, which is God, is more powerful and precious than the matter which is acted upon by God.

The place God holds in this cosmos is the same as that which the soul holds in man. What matter is in the universe, the body is in us; therefore, let the inferior serve the superior. Let us be brave in the face of chance events. Let us not tremble at injuries, wounds, chains, or poverty. What is death? Either an end or a transition. I do not fear ceasing to be, for it is the same as having never begun, nor do I fear passing over, because I will never be constrained in so narrow a place as this. [24] Farewell.

---

1. The phrase "id est deus" was regarded as a gloss by Schweighäuser.

LETTER 66

THE CONSTANCY OF THE
WISE MAN'S MIND

[1] AFTER MANY YEARS, I SAW MY OLD SCHOOLMATE CLARANUS. YOU needn't wait for me to add that he's grown old; in truth, his spirit remains vibrantly youthful and energetic, even as it wrestles with his frail body. Nature has dealt him an unfair hand, housing such a brilliant soul in an inadequate frame - or perhaps she intended to demonstrate to us that the most robust and contented mind can reside beneath any surface. Yet he conquers all impediments and, by holding himself in low regard, arrives at the point of holding all else in similar disdain.

[2] The one who said,

> *"Virtue appears all the more pleasing when it comes in a*
> *beautiful body,"*

seems to me to have been mistaken. For virtue requires no adornment; it is its own great glory and consecrates its bodily vessel. I have certainly come to view our Claranus in a different light - to me, he seems as beautiful and as upright in body as he is in mind.

[3] A great man can emerge from a humble cottage; a beautiful and expansive soul can inhabit a misshapen and diminutive frame. It

seems to me that nature produces certain individuals in this way to prove that virtue can arise in any place. If she could bring forth souls unencumbered, she would have done so. But as it is, she does something even more remarkable: she creates some who are impeded by their bodies and yet break through all that obstructs them.

[4] Claranus strikes me as one crafted to be an exemplar, that we might know a soul is not tainted by bodily deformity, but rather a body is graced by the beauty of the soul.

Though we spent only a handful of days together, our conversations were many. I'll gather them up and send them your way in due course.

[5] On this first day, the question arose: how can goods be equal when they fall into three different categories? As we see it, some goods are primary, such as joy, peace, and the safety of one's homeland. Others are secondary, manifested in unfortunate circumstances, like enduring torture or maintaining self-control during grave illness. The former goods we'll wish for ourselves directly; the latter, only if necessity dictates. There is still a third class, encompassing things like a modest gait, a composed and honest countenance, and gestures befitting a man of wisdom.

[6] How can these things be equal to each other, when some are to be wished for, others to be shunned? If we want to distinguish between them, let us return to the primary good and consider its nature: a mind that contemplates truth, skilled in discerning what to seek and avoid; assigning value to things not from opinion, but from nature; immersing itself in the whole universe and sending its thoughtful gaze upon all its activity; focused both in reflection and action; equally great and forceful, unconquered by both the harsh and the agreeable, submitting to neither fortune; rising above all that happens by chance or accident; most beautiful, most well-ordered both in grace and strength, sound and dry[1], unperturbed, fearless, unbreakable by any force, lifted up but not cast down by happenstance. Such a mind is virtue itself.

[7] This is virtue's appearance, if it could be seen all at once, showing itself completely. But in reality, virtue has many forms. They

are revealed according to the variety of life and the tasks at hand; virtue itself becomes neither less nor greater. For the highest good cannot diminish, nor can virtue move backward. But it transforms into other qualities, shaped to the condition of what it will undertake.

[8] Whatever virtue touches, it draws to a likeness of itself and imbues with its color. It graces actions, friendships, sometimes entire households which it has entered and set in order. Whatever it has handled, it makes lovely, remarkable, admirable.

Therefore, its power and greatness cannot rise further, since there can be no increase to the greatest. You will find nothing straighter than the straight, nothing truer than the true, nothing more temperate than the temperate.

[9] All virtue is without limit; only what can be measured is limited. Constancy has nowhere to advance, no more than do confidence, truth or faith. What can be added to the perfect? Nothing—otherwise it was not perfect to begin with. Therefore, nothing can be added to virtue either; if anything can be added, it was deficient. The morally right likewise admits no addition, for it is morally right because of the qualities I have recounted. Moreover, do you think that decorum, justice, and lawfulness are not of the same unvarying form, comprehended within fixed limits? The ability to increase is proof of imperfection.

[10] All good falls under the same rules. Private and public utility are linked—by Hercules, as inseparable as the praiseworthy and the desirable. Therefore, the virtues are equal to one another, as are the works of virtue and all people in whom they reside.

[11] The virtues of living creatures and animals, being mortal, are also fragile, fleeting, and uncertain. They depart and subside, and thus are not held in the same esteem. Yet for human virtues, a single rule applies. For right reason is one and simple. Nothing is more divine than the divine, more heavenly than the heavenly.

[12] Mortal things diminish, fall, wear away, grow, are depleted, and are replenished. Thus, in such an uncertain lot, there is inequality. But the nature of divine things is one. And reason is nothing other than a part of the divine spirit immersed in the human body. If reason

is divine, and no good exists without reason, then every good is divine. Further, there is no distinction among divine things; therefore, there is none among good things either. Thus, both joy and the strong, resolute endurance of torments are equal. For in each, the greatness of spirit is the same—in one relaxed and cheerful, in the other combative and strained.

[13] What? Do you not think the virtue of one who bravely storms the enemy's walls is equal to that of one who most patiently endures a siege? Great is Scipio, who encloses and confines Numantia and compels those unconquered hands to turn to their own destruction. Great too is the spirit of the besieged, who know their elimination is not final since death is at hand, and who breathe their last in the embrace of liberty. Equally, all other virtues are also mutually equivalent: tranquility, simplicity, generosity, constancy, equanimity, endurance. For beneath all these lies a single virtue, which keeps the spirit upright and unswerving.

[14] "What then? Is there no difference between joy and the inflexible endurance of pain?" None, as far as the virtues themselves are concerned. But a great difference between the circumstances in which each virtue is displayed. For in one, there is a natural relaxation and ease of spirit, while in the other, pain contrary to nature. Thus, these are intermediary matters that allow for the greatest difference. The virtue in each is equal.

[15] The subject matter does not change virtue—adversity does not make it worse, nor does cheerfulness and joy make it better. Therefore, it must necessarily be equal. For in both cases, what is done is done with equal correctness, prudence, and honor. Consequently, the goods are equal, beyond which neither in joy can one conduct oneself better, nor can the other amid those torments. And two things than which nothing can be done better are equal.

[16] For if things positioned outside of virtue can either diminish or augment it, then it ceases to be the one true good, which is moral rectitude. If you concede this point, all morality perishes. Why? I will tell you: because nothing moral can be done by an unwilling person under coercion[2]. All moral acts are voluntary. Mix in laziness,

complaining, evasiveness, fear—and the act loses its most excellent quality: self-approval. What is not freely chosen cannot be moral, for what fears is enslaved.

[17] Everything moral is secure and tranquil. If it refuses something, bemoans it, or judges it bad, then it has admitted perturbation and is tossed about in great discord. For the appearance of right calls from one direction, while the suspicion of evil pulls back from another. Therefore, whoever intends to act morally, whatever opposes it, even if he thinks it inconvenient, let him not consider it evil. Let him do it willingly, gladly. All moral action is unbidden and uncoerced, pure and unmixed with any evil.

[18] I know what objection might be raised here: "Are you trying to convince us that it makes no difference whether someone lies joyfully at a banquet or is stretched on the rack, wearing out his torturer?" I could reply that Epicurus, too, says a sage, if burned in the bull of Phalaris, will cry out, "This is pleasant and means nothing to me[3]!" Why marvel if I claim the one sprawling at the feast and the other standing strong in torment have equal goods, when Epicurus makes the more incredible claim that it is pleasant to be roasted?

[19] But I respond that there is indeed a great difference between joy and pain. If given the choice, I will seek the one and shun the other. The one accords with nature, the other against it. As long as they are judged so, they are separated by a vast interval. But when it comes to virtue, the two are equal, both that proceeding through delights and that through sorrows[4].

[20] Torment, pain, and any other disadvantage carry no weight, for they are overwhelmed by virtue. Just as the brightness of the sun obscures tiny lights, so virtue by its magnitude crushes and suppresses pains, annoyances, and injustices. And wherever virtue shines, whatever appears without it is extinguished. Disadvantages hold no more sway when they collide with virtue than a raincloud does in the sea.

[21] To know this to be true, consider that a good man will hasten towards anything noble without the slightest hesitation. Even if an executioner, torturer, and flames stand in his path, he will persevere,

focusing not on what he may suffer, but on what he must do. He will entrust himself to an honorable endeavor as a virtuous man should, judging it beneficial, safe, and favorable to himself. In his eyes, an honest but grim and arduous task will hold the same status as a good but poor, exiled, and haggard man.

[22] Come now, imagine on one side a good man abounding in riches, and on the other, one possessing nothing but his inner qualities. Both will be equally good men, even if fortune treats them differently. The same judgment applies to circumstances as it does to people: virtue is just as praiseworthy whether found in a healthy, free body or in one that is sick and shackled.

[23] Therefore, you should not praise your own virtue more if fortune has gifted you an unscathed body than if it is maimed in some way. To do otherwise would be like judging a master by the condition of his slaves. For all those things over which chance holds sway are in servitude—money, body, and honors—weak, fluid, mortal, and of uncertain possession. But the works of virtue are free and invincible, to be sought no more eagerly if fortune treats them kindly, nor less so if they are burdened by some adversity.

[24] What friendship is among men, desire is among circumstances. I do not imagine you would love a wealthy good man more than a poor one, nor a muscular, brawny one more than a slim, languid one. So, too, you should not desire or cherish a cheerful, peaceful situation more than one that is troubled and laborious.

[25] If this were the case, you would, given two equally good men, prefer the sleek and perfumed one to the dusty and unkempt one. Following this line of thought, you would eventually favor a man whole and uninjured in all his limbs to one who is feeble or one-eyed. Gradually, your disdain would reach the point where, given two equally just and prudent men, you would choose the one with styled, curly locks [over the bald and scruffy one]. Where virtue is equal in both, the inequality of other qualities is immaterial, for all else are not parts of a man, but merely accessories.

[26] Is there anyone who judges their own so unfairly that they love a

healthy child more than a sick one, or a tall and lofty child more than one who is short or of average height? Wild beasts do not distinguish between their offspring and lay themselves down equally to feed them all; birds distribute food impartially. Ulysses hurries back to the rocks of his Ithaca just as Agamemnon speeds to the noble walls of Mycenae. For no one loves their homeland because it is great, but because it is their own.

[27] What is the point of these examples? To show you that virtue looks upon all its works as its children with the same eyes, showing equal indulgence to all and even greater care for those that struggle, just as a parent's love leans more towards those who inspire pity. Virtue, too, does not love its works more when it sees them afflicted and oppressed, but like good parents, it embraces and cherishes them all the more.

[28] Why, then, is no good greater than another? Because nothing can be more fitting than what is already fitting, nothing flatter than what is already flat. You cannot say that one thing is more equal to another than a third thing; therefore, nothing is more honorable than what is honorable.

[29] If the nature of all virtues is equal, then the three kinds of goods [moral, desirable, and admirable] are on par. What I mean is this: to rejoice in moderation and to grieve in moderation are equal. The joy does not surpass the firmness of spirit that suppresses groans under torture; the former are desirable goods, the latter admirable, yet both are nonetheless equal because any inconvenience is over-shadowed by the power of a much greater good.

[30] Whoever judges these things as unequal turns their eyes away from the virtues themselves and looks at external factors; true goods have the same weight and are equally evident. Those false goods contain much emptiness. Thus, they appear impressive and grand to onlookers, but when weighed, they deceive.

[31] It is so, my Lucilius; whatever true reason commends is solid and eternal, strengthening the soul and always elevating it to future heights; those things praised rashly and considered good by popular opinion inflate us with empty joys. Conversely, those things which

threaten us with the appearance of evil instill fear in our minds, agitating them like animals faced with danger.

[32] Therefore, both these things needlessly elate and torment the soul; neither the one is worthy of joy nor the other of fear. Only reason is immutable and tenacious in judgment. For it does not serve the senses but commands them. Reason is equal to reason, just as right is equal to right; therefore, virtue is equal to virtue. Virtue is nothing other than right reason. All virtues are reasons. They are reasons if they are right. If they are right, they are also equal.

[33] As is the reasoning faculty, so too are the actions; therefore, all actions are equal. For since actions resemble the reasoning faculty, they also resemble each other. Moreover, I assert that actions are equal to one another insofar as they are honorable and righteous. There will, of course, be great variations depending on the subject matter, which is sometimes broader, sometimes narrower, sometimes illustrious, sometimes undistinguished, sometimes pertaining to many, sometimes to few. Yet in all these cases, that which is best is equal; they are honorable.

[34] Just as all good men are equal insofar as they are good, they still have differences in age: one is older, another younger. They have differences in body: one is handsome, another unsightly. They have differences in fortune: this one is rich, that one poor; this one is favored, powerful, known to cities and peoples, that one is unknown to most and obscure. But in that respect whereby they are good, they are equal.

[35] The senses do not judge concerning good and evil; what is useful and what is useless, they know not. The senses cannot pronounce judgment unless brought face to face with the matter at hand. They neither foresee the future nor remember the past; what may follow, they know not. But from reasoning springs the order and connection of things, and the unity of a life that shall run consistently straight. Reason, therefore, is the arbiter of good and evil; it regards things alien and external as cheap, and deems those that are neither good nor evil to be very paltry and trivial accessories. For reason, every good resides in the soul.

[36] However, reason considers certain things as primary goods, to which it comes by design, such as victory, good children, the safety of one's country. Others it deems secondary, which become apparent only in adversity, such as bearing a severe illness or exile with equanimity. Still others it judges intermediate, being no more according to nature than contrary to nature, such as walking prudently or sitting decorously. For sitting is no less natural than standing or walking.

[37] Those two aforementioned superior goods are different. The primary ones are according to nature: rejoicing in the devotion of one's children, in the well-being of one's country. The secondary are contrary to nature: bravely withstanding tortures and enduring thirst while a disease inflames the vitals.

[38] "What then? Is something contrary to nature good?" By no means; but that in which the good sometimes exists is occasionally contrary to nature. For to be wounded, to melt in the heat of a fever, to be afflicted with poor health—these are contrary to nature, but to maintain an indomitable spirit amid such trials is in harmony with nature.

[39] To express my point briefly, the raw material of good is sometimes contrary to nature, but good itself never is, since there can be no good without reason, and reason follows nature. "What, then, is reason?" you ask. It is the imitation of nature. "And what is the supreme good for humankind?" To conduct oneself according to nature's will.

[40] "There is no doubt," says Seneca, "that peace never provoked is happier than that reclaimed at the cost of much blood. There is no doubt that unshaken health is a happier state than having been dragged back from severe illnesses that threatened one's very life, by some force of will and endurance. Similarly, there will be no doubt that joy is a greater good than a mind stubbornly set on bearing tortures of wounds or fire."

[41] Not at all. Those things that come by chance admit the greatest variation, for they are judged by the utility of their recipient. The one purpose of goods is to be in harmony with nature; this is equal in all cases. When we support someone's opinion in the Senate,

it cannot be said that one agrees more than the other; all go towards the same opinion. I say the same about virtues: all are in harmony with nature. I say the same about goods: all are in harmony with nature.

[42] One passes away as a youth, another as an old man; someone else as a mere infant, granted nothing more than a glimpse of life. All of these were equally mortal, even if death allowed the life of some to proceed further, cut others off in their prime, and interrupted yet others at their very beginnings.

[43] One is released while dining. Another's death is an uninterrupted sleep. Intimacy extinguished another. Against these I set those pierced by the sword, those whose life breath was stopped by a serpent's bite, those crushed by collapse, or twisted joint by joint through a long contraction of the sinews. The end of some can be called better, of others worse; but death itself is equal for all. The means by which they depart are various; that into which they depart is one. No death is greater or lesser; for it has the same limit in all cases—the finish of life.

[44] I tell you the same thing about goods: one kind resides amidst pure pleasures, the other amidst sorrow and bitterness. The former manages fortune's indulgence, the latter conquers her violence. Both are equally good, though one travels a smooth and gentle path, and the other a rough one. All goods share the same end: they are good, they are praiseworthy, they attend upon virtue and reason. Virtue makes equal everything she acknowledges as her own.

[45] And don't be surprised to find this among our doctrines. According to Epicurus, there are two goods that constitute that highest, blessed state: a body free of pain and a mind free of disturbance. These goods do not increase if they are already complete. For how can that which is complete increase? The body is free of pain - what can be added to this painlessness? The mind is at harmony with itself and at peace - what can be added to this tranquility?

[46] Just as a clear sky, once purified into utter brilliance, cannot achieve any greater clarity, so too the perfect condition of a person caring for his body and mind, weaving his good from both, is to reach

the pinnacle of his desires, with neither passion in his mind nor pain in his body. If any external delights happen to come, they do not increase his highest good, but merely, if I may say so, spice it and add cheer. For the absolute good of human nature is content with peace of body and mind.

[47] I will give you, from Epicurus, a division of goods very similar to our own. For he has one class of goods he would prefer to have happen to him, like bodily tranquility free from all discomfort and the relaxation of a mind rejoicing in the contemplation of its own goods. But there is another class which, though he would rather they not occur, he nonetheless praises and approves - like that endurance of ill health and most severe pains I mentioned earlier, in which Epicurus spent his last, most blessed day. For he says he was suffering the torments of blocked bladder and ulcerated bowels, which could not increase in pain beyond what he felt, yet that day was nonetheless a blessed one. But only one who is in possession of the highest good can be said to live blessedly.

[48] Therefore, even in Epicurus' view there are goods you would prefer not to experience, but which, because circumstances brought them, you must welcome and praise and put on a level with the highest goods. One cannot say this is not a good equal to the greatest, when it provided the conclusion to a blessed life - a life for which Epicurus expressed gratitude with his dying breath.

[49] Permit me, Lucilius, best of men, to say something rather bold: if any goods could be greater than others, I would have deemed these goods that seem bitter greater than those soft and pampered ones. I would have called them greater, for it is a greater thing to break through difficulties than to manage enjoyments.

[50] By the same principle, I know, one can bear prosperity with grace and adversity with courage. The person who stands watch safely behind the rampart when no enemies assail the camp can be just as brave as the one who, hamstrung, catches himself on his knees and refuses to let go of his weapons. To the bloodied soldiers returning from the front lines, we say: "Well done and be blessed for your valor!" Thus I would praise more highly those good things that

have been tested and strengthened, that have struggled against fortune.

[51] Would I hesitate to praise more highly the mutilated and shriveled hand of Mucius than the unscathed hand of even the bravest man? Defying both enemies and flames, he stood firm, gazing at his own hand dripping away on the enemy's brazier, until Porsenna, favoring Mucius' punishment, begrudged his glory and ordered the fire removed against Mucius' will.

[52] Why should I not count this good among the foremost and consider it greater than those untested and unthreatened by fortune? For it is rarer to have conquered an enemy with a lost hand than with an armed one. "What then?" you ask, "Will you wish for such a good for yourself?" Why not? For one who cannot even wish for it, cannot do it.

[53] Or should I instead wish to offer up my joints for massage to my minions⁵? To have some woman, or some man turned womanish, manipulate my fingers? Why would I not deem Mucius more blessed, for handling the fire as though he had entrusted that hand to a masseuse? He corrected fully whatever had gone astray; unarmed and maimed, he finished the war, conquering two kings with that mutilated hand. Farewell.

---

1. Translating literally the Latin "sanus ac siccus," meaning mentally sound and free from destructive passions.
2. The manuscript readings for "coactum" vary, with some having "a coacto" or "aco acto," but the meaning is essentially the same.
3. Some manuscripts include an additional phrase here, "alterius in convivio iacentis," contrasting "one lying at a banquet" with one standing most bravely amidst tortures, but it is not in all copies.
4. The manuscript reading "terroris et" has been emended to "torreri sed" (but to be roasted) by Ludwig von Jan to align with the context.
5. The Latin term "exoletis" here refers to male slaves used for sexual purposes.

LETTER 67

HOW THE WISE MAN REGARDS EXTERNAL THINGS

[1] To begin with the usual, spring has started to reveal itself, but having already begun to turn into summer, it has grown cool again instead of warm as it ought to be at this time, and it is not yet to be trusted. For it often slips back into winter. Do you want to know how uncertain it still is? I don't yet trust myself to the true cold of the baths, but still temper its chill. "This means," you say, "enduring neither heat nor cold." Just so, my dear Lucilius; at my age I'm content with my own chilliness. I scarcely thaw out by midsummer.

[2] And so I spend most of my time bundled in clothing. I give thanks to old age for pinning me to my bed. Why should I not give thanks for this? I cannot refuse anything I ought to be unwilling to do. I converse at length with my books. Whenever one of your letters arrives, I feel as if I am with you, and I am so moved in spirit that I feel I am not writing back to you but speaking to you face to face. So let us examine together, as if conversing, the matter about which you inquire.

[3] You ask whether every good thing is desirable. "If it is good," you say, "to be tortured bravely, to burn with a stout heart, to endure illness with patience, it follows that these things are desirable. Yet I see nothing among them worth wishing for. At any rate, I have not yet

known anyone who has paid a vow because he was cut to pieces by the rod, twisted out of shape by gout, or stretched on the rack."

[4] Let me explain, my dear Lucilius, and you will understand that there is something in them worth wishing for. I would prefer to be free from torture; but if I must endure it, I will wish that I may conduct myself bravely, honorably, and courageously during it. Of course I prefer not to wage war; but if war is inevitable, I will wish that I may nobly bear wounds, hunger, and all other necessities of war. I am not so mad as to desire illness; but if I must be ill, I will wish that I may do nothing immoderate or effeminate. Thus, misfortunes themselves are not desirable, but the virtue by which we endure misfortunes is desirable.

[5] Some of our school think that patient endurance of all these things is not desirable, though not to be abhorred either, because only the pure good, the serene, and the trouble-free should be sought by vow. I disagree. Why? First, because it is impossible for anything to be good and yet not desirable. Second, if virtue is desirable, and nothing is good without virtue, then every good thing is desirable. Moreover, even the stout endurance of torture is desirable.

[6] I ask again: is courage not desirable? And yet it scorns and challenges dangers. Its most beautiful and wondrous aspect is this— not yielding to fires, marching out to face wounds, sometimes not even avoiding spears but receiving them full in the chest. If courage is desirable, then bearing torments with patience is also desirable, for this is a part of courage. But separate these things, as I have said, and there will be nothing to lead you astray. For enduring torments is not desirable in itself, but enduring them courageously is. That "courageously" is what I desire, and that is virtue.

[7] "But who has ever wished for this?" you ask. Some prayers are open and explicit when made in detail; others are hidden, when many things are encompassed in a single prayer. It is as if I were to pray for a morally upright life. But an upright life consists of various actions—within it are Regulus' [torture] chest, the wound Cato inflicted with his own hand, Rutilius' exile, the poisoned cup that transported Socrates from prison to heaven. Thus, when I prayed for

a morally upright life, I also prayed for these things, without which an upright life is sometimes impossible.

[8]

> *O thrice and four times blessed are they*
> *Who beneath Troy's lofty ramparts, before their fathers'*
> > *eyes,*
> *Met their fate!*

What difference does it make whether you wish this for someone or admit that it was desirable?

[9] Decius sacrificed himself for the republic; spurring his horse, he rushed into the midst of the enemy, seeking death. Following his example, another Decius, emulating his father's valor, charging into the thickest of the fray with the solemn and now familiar ritual words, concerned only with securing divine favor, considering a noble death to be desirable. Do you then doubt whether a memorable death in some virtuous deed is the best thing?

[10] When someone courageously endures torments, he employs all the virtues. Perhaps patience is the most visible and apparent. But courage is there, of which endurance, long-suffering, and forbearance are branches. Prudence is there, without which no plan is undertaken, which persuades bearing as bravely as possible what cannot be avoided. Consistency is there, which cannot be dislodged from its position and does not abandon its resolve when compelled by any force. There is that inseparable company of virtues: whatever is done honorably, a single virtue accomplishes, but with the assent of the whole council. And what is approved by all the virtues, even if it appears to be the work of one, is desirable.

[11] What? Do you think that only pleasant and leisurely things that are welcomed at decorated doors are desirable? Some blessings wear a grim countenance. There are prayers that are celebrated not with a crowd of well-wishers, but with the reverence and veneration of worshippers.

[12] Do you not think that Regulus longed to reach the

Carthaginians? Take on the spirit of that great man and withdraw a little from the opinions of the common crowd. Embrace the appearance of virtue at its most beautiful and magnificent, which we must worship not with incense or garlands, but with sweat and blood.

[13] Picture Marcus Cato applying his purest hands to that sacred breast, widening the insufficiently deep wounds. Which, then, will you say to him: "I wish things were as you wish" and "I am upset", or "Blessings upon what you do"?

[14] At this point our friend Demetrius comes to mind, who calls a secure life free from any incursions of fortune a "dead sea". To have nothing to rouse you, nothing to stir yourself to, nothing by whose threat and assault you may test the firmness of your spirit, but instead to lie in unshaken leisure—this is not tranquility; it is a flat calm.

[15] Attalus the Stoic used to say: "I prefer that fortune hold me in her camp rather than in her delights. I am racked, but acting bravely; it is well. I am being killed, but acting bravely; it is well." Listen to Epicurus, he will even say "it is sweet." I would never bestow a soft name upon such an honorable and severe matter.

[16] I am burned, but unconquered. Why should I not consider this desirable—not because the fire burns me, but because it does not conquer me? Nothing is more excellent than virtue, nothing more beautiful. Whatever is carried out by its command is both good and desirable. Farewell.

LETTER 68

THE PHILOSOPHER'S RETIREMENT FROM PUBLIC AFFAIRS

[1] I AGREE WITH YOUR PLAN: HIDE AWAY IN LEISURE. BUT HIDE THAT leisure itself as well. Know that you will be doing this in accordance not only with the precepts of the Stoics, but also their example. But you will act according to precept too, and prove it both to yourself and to whomever you wish.

[2] We do not dispatch ourselves to every republic, nor always, nor without any end in sight. Besides, when we have given the sage a republic worthy of him - that is, the world - he is not outside the republic even if he has retreated. Indeed, perhaps having left one tiny corner he passes into greater and more expansive realms. Placed in the heavens, he understands how lowly a place he sat when he ascended the [orator's] chair or tribunal. Lay this up in your heart: the sage is never more active than when divine and human matters have come into his view.

[3] Now I return to what I had begun to urge you to do: let your leisure be unknown. There is no need to proclaim your philosophy or quietude as if with a label. Give your purpose another name; call it health and frailty and indolence. To boast of leisure is lazy ambition.

[4] Certain animals obscure their tracks around their very lair lest they be found; you must do the same. Otherwise there will be no lack

of those who constantly pursue you. Many pass by what is open, but poke around in what is hidden and concealed. Locks entice a thief; a burglar passes by open doors. Such are the ways of the public, and of all the most ignorant: they are eager to burst in upon secrets. Therefore, it is best not to advertise your leisure.

[5] Yet there is a way of advertising it: to hide away too much and withdraw from the sight of men. That man buried himself in Tarentum, that one shut himself up in Naples, another for many years did not cross the threshold of his own house. Whoever imposes some story on his leisure attracts a crowd.

[6] When you have retreated, your aim should not be that men talk about you, but that you talk with yourself. And what should you talk about? What men most gladly do about others, think ill of yourself to yourself. You will grow accustomed both to speaking and to hearing the truth. But above all, dwell on what you perceive to be your greatest weakness.

[7] Each person is well acquainted with the weaknesses of their own body. Thus, one relieves an upset stomach with vomiting, another bolsters it with frequent meals, while yet another purges and exhausts the body with periodic fasting. Those whose feet are prone to pain either abstain from wine or avoid the baths. Though neglectful of other things, they take precautions against that which often plagues them; just so, there are certain parts of our mind that are, as it were, infirm[1] and require attentive care.

[8] What do I do with my leisure, you ask? I treat my own ulcer. If I were to show you a swollen foot, a bruised hand, or the withered sinews of a contracted leg, you would allow me to lie still and nurse my affliction. But the malady I suffer is greater than these, one I cannot display to you; an abscess and festering sore lies deep within my breast. Please, no applause, no accolades, proclaiming: "What a great man! He has scorned all things and fled the condemned madness of human existence."

[9] I have condemned nothing except myself. You have no reason to seek me out for the sake of progress. You are mistaken if you hope to find any aid here; it is not a physician but a sick man who dwells in

this place. I would prefer that when you depart, you remark: "I thought him a happy and learned man. I had perked up my ears, but now I am left disappointed. I saw nothing, heard nothing to stir my desire, nothing to draw me back again." If these are your thoughts and words, then some progress has been made. I would rather you forgive my retirement than begrudge it.

[10] "Do you commend leisure to me, Seneca?" you ask. "Are you lapsing into Epicurean sentiments?" It is indeed leisure I recommend to you, in which you may engage in greater and nobler pursuits than those you have abandoned. To knock at the haughty doors of the powerful, to keep record of childless old men [in hopes of inheritance], to wield great influence in the forum—such sway is both invidious and fleeting, and if you judge truly, degrading.

[11] Another may far surpass me in popularity at court, another in military renown and rank attained thereby, another in his throng of clients; but it is worthwhile to be outdone by all, if only I may outdo Fortune, whose equal I cannot be amid the crowd.

[12] Would that your spirit had chosen to pursue this path long ago! Would that we were not discussing the happy life [only] in sight of death! But even now, let us not delay[2]. For we are ready to believe experience about many things we would have thought superfluous and inimical to reason.

[13] Let us spur ourselves on, as those who have set out late are wont to do, wishing to make up for lost time with speed. This stage of life is optimal for these pursuits; the froth and frenzied passions of youth have settled. The indomitable vices of early adulthood, exhausted by their first ferocity, have not much vigor left to be extinguished.

[14] "And when," you ask, "will that which you learn at the very end of life benefit you, or for what purpose?" For this purpose: so that I may depart this life better than I entered it. Yet you should not think any age more suited to acquiring a sound mind than that which has tamed itself through many trials, through long and frequent penitence of its ways, and which comes to wholesome things with passions tempered. This is the opportune time for this

good; whoever arrives at wisdom as an old man, arrives by way of years. Farewell.

———————————

1. The Latin "causariae partes" literally means something like "parts that plead excuse," a unique phrase that suggests those parts of the mind that are weak, prone to troubles, and in need of special care or treatment.
2. The Latin "non moremur" means "let us not delay," urging immediate action. Some manuscripts have the alternate reading "non moraniur" meaning "we are not delaying," but this seems less fitting in context.

LETTER 69

VIRTUE IS THE ONLY GOOD;
ALL ELSE IS INDIFFERENT

[1] I DO NOT WISH FOR YOU TO BE CONSTANTLY CHANGING YOUR ABODE, leaping from one place to another, first because such frequent migration betrays an unsteady mind. Tranquility cannot take root unless you refrain from looking around and wandering. To steady your spirit, you must first arrest your body's flight.

[2] Secondly, remedies work best when applied continuously. Do not disrupt your peace and your forgetting of your former life. Allow your eyes to unlearn old sights, let your ears grow accustomed to more wholesome words. Whenever you venture out, you will encounter things in your very path that reawaken your cravings.

[3] Just as one who strives to cast off a love affair must avoid every reminder of the beloved body (for nothing reignites love more readily), so too, the person who wishes to renounce all desires that once inflamed his passions must turn both eyes and ears away from the things he has abandoned. The heart rebels swiftly.

[4] Wherever he turns, he will behold some immediate reward for his present occupation. No evil is without its compensation. Greed promises money; luxury, a host of varied pleasures; ambition, purple robes and applause and by this, power and all that power can achieve.

Vices lure you with repayment, but here you must live without recompense.

[5] Even in a whole lifetime, it is difficult to subdue and control vices swollen from such prolonged license—much less so if we chop up this brief time into segments. Constant vigilance and devotion scarcely bring a single endeavor to perfection.

[6] If you are willing to hear me, ponder and practice this: embracing death and, if circumstances warrant, inviting it. It matters not whether death comes to us or we go to it. Convince yourself that the words of the most unwise are false: "It is a fine thing to die one's own death." No one dies except by his own death. You might also reflect on this: no one dies except on his own day. You are not losing anything of your own time; for what you leave behind is not yours. Farewell.

LETTER 70

ON VOLUNTARY DEATH AND DEPARTING LIFE WELL

[1] After a long absence, I visited your beloved Pompeii. The sight transported me back to my youth. Whatever I did there as a young man, I felt I could still do, as if I had done it only moments ago.

[2] We have sailed swiftly through life, Lucilius, and just as on the sea, in the words of our Virgil, "The lands and cities recede," so too in the rapid course of time, we first leave childhood behind, then youth, then that middle ground between young and old, bordering on both, and finally the choicest years of old age itself. At last, the common end of humankind comes into view.

[3] In our great folly, we believe it to be a dreaded rock, but it is a harbor, to be sought in due time, never refused. One who arrives there in the first years of life should no more complain than one who swiftly completes a voyage. For as you know, some are toyed with and delayed by lazy winds, wearied by the tedium of dead calms, while others are borne with utmost speed by a steady gale.

[4] The same, I say, happens to us: some lives are brought with great haste to their necessary destination, which would come even to those who linger; others are made to endure and suffer. Life, as you are aware, is not always to be clung to. For living is not good, but

living well. Thus the wise man lives as long as he ought, not as long as he can.

[5] He will consider where he will live, with whom, in what manner, and what he will do. He reflects always on the quality of life, not the quantity. If many troubles arise that disturb his peace, he releases himself[1]. Nor does he do this only in dire necessity, but as soon as Fortune becomes suspect, he looks carefully to see if he should depart that day. It makes no difference to him whether he makes an end or accepts one, whether it comes sooner or later. He does not fear it as a great loss; no one can lose much from a mere dripping.

[6] To die sooner or later is of no relevance, but to die well or ill is of great import. And to die well is to escape the danger of living badly.

Thus I regard as most unmanly the words of that famous Rhodian who, when thrown into a cage by a tyrant and fed like some wild beast, replied to one who counseled him to starve himself, "A man may hope for anything while he has life."

[7] Even if this is true, not at every price should life be bought. Some things, though great and sure, I will not attain if the cost is a shameful admission of weakness. Should I reflect that Fortune has power over one who lives, rather than reflect that she has no power over one who knows how to die?

[8] Sometimes, however, even when certain death looms and one knows the ordained punishment, a wise person will not lend their own hand to the penalty. It would be for their own benefit to do so. It is foolish to die from fear of dying. Let the executioner come - wait for him. Why hasten to take up the task of another's cruelty? Do you envy your executioner or spare him?

[9] Socrates could have ended his life by abstaining from food, dying by starvation rather than poison. Yet he spent thirty days in prison awaiting death, not because he thought anything could change or that such a long time held many hopes, but to submit himself to the laws, to give his friends the gift of Socrates until the very end. What could be more foolish than to scorn death, yet fear the poison?

[10] Scribonia, a woman of dignity, was the aunt of Drusus Libo, a youth as foolish as he was noble, who hoped for greater things than anyone could hope for in that era, or he in any era. When he was carried from the Senate in a litter, sick and with a meager funeral procession, for all his relatives had impiously deserted him, no longer a defendant but a corpse, he began to deliberate whether to take his own life or await death. Scribonia said to him, "Why does it please you to take up someone else's troubles?" She did not persuade him; he laid hands on himself, and not without reason. For if he lives only to die three or four days later by an enemy's whim, he takes up someone else's troubles.

[11] Therefore, you cannot make a universal pronouncement about whether one should seize death or await it when an external force threatens it. For many factors can sway the decision either way. If one death involves torture while the other is simple and easy, why not choose the latter? Just as I would select a ship for a voyage and a house to live in, so I would choose the manner of death when departing from life.

[12] Moreover, just as a longer life is not always better, so a longer death is certainly worse. In nothing should we indulge the soul more than in death. Let it depart by whatever means it is drawn to, whether it seeks the sword, the noose, or some potion to fill the veins; let it proceed and break the bonds of servitude. Everyone must justify their life to others, but their death to themselves alone.

[13] The best death is the one that pleases you. It is foolish to dwell on these thoughts: "Someone will say I acted with too little courage, another that I was too rash, another that there was a more valiant way to die." Do you wish to reflect that the decision is in your hands, and reputation has no bearing on it? Focus only on this: how to steal yourself away from Fortune as swiftly as possible. Otherwise, there will arrive those who judge your act harshly.

[14] You will even find those who profess wisdom claiming that violence should not be inflicted upon one's own life, and that it is wrong for a person to become their own killer. They say one must await the end decreed by nature. Whoever says this does not see that

they are obstructing the path to freedom. Eternal law has done nothing better than giving us one way into life but many ways out.

[15] Should I wait for the cruelty of either disease or man, when I can depart through the midst of torments and shake off my adversities? This is the one reason we cannot complain about life: it holds no one back. Human affairs are in a good state, because no one is unhappy except by their own fault. Does it please you? Then live. Does it not please you? Then you may return to where you came from.

[16] To relieve a headache, you have often let blood. To diminish the body's strength, a vein is opened. There is no need for a gaping wound to cleave the heart; a lancet opens the way to that great freedom, and security is purchased at the cost of a pinprick.

So what is it that makes us lazy and inert? None of us reflect that we must someday depart from this dwelling. Just as the indulgence of a place and habit detains long-settled tenants even amidst mistreatment, so it is with us.

[17] Do you wish to be free in the face of this body? Live as one who will migrate. Propose to yourself that you must someday be deprived of this partnership; you will be stronger for the necessity of departing. But how will the thought of an end come to those who desire all things without end?

[18] Contemplation of nothing is so necessary. For other things perhaps are trained for superfluously. The mind is prepared to face poverty; yet riches have remained. We have armed ourselves for the contempt of pain; but the felicity of an intact and healthy body has never demanded from us a proof of this virtue. We have instructed ourselves to endure bravely the yearning for things lost; but fortune has preserved alive all those whom we love. The day will come which requires the practice of this one thing alone.

[19] You should not think that only great men possessed the strength to break the chains of human servitude; you should not judge that this can only be done by a Cato, who when he was unable to end his life by the sword, removed it with his bare hands. Men of the most wretched lot have with great spirit escaped to safety, and

when they were not allowed an agreeable death or to select the instruments of their death according to their own judgment, they seized whatever was available, and by their own force made weapons out of things that were not harmful by nature.

[20] Recently in a school for beast-fighters, one of the Germans, while being prepared for the morning spectacle, withdrew to relieve himself—no other secluded place was allowed him without a guard. There, he packed into his throat the whole wooden stick to which a sponge was attached for wiping the privates, and by blocking his gullet, he choked off his breath. This was heaping insult on death. Exactly so—it was filthy and disgusting; what is more foolish than to die squeamishly?

[21] What a brave fellow! Worthy of being permitted to choose his fate! How courageously he would have wielded a sword! With what spirit he would have hurled himself into the depths of the sea or over a steep cliff! Deprived of every means, he nevertheless found a way to bring about his own death and secure a weapon, so that you may know that nothing else but the will stands in the way of dying. Let this most vigorous man's act be judged however it seems fit, provided we agree on this—that the foulest death is preferable to the cleanest servitude.

[22] Since I have begun to use sordid illustrations, I will continue to do so; for each person will make greater demands upon himself, if he has seen that such acts can be despised even by the most despised of men. We think that the Catos, the Scipios, and the others whose names we are wont to hear with admiration, are beyond imitation; I shall now demonstrate that the virtue we admire in the leaders of civil wars can be found just as frequently in the arena of beast-fighters.

[23] When a man was recently being conveyed to the morning spectacle in a prison wagon, pretending to be pressed by sleep, he let his head droop so low that he inserted it into the spokes of the wheel, and he held himself in position on his seat until the revolving wheel snapped his neck. By the same vehicle in which he was being carried to his punishment, he made his escape.

[24] Nothing stands in the way of the soul that yearns to break free and depart. Nature keeps us under no guard in the open air. Those constrained by necessity can seek out a gentle exit, while those with ample means have many paths to assert their freedom. Let them choose carefully how they might best be liberated. Those lacking easy opportunities must seize the nearest one, no matter how unprecedented or novel. Ingenuity will not fail in finding a way to death for those with sufficient courage.

[25] You see how even the lowliest slaves, when goaded by pain, rouse themselves and deceive the most vigilant guards? That man is truly great who not only commands himself to die but devises the means.

I promised you more examples from the same source. [26] At the second naval spectacle, one of the barbarians took the lance he had been given to fight his adversaries and thrust it completely through his own throat. "Why, oh why," he cried, "do I not escape all this torment and mockery at once? Why do I, fully armed, await death?"

[27] This spectacle was all the more striking because men learn to die honorably rather than to kill.

What then? Will those whom long meditation and reason, the teacher of all things, have prepared for such trials not possess what even the desperate and guilty have? Reason teaches us that the approaches of fate are varied but the end is the same, and it matters not where the inevitable begins.

[28] That same reason advises us to die as we please if possible, and if not, to seize whatever means present themselves to do violence to ourselves. It is an injustice to live by robbery, but to die by robbery is most noble. Farewell.

---

1. Some later manuscripts have "if it is a pretense" instead of "if many."

LETTER 71

PHILOSOPHY EQUIPS US TO FACE ALL FORTUNES

[1] You keep consulting me about individual matters, forgetting that a vast sea divides us. Since a large part of advice depends on timing, it's inevitable that my opinion on certain issues will reach you only when the opposite course is already preferable. Advice, after all, must be adapted to circumstances - and our circumstances are not just moving, but hurtling along. Therefore, our decisions should be made on the spot; even that is too slow. Let them spring forth "under our hand," as the saying goes. But I will explain how to manage it.

[2] Whenever you wish to know what to avoid or what to pursue, look to the supreme good, the purpose of your whole life. For whatever we do ought to align with that; no one can properly arrange the details without having already settled on the main goal of their life. No artist, however well-prepared their paints, can create a likeness unless they've first determined what they wish to paint. The reason we make mistakes is because we deliberate about parts of life, but no one deliberates about the whole.

[3] The archer must know what he's aiming at in order to direct and control the arrow with his hands. Our plans go astray because they have no target to guide them. Not knowing which port you're

heading for, no wind is favorable. In a life lived at random, chance is bound to hold great sway.

[4] Some people, however, don't even realize what they don't know. Just as we often search for those standing right beside us, we tend to overlook the supreme good that lies close at hand.

Identifying the supreme good doesn't require many words or a long, roundabout argument. It can be pointed out with a finger, so to speak, not scattered across many ideas. What's the point of breaking it into tiny parts, when you can simply say: "The supreme good is that which is honorable"? And here's an even more wonderful truth: The honorable is the one and only good; everything else is false and fraudulent.

[5] Once you've convinced yourself of this and fallen passionately in love with virtue (mere affection is not enough), then whatever happens to you because of virtue will be a blessing and a joy, however it may appear to others. Being tortured will not shake your spirit if you can lie there more at peace than your torturers. Illness will find you uncomplaining to Fortune and unrelenting to the disease. In short, all apparent evils will be tamed and transformed into goods if you can rise above them.

Let this truth be clear: nothing is good except the honorable. And all hardships will rightly be called good if virtue has made them honorable.

[6] To many, we seem to promise more than the human condition allows; and not without reason. For they have regard only to the body. Let them turn their attention to the soul, and they will soon measure man by the standard of God. Rouse yourself, most excellent Lucilius, and leave behind that scholastic wordplay of the philosophers who diminish and wear down this most magnificent subject by reducing it to syllables. Those who invent such trivialities - not those who teach them and labor to make philosophy seem difficult rather than great - will make you just like themselves.

[7] Socrates, who recalled all of philosophy to rules of conduct and asserted that the highest wisdom was to distinguish between good and evil, said: "Follow these precepts if you would be happy, and

let some think you even a fool. Allow any man who so desires to insult you and work you wrong; but if only virtue dwells with you, you will suffer nothing. If you wish to be happy, if you would be a good man in earnest, let another despise you." No man can accomplish this unless he has come to regard all goods as equal, for the reason that no good exists without that which is honorable, and that which is honorable is in every case equal.

[8] What then? Is there no difference between the triumphal procession of Cato and his defeat at the polls? Or whether Cato is conquered or conquers in the battle-line of Pharsalia? Was this goodness of his, which could not be overcome even when his party met defeat, equal to the goodness by which he might have returned victorious to his native land and arranged a peace? And why should it not be equal? For it is by the same virtue that evil fortune is overcome and good fortune is ordered. Virtue, however, cannot be increased or decreased; its stature is uniform.

[9] But Gnaeus Pompeius will lose his army; the patricians, that most attractive Senatorial body and bulwark of the state, and the front-line of the Pompeian party, will be routed in a single engagement; the ruins of that great empire will be scattered all over the world, part falling in Egypt, part in Africa, part in Spain! And the poor state will not even have the privilege of being ruined once for all!

[10] Though all else be lost, Juba's familiarity with his own kingdom will avail him naught, nor will the resolute bravery of his people fighting for their king; even the men of Utica, crushed by their troubles, will waver in their allegiance; and the famous name of Scipio will forsake his ill-starred African army. For long ago destiny decided that nothing should injure Cato.

[11] "Nevertheless," people say, "he was conquered in the end." Well, count this also among Cato's "failures"; Cato will bear with an equally stout heart anything that thwarts him of his victory, as he bore that which thwarted him of his praetorship. On the day when he failed of election, he played; on the night when he intended to die, he read. He regarded in the same light both the loss of his praetorship

and the loss of his life; he had convinced himself that he ought to endure anything which might happen.

[12] Why should he [Cato] not endure a change in the republic with a brave and steady spirit? For what is exempt from the risk of change? Not the earth, not the sky, not even this whole fabric of the universe, though it be guided by the hand of God. It will not always maintain its present order, but some day in the future will drive it from its current course.

[13] All things move through fixed cycles; they are born, they grow, they are extinguished. Even these celestial bodies you see moving above us, and this seemingly solid ground on which we stand and are placed, will waste away and cease to be. There is nothing that does not have its old age. Nature sends all things to the same place at varying paces. Whatever is will one day not be, yet it will not perish but dissolve again.

[14] For us, to dissolve is to perish, for we look only at what is nearest; our sluggish mind does not see further, having surrendered itself to the body. Otherwise, it would bear the end of itself and its possessions more bravely if it hoped that, just as all things cycle through life and death, what is composed dissolves and what is dissolved composes again, turning in the eternal craft of the all-tempering God[1].

[15] And so, as Marcus Cato, having surveyed the generations, will say: "The whole human race, both that which is and that which is to be, is condemned to death. All those cities that anywhere hold sway, and that are the great glories of foreign empires, will one day be asked where they were, and will be razed by various kinds of destruction[2]; some wars will destroy, others sloth and peace turned to inertia will consume, and luxury, that destructive companion of great wealth. All these fertile fields will be hidden by a sudden flood of the sea or carried away by the collapse of the subsiding ground into an abrupt chasm[3]. Why then should I be indignant or grieve, when by a small moment I precede the fate of the world?"

[16] The great soul obeys God and endures whatever the law of the universe commands without hesitation; it is released either into a

better life to dwell more radiantly and tranquilly among divine things, or at least[4] without any inconvenience of its own it will be mingled again with nature and return to the whole.

Therefore, an honorable life is no greater good for Marcus Cato than an honorable death, since virtue does not increase. Socrates used to say that truth and virtue were the same. Just as truth does not grow, neither does virtue; it has its own measures, it is complete.

[17] Therefore, you should not be surprised that all goods are equal—both those to be chosen on purpose and those thrust upon us by circumstance. For if you were to accept this inequality, counting being bravely tortured among the lesser goods, you would also number it among the evils. You would call Socrates unfortunate in prison, Cato unfortunate as he fiercely reopened his own wounds, and Regulus the most miserable of all as he paid the penalty for keeping faith even with his enemies. Yet no one, not even the most delicate, has dared to say this. They deny that these men were happy, but they still deny they were wretched.

[18] The Old Academics admit that one may be happy even amidst such tortures, but not perfectly or completely so. This view is utterly unacceptable; if a man is not happy, he has not attained the highest good. The highest good has no grade above it, as long as virtue remains—if adversity does not diminish it, if it endures unharmed even when the body is shattered. And endure it does. For by virtue I mean a lofty and courageous spirit, aroused by whatever assails it.

[19] This spirit, often adopted by youths of noble character who are struck by the beauty of some honorable pursuit, leads them to despise all the gifts of fortune. Wisdom will surely imbue and entrust us with this spirit, convincing us that the only good is that which is honorable. This cannot be lessened or increased, any more than you can bend the ruler by which straightness is tested. Any alteration you make is a detriment to its rectitude.

[20] We will say the same, then, about virtue: it too is straight, brooking no bending. What is already rigid cannot be made more tense. Virtue judges all things, but nothing judges virtue. If virtue

itself cannot become more upright, then neither can the acts which spring from it be more or less upright in relation to each other. For they must correspond to virtue; thus, they are equal.

[21] "What then?" you ask. "Are lounging at a banquet and being tortured on the rack equal?" Does this seem astonishing to you? You may find this even more amazing: lounging at a banquet is an evil, while being tortured on the rack is good—if the former is done in a disgraceful manner and the latter in an honorable one. It is not the matter, but the virtue, which makes these things good or bad. Wherever virtue appears, all things are of the same measure and value.

[22] Now the man who judges everyone's mind by his own threatens to gouge out my eyes, because I claim that there are equal goods in those who make honorable judgments and those who honorably face great dangers. I maintain that the goods of one who triumphs are on par with one who rides unconquered in spirit before the victor's chariot. For people think that whatever they cannot do themselves is impossible; they pass judgment on virtue based on their own weakness.

[23] Why marvel if being burned, wounded, slain, or bound is sometimes not only welcome but even pleasurable? To the self-indulgent, frugality is a penalty; to the lazy, work is a punishment; the soft pity the industrious; to the idle, studying is torture. In the same way, we consider the things to which we are all too weak to be hard and intolerable, forgetting how many find it torment to be deprived of wine or roused at dawn. These things are not difficult by nature, but we are fluid and soft.

[24] Great matters must be judged with greatness of spirit; otherwise, what is really our own defect will seem to be theirs. So it is that some things which are perfectly straight, when plunged into water, give the appearance of being crooked or fractured to those looking at them. It matters not only what you see, but with what eyes you see it; our mind's vision is too clouded to perceive the truth.

[25] Give me an uncorrupted youth with a vigorous mind, and he will say that the one who bears all the burdens of adversity with a stiff neck and stands above Fortune seems to him more blessed. It is no

wonder not to be shaken in tranquil times; but marvel instead at one who rises when all others are beaten down, who stands when all others lie prostrate.

[26] What evil is there in tortures and in other things we call adversities? This, I think: that the mind caves in, bends, and collapses. None of which can happen to the wise man; he stands upright under any weight. Nothing makes him less than he is; he does not complain that anything which must be endured has befallen him. For he knows his own strength; he knows he was born to bear burdens.

[27] I do not withdraw the wise man from the category of man, nor do I deny him the sense of pain as though he were some rock that has no feelings at all. I remember that he is made up of two parts: the one irrational - this is bitten, burned, and pains; the other rational - this has unshakable opinions, is undismayed and unconquered. The Supreme Good of man lies in the latter. Before this is completely attained, the mind wavers in uncertainty; but when it is perfected, it has an immovable fixity.

[28] And so the person who has begun the journey, proceeding towards the heights as a devotee of virtue, even if he approaches the perfect good but has not yet put the final touches upon it, will still occasionally slip backwards and relax somewhat the intensity of his mental focus. For he has not yet crossed beyond into certainty; he still moves upon slippery ground. But the truly happy man who has attained perfect virtue loves himself most of all when he has most bravely endured trials, and he not only bears but embraces those things that others dread, if they are the price of some honorable duty. He much prefers to hear himself called "noble" rather than "fortunate."

[29] I come now to the point which your anticipation summons me to address, lest our virtue seem to wander beyond the bounds of nature. The wise man will both tremble and feel pain and turn pale, for all these are sensations of the body. Where then is misfortune, where is that true evil? There doubtless, if these feelings drag down the mind, if they lead it to an admission of servitude, if they cause it to regret its own self.

[30] The wise man indeed conquers fortune by his virtue, but many who profess wisdom have sometimes been terrified by the most trifling threats. Here the fault is ours, who demand the same conduct from the wise man as from the learner. I still commend to myself those principles which I praise, but have not yet convinced myself of them. Even if I had done so, I would not yet have them so ready or so well-practiced that they would rush to meet every crisis.

[31] Just as wool takes on some colors at once, but will not absorb other dyes unless it is soaked and boiled repeatedly, so with other systems of doctrine - when minds have grasped them they immediately display their quality, but this Stoic teaching, unless it has gone deep and remained long in the soul, and has not merely tinged but thoroughly permeated it, does not fulfill any of its early promises.

[32] This can be imparted quickly and in very few words: virtue is the only good, and certainly nothing is good without virtue, and virtue itself is situated in our better part, that is, the rational part. What then will this virtue be? A true and immovable judgment. For from this will come all mental impulses, and by its agency every external appearance that stirs an impulse will be clarified.

[33] It will be in agreement with this judgment to consider all things that have been touched by virtue both good and equal to each other.

Bodily goods are indeed good for the body, but they are not absolutely good. There will indeed be some value in them, but no true worth; they will differ from each other by wide intervals; some will be less, others greater.

[34] Even among those who pursue wisdom, we must acknowledge there are great differences. One has already progressed so far that he dares to lift his eyes to face Fortune, but not persistently, for they fall back, dazzled by her excessive splendor. Another has advanced to the point where he can meet her gaze—provided he has already reached the heights and is full of confidence.

[35] It is inevitable that those who are still imperfect will stumble, now making progress, now slipping back or collapsing. They will surely slip, unless they persist in pushing forward and striving. If they

slacken at all in their dedication and faithful effort, they must regress. No one finds progress in the same place he left it. Let us therefore press on and persevere.

[36] More remains than we have already accomplished, but to will progress is itself a great part of progress.

I am conscious of this truth; I both desire it and desire it with my whole mind. I see that you too are spurred on, hastening with great zeal toward all that is most beautiful. Let us make haste; only then will life truly be a blessing. Otherwise, it is merely a delay—a disgraceful one at that, mired as we are in sordid things. Let us strive to make all our time our own. But it will not be ours until we first begin to be our own masters.

[37] When will it come to pass that we despise both kinds of fortune? When, with all our passions suppressed and brought under our own control, will we be able to utter the words, "I have conquered"? Do you ask whom I have conquered? Neither Persians, nor the far reaches of Media, nor any warlike peoples that may lie beyond the Dahae. No, I have conquered greed, ambition, and the fear of death—the things that conquer the conquerors of nations. Farewell.

---

1. Haase adds "ut" here.
2. Some later manuscripts read "exitii" (destruction) instead of "exhilii" or "exilii" (exile).
3. Some later manuscripts read "repentina" (sudden) instead of "repentini".
4. Gemoll emends "si" to "sui".

LETTER 72
THE SINGLE PATH TO
LASTING HAPPINESS

[1] REGARDING YOUR QUERY, THE MATTER HAD ONCE BEEN CLEAR TO ME, for I had thoroughly learned it. But it has been some time since I last tested my recollection, and so my memory does not easily cooperate. Just as books grow sticky with disuse, so too, I feel, has my mind become; it must be unfurled and its stored contents frequently shaken out to be ready whenever occasion demands. Let us therefore postpone this matter for the present, as it requires much effort and diligence. As soon as I can hope for a longer stay in one place, I shall take it in hand.

[2] For there are some things one can write even in a carriage, while others require a couch, leisure, and seclusion. Nevertheless, let something be accomplished even during these busy days—indeed, during all of them. For new preoccupations will never fail to arise; we sow them, and so from one springs many. Then we grant ourselves a respite, saying, "When I have finished this, I shall apply myself with complete focus," and "If I sort out this troublesome affair, I shall devote myself to study."

[3] But philosophy is not to be postponed until you have leisure; all other pursuits must be neglected so that we may attend to that one

pursuit for which no amount of time is sufficient, even if life is prolonged from childhood to the uttermost limits of human existence. It makes little difference whether you abandon philosophy or merely interrupt it, for when interrupted it does not stay put. Instead, like things that spring back when stretched, it returns to its starting point, losing what it gained from continuity. We must resist preoccupations—not unravel them, but banish them entirely. No time is ill-suited for salutary study, yet many fail to study amid those very things for which study is necessary.

[4] "But some event will occur to hinder it," you say. Certainly not for one whose spirit is joyous and eager in every pursuit. For the joy of those still imperfect is fragmented, while the wise person's delight is woven into one continuous whole, broken by no cause or fortune; always and everywhere, the sage is tranquil[1]. For the sage's joy depends not on externals, nor does it await the favor of fortune or man. The sage's happiness is homegrown—it would depart from the soul if it entered from without; it is born within.

[5] At times, something external may intervene to remind the sage of mortality, but it is slight and merely grazes the surface. Some minor inconvenience, I say, may be added, but that supreme good is unshakable. What I mean is this: there are some external drawbacks, just as on a robust and solid body there may be eruptions of rashes and small ulcers, but no deep-seated malady.

[6] The difference, I say, between a man of perfect wisdom and one who is still progressing is like that between a healthy man and one recovering from a severe and prolonged illness, for whom "healthier" means only a lighter attack. The latter, unless he takes great care, is weighed down again and relapses; but the wise man cannot fall back, or indeed fall ill at all. For the body, health is only temporary—the doctor cannot guarantee it even if he restores it, and often has to be summoned again for the same patient who called him before. But the mind, once healed, is healed completely.

[7] Let me explain what I mean by a healthy mind: if it is content with itself, if it has confidence in itself, if it understands that all the

prayers of mortals, all the benefits which are given and sought, have no bearing at all upon the happy life. For a thing is incomplete if something can be added to it, and impermanent if something can be subtracted from it; but a man whose gladness will be permanent must rejoice in himself alone. All the things that the crowd gapes after, flow away this way and that. Fortune gives us nothing to have and to hold. But even these chance gifts please us when reason has tempered and blended them—it is reason that makes even external goods agreeable to us, though to the greedy their enjoyment is thankless and tormenting.

[8] Attalus used to employ the following simile: "Did you ever see a dog snapping with open jaws at bits of bread or meat that his master tosses him? Whatever he catches, he swallows whole in a flash, and always opens his jaws in the hope of something more. So it is with us—whatever Fortune has thrown to us while we wait expectantly, we gulp down without chewing, in one swift motion, and then stand alert and stretch out our hands for another helping." The wise man is not like this; he is full. Even if something comes his way, he accepts it calmly and sets it aside.

[9] His joy is immense, constant, and his own. Suppose a man has good intentions, has made progress—yet much still remains before he reaches the top; such a one wavers, now lifted to heaven, now brought down to earth. The untrained and the novice have no limit to their plunging downward—they fall into the void, the bottomless Epicurean pit.

[10] There is yet a third class, that of those who toy with wisdom —they have not indeed touched it, but are within sight of it, and have it, so to speak, within striking distance. These men are not shaken, nor do they drift back either. Though not on dry land, they are already in port.

[11] Therefore, since there are such great differences between those at the top and those at the bottom, and since even the middle group is battered by waves and faces grave danger of slipping back, we should not indulge in occupations. They must be shut out; once

they gain entrance, they will bring in others to replace them. Let us resist them at the start—it is better that they never begin than that they stop. Farewell.

---

1. "tranquillus" (tranquil) is a reading by Haase, while the manuscripts have "tranquillum" (tranquility).

LETTER 73
JUSTICE AND GRATITUDE TOWARD GOOD GOVERNANCE

[1] In my view, those who believe that the devoted followers of philosophy are stubborn, obstinate, and contemptuous of magistrates, kings, or the administrators of public affairs are quite mistaken. On the contrary, no one is more grateful to such leaders than the philosophers, and not without reason. For no one benefits more from public peace and stability than those who are able to enjoy tranquil leisure thanks to it.

[2] Therefore, those who greatly profit in their pursuit of a good life from public security must necessarily revere the provider of this benefit as a parent, certainly much more so than those restless individuals in the thick of public life, who owe much to their rulers but also charge much to their account. No act of generosity can ever fully satisfy the ever-growing desires of the latter, which only increase the more they are fulfilled. Whoever thinks about receiving has forgotten what he has already received, and ingratitude is the greatest evil born of desire.

[3] Moreover, none of those engaged in public affairs consider how many they surpass, but only by whom they are surpassed. It brings them less joy to see the many behind them than distress to see even one ahead. All ambition shares this vice: it never looks back. But

ambition is not alone in its instability; all desires are the same, for they always begin at the end.

[4] But that man of integrity and purity, who has left behind the senate, the forum, and all involvement in public affairs to withdraw to nobler pursuits, loves those who safely permit him this freedom. He alone offers them his sincere testimony and owes them a great debt, though they know it not. Just as he venerates and admires his teachers, by whose aid he escapes the paths of the crowd, so too does he revere those under whose protection he can cultivate the noble arts.

[5] "But," one might object, "the king protects others too by his might." Who denies it? But just as a merchant who has conveyed more numerous and precious goods judges that he owes more to Neptune than a mere passenger, even though both enjoyed the same calm seas, and pays his vow with greater zeal—and among the merchants themselves, the one transporting perfumes, purple dyes, and gold is more profuse in his gratitude than he who heaped up only the cheapest goods, mere ballast—in the same way, while the benefit of this peace extends to all, it reaches more deeply those who make good use of it.

[6] For there are many among these toga-clad citizens for whom peace is more laborious than war. Or do you think that those who squander their peace on drunkenness, lust, or other vices that must be shattered even by war, owe the same debt for it? Unless perhaps you consider the wise man so unjust that he judges he owes nothing man-by-man for the common goods. I owe the most to the sun and moon, and they do not rise for me alone. I am privately indebted to the god who regulates the seasons and the year, although the times are not apportioned in my honor[1].

[7] The foolish greed of mortals distinguishes possession and ownership, believing that nothing is one's own which is public. But the wise man judges nothing more his own than that in which he has fellowship with the human race. For things would not be so common if a part of them did not pertain to each individual; even what is common from the smallest portion makes one a partner.

[8] Now consider that great and true goods are not divided in such

a way that only a small amount falls to each person; they come whole to every individual. From a public handout[2], men carry away only as much as has been promised per head. A feast, a distribution of meat, and whatever else is grabbed by hand, is divided into portions. But these indivisible goods - peace and liberty - belong as much to all as to each one.

[9] Therefore, he reflects through whom he obtains the use and enjoyment of these things, through whom public necessity does not call him to arms, to keep watch, to defend the walls, and to the manifold tribute of war, and he gives thanks to his helmsman. This is what philosophy teaches above all - to incur benefits well, to repay them well;

[10] and sometimes the repayment is the acknowledgment itself. He will therefore confess that he owes much to him by whose governance and providence he obtains rich leisure, control of his own time, and tranquility undisturbed by public occupations.

> *"O Meliboeus, a god has granted us this peace -*
> *For that god shall be forever mine."*

[11] If even those leisure times owe much to their creator, whose greatest gift is this:

> *"As you see, he has allowed my cattle to roam and myself*
> *To play what I wished on my rustic reed,"*

How highly do we value this leisure which is spent among the gods, which makes gods?

[12] Yes, Lucilius, that is what I proclaim—and I summon you to heaven by a shortcut.

Sextius used to say that Jupiter has no more power than a good man. Jupiter may have more to bestow upon mankind, but between two good men, the one who is richer is not therefore better—just as, between two pilots of equal skill in steering, you would not call the one with the larger and more impressive ship superior.

[13] In what way does Jupiter surpass the good man? His goodness lasts longer; but the wise man thinks no less of himself because his virtues are confined to a shorter span. Just as, of two wise men, the one who dies older is not happier than the one whose virtue is bounded by fewer years, so too God does not surpass the wise man in happiness, even if He surpasses him in length of years.

[14] Virtue is not greater by virtue of being longer. Jupiter possesses all things, but He has surely relinquished the possession of them to others; the only use that belongs to Him is that He is the cause of the use of all things. The wise man looks upon all things in the possession of others as calmly as does Jupiter and regards himself with even greater reverence because Jupiter cannot use them but the wise man does not wish to.

[15] Let us therefore believe Sextius as he points out the most noble path and proclaims: "This is the way to the stars," this is the way through frugality, this is the way through temperance, this is the way through courage.

The gods are not fastidious or envious; they open the door to those approaching and lend a hand as they climb.

[16] Do you marvel that man goes to the gods? God comes to men —nay, He comes nearer still, He comes into men. No mind is good without God. Divine seeds are scattered throughout mortal bodies; if a good cultivator receives them, they spring up resembling their source and equal to those from which they came. If a bad cultivator receives them, like barren and marshy soil, he kills them and produces weeds instead of grain. Farewell.

---

1. Hense suggests the possibility of "tempora" (times) after "honorem" (honor).
2. Latin: congiarium, a gift or handout given by emperors to the people.

LETTER 74

THE EQUALITY OF ALL GOODS AND THE NATURE OF VIRTUE

[1] Your letter delighted me and roused me from my sluggishness. It also stirred my memory, which has grown dull and slow.

Why, my dear Lucilius, would you not consider this conviction the greatest instrument of a happy life: that the only good is that which is honorable? For whoever judges other things to be good falls under the control of fortune and becomes dependent on another's will. But one who has defined every good by the standard of honor is happy within himself.

[2] One man grieves at the loss of his children, another is anxious about the sick, another troubled by those suffering disgrace and infamy. You will see one tortured by his love for another man's wife, another by his love for his own. There will be no lack of those tormented by rejection, and some vexed by the very honors they receive.

[3] But the largest crowd of miserable people out of the whole mass of mortals is the one harassed by the anticipation of death looming on all sides. For there is nowhere it does not approach from. And so, as if traveling through hostile territory, we must look around to this side and that, turning our head at every noise—

unless this fear is cast out from our breast, we live with trembling hearts.

[4] You will encounter those driven into exile and stripped of their possessions. You will encounter those suffering the worst kind of poverty—being poor in the midst of riches. You will encounter shipwrecked people or those who have suffered things similar to shipwreck, whom either popular rage or envy (that weapon most dangerous to the best people) has struck down unawares and unsuspecting, like a sudden storm that often rises up just when we are most confident of clear skies, or like a sudden bolt of lightning, whose strike makes even those nearby tremble. For just as in the latter case whoever stood closest to the fire is left stunned as if struck himself, so in these calamities caused by some violent force, the disaster crushes one person, but the fear crushes the rest, and makes those who can suffer the same feel equal sadness.

[5] The misfortunes of others, especially when sudden, disquiet all our minds. Just as birds are frightened even by the sound of an empty sling, so we are disturbed not just by the blow but by the mere crack. No one, therefore, can be happy who has entrusted himself to this belief. For only that which is unafraid is happy; living among things held in suspicion is miserable.

[6] Whoever surrenders himself largely to happenstance creates for himself an enormous source of disturbance that he cannot untangle. The one path to safety for one proceeding through life is to despise external things and be content with honor. For he who thinks anything better than virtue, or any good besides it, opens wide his lap to catch those things fortune tosses out and anxiously awaits her missiles.

[7] Picture this scene in your mind: Fortune is staging a show and showering the gathered mortals with honors, riches, and favors. Some of these gifts are torn to pieces as the crowd snatches at them greedily; others are divided up through shaky alliances; and still others are seized, much to the detriment of those who eventually gain them. Some of these baubles fall to those who aren't even paying attention, while others are lost because they are too eagerly sought

after—in the frantic scramble to grab them, they are knocked away. Indeed, no one who succeeds in seizing some plunder, however luckily, enjoys their spoils without later regretting it.

And so, as soon as the wisest of spectators sees the cheap little gifts being brought out, he flees the theater, knowing that a high price is paid for things of little worth. No one grapples with him as he departs; no one strikes the man leaving the show. The real battle is around the prizes on stage.

[8] The same thing happens with the glittering prizes that Fortune tosses down from above. Wretched, we grow anxious and unsettled, wishing we had more hands to grasp with, looking now this way and now that[1]. The things that inflame our desires seem to come too slowly, reaching only a few while being awaited by all.

[9] We long to rush headlong for these falling gifts. If we snatch something, we rejoice, and the foolish hope of snatching more deceives some of us. We pay a steep price for worthless plunder— some great loss—or we are cheated and left empty-handed[2]. So let us withdraw from these games and give way to the greedy grabbers. Let them gaze upon those dangling goods and dangle more precariously themselves.

[10] Whoever resolves to be happy should believe that there is only one good: that which is honorable. For if he considers anything else to be good, he first speaks ill of Providence, since many misfortunes befall righteous men and since whatever she has given us is short-lived and paltry if you compare it to the lifespan of the entire universe.

[11] From this way of thinking springs our tendency to be ungrateful interpreters of divine gifts. We complain that the things granted to us are infrequent, few, uncertain, and fleeting. Hence our reluctance to live or die—we are filled with hatred of life and fear of death. All our plans are adrift, and no happiness can fulfill us. The reason is that we have not yet attained that immense and unsurpassable good, the point at which our desires must necessarily cease, because beyond the highest point there is no place to go[3].

[12] You ask why virtue needs nothing? It finds joy in the present,

not coveting what is absent. Nothing is too small for virtue that suffices.

Abandon this judgment, and you will find no constancy in piety or in loyalty. For one who desires to uphold both must endure many things commonly called evils, and must relinquish many things we indulge in as goods.

[13] Bravery perishes when it must hazard its own safety. Greatness of spirit cannot tower aloft unless it has scorned as paltry all that the masses pray for as supreme goods[4]. Gratitude and reciprocity perish if we fear toil, if we acknowledge anything more precious than loyalty, if our eyes are not fixed on the highest good.

[14] But to pass over all that—either those things called good are not truly good, or man is happier than God, since God has no enjoyment of the things prepared for us. For lust does not tempt Him, nor savory feasts, nor wealth, nor any of those enticements that allure mankind and lead him on through base pleasure. Therefore, either it is not unbelievable that God lacks goods, or the very fact that God does not have them proves they are not goods.

[15] Consider too that many things seeming to be goods are found more abundantly in animals than in humans. They eat more greedily, are not equally wearied by lust, have greater and more consistent strength. It follows that animals are far happier than man, for they live without wickedness or deceit. They enjoy pleasures more fully and readily, with no fear of shame or regret.

[16] Therefore contemplate whether something by which man is surpassed by God can be called good. Let us keep the supreme good in the soul; it fades if it passes from the best part of us to the worst and is transferred to the senses, which are more nimble in dumb animals. The height of our happiness must not be placed in the flesh. The only true goods are those bestowed by reason—sound, everlasting goods that cannot fall away, or even diminish or shrink.

[17] All other "goods" are goods in opinion only. They share the name of good with the true goods, but the essence of goodness is not in them. Let us therefore call them "conveniences," or, to use our own tongue, "advantages." But let us realize they are our chattels, not our

possessions. And let them be with us, but in such a way that we remember they are outside us. Even if they are with us, let them be counted among the slavish and lowly things for which no one should puff himself up. For what is more foolish than for someone to please himself by something he did not create?

[18] All these external goods should be additions, not attachments; so that if they are taken away, they part from us without tearing off any piece of ourselves. Let us use them, not boast of them, and use them sparingly, as if they were merely loaned to us and will soon depart. Whoever possesses such things without reason will not hold them for long, for prosperity itself, unless reined in, exerts its own pressure. If one entrusts himself to these most fleeting things, he will quickly be deserted and, even if not deserted, will suffer. Few are granted the power to lay down their happiness gently; the rest tumble down along with the things that lifted them on high, and those same things crush them.

[19] Therefore, let us apply wisdom to impose moderation or frugality on these things, since unrestrained license assuredly squanders and drives away its own riches. Nothing immoderate has ever lasted, unless that moderating reason put a check on it. The fate of many cities will show you this, whose excessive, luxurious dominions collapsed right at their peak, and whose gains made through virtue were ruined by intemperance. We must fortify ourselves against such disasters. But no wall is impregnable to fortune; let us be equipped within. If that part is secure, a person can be assailed but not captured.

[20] Do you wish to know what this equipment is? Let him be angry at nothing that happens to him, and let him know that those very things by which he seems to be injured are part of the conservation of the universe and are of those things which fulfill the course and function of the world. Let a person be pleased with whatever has pleased God; for this very reason let him marvel at himself and his possessions, because he cannot be conquered, because he holds evils themselves under him, because by reason, than which nothing is stronger, he subdues chance and pain and injustice.

[21] Love reason! This love will arm you against the hardest things. The love of their young drives wild beasts against the spears of hunters, and their wild and reckless impulse renders them fearless; sometimes the desire for glory sends youthful spirits into contempt of both sword and flame; the mere semblance and shadow of virtue impels certain people to a self-imposed death. How much more powerful than all these is reason, how much more unwavering, so much more vehemently will it pass through fears and dangers themselves!

[22] "You accomplish nothing," says the objector, "by denying that anything except the honorable is good; this fortification will not make you safe from fortune and immune to her. For you say that dutiful children, a well-governed country, and good parents are among the goods; you cannot behold their dangers and be untroubled. The siege of your country, the death of your children, the slavery of your parents—these will shake you."

[23] I shall set forth the usual responses given in our defense against these critics, and then I will add what further counterarguments I think should be made.

The situation is different with things whose loss entails the substitution of some inconvenience, as when sound health is impaired and turns to sickness, or keen eyesight is destroyed and its loss afflicts us with blindness. When the knees are hamstrung, it is not just speed that is lost, but feebleness takes its place. This danger does not apply to the examples I cited a moment ago. Why? Because if I have lost a good friend, I do not then have to endure perfidy in his stead, nor if I have buried worthy children do I have impiety sneaking in to replace them.

[24] Moreover, in those cases it is not friends or children who are destroyed, but their bodies. A good, however, is lost in only one way —by turning into an evil, which nature does not allow, since every virtue and every work of virtue remains uncorrupted. Furthermore, even if friends have perished, even if children who lived up to their father's prayers have died, there is something to take their place. Do

you ask what that is? It is that which had made them good in the first place—virtue.

[25] Virtue leaves no room vacant; it takes complete possession of the soul and removes all sense of loss. Virtue alone is sufficient, for the strength and beginnings of all goods exist in virtue itself. What does it matter if running water is cut off and flows away, as long as the source from which it flowed remains unharmed? You will not say that a man's life is more just if his children are spared than if they pass away, nor better ordered, nor more sensible, nor more honorable. Therefore, his life is not better, either. The addition of friends does not make one wiser, nor does their subtraction make one more foolish; therefore, it does not make one happier or more wretched. As long as your virtue remains intact, you will not feel the loss of anything that has departed.

[26] "What then?" you say. "Is a man not happier when surrounded by a throng of friends and children?" Why should he not be? For the highest good is neither impaired nor increased; it remains in its own measure regardless of how Fortune has conducted herself. Whether a long old age falls to a man's lot, or whether the end comes for him short of old age, the measure of the highest good is unaltered, despite the difference in years.

[27] Whether you draw a larger or smaller circle pertains to its dimensions, not its shape. Even if one remains for a long time while you instantly erase the other and merge it into the dust on which it was drawn, both shared the same form. What is right is judged neither by its size, nor its number, nor its duration; it can no more be prolonged than contracted. Compress an honorable life from a span of a hundred years into as brief a time as you wish, even a single day; it remains equally honorable.

[28] In one moment, virtue may spread itself more widely - governing kingdoms, cities, and provinces, enacting laws, nurturing friendships, apportioning duties among kin and children. In the next, it may be confined to narrow limits by poverty, exile, or bereavement. Yet it is not diminished if it withdraws from a loftier pinnacle to a private state, from a palace to a humble abode, from

open and expansive freedom to the confines of a meager house or room.

[29] Virtue remains equally great even when it has retreated and is excluded from all sides. For still it maintains its grandeur of spirit, its uprightness, its perfected wisdom, its unbending justice. Therefore it is equally blessed. For blessedness depends on one thing alone, found in the mind itself: a greatness that is firm, stable, and tranquil, which cannot be attained without knowledge of matters both divine and human.

[30] Here is what I said I would respond to next. The sage is not afflicted by the loss of children or friends. For he bears their death with the same resolute spirit with which he anticipates his own. This he fears no more than he grieves for that. Virtue, after all, rests in conformity; all its works harmonize and fit together with it. This harmony is lost if the soul, which ought to be elevated, is instead laid low by grief or longing. All trembling, worrying, or holding back in any endeavor is dishonorable. For what is honorable is untroubled, unencumbered, unafraid, ready to act.

[31] "What then?" you ask, "Will the sage not experience something like a perturbation? Won't his complexion change, his expression be agitated, his limbs grow cold? And all the other involuntary reactions driven not by the command of the mind, but by an unthinking impulse of nature?" I admit it. But his conviction will hold firm that none of those things are evil or worth disturbing a healthy mind over. All that must be done, he will do boldly and readily.

[32] For this is the hallmark of folly, to do what one does in a cowardly and stubborn way, to drive the body in one direction and tear the mind in another, to be split between the most contradictory impulses. Even in those very things by which the fool prides and admires himself, he is despised. He does not even do gladly the things he boasts of. But if some evil is feared, he is weighed down by it in anticipation, as if it had already arrived. Whatever he fears he may suffer, he already suffers in fearful expectation.

[33] Just as in the body, telltale signs precede the onset of a lingering malady—a certain listless feebleness, a weariness without

any exertion, yawning, and a shudder running through the limbs—in the same way a weak spirit is shaken long before it is overcome by afflictions. It anticipates them and falls before its time.

But what could be more foolish than to be tormented by the future, not sparing oneself anguish but rather summoning miseries and bringing them near? If you cannot dispel them, it is best to defer these troubles. Do you wish to know that no one should be tortured by the future? [34] Whoever hears that they must suffer punishments after their fiftieth year will not be perturbed unless they have leapt over the intervening time and plunged themselves into that worry destined for a later age. In the same way, it happens that minds which are willingly sick and seizing upon causes for grief are saddened by things old and long forgotten. Both the past and the future are absent; we feel neither[5]. But there is no pain except from what you feel. Farewell.

---

1. The words "now this way" are omitted in certain manuscripts.
2. The phrase "or we are cheated and left empty-handed" is based on an emendation by Buecheler; the manuscript tradition is uncertain here.
3. Reading "the highest point" based on later manuscripts; the earliest manuscripts have "the highest" or "the summit."
4. Alternative reading: "proximate goods".
5. The text is uncertain here. Some manuscripts read "we may feel" or "I may feel" instead of "we feel".

LETTER 75
AVOIDING LUXURY AND CULTIVATING MODERATION

[1] You complain that my letters to you are rather carelessly written. Now who speaks carefully unless he also desires to speak affectedly? I prefer that my letters should be just what my conversation would be if you and I were sitting in one another's company or taking a walk together—spontaneous and easy. I aim for my letters to be free from anything contrived or artificial.

[2] If it were possible, I would rather reveal my feelings to you than express them in words. Even if I were arguing a point, I should not stamp my foot, or toss my arms about, or raise my voice; but I should leave such tricks to the orator, and be content to have conveyed my feelings to you in a way that neither amplified nor disparaged them.

[3] There is one thing I would like to prove to you: that I really do feel the sentiments I utter, and that I not only feel them, but am devoted to them. When men kiss their mistress and when they kiss their children, the very way they embrace is different. From even such a holy and restrained embrace as the latter, it is readily apparent that there is affection behind it. I do not wish my letters to you on matters of such importance to be dry and sterile. For although philosophy

does not renounce clever writing, nevertheless we should not devote too much effort to mere words.

[4] Let this be the kernel of my idea: let us say what we feel, and feel what we say; let our speech harmonize with our life. That man has fulfilled his promise who remains the same whether you see him or hear him.

[5] We shall see what sort of man he is and how great a man he is; for he should be one and the same. Our words should aim not to please, but to help. Still, if eloquence comes readily to hand, if it flows either spontaneously or with little effort, let it be ours to follow up the noblest of subjects with the fairest of language. Let the language be such that the thought stands out, rather than the style. Other arts pertain wholly to cleverness and wit; but the one we now discuss deals with the soul.

[6] A sick man does not call for an eloquent physician; but if it happens that the physician who can cure him likewise discourses elegantly about his treatment, the patient will take it in good part. However, the patient will not congratulate himself on having discovered a physician who is eloquent to boot. For the case is no different from that of a skilled pilot who is also handsome.

[7] Why do you stroke my ears? Why do you entertain me? There is other business at hand; I am to be cauterized, operated on, or put on a diet. That is what you have been called in for.

You are required to treat a disease that is chronic and serious, one that affects the general public. You have as serious a business on your hands as a physician during a plague. Are you concerned about words? Rejoice this instant if you can cope with things. When will you learn all that there is to learn? When will you impress upon yourself what you have learned, so that it cannot slip away? When will you put it all to the test? For it is not sufficient merely to commit these things to memory, like other matters; they must be practically tested. He is not happy who only knows them—he must do them. "What," you say, "are there no degrees of happiness below your 'happy' man?"

[8] Are there no degrees below wisdom? Is the descent from there sheer? No, I think not. For the one making progress, though still

numbered among the foolish, is nevertheless separated from them by a wide interval. Even among those progressing, there are great distinctions. They are divided, as some see it, into three classes: the first are those who do not yet possess wisdom but have already taken their stand in its vicinity.

[9] Yet even what is near is still outside[1]. You ask who these are? Those who have already put aside all passions and vices, who have learned what must be embraced, but their confidence is still untested. They do not yet have their good in use, but they can no longer slip back into the faults they have fled. They are already at a point from which there is no backward slide, but this is not yet clear to them about themselves—as I remember writing in a certain letter, "they do not know that they know." They have already attained the enjoyment of their good, but not yet confidence in it.

[10] Some encompass this class of progressors I have spoken of in such a way as to say that they have already escaped the diseases of the mind but not yet the passions, and still stand on slippery ground, because no one is beyond the danger of wickedness unless he has shaken it off entirely. But no one has shaken it off except the one who has taken on wisdom in its place.

[11] I have often discussed the difference between diseases of the mind and passions. I will remind you now as well: diseases are inveterate and hardened vices, like greed and ambition; these have entwined the mind too tightly[2] and have begun to be its perpetual evils. To define it briefly, a disease is a persistent perverse judgment that deems very desirable what is only slightly so. Or if you prefer, let us define it this way: to pursue too eagerly things that should be pursued slightly or not at all, or to value highly things that should be valued little or not at all.

[12] Passions are reprehensible, sudden, and agitated movements of the mind which, when frequent and neglected, have created a disease, just as a single flow of rheum, not yet a habit, produces a cough, but chronic and inveterate rheum leads to consumption. And so those who have progressed the most are free from diseases but still feel passions—they are next to the perfected.

[13] The second class is of those who have laid aside both the greatest evils of the mind and their passions, but not so completely as to have secure possession of their state. For they can relapse into the same faults.

[14] The third category of people, while escaping many grave vices, is not immune to all faults. They have fled from avarice, yet still feel the pangs of anger. No longer enticed by lust, they remain susceptible to ambition. They may have conquered desire, but fear still holds sway. Even amidst this fear, they stand firm against certain threats while yielding to others. They scorn death, yet recoil from pain.

[15] Let us reflect on this point. We should count ourselves fortunate to be counted among their number. Through a grand blessing of nature and diligent, unceasing devotion to study, one may attain the second rank. But even this third hue is not to be despised. Consider the abundance of evil you see around you, how no sin lacks for precedent, how wickedness advances day by day, how much is transgressed in public and private. You will understand it is enough of an accomplishment if we are not counted among the worst.

[16] "But I," you protest, "hope that I can ascend to a higher order." Would that I could promise this for us, rather than merely wish it! We are preoccupied, striving for virtue while beset by vices on all sides. It pains me to admit: we attend to virtuous pursuits only in our spare moments. Yet what a magnificent reward awaits us if we can break free from our preoccupations and tenacious afflictions! We will be driven neither by desire nor by fear.

[17] Unperturbed by terror, uncorrupted by pleasures, we will dread neither death nor the gods. We will recognize that death is no evil, and that the gods are not malevolent forces. That which causes harm is as feeble as that which is harmed; the greatest powers are free from the capacity to injure.

[18] If we can but escape from this mire and ascend to those lofty, exalted heights, perfect serenity and freedom await us, our misconceptions banished at last. And what does this freedom entail? Fearing neither mortals nor gods, desiring neither the base nor the excessive,

wielding ultimate power over oneself. To be one's own master - an inestimable good! Farewell.

---

1. Some later manuscripts read "extra" (outside) instead of "ex ora" (from the edge).
2. Rossbach's conjecture "nimio" (too much), other manuscripts read "nimia" or "ninia."

    Later manuscripts read "artius" (more tightly) instead of "actus."

LETTER 76

ON OLD AGE AND THE APPROACH OF DEATH

[1] You threaten me with enmity if I fail to inform you of any of my daily activities. Behold how simply I live with you: I shall entrust you with this matter as well. I am attending the lectures of a philosopher; indeed, it has been five days now that I have been going to his school and listening to him discourse from the eighth hour onward. "At your ripe age?" you say. But why not at my ripe age? What, after all, is more foolish than refusing to learn simply because one has not been learning for a long time?

[2] "What then?" you say, "Shall I do the same as the gilded youth and the new recruits?" I am content if this is the only thing that discredits my old age. This school welcomes men of all ages. "Are we to grow old only so that we may follow the young?" I will go to the theater as an old man, and be carried to the circus, and no pair of gladiators shall fight without me. Am I then to blush to go to a philosopher?

[3] One should learn as long as one is ignorant—if we may trust the proverb, as long as one lives. And no other occupation is more suited to the old than that of learning; one should learn how to live as long as one lives. Yet I do also teach something there. You ask what I teach? That even an old man should keep learning.

[4] I am ashamed of mankind, though, every time I enter the lecture hall. On my way to the home of Metronax[1] I must pass, as you know, right by the Neapolitan theater. It is packed, and the crowd is judging with great zeal the merits of the flute-player; even the Greek trumpeter and the herald draw a crowd. But in that other place, where the question discussed is what makes a good man, and the lesson taught is how to be a good man—very few attend, and most of these think the others are engaged in no good business; they are called idle triflers. Let such mockery fall to my lot; I must listen calmly to the railings of the ignorant, and go bravely onward toward excellence, scorning the scorn itself.

[5] Onward, Lucilius, and make haste, lest the same fate befall you as befell me—that you reach old age still needing to learn. Nay, hurry all the more because you have undertaken a task that you will barely have time to learn thoroughly as an old man. "How much progress shall I make?" you ask.

[6] As much as you try to make. Why wait? Wisdom does not fall to one's lot by chance. Money will come of its own accord, honors will perhaps be offered to you, influence and authority may be thrust upon you; but virtue will not fall into your lap. Neither is she to be gained by light effort or small toil; but the reward is great to strive for all virtues at once. For the only true good is that which is honorable; in all those other things that meet with popular approval, you will find no truth or certainty.

[7] But why is there only one good, which is moral rectitude? I will explain, since you judge that I did not fully develop this point in my previous letter and think the matter was more praised by me than proven. I will condense what has been said into a brief argument.

[8] All things are defined by their own particular good. A vine is valued for its fruitfulness and the flavor of its wine, a stag for its speed. In judging the strength of beasts of burden, you ask about their ability to carry a load, as that is their sole use. In a hunting dog, the primary qualities are its keen scent in tracking game, its swiftness in pursuit, and its boldness in seizing and attacking its quarry. The

best attribute for any creature should be that for which it is born and by which it is judged.

[9] What is best in humans? Reason. By this we surpass the animals and follow the gods. Perfect reason, therefore, is the characteristic good of humans; all else we share with animals and plants. You may say: "But humans have strength." So do lions. "Humans have beauty." So do peacocks. "Humans have speed." So do horses. I do not claim that humans are surpassed in all of these qualities. I am not asking what humans have that is greatest in itself, but what is uniquely theirs. The human body? Trees also have form. The impulse for voluntary motion? Beasts and worms also move of their own volition. Voice? But how much louder is the bark of a dog, shriller the cry of an eagle, deeper the bellow of a bull, sweeter and more versatile the song of the nightingale!

[10] What is unique to humans? Reason. When right and perfected, it alone fulfills human happiness[2]. Therefore, if every being is praiseworthy when it has perfected its own good and attained the end intended by its nature, and if the good peculiar to humans is reason, then a human has reached the end intended by nature and is praiseworthy if reason has been perfected in him. This perfected reason is called virtue and is the same as moral rectitude.

[11] Virtue, therefore, is the one and only good in humans because it is the only thing that belongs uniquely to humans. Now we are not seeking to know what the good is in general, but what is the good of humans in particular. If humans have no other attribute that is uniquely theirs except reason, then this will be their sole good, but it must be deemed equal in value to all the rest combined. If someone is wicked, they will be condemned, I think; if good, they will be approved. Therefore, this is the one thing in humans that determines whether they are approved or condemned.

[12] You do not doubt whether this is good, but you question whether it is the only good. If someone possesses all other assets such as health, wealth, many ancestral masks, and a crowded atrium, but is admittedly wicked, you will disapprove of them. Likewise, if someone lacks all the advantages I have just mentioned—is poor, without a

throng of clients, without noble lineage or a long ancestral line—but is admittedly good, you will approve of them. Therefore, this is the one and only good in humans: whoever has it, even if lacking in all else, is praiseworthy, and whoever does not have it, though abounding in everything else, is condemned and rejected.

[13] The same condition applies to things as it does to men. A ship is not deemed good because it is painted with precious colors, has a silver or gold prow, features elaborately carved ivory, or is loaded with royal treasures and riches. Rather, a good ship is stable and sturdy, tightly constructed to keep out water, robust enough to withstand the onslaught of the sea, responsive to the helm, swift, and untroubled by the wind.

[14] You would call a sword good, not if it has a gilded belt or a jewel-encrusted sheath, but if it has a keen edge for cutting and a point strong enough to pierce any armor. With a ruler, we ask not how attractive it is, but how straight. Each thing is praised according to the standards appropriate to it and its own special qualities.

[15] Therefore, in a person too, it does not matter how much land he plows, how much interest he collects, how many people greet him, how expensive a couch he reclines on, or how translucent a cup he drinks from. What matters is how good he is. And he is good if his reason is well-developed, straight, and aligned with the intentions of his own nature.

[16] This is called virtue—the one and only good of humankind. For since reason alone perfects a person, only perfect reason makes him happy; and this alone is the good by which he is rendered happy. We say that other things are also good when they spring from virtue and are infused with it—that is, all of virtue's works. But virtue itself is the only good because there is no good without it.

[17] If every good resides in the soul, then whatever strengthens, uplifts, and enlarges the soul is good. Virtue makes the soul stronger, loftier, and greater. Other things that provoke our desires also depress the soul and weaken it, and when they seem to elevate it, they actually inflate it with much empty vanity and lead it astray. Therefore, the only good is that which will make the soul better.

[18] All of life's actions are moderated with regard for what is honorable and dishonorable. The rationale for what we should and should not do is derived from these considerations. Let me explain what this means: A good man will do what he thinks is honorable, even if it requires hard work, causes harm, or involves danger. By contrast, he will not do what is dishonorable, even if it brings money, pleasure, or power[3]. He will be deterred from the honorable by nothing, and tempted to the dishonorable by nothing.

[19] Therefore, if a person is resolved to always pursue what is honorable and shun what is base, considering these two factors in every action of life - recognizing no good except what is honorable, no evil except what is disgraceful - if virtue alone is unperverted and holds steadfast to its course, then virtue is the sole good, which cannot be corrupted and cease to be good. It escapes the danger of change; folly may creep toward wisdom, but wisdom never slips back into folly.

[20] As I mentioned before, if you recall, the things coveted and feared by the masses have often been trampled underfoot by the impulsive charge of the unthinking. There have been those who thrust their hands into flames, whose laughter no torturer could still, who shed no tear at the funeral of their children, who met death without trembling. For love, anger, and desire have demanded facing dangers. What brief bursts of a stimulated spirit can accomplish, how much more so can virtue achieve, which relies not on impulse or suddenness, but on steady strength that endures perpetually?

[21] It follows, then, that things often scorned by the rash but always by the wise are neither good nor evil. Thus, virtue itself is the only good, which strides proudly between favorable and unfavorable fortune, greatly despising both.

[22] If you accept the view that anything besides moral uprightness is good, every virtue will be undermined. For no virtue can be maintained if it looks beyond its own sphere. If this is so, it opposes reason, the source of the virtues, and truth, which cannot exist without reason. But any view that opposes truth is false.

[23] You must necessarily concede that the good man possesses

the highest reverence toward the gods. So whatever befalls him, he will endure with equanimity, knowing it has happened by divine law, the force that drives the universe. If this is the case, his only good will be that which is honorable - for this consists of obeying the gods, not burning with anger at sudden events or bemoaning one's lot, but patiently accepting fate and carrying out its commands.

[24] If anything other than moral rectitude is good, we will be pursued by a greed for life and for the things that equip us for life - an intolerable, limitless, unsettled condition. Therefore, the honorable is the only good, and it is that which has a limit.

[25] We have said that the life of humans would be happier than that of the gods, if those things which the gods cannot use, such as money and honors, are truly good. Consider this also: if souls remain after being released from bodies, a happier state awaits them than they had while dwelling in the body. However, if those things that we use through the body are good, it will be worse for souls when released, which is contrary to belief—that souls enclosed and besieged should be happier than those free and in the universe.

[26] I had also said that if those things which befall both humans and dumb animals are good, then dumb animals too would live a blessed life—which is impossible. All things must be endured for the sake of what is honorable; this would not be so if there were any other good besides the honorable.

Although I had pursued these arguments more broadly in a previous letter, I have compressed and briefly run through them here.

[27] But you will never hold such an opinion to be true, unless you raise up your soul and ask yourself: if circumstances should require you to die for your country and to ransom the welfare of all citizens with your own, would you extend your neck not only patiently but even gladly? If you would do this, there is no other good. For you abandon all else in order to have this good. See the great power of honor: you will die for the republic, and do so immediately, knowing it must be done.

[28] Sometimes, from a most beautiful deed, great joy is derived even in a short and fleeting time; and although the doer, once dead

and removed from human affairs, gains no fruit from the accomplished work, still the very contemplation of the future deed brings delight. The brave and just man, when he has weighed the price of his death—the liberty of his country, the welfare of all for whom he pays out his soul—is in the highest pleasure and rejoices in his own peril.

[29] But even he from whom this joy is snatched away—the joy that pondering a great and final work provides—will without hesitation leap to his death, content to act rightly and dutifully. Even now, confront him with the many things that would dissuade him; say, "Your deed will quickly be followed by oblivion and the scant gratitude of the citizens." He will reply, "All those things are outside my work. I am the one who scorns them. I know this deed to be honorable; therefore, wherever it leads and calls me, I go."

[30] This, then, is the one true good – not only can a perfect soul attain it, but so too can one of noble character and natural ability. All else is trivial and fleeting, leaving those who possess it anxiously clutching their treasures. Even when amassed in abundance by fortune's favor, these things weigh heavily on their owners, forever burdening and sometimes crushing them. None of those you see arrayed in royal purple are truly happy – no more than actors who don a scepter and robe on stage. While the audience watches they strut about, lofty and tragic, but the moment they exit they remove their costumes and return to their true stature.

[31] None of those placed on a higher plane by wealth and honors are truly great. Why, then, do they appear so? You are measuring them along with their pedestals. A dwarf is not tall, even if he stands atop a mountain; a colossus retains its grandeur even placed in a well.

[32] This is the error we labor under, the way our perceptions are distorted – we assess a person not by what he is, but by the adornments draped upon him. But if you wish to appraise a man accurately and understand his true nature, view him unadorned. Let him remove his inheritance, his titles, and all the other trappings of fortune; let him even shed his very body. Examine his soul – its

quality and magnitude, and whether its greatness is its own or borrowed.

[33] If he can gaze with steady eyes at flashing swords, certain it makes no difference whether his life departs through mouth or throat, call him happy. If, when faced with bodily tortures – whether by chance or a tyrant's whim – and bonds, and exile, and all the imagined horrors that haunt the mind, he can hear it calmly and say:

> *"No form of toil*
> *Comes new or unexpected to me, maiden.*
> *Within my mind I have already faced it all."*

You spring this on me today, but I have always warned myself and steeled my human spirit for human trials.

[34] A blow foreseen falls more softly. But to fools who trust in fortune, every turn of events appears novel and unforeseen. Much of misfortune's power over the uneducated comes from its suddenness. Know this – hardships once thought unbearable are endured more stoically once made familiar.

[35] Thus the sage accustoms himself to future misfortunes. What others make light through long suffering, he lightens through long reflection. At times we hear the inexperienced say, "I didn't realize this was in store for me." The sage knows all things are in store for him. Whatever has happened, he says, "I knew it." Farewell.

---

1. A philosopher.
2. Some scholars suspect the phrase "quid in homine implevit".
3. Some manuscripts read "even without money" instead of simply "even if" in the phrase "even if it is laborious"

LETTER 77

THE VANITY OF RICHES AND
FALSE HAPPINESS

[1] The Alexandrian ships suddenly appeared to us today, the ones customarily sent ahead to announce the impending arrival of the following fleet; they call them "mail boats." The sight of them is welcome to [the residents of] Campania; the entire crowd gathers on the piers of Puteoli and, simply from the type of sails, recognizes the Alexandrian ships even in the midst of a great throng of vessels. For they alone are permitted to extend the topsail, which all ships use on the open sea.

[2] Indeed, nothing aids a ship's progress as much as the topmost part of the sail; that is the main source of propulsion. And so, whenever the wind has freshened and is greater than is advantageous, the yard-arm is lowered; a blast from lower down has less force. When they have entered between Capreae and the promontory from which "Pallas gazes forth from her turbulent peak upon the swelling sea," the other ships are ordered to be content with their regular sail; the topsail is the distinguishing mark of the Alexandrian fleet.

[3] Amid all this bustle and hurry to the shore, I felt great pleasure from my own indolence, because, although about to receive letters from my own folk, I was in no rush to know the state of my affairs there, what news they brought; now at length nothing is either lost or

gained by me. This attitude would be appropriate even were I not an old man - but at my age, how much more so! However little I might possess, still I would have more provisions for the journey than road left to travel, especially since I have embarked upon a road which it is not necessary to see through to the end.

[4] A journey is incomplete if you halt midway or short of your intended destination; life is not incomplete if it is honorable. Wherever you leave off, if you leave off well, it is a whole. But often one must leave off bravely, and not for the weightiest reasons; for those reasons which hold us back are not weighty either.

[5] Tullius Marcellinus, whom you knew very well, a quiet young man who became old before his time, fell ill with a chronic and troublesome malady which demanded much of him, though it was not incurable. He began to ponder death. He called together several friends. Each one, either because he was timid, urged upon Marcellinus the course he himself would have adopted, or else played the flatterer and sycophant, offering the advice he suspected the deliberating man would find more agreeable. Our Stoic friend, a rare man who praised Marcellinus in the terms he deserved, a man bold and steadfast, seems to me to have given the best counsel.

[6] For this is how he began: "Do not torture yourself, my dear Marcellinus, as if you are deliberating over some great matter. Living is not a great matter; all your slaves live, as do all animals. What is great is to die honorably, prudently, bravely. Consider how long you have been doing the same things: food, sleep, lust—this is the circle in which we run. Not only a prudent man or a brave or miserable man, but even a fastidious man may wish to die."

[7] He did not need someone to persuade him, but to assist him; his slaves were refusing to obey. First, he removed their fear and pointed out that the household would be in danger only when it was uncertain whether the master's death had been voluntary; otherwise, it was setting just as bad an example to kill a master as it was to prevent his suicide.

[8] Next, he reminded Marcellinus himself that it was not inhumane, just as the remains of a dinner are distributed to the attendants

after the meal is finished, to hand over something to those who had been the servants of his entire life now that life was finished. Marcellinus was an agreeable and generous man, even when it came to his own property. And so he distributed little sums to his tearful slaves and even consoled them unprompted.

[9] He had no need of a sword or bloodshed; he fasted for three days and ordered a tent to be set up in his very bedroom. Then a bathtub was brought in, in which he lay for a long time, with hot water poured over him now and then. Gradually he grew faint, as he said, not without a certain pleasure, the sort which a gentle dissolution is accustomed to bring—not unfamiliar to us, whom at times our spirit has left.

[10] I have lapsed into a little story that is not displeasing to you. For you will learn that the end of your friend was not difficult or miserable. For although he took his own life, still he passed most gently and slipped out of life. But not even this little story will have been useless. For necessity often demands such examples. Often we must die and are unwilling; we die and are unwilling.

[11] No one is so ignorant as not to know that we must die some day; nevertheless, when the time comes closer, he turns away, trembles, laments. Would not everybody think him the greatest of fools who wept because he was not alive a thousand years ago? Equally foolish is he who weeps because he will not be alive a thousand years from now. These two are the same; you will not be, nor were you. Both times are foreign to you.

[12] You have been cast into this tiny point of time; however much you extend it, how far will you extend it? Why weep? Why pray? You waste your efforts.

> *Cease to hope that the decrees of the gods can be changed by*
> *prayer.*

They are fixed and determined, and they sweep all things along in their great and everlasting compulsion. You will go where all else goes. What is new to you? You were born to this law. This befell your father, your mother, your ancestors, all who came before you; and it will befall all after you. An unconquerable and unchangeable series has bound and draws all things together.

[13] Imagine the multitude of the dying who will follow you! Picture the throng who will accompany you! You would be braver, I think, if many thousands were to die along with you; and yet, at this very moment when you hesitate to die, many thousands of men and animals are breathing their last, in various ways. But did you not suppose that you would someday arrive at the point toward which you have always been heading? No journey is without its end.

[14] Do you think I will now cite examples of great men? No, I will cite boys. The story is told of a Spartan lad, captured while still too young to bear arms, who cried out in his native Doric tongue, "I will not be a slave!" and made good on his word. As soon as he was ordered to perform a degrading and servile task—to fetch a chamber pot—he dashed his head against a wall and shattered it.

[15] Freedom is so near at hand, and yet someone remains a slave? Would you not rather have your son die like this than grow old in idleness? What reason is there, then, for you to be disconcerted if even a child can muster a courageous death? Suppose you refuse to follow; you will be led. Take charge of what is not yours to control. Will you not take on a boy's spirit and say, "I will not serve"? Unhappy man, you are a slave to men, a slave to your affairs, a slave to life. For life, if the virtue to die is lacking, is slavery.

[16] What reason do you have to wait? You have exhausted the very pleasures that delay you and hold you back. No pleasure is new to you, none not already grown odious through satiety. You know the taste of wine, of honey-wine. What difference is it to you whether a hundred or a thousand bottles pass through your bladder? You are nothing but a filter[1]. You are expertly acquainted with the flavor of oysters and of mullet. Your self-indulgence has left nothing untasted for the years to come. And yet these are the things from which you are torn away unwillingly.

[17] What else is there that you would be pained to have torn from you? Friends? For who can be a friend to you[2]? Your country? Do you

consider it so precious that you would put off dinner for it? The sun? If you could, you would extinguish it. What have you ever done that was worthy of the light? Admit that it is not longing for the Senate chamber, the Forum, or the world of nature herself that makes you tardy to die; it is unwillingly that you leave the meat-market, in which you have left nothing behind.

[18] You fear death, yet how blithely you disregard it amid your mushroom-feasts! You wish to live—for you know how to live, yes? You fear to die. But tell me, is this life of yours not itself a death? When Gaius Caesar (as some manuscripts name him; others have simply "Caesar") was passing along the Latin Way, a man from a group of prisoners, his aged beard hanging down upon his breast, called out to him, begging for death. "For surely," said Caesar, "you are now alive?" This is the reply we must make to those who view death as their deliverer: You fear to die—but are you now truly alive?

[19] "But I," he objects, "I wish to live, for I do many worthy things. Unwillingly do I relinquish life's duties, which I discharge with loyalty and zeal." What's that you say? Are you unaware that one of life's duties is to die? You are forsaking no duty, for there is no fixed number that you are bound to fulfill.

[20] No life is not short. For if you consider the nature of things, even the life of a Nestor or an Sattia—who ordered it inscribed on her tomb that she had lived to ninety-nine—is brief. You see some who glory in their long old age. But who could have endured it if they had reached their hundredth year? A life, like a story, is judged not by its length, but by the quality of its contents. It matters not at what point you end. End where you will, only make sure the conclusion is a good one. Farewell.

---

1. The Latin text is incomplete here. "es" ("you are") was added by later manuscripts to complete the thought.
2. The phrase "amicos? quis enim tibi potest" ("Friends? For who can [be a friend] to you?") was added by scholars to complete the thought, as the original text seems to be missing some words.

LETTER 78

REMEDIES AND CONSOLATIONS FOR SICKNESS AND PAIN

[1] IT TROUBLES ME THAT YOU ARE AFFLICTED WITH FREQUENT COLDS and low-grade fevers, which tend to follow prolonged colds that have become chronic, because I myself have experienced this kind of ill health. In the beginning, I disregarded it, for my youth could still withstand such assaults and hold out against disease with defiance. But eventually I succumbed, and it reached the point that I myself wasted away, reduced to utter emaciation.

[2] Often I was tempted to take my own life, but the thought of my indulgent father's old age held me back. For I considered not how bravely I might die, but how little braveness he would have to bear my loss. And so I commanded myself to live on, for at times, living too requires an act of bravery.

[3] I will tell you what consoled me then, but first let me say this: the very things that brought me peace of mind had the power of medicine[1]. Honorable consolations turn into remedies, and whatever lifts the spirit benefits the body as well. My studies were my salvation, and I credit philosophy for my recovery and convalescence. I owe my life to philosophy, and to her I owe no less.

[4] My friends greatly contributed to my good health, for their encouragements, vigils, and conversations raised my spirits. Nothing,

dear Lucilius, best of men, restores and aids the sick so much as the affection of friends; nothing so steals away the expectation and dread of death. I did not feel I would die if I left them behind[2]. Indeed, I thought I would live, not with them, but through them. It seemed I would not be breathing my last, but passing it on[3]. This gave me the will to help myself and endure any torment, for it is a wretched thing indeed to have abandoned the intention to live without retaining the resolve to die.

[5] Therefore, apply yourself to these remedies. Your doctor will advise how much to walk and exercise, as an idle convalescence tends toward indolence. He will tell you to read aloud and exercise your breath, whose passages and repository are strained; to sail and shake up your organs with gentle rocking; what foods to eat, when to drink wine for strength, when to refrain lest it provoke and aggravate your cough. But I instruct you to do something that is the remedy not only for this illness but for your whole life: despise death. Nothing is grim once we have escaped the fear of it.

[6] Three things are burdensome in any illness: fear of death, bodily pain, and the interruption of pleasures. Enough has been said about death, but I will say this one thing - that it is a fear not of illness but of nature. Many have had death postponed by illness and found it to be their salvation to seem to be dying. You will die, not because you are sick, but because you are alive. This fate awaits you even when you have recovered; when you get well, you escape not death but only ill health.

[7] Let us now return to that particular affliction of ours: disease brings great torments, but these are made tolerable by their intermittency. For the strain of the severest pain finds its end. No one can suffer intense pain for long; our nature, which holds us most dear, has so arranged it that pain is either tolerable or brief.

[8] The greatest pains are situated in the body's thinnest parts; the nerves, joints and all else that is delicate rages most fiercely when defects seize upon constricted spaces. Yet these parts swiftly grow numb and lose the sensation of pain through the very pain itself, whether because the breath, barred from its natural course and

turned for the worse, loses that potency by which it thrives and alerts us, or because the corrupted humors, having nowhere to flow, crush themselves and eject sensation from the parts they have overfilled.

[9] Thus gout, both in the feet and hands, and all pains of the vertebrae and sinews[4], subside when they have numbed the parts they were torturing[5]. In all of these, the initial gnawing causes distress; their force is extinguished by endurance, and the end of pain is to become insensible. Pain in the teeth, eyes, and ears is sharpest for this very reason, because it originates in constricted parts of the body, no less, I assure you, than in the head itself; yet if it becomes too intense, it turns into delirium and stupor.

[10] This, then, is the solace for overwhelming pain: you must cease to feel it if you feel it too much. The trouble is that the inexperienced, when in bodily distress, are loath to content themselves with their minds. Their association has been too much with the body. Therefore, the great and wise man detaches the mind from the body, and consorts much with that better, divine part, attending only as needed to this querulous and fragile portion.

[11] "But," one objects, "it is irksome to do without our accustomed pleasures, to fast, to feel thirst and hunger." These things are hard at first abstention, but then desire abates as the very organs through which we desire grow weary and deficient[6]. Then the stomach becomes peevish, then that for which there was such avidity for food becomes an object of loathing[7]. Desires themselves expire, and surely it is not painful to lack that which you have ceased to crave.

[12] Add, too, that no pain is unremitting—it is certainly intermittent or at least diminished. Add that you can guard against its onset and resist its approach with remedies, for every pain, especially one that is habitual, sends forth advance warnings. Surely the endurance of illness is tolerable if you disdain that with which it threatens at the last.

[13] Do not aggravate your own misfortunes, burdening yourself with grievances. Pain is slight if opinion has not exaggerated it; conversely, if you begin to encourage yourself, saying, "It is nothing - a trifling matter at most; keep a stout heart and it will soon cease," then

in thinking it slight, you will make it slight. Everything depends on opinion; ambition, luxury, greed, hark back to opinion. It is according to opinion that we suffer. Each one is as wretched as he has convinced himself that he is.

[14] I think we should cast away all complaints about past sufferings and such words as: "No one was ever worse off than I. What sufferings, what evils have I endured! No one thought I would recover. How often my family bewailed me, and the doctors gave me over! Those placed upon the rack are not torn asunder more cruelly[8]." Even if all this is true, it is over and done. What benefit is there in reviewing past sufferings and in being unhappy, just because once you were unhappy? Besides, every one adds much to his own ills, and tells lies to himself. And that which was bitter to bear is pleasant to have borne; it is natural to rejoice at the ending of one's ills.

Two elements must therefore be rooted out once for all - the fear of future suffering, and the recollection of past suffering; since the latter no longer concerns me, and the former concerns me not yet.

[15] When set in the very midst of troubles one should say:

> Perchance some day the memory of this sorrow will even
>   bring delight.

Let such a one fight against them with his mind; if he conquers them by giving in, he will be conquered; but if he strives against his sufferings, he will conquer. As it is, people are seeking out excuses for their ills - what they suffer by too readily submitting to, they could overcome by continued resistance.

[16] Consider the athletes who endure blows to the face and the body. They bear all the torture for the hope of glory, not merely because they are fighting but in order to fight. The training itself is a torture. So let us also win the way to victory in all our struggles, - for the reward is not a garland or a palm or a trumpeter who calls for silence at the proclamation of our names, but rather virtue, steadfast-

ness of soul, and a peace won for all time, if fortune has once been utterly vanquished in any combat.

[17] "I am in great pain," you say. Well then? If you bear it like a woman, do you not feel it all the same? Just as an enemy is more dangerous to those who flee, so every chance mishap presses harder upon those who give way and turn their backs. "But it is a heavy burden," you protest. What? Are we only strong so that we may bear light loads? Would you rather have your illness be long or short and severe? If it is long, it allows for intervals of respite, grants time for recovery, and gives much time of necessity as it arises and subsides. A brief and rapid illness will do one of two things: either it will quench or be quenched. What does it matter then whether it no longer exists or I no longer exist? In either case, there is an end to the pain.

[18] This too will help: turn your mind to other thoughts and depart from the pain. Ponder what you have done with honor and courage; reflect upon the noble roles you have played. Let your memory dwell upon those things you have most admired. Then, call to mind all the bravest and most victoriously pain-defiant individuals: the one who persevered in reading a book while having his varicose veins cut out; the one who did not cease laughing while the enraged torturers tried out every instrument of their cruelty upon him. Shall pain not be conquered by reason when it has been vanquished by laughter?

[19] You may now mention anything you wish - catarrhs, the violence of chronic coughing that brings up parts of our entrails, fever that scorches our very vitals, thirst, limbs so wrenched that the joints protrude in different directions. Yet worse than these are the flames, the rack, the red-hot plates, and the instrument that reopens wounds while they are still swollen and drives their imprint even deeper. In the midst of such tortures, however, someone has not groaned. "That's not enough," you say? He has not begged for mercy. "Still not enough?" He has not answered back. "Still not sufficient?" He has laughed, and heartily too. After hearing this, do you still wish to scoff at pain?

[20] "But," you object, "my illness does not allow me to be active

and has withdrawn me from all my duties." It is your body that disease constrains, not your mind as well. So, illness may hamper the feet of a runner and shackle the hands of a cobbler or artisan. But if your mind is accustomed to being active, you will advise, teach, listen, learn, inquire, and remember. What's more - do you think you are doing nothing if you are a patient who bears their illness with self-control? You will demonstrate that disease can be overcome, or at the very least, endured.

[21] Believe me, there is room for virtue even upon a bed of sickness. It is not only arms and battlefields that offer proof of an indomitable spirit unafraid of terrors; a man's bravery shines through even beneath his bedclothes. You have a mission before you: to wrestle nobly with disease. If it exacts nothing from you, if it fails to gain any concession, you set a shining example. Oh, what ample matter were there for renown, if we could have spectators of our sickbed! Be your own spectator, your own applauder.

[22] Moreover, there are two types of pleasures. Bodily pleasures are inhibited by sickness but not wholly removed. Indeed, if truth be told, they are sharpened; drink tastes better to the thirsty man, food is more welcome to the hungry one. Whatever comes after privation is greedily devoured. But as for the pleasures of the mind, which are higher and surer, no physician denies those to the sick man. Whoever pursues these and well understands them scorns all the blandishments of the senses. "Oh, what an unhappy invalid!"

[23] And why? Because he does not mix snow with his wine? Because he does not revive the chill of his drink—mixed as it is in a good-sized bowl—by chipping ice into it? Because no Lucrine oysters are opened right at his dining table? Because there is no mob of cooks around his dining hall, bringing in their very cooking stoves along with their viands? For this is the latest invention of luxury: to avoid any warming of the food, to avoid having anything too tepid for a palate already hardened, the kitchen accompanies the dinner all the way to the table. "Oh, what an unhappy invalid!" He will eat as much as he can digest. No boar will lie before his eyes, banished from the table as a common dish, nor will the breasts of

birds be piled upon his platter, for to see the entire birds is nauseating.

[24] But what evil has befallen you? You will dine like an invalid, nay, sometimes like a sound man. But all these things are easily endured—gruel, warm water, and whatever else seems unbearable to those dissolute with luxury and sick more in mind than in body. We must only cease to shudder at death. And we shall cease, if we have learned the bounds of good and evil; only then will neither weariness of life nor fear of death assail us.

[25] For surfeit of self can never seize upon a life that surveys all the manifold wonders of the vast and varied universe; only idle leisure is wont to make men hate their lives. To one who roams among the truths of nature, the vision never palls; it will be the false and lying that cloy.

[26] And again, if death comes near with summons, even if it be untimely, even if it cut one off in one's prime, a man has had a taste of all that the longest life can give[9]. The great mysteries of nature he knows in good part. He knows that honesty does not grow with time, and those who measure life by vain and therefore endless pleasures inevitably find all of life too short.

[27] If death summons and calls, though it come prematurely, though it pluck one in one's mid-career, a very long journey's joys have been tasted to the full. The mind schooled in the ways of nature knows that honest things do not grow greater with time; those who measure life by vain and therefore endless pleasures inevitably find all of life too short.

[28] Refresh yourself with these thoughts and, in the meantime, devote attention to our correspondence. A time will come when we shall be united and brought together once more; however brief that time may be, we shall make it long through the art of savoring it. For, as Posidonius says, "A single day in the life of the learned unfolds more expansively than the longest lifetime of the ignorant."

[29] Until then, hold fast to this precept, cling to it with all your might: do not succumb to adversity, do not trust in prosperity, and keep the full scope of Fortune's power before your eyes, treating it as

though whatever she can do, she will do. Whatever has been long anticipated comes more gently when it arrives. Farewell.

---

1. Some later manuscripts have "dixerim" (I would have said) or "dixeris" (you would have said) instead of "dixero" (I will have said).
2. Some later manuscripts have "relinquerent" (they were leaving behind) instead of "relinquere" (to leave behind).
3. Muretus suggests "tradere" (to hand over) instead of "trahere" (to drag out).
4. Later manuscripts read "nervorumque" ("and of the sinews"), while earlier versions have variations like "et nervorumq." or "et nervorum."
5. Later manuscripts have "hebetavit" ("it has numbed"), while older ones read "hebetabit" ("it will numb").
6. Muretus reads "per quae" ("through which"), while the manuscripts have "per se quae" ("through itself which").
7. Madvig suggests "cuius" ("for which"), while the manuscripts read "quibus" ("for which things").
8. Some later manuscripts read "distrahuntur" (torn asunder) here instead of "detra(h)untur" (drawn off).
9. The text has "longissimae" ("exceedingly long") corrected by Madvig to "longissime" ("to the greatest extent, furthest"), perhaps indicating Seneca intended to suggest a life need not be long to be fully lived.

LETTER 79

THE GROWTH OF KNOWLEDGE AND PURSUIT OF WISDOM

[1] I EAGERLY AWAIT YOUR LETTER TELLING ME WHAT NEW SIGHTS YOUR journey around Sicily has shown you, and most of all, more certain information about Charybdis herself. I am well aware that Scylla is a rock, and not a particularly daunting one for sailors. But I long to know whether Charybdis lives up to her legends. If you happen to observe her—and she is worth observing—do let me know: Is she driven into a whirlpool by only one wind, or does every storm churn up the sea there equally? Is it true that anything caught in the vortex of that strait is dragged down for many miles, only to emerge near the shore of Tauromenium?

[2] If you write to me about all this, then I will dare to ask you to climb Mount Etna in my honor as well. Some deduce that Etna is being consumed and gradually subsiding, because she used to be visible from further out at sea. This could be happening not because the mountain's height is diminishing, but because the fire has died down and is being emitted with less force and abundance—for the same reason the smoke is lazier during the day. Neither explanation is incredible: that a mountain devoured daily bit by bit is shrinking, or that it remains the same size because the fire does not actually eat

away at the mountain itself, but rages in some infernal valley, feeding on other things. The mountain provides not its fuel, but its chimney.

[3] In Lycia there is a well-known region the inhabitants call Hephaestion, where the ground is perforated in many places and harmless flames flicker around it without damaging any of the plants. The land is thus fertile and grassy, the fire not fierce enough to scorch, but merely shining with subdued, languid power.

[4] But let us save these questions for when you write to me about how far the snows lie from the crater itself—snows that not even summer melts, so safe are they from the neighboring fire. Yet you should not consider this a burdensome request from me. Even if no one asked, you would have done it to indulge your own obsession!

[5] What can I give you not to describe Etna in your poem, not to touch on this stock theme of all poets? Ovid was not at all deterred from treating it by the fact that Virgil had already done so to perfection. Nor did either of them frighten off Cornelius Severus. Besides, this subject has worked out well for all who came before me. They seem not to have preempted what could be said about it, but to have opened the way.

[6] It matters greatly whether you approach a subject already exhausted or one just barely touched. Knowledge grows daily, and prior discoveries do not impede new ones. Moreover, the last thinker has the best condition—he finds the words ready, which when arranged anew take on a fresh appearance. Nor does he lay hands on them as if they belong to another.

[7] For they are public property. Unless I mistake your character, Aetna [the great volcano] must make your mouth water. You long to write something grand and on par with your predecessors. Your modesty, which is so great in you, does not allow you to hope for more—so much that you seem to me ready to rein in your intellectual powers if there were a risk of surpassing them. Such is your reverence for those who came before.

[8] Among other benefits, wisdom has this one: no person can be outdone by another, except during the ascent. When you have reached the summit, it is a draw—there is no room for further

growth, the game is over [lit: one stands still]. Does the sun add to its size? Does the moon advance further than usual? The seas do not grow. The universe keeps the same character and measure.

[9] Things that have fulfilled their proper magnitude cannot be puffed up more. All sages, whoever they may be, will be equals and peers. Each will have his unique gifts: one will be more affable, another quicker, another more fluent in speech, another more eloquent. But the quality in question, that which makes one happy, is equal in all.

[10] Whether your beloved Aetna can collapse and cave in on itself, whether that lofty and conspicuous peak visible across the vast sea can be lessened by the incessant force of its fires, I do not know. But virtue cannot be brought down by flames or ruin. Its majesty alone knows not how to be humbled. It can neither be advanced further nor drawn back. Its magnitude, like that of the celestial bodies, is fixed. Let us try to raise ourselves up to it.

[11] Already much of the work is done—or rather, if I wish to confess the truth, not much. For it is no great feat to be better than the worst. Who would boast of eyes that can only sense daylight faintly? Though one may be satisfied in the meantime to have escaped the darkness, he does not yet enjoy the blessing of full light.

[12] Our soul will then have reason to rejoice when, released from this darkness in which it is submerged, it sees with clarity not by feeble vision, but lets in the full light of day and is restored to its rightful place in the heavens, reclaiming the station allotted to it by birth. Its very origins beckon it on high. But even before it is released from this prison, when it has cast off vice and, pure and weightless, flashes forth into divine thoughts, it will be there.

[13] This, my dearest Lucilius, is what we must devote ourselves to, this is where we must rush with all speed, even if few know it, even if no one does. Glory is the shadow of virtue; it will attend virtue even against its will. But just as a shadow sometimes precedes, sometimes follows, or is at our back, so too glory at times goes before us and presents itself to be seen, at times it is behind us, and greater the later it comes, when envy has retreated.

[14] How long did Democritus seem to rave? Fame barely accepted Socrates. How long was Cato ignored by the state? It rejected and misunderstood him, until it lost him. Rutilius' innocence and virtue would have gone unknown, had he not suffered injustice; in being wronged, he shone forth. Did he not give thanks for his lot and embrace his exile? I speak of those whom fortune has made illustrious by tormenting them. How many have become known only after their deaths! How many has fame not taken up, but unearthed!

[15] You see how greatly Epicurus is admired, not only by the more educated, but also by this ignorant crowd. He was unknown in Athens itself, near which he had hidden himself away. And so, many years after surviving his dear Metrodorus, in a certain letter, having sung the praises of their friendship with fond remembrance, he added this at the very end - that it had not harmed Metrodorus and himself, amidst such great blessings, that noble Greece had not only not known them, but had scarcely even heard of them.

[16] Was Epicurus not discovered then, only after he had ceased to be? Did his renown not shine forth? Metrodorus too admits this in a certain letter - that he and Epicurus had not become sufficiently well-known; but that after them, those who wished to follow in their footsteps would have a great and ready-made name.

[17] No virtue lies hidden, and to have lain hidden is not to its own detriment. There will come a day that publishes what was concealed and suppressed by the spite of its own time. Few are born who take into consideration the people of their own age. Many thousands of years, many generations will come after; look to them. Even if the spite of all the living should enjoin silence, there will come those who judge without offense or favor. If there is any reward for virtue from fame, not even this perishes. The talk of posterity will indeed be nothing to us; yet it will honor and frequent us even when we do not feel it.

[18] Virtue always rewards those who embrace her, both in life and in death, as long as they follow her with true faith. She cares not for those who adorn themselves with false colors, painting themselves in her likeness. Virtue remains unchanged, whether she is

sought out intentionally or encountered suddenly and unexpectedly. Pretense profits nothing. A superficial veneer may deceive a few, but truth is consistent in every aspect of itself. Deceptions have no substance. Lies are thin and fragile; they become transparent under careful inspection. Farewell.

LETTER 80

FAME AND GLORY AS THE SHADOW OF VIRTUE

[1] Today I am free, not only because of my own doing, but also thanks to a public spectacle that has drawn away all bothersome folks to the arena. No one will burst in, no one will impede my train of thought, which proceeds more boldly with this very assurance. The door does not creak open every minute, nor will the curtain be lifted; it will be possible to walk safely, which is more necessary for one walking by himself and following his own path. So then, do I not follow those who went before? I do, but I allow myself to discover something, to change, and to leave things out. I do not serve them, but I assent to them.

[2] And yet, I spoke a grand word in promising myself silence and seclusion without interruption. Behold, a great clamor carries from the stadium, and though it does not jar me from myself, it does transfer me to contemplation of this very matter. I ponder how many exercise their bodies, how few their minds; what a great concourse happens for spectacles untrustworthy and frivolous, what great solitude surrounds the noble arts; how feeble in spirit are those whose arms and shoulders we admire.

[3] I mull over this point especially: if the body can be trained by exercise to such endurance that it withstands the blows and kicks

from multiple opponents, that someone might endure the fiercest sun in the hottest dust, drenched in his own blood, and last the day; how much more easily might the mind be strengthened, so that it receives fortune's strikes invincibly, so that thrown down and trampled, it rises again.

For the body needs many things to be strong; but the mind grows from itself, nourishes itself, trains itself. The body requires much food, much drink, much oil, and long exertion; but virtue will come to you without equipment, without expense. Whatever can make you good, you already have within you.

[4] What do you need in order to be good? To wish it. And what better thing could you wish for than to free yourself from this slavery that oppresses everyone, which even slaves of the lowest condition, born in this squalor, try to strip off by any means? They count their savings, scraped together by defrauding their bellies, as the price of their lives. You, who think yourself born for freedom, will you not yearn to attain it at any cost?

[5] Why do you look to your strongbox? Freedom cannot be bought. And so the term "freedom" is vainly entered in the account books, for neither those who bought it nor those who sold it truly possess it. You must grant yourself this boon; seek it from yourself.

First free yourself from the fear of death, for that places a yoke upon us; then from the fear of poverty.

[6] If you wish to know that there is nothing evil in poverty, compare the faces of the poor and the rich; the poor man smiles more often and more genuinely; no anxiety lingers in the depths of his heart. Even if some concern does come, it passes like a light cloud. The merriment of those who are called happy is feigned, while their sadness is heavy and festering—all the heavier because sometimes they may not openly appear wretched, but amid troubles gnawing at their very hearts, they must play the part of the happy man.

[7] I must use this example quite often, for no other more effectively illustrates this farce of human life, which assigns us the parts we play so poorly. The actor who strutted on the stage declaiming grandly,

"Behold, I am master of Argos; Pelops left me this realm
Which stretches from the Pontic Sea to Helle's waves,
From the Ionian Sea to the Isthmus,"

is a slave who earns five measures of grain and five denarii. The one who, arrogant and mighty, puffed up by confidence in his own strength, says:

[8] "If you don't fall silent, Menelaus, you'll perish by this right hand!" receives a daily pittance and sleeps on a cot. You can say the same about all those delicate people whose litters bear them high above the heads of men, above the swarming crowd; all their happiness is a mask. Scorn them and you will see them stripped bare.

[9] When you intend to buy a horse, you order its blanket removed; you pull off the garments of slaves for sale so that no bodily flaws may escape notice. Do you judge a man while he is wrapped in a disguise? Slave-dealers hide under some sort of concealment any defect which may give offense, and for that reason the very trappings arouse the suspicion of the buyer. If you catch sight of a leg or arm bound up in cloths, you demand that it be stripped and the body itself revealed to you.

[10] Do you see yonder Scythian or Sarmatian king, his head adorned with the badge of his office? If you wish to appraise him and know his full worth, take off his diadem; much evil lurks beneath it. But why speak of others? If you wish to set a value on yourself, lay aside your money, your estates, your honors, and look into your own soul. At present, you accept the opinion of others about yourself. Farewell.

LETTER 81

ON DEALING WITH INGRATITUDE AND THE NATURE OF FRIENDSHIP

[1] You complain of having encountered an ungrateful person. If this is your first such experience, then you should thank either your good fortune or your sound judgment. But in this case, good judgment can do nothing except make you uncharitable. For if you wish to avoid this danger, you will not confer benefits, and so, to keep them from being lost with another, they will be lost to yourself. It is better that benefits go unacknowledged than that they not be given at all. Even after a poor harvest one should sow again; often the steady barrenness of an unproductive soil is compensated by one year's abundance.

[2] It is worth it to find a grateful person, even if it means experiencing ingratitude. No one has so sure a hand in conferring benefits that they are not often deceived; benefits must roam so that some may eventually stick. After a shipwreck, people still brave the seas. A defaulting debtor[1] does not drive the moneylender from the marketplace. Life will soon grow dull in sluggish idleness if we abandon whatever offends us. In fact, let this very matter make you more charitable. For when the outcome of something is uncertain, to succeed sometimes, one must try often.

[3] But enough about that topic; I have spoken of it at length in the

books which I have written On Benefits. Here, I think we should rather explore a matter which I feel has not been sufficiently explained: whether a person who has helped us and later harmed us has squared the account and absolved us of our debt. You might add this point too: what if they harmed us far more later than they had previously helped us?

[4] If you seek the strict ruling of a rigid judge, they will absolve the one consideration from the other and say: "Although the injuries outweigh the benefits, let the balance of injury be pardoned for the sake of the benefits." The harm was greater, but the help came first. So let the timing also be taken into account.

[5] The following points are too obvious for you to need reminding: one must ask how gladly the person helped and how reluctantly they harmed, since it is the intention behind both benefits and injuries that matters. "I did not want to confer a benefit; I was won over by either a sense of shame, the persistence of the requester, or by hope."

[6] The spirit in which each thing is owed depends on the spirit in which it is given, and it is not the magnitude of the action, but the quality of the intent behind it which is weighed. Now, let us do away with guesswork. The first act was a benefit, and this latest one, which exceeded the measure of the prior benefit, is an injury. A good person balances the two sides of the ledger in such a way as to shortchange themselves - they add to the benefit and subtract from the injury. That other, more lenient judge, which I prefer to be, will bid you forget the injury and remember the service.

[7] "Surely," you say, "it is in accordance with justice to repay each person what is due - gratitude for a benefit, retaliation or at least ill-will for an injury." That would hold true if it were one person who inflicted the injury and another who conferred the benefit; for if it is the same person, the force of the injury is extinguished by the benefit. For if someone deserves to be pardoned even if no previous services were rendered, then after receiving benefits the offender deserves more than forgiveness.

[8] I do not assign equal value to benefits and injuries. I esteem a

benefit more highly than an injury. Not all who are grateful know how to be indebted for a benefit; even a thoughtless, crude person, one of the masses, can be grateful, especially while the memory of receiving is still fresh; but he does not know how much he ought to repay for it. Only the wise man knows the exact worth of each thing. For the fool I was just speaking of, even if he is well-intentioned, either repays less than he ought, or at a time other than he ought, or in a place where he ought not. What ought to be returned, he squanders and throws away.

[9] In some matters there is a marvelous propriety of words, and the custom of old-fashioned speech denotes certain things by the most effective and duties-teaching signs. Thus, for example, we are accustomed to say: "He returned a favor to him." To return is to bring back voluntarily what you owe. We do not say "He paid back a favor," for those who are asked to repay also pay back, as do those who do so unwillingly, at any time, and through another. We do not say "He replaced the benefit" or "He discharged it"; no word that applies to a debt has found favor with us.

[10] To return means to bring back the thing to the person from whom you received it. This phrase signifies a voluntary return; he who has returned a favor has served as his own reminder.

The wise man will thoroughly consider everything - how much he has received, from whom, when, where, how. And so we say that only the wise man knows how to return a favor; just as no one knows how to confer a benefit except the wise man, who finds more joy in giving than others find in receiving.

[11] Someone counts this among those things we Stoics seem to say that are surprising to all - the Greeks call them παράδοξα[2] - and he objects: "No one, then, knows how to return a favor except the wise man? Then does no one else know how to repay his creditor what he owes, or to pay the price to a seller when he buys something?"

To avoid making ourselves unpopular, be aware that Epicurus says the same thing. Metrodorus certainly says that only the wise man knows how to return a favor.

[12] The same person also expresses surprise when we say, "Only

the wise man knows how to love. Only the wise man can be a true friend." Yet both love and friendship involve returning gratitude—indeed, this is more common and applies to more people than true friendship. He is also surprised when we say that loyalty is found only in the wise, as if he himself did not say the same thing. Or do you think that a person who does not know how to return gratitude can be considered loyal?

[13] Therefore, let them cease to slander us as making unbelievable claims, and let them understand that the wise man possesses true virtues while the masses have only images and semblances of virtues. No one knows how to return gratitude except the wise man. Even the fool may return it as best he can, in whatever way he knows how; it is the knowledge rather than the will that he lacks. Willingness cannot be taught.

[14] The wise man will weigh all factors against each other, for the same thing can become greater or smaller depending on the time, place, and cause. Often, a timely gift of a thousand denarii can accomplish what an influx of riches into a household cannot. There is a great difference between making a gift and coming to someone's aid, between saving someone through your generosity and equipping them [for success]. Often, what is given is small, but its consequences are great. And how much difference do you think it makes whether someone takes what he lacks from his own resources, which he has at his disposal, or receives a benefit so that he may give to others?

[15] But let us not retread the same ground that we have already sufficiently examined. In comparing benefits and injuries, a good man will certainly judge as fairly as possible, but he will favor the benefit; he will be more inclined in that direction.

[16] The person [involved] often carries the greatest weight in such matters: "You gave me a benefit in [the form of] a slave, but you wronged me in [the form of] a father. You saved my son, but you took away my father." And so on, through all the other points of comparison that follow. If the difference is small, he will overlook it. Even if it is large, but if the injury can be forgiven without compromising

loyalty and duty, he will let it go—that is, if the wrong pertains to him alone.

[17] The main point is this: he will be accommodating in making the exchange. He will allow more to be credited to his account. He will be reluctant to cancel out a benefit by balancing it against a wrong. He will lean and incline in this direction, desiring to owe gratitude, eager to repay it. For someone is mistaken if he more gladly accepts a benefit than returns it. Just as the borrower is more cheerful when repaying a loan than when taking it out, so should the person who rids himself of the immense debt of a benefit received be happier than the one who is just now being placed under obligation.

[18] The ungrateful are mistaken in this too: they count anything extra given to a creditor beyond the principal as extraordinary, but they think the use of benefits should be free. Yet those benefits grow with time; the longer the repayment is delayed, the more must be repaid. The ungrateful man is one who returns a benefit without interest. Thus, when weighing receipts and expenditures, this too shall be taken into account.

[19] We must do everything to be as grateful as possible. For this goodness is our own, just as justice, contrary to popular belief, is not something directed towards others; a large part of it returns to oneself. No one who benefits another fails to benefit himself—I don't mean because the one helped will want to help in return or because good examples come back around to their author, while bad examples rebound upon those who would tolerate injuries which their own conduct has shown are possible. Rather, I mean that the reward for all the virtues lies in the virtues themselves. For they are not practiced for a prize; the recompense for a good deed is to have done it.

[20] I am grateful, not so that another will be more likely to help me, prompted by my previous example, but so that I might do a most pleasant and beautiful thing. I am grateful not because it is expedient, but because it delights me. To prove this is so: if I may not be grateful unless I appear ungrateful, if I can return a benefit only by a semblance of injury, I will pursue the honorable course with utmost equanimity, even through the midst of infamy. No one seems to me to

esteem virtue more highly or be more devoted to it than one who has lost the reputation of a good man in order not to lose his conscience.

[21] Thus, as I said, in being grateful you do more good to yourself than to another. For he has obtained an ordinary, everyday occurrence—getting back what he gave—while you have obtained something great, springing from the most blessed state of mind: to have been grateful. For if wickedness makes people wretched while virtue makes them blessed, and if being grateful is a virtue, then you have rendered an ordinary service but obtained an inestimable one: the consciousness of gratitude, which comes only to the divine and fortunate mind. But the opposite state is beset by the height of wretchedness; no ungrateful person will be wretched if I defer calling him so —he is wretched immediately.

[22] Let us therefore avoid being ungrateful, not for another's sake, but for our own. The least and lightest portion of evil flows over to others; the worst and densest part, so to speak, stays home and weighs down the possessor. As our Attalus used to say, "wickedness itself drinks the greatest part of its own poison." The venom that snakes produce for the ruin of others is harmless to themselves; this is not like that—it is most harmful to those who have it.

[23] The ungrateful man torments and consumes himself; he despises the gifts he has received because he must repay them, diminishing their worth, while inflating and magnifying the injuries done to him. What could be more wretched than a man who forgets the good turns done to him but clings to the wrongs?

[24] The wise, in contrast, adorns every kindness and commends it to their own heart, delighting in the constant recollection of it. To the wicked, there is but one fleeting pleasure: the moment they receive a boon. But the sage derives lasting, perpetual joy from it. For he rejoices not in the receiving, but in having received—an immortal, enduring gladness. He spurns the injuries done to him, not through negligence, but by choice.

[25] He does not twist everything for the worse or seek someone to blame for misfortune, attributing men's failings to fate instead. He finds no fault with words or expressions, but interprets all that

happens with goodwill to ease the sting. He remembers the service done rather than the offense given. As much as he can, he dwells on the earlier, fonder memory and does not change his disposition toward those who have served him well—unless a great many misdeeds tip the scales and the difference is so stark that even he cannot overlook it. But even then, he only goes so far as to be the same after the greater injury as he was before the kindness. For when wrongdoing merely matches the good received, some measure of goodwill still remains in his soul.

[26] Just as a defendant is acquitted when the votes are equal and human judgment always leans toward mercy in cases of doubt, so too the wise man's heart, when injuries and merits are evenly weighed, will cease to feel indebted but not cease to wish to be indebted. In this, he is like those who repay their debts after the ledgers have been wiped clean.

[27] But no one can be truly grateful unless he scorns the things that drive the masses to madness. If you wish to repay a kindness, you must be willing to go into exile, to shed your blood, to endure poverty, to sully your innocence and expose it to shameful rumors.

[28] Gratitude comes at no small cost. We value nothing more highly than a favor when we are asking for it, and nothing more cheaply once we have received it. Do you wonder what makes us forget the boons we have obtained? It is our eagerness to obtain more. We dwell not on what we have gained, but on what we still desire. Riches, honors, power—all those things we falsely prize but which are cheap at their true value—distract us from the righteous path.

[29] We do not know how to judge matters on which we should consult nature, not popular opinion. Those coveted things contain nothing so grand that they should sway our minds, except that we have grown accustomed to marveling at them. They are praised not because they ought to be desired, but desired because they have been praised. When the delusion of each individual has created a collective madness, the madness of the masses reinforces the delusion of the individual.

[30] But just as we have believed those things, let us also trust this

same people when they proclaim that nothing is more honorable than a grateful spirit. All cities and even tribes from barbarous regions will shout this in unison. On this point, good and bad men will agree.

[31] There will be those who praise pleasures, and those who prefer labors; some will say pain is the greatest evil, while others won't even call it an evil at all. Some will admit riches as the supreme good, but another will say they were discovered for the ruin of human life, and that no one is wealthier than he for whom Fortune cannot find a gift. Amidst such a great diversity of opinions, everyone will affirm to you with one voice, as they say, that favors must be repaid to the well-deserving. On this, the discordant crowd will consent.

Meanwhile, we return injuries for benefits, and the primary reason anyone is ungrateful is that he could not be grateful enough. [32] The madness has been carried to such a point that it is most dangerous to confer great benefits on anyone, for since he thinks it base not to repay, he does not wish to have anyone to whom he should repay. Keep what you have received; I do not ask it back, I do not demand it. Let it be safe to have done a good turn. No hatred is more pernicious than that which springs from shame at the desecration of a benefit. Farewell.

---

1. The original Latin uses the term "decoctor", which Muretus notes is from an old manuscript. Other versions have terms like coctor, coactor, or tortor.
2. In philosophical contexts, "paradoxa" often refers to statements or propositions that seem self-contradictory, absurd, or counter-intuitive, but may nonetheless be true or reveal a deeper truth upon further examination.

LETTER 82

THE SECURITY AND FREEDOM OF THE WISE MAN'S SPIRIT

[1] I HAVE CEASED TO BE ANXIOUS ABOUT YOU, MY FRIEND. "WHAT GOD," you ask, "has stood surety for him?" The one who never deceives—a soul which loves rectitude and goodness. The better part of yourself is on safe ground. Fortune can inflict injury upon you, but what matters more is that I have no fear of you doing injury to yourself. Continue as you have begun, and settle yourself in this way of living —not luxuriously, but calmly and steadfastly.

[2] I would rather be ill at ease than enjoy excessive ease—being uncomfortable, as people commonly understand it: experiencing hardship, enduring difficulties, laboring intensely. We often hear this sort of language in praise of certain persons' lives, for whom there is envy: "He lives luxuriously"; that is, "He is a weakling." For the mind grows soft and effeminate little by little, and is dissolved into a state of idleness and lethargy in which it languishes. What then? Is it not better for a man even to grow stiff and numb? Later those same indulgent people fear that to which they have made their lives resemble. There is a great difference between leisurely repose and being buried alive.

[3] "What then," you say, "is it not better to lie idle than to whirl round in these vortices of duties?" Both things are to be regarded as

hateful—both tension and torpor. I think that he who lies perfumed amid roses is no less dead than he who is dragged along by the executioner's hook.

Leisure without study is death—a tomb for the living man.

[4] What good is it to have withdrawn from active life? As if the causes of our anxieties do not follow us across the seas! What hiding-place is there where the fear of death does not enter? What peaceful haunts are so fortified and so far withdrawn that pain does not fill them with dread? Wherever you hide yourself, human ills will make an uproar all around. There are many external things which encompass us, causing us to lose our way or weighing us down, and many things within which, even amid solitude, fret and ferment.

[5] Therefore, we should surround ourselves with philosophy—an impregnable wall which fortune, despite assailing it with many siege-engines, cannot pass. The soul stands on unassailable ground when it has abandoned external things; it is independent in its own fortress; and every missile falls short of it. Fortune has not, as we imagine, long arms; she can seize none except him who clings to her.

[6] Let us then recoil from her as far as we are able; this can be accomplished only through knowledge of self and of nature. The soul should know whither it is going and whence it came, what is good for it and what is evil, what it seeks and what it avoids, and what is that essence which distinguishes things to be desired and things to be shunned, tames the madness of our desires, and calms the fierceness of our fears.

[7] Some think that even without philosophy, they can overcome these hardships on their own. But when misfortune catches them off guard, a belated confession is wrung from their lips. Grand words desert them when the torturer demands their hand, when death draws near. You could say to such a one: "You readily provoked dangers when they were absent; but behold the pain you claimed was bearable, behold the death you spoke so spiritedly against; the whips crack, the sword flashes—

Now, Aeneas, now is the time for courage, for a robust spirit.

[8] But only diligent meditation will make that spirit robust. You must train not your tongue, but your mind. Prepare yourself to face death, which no one can exhort you to or build you up for, who tries to persuade you with quibbles that death is no evil. For I delight, excellent Lucilius, in mocking the absurdities of the Greeks, which I have not yet rejected despite my astonishment at them.

[9] Our Zeno uses this syllogism: "Nothing glorious is evil; but death is glorious; therefore death is not evil." You have made progress; I am freed from fear. After this, I will not hesitate to bare my neck. But do you not wish to speak more seriously and not elicit laughter from one about to die? By Hercules, I could not easily tell you which is more foolish—the one who thought he could extinguish the fear of death with this question, or the one who endeavored to refute it, as if it mattered.

[10] For Zeno posed a counter-question stemming from the fact that we place death among the indifferent things, which the Greeks call ἀδιάφορα[1]. He says, "Nothing indifferent is glorious; but death is glorious; therefore death is not indifferent." You see where this question sneaks in by stealth. Death is not glorious, but to die bravely is glorious. And when you say, "Nothing indifferent is glorious," I grant you this, so long as I may say that nothing is glorious except concerning indifferent things. I mean by indifferent things those that are neither good nor bad, like disease, pain, poverty, exile, death.

[11] None of these things are intrinsically glorious, yet nothing is glorious without them. For it is not poverty that is praised, but the man who is not humbled or bent by poverty. Exile is not praised, but he who went into exile as if he had sent himself. Pain is not praised, but the one whom pain could compel to do nothing. No one praises death itself, but rather the one whose spirit death snatched away before it could dismay him.

[12] None of those things are inherently noble or glorious, but whatever virtue has approached and handled, it makes noble and glorious; those things are neutral, and it matters whether wickedness or virtue has laid a hand on them. For that death which is glorious in Cato's case is straightaway shameful and blush-worthy in Brutus's.

This is the Brutus who, when about to die, looked for ways to delay his death; he withdrew to relieve his bowels, and when summoned to his death and ordered to offer his neck, he said, "I will offer it, in such a way will I live!" What madness it is to flee, when you cannot turn back! "I will offer it," he says, "in such a way will I live." He nearly added, "even under Antony." O what a man, deserving to be given to life!

[13] But, as I had begun to say, you see that death itself is neither bad nor good; Cato used it most honorably, Brutus most basely. Everything that does not have honor, once virtue is added, takes it on. We call a room well-lit; this same room is utterly dark at night.

[14] The day pours light into it, the night takes it away. So it is with those things we call indifferent and neutral—riches, strength, beauty, honors, power, and on the other hand, death, exile, ill health, pains, and whatever else we have feared to a lesser or greater degree—either wickedness or virtue gives them the name of good or evil. A lump of matter is inherently neither hot nor cold; thrown into a furnace it becomes hot, plunged into water it becomes cold. Death is made honorable by that which is honorable, that is, virtue and a soul that scorns extremities.

[15] There is also, Lucilius, a big difference among these things we call "indifferent." For death is not indifferent in the same way as whether you have an odd or even number of hairs. Death is among those things which, while not evil, still have the appearance of evil. There is an inborn self-love, a deep-seated desire to persist and preserve oneself, and an aversion to dissolution, because it seems to snatch many good things from us and lead us out from this abundance of things to which we have grown accustomed. That other matter also estranges us from death: we know these present things, but what we will pass into, we do not know what it is like, and we shudder at the unknown. There is, besides, a natural fear of the darkness into which death is believed to lead us.

[16] And so, even if death is something indifferent, it is not something that can be easily disregarded. The mind must be toughened by great practice to endure its sight and approach.

We should hold death in greater contempt than we are accustomed to. For we have believed many tales about it. Many intellects have vied to amplify its ill repute. They have depicted the infernal prison, the land oppressed by perpetual night, where "the vast guardian of Orcus, reclining in a bloody cave upon half-gnawed bones, eternally barks, terrifying the bloodless shades."

Even when you have convinced yourself that these are mere fables, and that nothing remains for the dead to fear, another unease creeps in. For people fear just as much that they will be in the underworld as that they will be nowhere at all.

[17] To combat these notions, which lengthy credulity has clouded our minds with, why should it not be glorious to face death bravely, among the greatest works of the human spirit? The soul will never rise to virtue if it believes death to be an evil; it will rise if it considers death to be indifferent. It is not in the nature of things for anyone to approach with a great spirit that which he judges to be an evil; he will come to it sluggishly and hesitantly. There is no glory in what is done by the unwilling and the reluctant; virtue does nothing because it must.

[18] Add to this that nothing is done honorably unless the whole mind has applied itself and been present, with no part of itself dissenting. But when one approaches an evil, either from fear of worse or hope of goods which might be worth enduring the suffering of a single evil to attain, then the judgments of the doer are in conflict. On one side, they command him to carry out his purpose; on the other, they pull him back and urge him to flee from the suspect and perilous matter. Therefore he is pulled apart in different directions, and if this happens, glory perishes. For virtue carries out its resolves with a harmonious spirit. It does not fear what it does.

> *"Do not yield to misfortunes, but go forth more boldly*
> *Where your fortune will allow."*

[19] You will not go forth more boldly if you believe those things to be evils. This notion must be rooted out from your breast; otherwise,

the suspicion that death is an evil, delaying your initiative, will cause hesitation. The soul will flinch from the thing it must charge.

Our philosophers certainly wish Zeno's line of questioning to be seen as true, and the other which is set against it to be fallacious and false. I myself do not reduce these matters to the law of dialectic and those knots of that most indolent artifice. I judge that this whole genus of arguments, by which the one being questioned supposes himself to be hemmed in and gives one answer when led to the admission but thinks another, ought to be driven out. In the case of truth, we must act more simply; against fear, more bravely.

[20] I would prefer to unravel and examine the very arguments they put forth, not to impose my views, but to persuade. When a general leads his army into battle, ready to die for their wives and children, how does he exhort them? I present to you the Fabii, who took upon their single house the entire war effort of the republic. I show you the Spartans, positioned in the very narrows of Thermopylae. They hope for neither victory nor return. That place will be their sepulcher.

[21] How do you exhort men to block the downfall of their entire nation with their own bodies, to yield their lives rather than their position? You might say, "What is evil is not glorious; death is glorious; therefore, death is not evil." Oh, what a persuasive harangue! Who, after this, would hesitate to throw himself upon the swords of the enemy and die standing? But consider how bravely Leonidas addressed his men! "Comrades," he said, "eat your lunch now as if you will dine in the underworld." The food did not swell in their mouths, stick in their throats, or slip from their hands; with cheer they promised to attend both lunch and dinner.

[22] And what of that Roman general who, sending soldiers to occupy a position through the midst of a vast enemy force, addressed them thus: "It is necessary, comrades, to go there, whence it is not necessary to return." You see how straightforward and imperious virtue is. Which of your circumlocutions can make a mortal braver or more upright? They break the spirit, which should never be more

unrestrained or less forced into petty quibbling than when something great is being composed.

[23] The fear of death must be stripped away not from three hundred, but from all mortals. How do you teach them that it is not an evil? How do you overcome the opinions of an entire era, with which infancy is imbued from the outset? What aid do you find for human frailty? What do you say to inflame them to rush into the midst of dangers? With what oration, with what powers of intellect, do you turn aside this consensus of fear, this conviction of the human race that stands arrayed against you? Do you construct captious words for me and weave little questions? Great monsters are slain by great weapons.

[24] In Africa, they assailed that savage serpent, more terrible to the Roman legions than the war itself, in vain with arrows and slings. Not even to the Pythian god was it revered when, due to its immense size and solid mass of its body, it rejected iron and whatever human hands had hurled. In the end, it was crushed by millstones. And against death do you toss such tiny darts? Do you meet the lion with an awl? What you say is sharp—nothing is sharper than the awn. But subtlety itself renders some things useless and ineffectual. Farewell.

---

1. The Greek term "ἀδιάφορα" (adiaphora) is the plural form of the noun "ἀδιάφορον" (adiaphoron), which is derived from the adjective "ἀδιάφορος" (adiaphoros), meaning "indifferent" or "not different." In philosophical contexts, particularly in Stoicism, "adiaphora" refers to things that are considered neither good nor bad, but morally neutral or indifferent.

LETTER 83

APPLYING PHILOSOPHICAL PRECEPTS TO DAILY LIFE

[1] You bid me give you an account of each separate day, and of the whole day too. You must think well of me if you deem me worthy of passing no moment that I would wish to conceal. Indeed, we should live as though we were living in plain sight of all; and we should think as though someone could peer into our inmost heart—as indeed someone can. For what does it avail that anything is hidden from man? Nothing is shut off from the sight of God. He is witness to our souls, and he comes into the very midst of our thoughts—comes into them, I say, as one who may at any time depart.

[2] I will therefore do as you bid, and will gladly inform you by letter what I am doing, and in what sequence. I will keep watch over myself, and—a most useful habit—will review each day. For this is what makes us wicked: that no one of us looks back over his own life. Our thoughts are devoted only to what we are about to do. And yet our plans for the future always depend on the past.

[3] Today has been uninterrupted; no one has filched the slightest part of it from me. The whole time has been divided between rest and reading. A brief space has been given over to bodily exercise, and on this ground I can thank old age—my exercise costs very little effort; as

soon as I stir, I am weary. And weariness is the aim and end of exercise, no matter how strong one is.

[4] Do you ask about my sparring partners? One is enough for me—the young slave-boy Pharius, as you know, a pleasant fellow; but he will soon be changed. At my time of life, I need one who is of still more tender years. Pharius, at any rate, says that he and I are at the same period of life; for we are both losing our teeth. Yet even now I can scarcely catch up with him as he runs, and within a very few days I shall not be able to reach him at all; so you see what profit we get from daily exercise. Very soon does a wide interval open between two persons who travel different ways. He is mounting uphill, I am going down, and you know how much quicker the latter is. Were I to say that I am not descending but falling, I should be deceiving you; for old age does not fall headlong, it slides downwards.

[5] Well, this has been a great achievement for my day; the bath had been made ready, though in an under-heated state which I can stand when I am most robust and when there is not a flaw in my bodily processes. In the days when I was a lusty hero, I used to celebrate the New Year by taking a plunge into the canal [the frigid Aqua Virgo], in the same way as I used to do on the Kalends of January in memory of my vow and my toughening practice. After this I passed into the cold pool, which is big enough to swim in when I have grit. Now I have abandoned both these customs: the chilling of the body is all that remains from my old-time pluckiness.

[6] After my plunge, I take some dry bread and eat without a table, a lunch that requires no hand-washing afterward. Then comes a very short nap. You know my habit; I avail myself of a scanty bit of sleep—unharnessing, as it were, for a mere instant. For I am satisfied with just barely ceasing to be awake. Sometimes I know that I have slept; at other times, I have a mere suspicion.

[7] Hear how the clamor of the circus resounds! My ears are struck by a sudden, universal shout. Yet it does not shake my thoughts, nor even interrupt them. I bear the din with utmost patience. The many voices merged into one are to me like the crashing of waves or the battering of the forest by the wind—sounds without meaning.

[8] So then, what have I set my mind to now? I will tell you. A thought from yesterday remains with me: what did those most sagacious men intend, who made the weightiest proofs of the most important matters so trivial and convoluted that, even if true, they still resemble falsehoods?

[9] Zeno, that great man, founder of our most valiant and holy sect, wishes to deter us from drunkenness. Hear, then, how he reasons that a good man will not become drunk: "No one entrusts a secret to a drunken man; but one will entrust it to a good man; therefore, the good man will not get drunk." Observe how, by a similar line of questioning, this can be ridiculed—for it suffices to offer one example out of many: "No one entrusts a secret to a sleeping man; but one entrusts it to a good man; therefore, the good man does not sleep."

[10] Posidonius pleads the cause of our friend Zeno in the only possible way, but not, I think, with real success. For he says that the word "drunken" is used in two ways: first, of a man who is loaded with wine and has lost control of himself; second, of a man who is accustomed to getting drunk and is a slave to the habit. Zeno, he claims, refers not to the man who is drunk, but to him who is accustomed to getting drunk.

[11] But to this man, no one would entrust secrets which might be blurted out under the influence of wine. However, this is false. For the original question refers to the man who is actually drunk, not the one who will become so. You will surely admit there is a vast difference between a drunk man and a drunkard. The man who is drunk may be in that state for the first time and not have the vice, while the drunkard is often free from drunkenness. Therefore, I understand the common meaning of the word, especially when employed by a man who professes careful choice of language and who weighs his words. Furthermore, if this is what Zeno meant and wished us to think, he sought to profit by verbal ambiguity—which ought not be done when the truth is being sought.

[12] While one may indeed hold this opinion, it is false to claim that a person who is often drunk cannot be entrusted with a secret.

Consider how many soldiers, not always sober, have been entrusted with confidential information by their commander, tribune, or centurion. Regarding the assassination of C. Caesar [Julius Caesar], I mean the one who held power over the republic after defeating Pompey, Tillius Cimber[1] was trusted just as much as C. Cassius. Cassius drank water his entire life, while Tillius Cimber was excessive in his wine consumption and prone to drunken brawls. Caesar himself spoke on this matter, saying, "Shall I tolerate anyone who cannot tolerate wine?"

[13] Each person can now name those whom they know to be poorly trusted with wine but well trusted with secrets. However, I will relate one example that comes to mind, lest it be overlooked. For life must be instructed with illustrious examples, and we should not always resort to ancient ones.

[14] L. Piso, the guardian of the city, was drunk from the moment he first became so. He spent the greater part of the night at banquets and slept until nearly the sixth hour [noon]; this was his morning routine. Nevertheless, he administered his duties, which included the protection of the city, with the utmost diligence. The divine Augustus gave him secret instructions when he placed him in charge of Thrace, which he had thoroughly subdued, and Tiberius did the same when setting out for Campania, leaving behind many suspicious and unpopular matters in the city.

[15] I believe that because Piso's drunkenness had turned out well, Tiberius later appointed Cossus as prefect of the city, a serious and temperate man, but one who was submerged and soaked in wine, to the point that he was sometimes carried out of the Senate, which he had entered from a banquet, overcome by an unshakable sleep. Nevertheless, Tiberius wrote many things to him in his own hand, which he deemed too sensitive to entrust even to his own ministers. No secret, either private or public, ever slipped from Cossus.

[16] Therefore, let us set aside those rhetorical declarations: "The mind is not in its own power when bound by drunkenness. Just as casks themselves burst with new wine, and the heat forces everything that lies at the bottom to the top, so when wine is seething, whatever

hidden things lie at the bottom are brought forth and revealed. Just as those burdened with wine do not contain their food when it overflows, neither do they contain secrets. They pour forth equally what is their own and what belongs to others."

[17] Though this frequently occurs, it is also true that we tend to deliberate on essential matters with those we know to be more fond of drinking. Thus, the claim made in defense - that a habitual drunkard cannot keep a secret - is false. How much better would it be to openly denounce drunkenness and lay bare its vices, which even a tolerably decent person would shun, let alone one who is perfect and wise, who is content merely to quench his thirst. Such a man, even if the gaiety of company sometimes induces him to prolong his drinking, still stops short of drunkenness.

[18] As for the question of whether a wise man's mind is unsettled by excessive wine, causing him to act like a typical drunk - we will consider that later. For now, if you wish to prove that a good man ought not to get drunk, why resort to syllogisms? Proclaim how shameful it is to pour down more than one can hold, to be ignorant of the capacity of one's own stomach. Describe the many disgraceful acts that drunken men commit, things they would blush to do when sober. Drunkenness is nothing other than voluntary madness. Imagine the condition of a drunkard prolonged over several days - would you have any doubt about his insanity?

[19] Even now, the insanity is no less severe, only shorter in duration. Recall the example of Alexander of Macedon, who during a feast stabbed Clitus, his dearest and most loyal friend. Upon realizing his crime, Alexander wished to die - and certainly, he should have[2]. Drunkenness inflames and lays bare every vice, removing the sense of shame that hinders evil intentions. More people refrain from prohibited acts out of fear of disgrace than from a virtuous will.

[20] When the overwhelming force of wine has seized the mind, whatever evil lay hidden emerges. Drunkenness does not create vices, but brings them into the open. The lustful man won't even wait for the bedroom then, but without delay gives free rein to his desires. The immodest openly parade their perversions. The insolent lose

control over both their tongues and hands. The arrogance of the proud swells, the cruelty of the harsh turns savage, the spite of the petty turns malicious.

[21] Every vice is unleashed and displayed[3]. Add to this the drunkard's obliviousness to himself, his barely intelligible speech, his unsteady eyes, his faltering step, the spinning in his head. The very room seems to whirl about as if caught in a tornado, and his stomach churns as the wine ferments and stretches his innards. Yet all this is somehow bearable while the drunkenness runs its course. But what happens when it is aggravated by sleep, and the drunkenness turns to queasiness?

[22] Consider the disasters that public drunkenness has caused. It has betrayed the fiercest and most warlike nations to their enemies. It has breached city walls defended by years of stubborn[4] warfare. It has forced the most defiant, those who scorned the yoke, to submit to foreign domination. It has conquered invincible armies with wine when weapons failed.

[23] Alexander, whom I just mentioned, was kept safe through so many journeys, so many battles, so many winters in which he overcame the challenges of weather and terrain, so many rivers falling from unknown sources, so many seas; yet intemperate drinking and that Herculean, fateful cup destroyed him.

[24] What glory is there in holding much liquor? When you claim the prize and your collapsed drinking companions, sprawled in slumber and vomit, refuse your urgings to drink more; when you outlast the entire party; when your magnificent prowess conquers all and no one has a stomach for wine like you do as you defeat an entire cask - what then?

[25] As for Mark Antony, a great man of noble character, what else ruined him and diverted him into foreign customs and un-Roman vices than drunkenness and his love for Cleopatra, no less potent than wine? This made him an enemy of the republic, inferior to his enemies. This made him cruel, as the heads of leading citizens were brought to him at dinner. Amidst the most sumptuous feasts and regal luxury he examined the faces and hands of the proscribed,

heavy with wine yet still thirsty for blood. It was intolerable that he did this while drunk; how much more intolerable that he did this because of the drunkenness itself!

[26] Cruelty nearly always follows excessive drinking; for the mind's health is corrupted and aggravated. Just as chronic illnesses make people irritable and difficult, enraged at the slightest offense, so too does constant drunkenness incite the passions. For when people are often not in their right mind, the habit of madness persists, and the vices conceived in wine prevail even without it.

[27] Tell me, then, why the wise man ought not to get drunk. Demonstrate the shamefulness and unsuitability of the matter, not with words, but with facts. Prove, as is quite easy to do, that these so-called pleasures, when they exceed moderation, are punishments. For if you try to argue that the wise man can be thoroughly intoxicated with much wine and maintain his proper course even while inebriated, you might as well gather that he will not die from drinking poison, will not fall asleep from taking a sleeping potion, and will not purge and void from his gut whatever is lodged there after taking hellebore [an ancient purgative]. But if his feet are unsteady and his tongue is incoherent, on what basis do you suppose that he is sober in one part and drunk in another? Farewell.

---

1. Some manuscripts refer to him as "Tillius Cimber," while others use variations such as "illinc imbro" or "illic imbro."
2. Reading "debuit" (should have) over alternatives like "meruit" (deserved to).
3. Lipsius suggests reading "laxatur" (is loosened) rather than the obscure manuscript readings "taxatur" or "texatur".
4. Some later manuscripts read "pertinaci" (stubborn) instead of "pertinacia" (stubbornness).

LETTER 84

THE WISDOM OF BEES AND DIGESTING OUR MENTAL NOURISHMENT

[1] These travels, which shake off my lethargy, I judge beneficial for both my health and my studies. You can see how they aid my health: since love of literature makes me lazy and neglectful of my body, I get exercise through the efforts of others. As for why they benefit my studies, I will explain. I have not withdrawn from my reading, which I consider essential, first so that I am not content with only myself, and second so that after learning what others have found, I may form my own judgments about their discoveries and reflect on future inquiries. Reading nourishes the mind and refreshes it when fatigued by study—yet still with study.

[2] We should neither merely write nor merely read; the one will drain our strength and exhaust it—I speak of writing—while the other will relax and dilute it. We must alternate between the two, using one to regulate the other, so that the pen gives form to the collected fruits of reading.

[3] We ought to imitate bees, they say, who flit about and cull the flowers suitable for making honey, then arrange whatever they've gathered, distributing it throughout the honeycomb. As our own Virgil says, "They pack the liquid honey and swell their cells with sweet nectar[1]."

[4] It's not fully understood whether bees extract from flowers a juice that becomes honey instantaneously, or whether they transform what they've collected into this flavor through some blending and the particular property of their breath. Some believe bees possess the skill not of making honey but of gathering it. They say a honey is found on the leaves of reeds in India, produced either by the dew of that climate or the sweet, richer moisture of the reed itself. In our own plants too, the same potency is said to be present, though less obvious and notable—which the creature born for this purpose tracks down and collects. Some think the material bees have plucked from the most tender blooming flora is converted to this special quality by means of ripening and arrangement—not without some sort of leavening, if I may put it that way, which binds the various elements into one.

[5] But lest I digress from my subject, we too should imitate these bees and set apart whatever we've amassed from our diverse reading —for things kept separate are better preserved. Then, applying the care and skill of our own minds, we should blend those various extracts to create a unified flavor. Even if the source is apparent, the end product should nevertheless appear distinct from its origin. We see this process occur naturally in our own bodies, without any effort on our part:

[6] The nourishment we consume, as long as it retains its original quality and floats undigested in our stomachs, is but a burden. Yet once it has been transformed from its original state, only then is it absorbed into our strength and lifeblood. We must strive for the same in matters that nourish our minds, never allowing the things we have learned to remain intact and foreign to us.

[7] Let us thoroughly digest these mental meals. Otherwise, they will merely enter our memory and not our true understanding. We must absorb teachings faithfully and make them our own, blending the many parts into a unified whole, just as a single sum is derived from smaller, disparate numbers when a single calculation binds them together. This is what our minds must do: conceal all the

elements by which they have been aided, revealing only the final product of those efforts.

[8] Even if a likeness to one you deeply admire should appear in your work, I wish for you to be like a son, not a mere portrait. For a portrait is a lifeless thing. "What then?" you may ask. "Will it not be discerned whose style you are imitating, whose reasoning, and whose ideas?" I think sometimes it may not even be discernible, if the likeness is true. For a genuine likeness impresses its own form upon all the features it has derived from its chosen model, blending them into a unified whole. Do you not see how many voices comprise a chorus?

[9] Yet from them all, a single sound is produced. Some voices are high, some low, and others in between. Women's tones join with men's, and flutes interweave their notes throughout.

[10] In that chorus, the sound of each individual voice is obscured, yet the harmony of all rings forth. I speak of the chorus as the ancient philosophers knew it. In our productions today, there are more singers on stage than there were spectators in the theaters of old. When a throng of singers fills every aisle, and the orchestra pit is encircled by brass players, and every type of flute and instrument resounds from the stage, a unified melody arises from the discord.

This is how I wish our minds to be: possessed of many skills, much wisdom, and examples from many eras, all working together in concert.

[11] "But how," you ask, "can this be accomplished?" Through constant devotion; if we take no action except what reason dictates. If you are willing to listen to reason, it will tell you: Abandon those things which have long enticed you, for which you rush about. Abandon riches, for they are either a danger to possess or a burden. Abandon the pleasures of the body and mind; they soften and weaken you. Abandon ambition; it is a swollen, empty, and fickle thing, having no limit, as worried about seeing someone ahead as behind[2]. Ambition suffers from envy, and indeed from a double envy; you see, then, how wretched one must be, if he both envies and is envied.

[12] You marvel at the mansions of the powerful, the tumultuous

mob crowding their doorsteps paying respects? They hold many insults for you as you enter, and even more once inside. Pass by those storied steps of the wealthy and their lofty, grand entryways; you will stand there not only on a precipice, but on slippery ground. Direct yourself instead toward wisdom and seek out her most tranquil yet expansive domains.

[13] Whatever seems to tower above in human affairs, however small it may be and however much it stands out compared to the lowest - the paths to reach it are still difficult and steep. The way to the peak of dignity is arduous; but if you are willing to scale this summit, to which Fortune herself bows down, you will indeed look down upon all that is considered most exalted, yet you will still come to the top along level ground. Farewell.

---

1. Virgil, Georgics 4.164-165.
2. The Latin here is uncertain. Some manuscripts say "worried that it sees itself behind" rather than "worried about seeing someone behind."

LETTER 85

COUNTERING OBJECTIONS TO STOIC DOCTRINE

[1] I HAD SPARED YOU, LUCILIUS, AND PASSED OVER WHATEVER KNOTTY points remained, content to give you but a taste of what our school teaches: that virtue alone suffices for the perfection of the happy life. Yet now you bid me include every argument, whether invented by our school or devised to criticize it. Were I to comply, this would be not a letter, but a book. I swear to you again and again, this sort of argumentation brings me no delight. I am ashamed to enter the fray armed only with a pen to champion the cause of gods and men.

[2] "The wise man is also temperate. The temperate man is also steadfast. The steadfast man is unperturbed. The unperturbed man is free from sadness. The man free from sadness is happy. Therefore, the wise man is happy, and wisdom suffices for a happy life."

[3] Some Peripatetics respond to this syllogism by interpreting "unperturbed," "steadfast," and "free from sadness" to mean one who is rarely and only moderately perturbed, not one who never is. Likewise, they say a man is called "free from sadness" when he is not prone to sadness nor often or excessively overcome by this failing. For they deny it is in human nature for a mind to be entirely immune to sadness. The wise man is not vanquished by grief but is yet touched by it—and so forth, splitting hairs in defense of their school.

[4] With these arguments they do not banish the emotions but merely temper them. Yet how little do we grant the wise man if he is merely stronger than the weakest, more joyful than the gloomiest, more self-controlled than the most dissolute, and greater than the basest? What if Ladas[1], marveling at his own speed, were to look back at the lame and feeble?

> *She could skim the topmost blades of grass*
> *Untouched, nor bruise the tender ears of grain with her*
> > *race.*
> *Wafted high, she could course the middle sea*
> *Nor dip her speeding feet in its swelling surge.*

This is swiftness judged by its own merits, not praised by comparison with the slowest. Would you deem a man healthy who has but a mild fever? Good health does not mean a moderate illness.

[5] "But," they say, "the wise man is called unperturbed in the way that pitted olives are called 'pitless'—not that there is no hardness in their kernels, but there is less of it." False! For in the good man I do not understand a diminution of evils, but a complete absence of them; there must be none at all, not merely small ones. For if there are any, they will grow and at times impede him. Just as a large, fully developed cataract blinds the eyes, so a moderate one disturbs them.

[6] If you allow the wise man any passions at all, his reason will be no match for them and will be swept away as if by a torrential stream —especially since you assign to him not one passion with which to struggle, but all of them. A mob of even moderate vices has more power than the violence of any one great vice.

[7] He has a desire for money, but only in moderation. He has ambition, but it is not inflamed. He has a temper, but it can be placated. He has inconsistency, but it is less fickle and changeable. He has lust, but not of a crazed sort. It would be better to deal with a man who had one vice in its entirety than with one who had all vices, albeit to a lesser degree.

[8] Moreover, it makes no difference how great a passion is;

however great it is, it knows not how to obey, it does not accept advice. Just as no animal obeys reason, neither wild beast nor tame and gentle one (for their nature is deaf to persuasion), so the passions do not follow or listen, however small they are. Tigers and lions never cast off their wildness; they may lower it at times, but when you least expect it, their softened fierceness is roused again. Vices never genuinely grow tame.

[9] Furthermore, if reason prevails, the passions will not even begin; if they begin against the will of reason, they will persist against its will. For it is easier to stop them at the outset than to control their force once started. Therefore, this "moderation" is both false and useless—it should be regarded the same as if someone said we should be mad in moderation, or ill in moderation.

[10] Only in the case of virtue is no moderation possible; the evils of the mind, once they have become chronic and hardened (we call them diseases) are beyond control—for example, greed, cruelty, and unrestrained power. Therefore, the passions, too, are beyond control.

[11] For it is from the passions that we pass over to the vices I have named. Again, if you grant any authority to sadness, fear, desire, and the other wrong impulses, they will cease to be under our control. Why? Because the means of stimulating them lie outside ourselves. And so they will grow in proportion to the magnitude of the causes by which they are excited. Fear will grow greater the more numerous or the nearer the objects of terror it beholds, and desire will become sharper in proportion as the hope of a greater gain has summoned it to action.

[12] If the existence of the passions is not in our power, neither is the extent of their power; for if you have permitted them to get a start, they will increase along with their causes, and they will be as great as they grow to be. Moreover, add now the fact that these passions, however small they are, grow greater. Destructive things never maintain a limit. However trifling diseases may be at the start, they creep on apace; and sometimes the slightest aggravation of ill health overthrows the enfeebled body.

[13] But what folly it is to imagine that we can termini passions

whose beginnings lie outside our control! How have I the power to bring to an end that which I lacked the power to prevent from getting started—when it is easier to exclude than to suppress?

[14] Some have made a distinction, saying: "The temperate and prudent person is tranquil in the disposition and state of his mind, but not in outcome. For as far as the state of his own mind, he is not perturbed, saddened or afraid, but many external causes befall him which bring disturbance."

[15] What they mean is this: a person is not irascible, but still gets angry sometimes; he is not timid, but still fears sometimes. That is, he lacks the vice of fear but not the emotion. But if this is accepted, then through frequent occurrence, fear will turn into a vice, and anger admitted into the mind will unravel that state of a mind obedient to reason.

[16] Moreover, if one does not disregard external causes when they come and fears something, then when it is necessary to bravely face weapons and fires for the sake of country, laws and liberty, he will go out hesitantly with a shrinking spirit.

[17] But this inconsistency of mind does not befall the wise person. I judge that we must also be careful not to mix together two things which should be proven separately. For it is deduced on its own that the good is solely that which is honorable; again on its own, that virtue is sufficient for a happy life. If the honorable is the only good, all concede that virtue is enough for living happily. Conversely, if virtue alone makes one happy, it does not follow that the honorable is the only good.

[18] Xenocrates and Speusippus think that one can become happy by virtue alone, but that the honorable is not the only good. Epicurus also judges that one who has virtue is happy, but that virtue itself is not enough for a happy life, because what makes one happy is the pleasure that comes from virtue, not virtue itself. [This is] an inept distinction. For he denies that virtue is ever without pleasure; so if it is always joined to it and inseparable, it is sufficient alone. For it has pleasure with it, without which it is not, even when alone.

[19] But it is absurd to say that one will indeed be happy with virtue alone but not perfectly happy. I do not see how this can be. For the happy life contains within itself a perfect, unsurpassable good. If this is so, it is perfectly happy.

If the life of the gods has nothing greater or better, and the happy life is divine, then it has nothing to which it can be raised further.

[20] Moreover, if the happy life lacks nothing, then every happy life is perfect - and a life that is happy is also supremely happy. Do you have any doubt that the happy life is the supreme good? Therefore, if it possesses the supreme good, it is supremely happy. Just as the supreme good admits of no addition (for what could be above the supreme?), neither does the happy life, which cannot exist without the supreme good. But if you suggest that one person is happier than another, you will also be suggesting that this other person is much happier. You will be creating innumerable degrees of the supreme good, when I understand the supreme good to be that which has no degree above it.

[21] If someone is less happy than someone else, it follows that he will desire the life of that happier person more than his own. But the happy person prefers nothing to his own life. Either of these alternatives is incredible: that something remains for the happy person which he would prefer to his present life, or that he does not prefer that which is better than what he already has. The wiser he is, the more he will strive for what is best and desire to attain it by every means. But how can one be happy who can still desire - indeed, must desire?

[22] Let me tell you what causes this error: people are ignorant that the happy life is a unity. Its quality, not its size, establishes it in the ideal state. And so it makes no difference whether it is long or short, spread out or more confined, distributed among many places and parts or concentrated in one. If someone tries to evaluate it by number, measure, or parts, he deprives it of its distinctive quality. And what is the distinctive quality of the happy life? Its fullness.

[23] The goal of eating and drinking, I suppose, is to satisfy

hunger and thirst. One person eats more, another less - what difference does it make? Both are now satisfied. One person drinks more,
another less - what difference does it make? Neither is thirsty. This
person has lived more years, that one fewer - it makes no difference if
many years have made the one as happy as few have made the other.
The person whom you call less happy is not happy at all; the term
does not admit of diminution.

[24] "The brave man is without fear; he who is without fear is
without sadness; he who is without sadness is happy." This is a chain
of reasoning characteristic of our school [the Stoics]. But certain
objectors try to refute it as follows: "You Stoics are assuming as
admitted a premiss which is false and distinctly controverted, namely,
that the brave man is without fear." "What!" they say, "will the brave
man have no fear of evils that threaten him? That would be the mark
of a madman, a lunatic, rather than of a brave man." "What we mean,"
they say, "is that he will fear such things to a moderate degree, but not
to the extent of being absolutely free of fear."

[25] Those who argue thus find themselves mired once more in
the same quandary, holding that lesser vices take the place of virtues.
For one who feels fear, albeit more rarely and to a lesser degree, is not
free from moral failing, but merely afflicted less grievously. "But surely," they object, "I consider a person mad who does not dread
impending ills." What you say is true, if those things are in fact ills;
but if that person recognizes that they are not ills and judges moral
baseness alone to be evil, then they ought to face dangers with equanimity and scorn what others fear. Or if it is the mark of a fool and a
madman not to dread ills, then the wiser a person is, the more they
will feel dread.

[26] "So in your view," they say, "the brave person will offer themselves up to dangers." By no means; the brave will not dread those
things but will avoid them. Caution befits them, while fear does not.
"What then?" they ask, "Will they not dread death, imprisonment, fire,
all the other arrows of fortune?" No. For they know that those things
are not evils, but only seem so. They reckon all such things among
the bugbears that terrify human life.

[27] Go ahead and describe captivity, floggings, chains, destitution, the mangling of limbs by disease or violence, and whatever other misfortune you might add: the sage counts them all among the empty fears that frenzied minds conjure. Such things are to be dreaded by the timid. Or do you imagine something to be an evil, to which we must sometimes come of our own free will?

[28] Do you ask what is evil? It is yielding to those things called evils, and surrendering to them our own freedom, for the sake of which we should endure all things. Freedom perishes unless we despise those things that would place a yoke upon us. People would not be in doubt as to what befits a brave person if they understood what bravery is. For it is not reckless rashness, nor a love of danger, nor a fondness for things that inspire dread; rather, it is the knowledge to discern what is and is not evil. Bravery takes most diligent care for its own security, and likewise endures with utmost patience those things that wear a false appearance of evil.

[29] "What then? If a sword is held to the neck of the brave, if their body is pierced through now here, now there, if they see their own entrails in their lap, if, in order to feel the torment more keenly, they are allowed to recover before fresh blood is let into their dried-up veins - do they feel no fear?" That person does feel pain, you will say, do they not? Indeed they do feel pain. For no virtue relieves a person of sensation. But they do not feel dread; unconquered, they gaze down from on high at their own sufferings. Do you ask what their state of mind is then? It is like that of those urging comfort to a sick friend.

[30] "What is evil does harm; what does harm makes a person worse. But pain and poverty do not make a person worse; therefore they are not evils." "False," is the objection, "for what you propose does not follow; indeed not everything that does harm also makes a person worse. A storm and tempest do harm to a ship's pilot, yet they do not make the pilot a worse one for all that."

[31] Some of the Stoics respond to this objection as follows: a helmsman is made worse by storms and gales, because he cannot accomplish his intended goal and maintain his course; he is not made

worse in his skill, but in the execution of his work. To which the Peripatetic replies, "Therefore, poverty, pain, and anything else of that sort will also make the wise man worse. For while it will not rob him of his virtue, it will hinder his works."

[32] This would be rightly said, were the situation of a helmsman and a wise man not dissimilar. For the wise man's purpose in conducting his life is not to accomplish what he attempts at all costs, but to do everything rightly. The helmsman's purpose, however, is to bring his ship into port at all costs. The [practical] arts are servants; they must deliver what they promise. Wisdom is the mistress and ruler; the arts serve life, wisdom commands it.

[33] I think the objection should be answered differently: neither the helmsman's skill nor the very practice of his skill is made worse by any storm. The helmsman did not promise you good fortune, but beneficial service and knowledge of steering the ship. This becomes more apparent the more some random force opposes him. The helmsman who can say, "Neptune, I will never steer this ship except rightly" has satisfied his art; a storm does not impede the helmsman's work, but his success.

[34] "What then?" he says, "Does the circumstance that prevents the helmsman from reaching port, that renders his efforts futile, that either drives him back or detains and disables him, not harm him?" Not as a helmsman, but as a voyager; otherwise he is not a helmsman at all. It hinders the helmsman's art so little that it even exhibits it; for, as they say, anyone is a helmsman in calm weather. These things harm the voyage, not the one directing it, insofar as he is its director.

[35] A helmsman has two roles: one in common with all who have boarded the same ship—he too is a passenger; the other unique to him—he is the helmsman. The storm harms him as a passenger, not as a helmsman.

[36] Moreover, the helmsman's skill is a good that belongs to others; it pertains to those whom he conveys, just as a doctor's skill pertains to those he cures. The good of the wise man is shared—it belongs both to those with whom he lives and also to himself. And so

a helmsman is perhaps harmed when his service, promised to others, is hindered by a storm; but a wise man is not harmed by poverty, by pain, or by the other storms of life.

[37] For not all of the sage's works are prohibited, only those pertaining to others; he himself is always in action, then most mighty in effect, when fortune opposes him. For then he carries out the very business of wisdom, which we have said is both the good of others and his own.

[38] Moreover, he is not prohibited from benefiting others even when some necessities press upon him. Poverty may prohibit him from teaching how the republic should be managed, but it teaches him how poverty itself should be handled. His work extends through his whole life.

Thus no fortune, no circumstance, excludes the acts of the sage. For the very thing by which he is prohibited from doing other things, is what he does. He is suited to both circumstances: a guide of good things, a conqueror of bad.

[39] In this way, I say, he has trained himself to display virtue just as much in favorable conditions as in adversity, and to gaze not at virtue's raw material, but at virtue itself. And so neither poverty nor pain nor anything else that turns away the inexperienced and drives them headlong, prohibits him. Do you think he is oppressed by evils?

[40] He makes use of them. Phidias knew how to make statues not only from ivory; he made them from bronze. If you had offered him marble or an even cheaper material, he would have made the best that could be made from it. So the sage, if allowed, will unfold virtue in riches; if not, in poverty. If possible, in his homeland; if not, in exile. If possible, as a commander; if not, as a soldier. If possible, in wholeness of body; if not, in physical weakness. Whatever fortune he receives, he will make something memorable from it.

[41] There are skilled tamers of wild beasts who subdue the fiercest animals, terrifying to behold, to endure a man's touch, and not content merely to have driven out their ferocity, they tame them even to share their quarters. The lion's trainer thrusts his hand into

its mouth, the tiger is kissed by its keeper, the tiny Ethiopian bids the elephant to sink down on its knees and walk a tightrope. In the same way, the sage is skilled in taming evils. Pain, want, disgrace, imprisonment, exile - everywhere dreaded - when they encounter the sage, are rendered tame. Farewell.

---

1. A famously swift runner in ancient Greece.

LETTER 86

REFLECTIONS ON SCIPIO'S VILLA AND THE EXCESS OF LUXURY

[1] As I lie here in the very villa of Scipio Africanus, having paid homage to his spirit and the altar which I suspect to be the tomb of so great a man, I write these words to you. I am convinced that his soul has returned to the heavens from whence it came, not because he led great armies (for Cambyses the madman also had these, and used his madness to good effect), but because of his exceptional moderation and sense of duty, which I judge more admirable when he left his homeland than when he defended it. Either Scipio had to remain in Rome, or Rome had to remain free.

[2] "I wish," he said, "to take nothing away from the laws, nothing from our traditions. Let the rule of justice be equal among all citizens. Enjoy my good service without me, O homeland. I was the reason for your liberty, and I shall also be the proof of it. I depart, if I have grown beyond what is expedient for you."

[3] How could I not marvel at this greatness of soul, by which he withdrew into voluntary exile and unburdened the state? Things had been brought to such a pass that either liberty would wrong Scipio, or Scipio would wrong liberty. Neither was righteous. And so he yielded to the laws and retired to Liternum, intending to credit his exile to the Republic as much as Hannibal's defeat.

[4] I saw a villa built of quarried stone, surrounded by a wall, groves, and towers rising on either side to defend the villa, with a cistern lying below the buildings and gardens, ample enough to serve even an army. The bathhouse was cramped and dimly lit in the ancient style, for our ancestors did not believe a bath was warm unless it was dark. I thus took great pleasure in contemplating the ways of Scipio and comparing them to our own.

[5] In this nook, that scourge of Carthage to whom Rome owes her only being captured once, would wash his body when weary from rustic labors. For he worked the land himself, as was the custom of men of old, to keep himself in fighting trim. Beneath this dirty roof he stood; this cheap floor supported him.

[6] But now, who could bear to bathe in such simplicity? One would think himself impoverished and unkempt, unless his walls glowed with large and costly mirrors, unless Alexandrian marbles were offset by inlays of Numidian stone, unless an intricate molding, richly varied like a painting, ran round the walls, unless the ceiling were hidden by glass, unless Thasian stone (once a rarity even in temples) lined the pools into which we let down our bodies, wasted by copious sweating[1], unless the water poured from silver spigots.

[7] And I have been speaking so far of the ordinary pipes; what when I come to those of the freedmen? What a wealth of statues, of columns that support nothing, but are placed for decoration and expense! What quantities of water cascading noisily down steps! We have become so luxurious that we will tread on nothing but precious stones.

[8] In this bathhouse of Scipio's, there are the tiniest of cracks, more than windows, cut out of the stone wall to let in light without weakening the structure. But nowadays they call baths "moth-holes" unless they're built to admit the sun all day long through huge windows, unless people can both bathe and get a tan at the same time, unless they have a view of fields and sea from the bathing-pool. And so the baths that drew crowds and admiration when they were first opened are now rejected and consigned to the ranks of the old-

fashioned whenever luxury dreams up some new excess to eclipse itself.

[9] In the old days, though, baths were few and far between, with no decoration to speak of. Why embellish something that costs a quarter-cent to use, a functional facility, not a pleasure dome? The water didn't keep pouring in, always fresh as if from a hot spring, and they didn't think it mattered how crystal-clear the water was that they washed their dirt off in.

[10] But good gods, what a pleasure it is to enter those dim baths with their common stucco walls, knowing that it was a Cato, a Fabius Maximus, or one of the Cornelii who temperated the water with his own hand! For this, too, was a duty that the most eminent aediles performed - inspecting the places that welcomed the public, demanding cleanliness and a temperature both comfortable and healthy, not like the one recently invented that's more like a conflagration, so much so that a slave convicted of some crime ought to be bathed alive. These days there seems to be no difference between the baths being on fire and them being heated.

[11] How some people nowadays condemn Scipio as a boor for not letting daylight into his caldarium through wide windows, for not stewing himself in plenty of sunlight or taking his time to digest his food right there in the bath. Poor, unfortunate man - he didn't know how to live! He didn't bathe in filtered water, but often in cloudy water, virtually muddy when it rained harder. It made little difference to him if he bathed like that; he went there to wash off sweat, not to anoint himself with perfume.

[12] What sort of comments do you think some people today would make? "I don't envy Scipio; he truly lived in exile if that's how he bathed." In fact, if you only knew, he didn't bathe daily. For as those who've handed down the old customs of the city say, they washed their arms and legs every day, obviously the parts that got dirty from work, but bathed all over only once every eight days. At this point someone will say: "Well, it's clear to me they were absolutely filthy back then. How do you think they smelled?" Of military

service, of hard work, of being a man. Now that fancy baths have been invented, people are dirtier than ever.

[13] In describing a man infamous and excessively notable for his decadence, what does Horatius Flaccus say?

"Buccillus reeks of perfume."

If you were to present Buccillus now, it would be as if a goat reeked—he would be in the position of Gargonius, whom that same Horatius contrasted with Buccillus. It is not enough to apply perfume, unless it is renewed two or three times a day, lest it fade on the body. What's more, they glory in this scent as if it were their own!

[14] If these things seem too grim for you, you will attribute it to my villa, where I learned from Aegialus, a most diligent head of household (for he is now the owner of this land), that an old arbor can be transplanted. This is necessary for us old men to learn, none of whom plants an olive grove for any other reason[2].

[15] That tree will also protect you, which,

"Slow-growing, will make shade for late-born descendants,"

as our own Vergil says, who considered not what would be said most truly, but most fittingly, and wished not to teach farmers, but to delight readers.

[16] Now, to pass over everything else, I will note down this thing that I had to discover today. Vergil writes:

"In spring is the sowing of beans; then you too, alfalfa, the crumbling
Furrows receive, and millet's annual care comes due."

You may judge from this whether those crops are to be planted at one time and whether the sowing of both is in spring: it is the month of June in which I write to you, already sloping toward July; on the same day I saw them reaping beans and sowing millet.

[17] I will return to the olive grove, which I saw transplanted in two ways: the trunks of large trees with their branches trimmed and reduced to one foot along with their own ball of roots, once the roots were cut off, leaving only the head itself from which they had hung. He dipped this in manure, lowered it into a trench, then not only heaped earth upon it, but trampled it and pressed it down.

[18] He claims that nothing is more effective than this method of planting, as he calls it, for keeping out cold and wind. Furthermore, the tree is less disturbed, allowing the emerging roots to spread out and take hold of the soil. While still soft and tenuously attached, even a light disturbance can tear them away[3]. Before covering it, he scrapes[4] the turnip-like[5] part of the tree. For, as he says, new roots sprout from any part of the bare wood. No more than three or four feet of the trunk should protrude above ground. It will soon be clothed with growth from the bottom, and unlike old olive groves, no large part will be withered and shriveled.

[19] The other method of planting was this: he planted stout branches without hard bark, such as those of young trees tend to be, in the same way. These are a bit slower to rise, but when they have sprouted like a seedling, they have nothing disagreeable or sorry-looking about them.

[20] I have also seen this: an old vine transplanted from its own arbor. Its hair-like roots, if possible, should also be gathered up, and then the vine should be spread out more freely, so that it may take root even from the main stem. And I have seen them planted not only in February but even at the end of March; they take hold and embrace elm-trees not their own.

[21] He says that all those trees that are, so to speak, on a large stalk, should be watered with cistern water, and if this helps, we have rain under our control.

I do not intend to lecture you at greater length, lest, just as Aegialus made me his adversary, I make you mine. Farewell.

---

1. Some manuscripts say "wasted", others "emptied out".

2. The following corrupt passage has been omitted: quod vidi illud arborum trimum et quadrimum fastidiendi fructus aut deponere.
3. The manuscript reads "ceteras" or "conteras" here, but later manuscripts and Erasmus suggest the correction to "cereas," meaning soft or pliable.
4. Pincianus corrects the manuscript reading "radix" (root) to "radit" (he scrapes).
5. Some manuscripts read "parum" (too little) here, but Ludwig von Jan suggests the emendation to "rapum" (turnip).

LETTER 87

THE EQUALITY OF GOODS
AND THE MARKS OF THE
WISE MAN

[1] I suffered a shipwreck before ever setting foot on a ship. I won't elaborate on how it happened, lest you think this is one of those Stoic paradoxes - though I assure you, none of them are false or as astonishing as they first appear. I can prove it to you if you wish, or even if you don't. What this journey has taught me is how many unnecessary things we possess, and how easily we could do without them if we put our minds to it. When necessity forces us to shed these extras, we don't even feel their absence.

[2] Accompanied by a handful of slaves (as many as could fit in one carriage), my dear Maximus and I have been living most joyously these past two days, carrying nothing except what's on our persons. My mattress lies on the ground, and I upon it. One cloak serves as a blanket, the other a coverlet.

[3] As for lunch, nothing could be more frugal. It took no time at all to prepare, and consisted of dried figs and writing tablets - the figs serve as a relish if I have bread, or in place of bread if I don't. Each day feels like a fresh new year to me, rendered auspicious and joyful by virtuous thoughts and greatness of spirit. The soul is never grander than when it has cast off external encumbrances, made

peace with itself by fearing nothing, and found riches by craving nothing.

[4] The carriage I'm riding in is a rustic affair, its axles creaking in protest with every turn of the wheel. The mule driver is barefoot, and not on account of the summer heat. I can barely bring myself to acknowledge this ramshackle conveyance as my own[1]. A perverse sense of shame over doing what's right persists in me. Whenever we encounter a grander equipage, I blush involuntarily - proof that the principles I endorse and praise have not yet taken firm and unshakable root. The man who's ashamed of a shabby carriage will boast of a costly one.

[5] I still have progress to make. I do not yet have the courage to openly embrace frugality; I still worry about what other travelers think. What I ought to do is proclaim, in defiance of the whole human race: "You're mad, you're deluded, you're stunned by superfluities! You judge no one by their true worth. When taking stock of a man's wealth, you, who are the most painstaking of accountants, reckon up the following items to decide whether to lend him money or do him favors (for you now record even kindnesses as expenditures):

[6] 'He has extensive properties, but he's deeply in debt. He has a beautiful house, but it was bought with borrowed money. No one could put on a finer spectacle with a retinue of slaves, but he cannot pay his bills. If he settles with his creditors, he'll have nothing left.' You ought to investigate how much of a man's wealth is truly his own."

[7] You think a man is rich because his gold plate goes with him even on his travels, because he farms land in every province, because he unfurls a large account book, because he owns as much land near the city as would stir envy if held in the wastelands of Apulia. When you have said all this, he is still poor. Why? Because he is in debt. "How much?" you ask. Everything. Unless perhaps you think it matters whether one has borrowed from another man or from Fortune.

[8] What is the point of fat mules all of one color? What of those

engraved carriages? "Trotting horses decked in purple and embroidered carpets, with golden necklaces hanging down on their chests, champing yellow gold under their teeth[2]." These things can make neither the master nor the mule any better.

[9] Marcus Cato the Censor, whose birth was as beneficial to the republic as Scipio's—for the one waged war on our enemies, the other on our morals—used to ride a nag, with saddle bags thrown over it so he could carry his necessaries. Oh how I would love for him to meet now on the road one of these fancy dandies with his outriders and Numidians and clouds of dust before him! No doubt this man would seem more refined and better attended than Marcus Cato— this man who, amid those dainty outfits, is pondering whether to apply himself to the sword or the carving knife.

[10] What a glory to the age it was to be satisfied with a single horse for a triumphal general, a censor, and above all, a Cato—and not even a whole horse at that! For saddlebags hanging down on either side took up part of the mount. Would you not therefore prefer that single steed, rubbed down by Cato himself, to all the plump cobs and Spanish jennets and pacers?

[11] I see there will be no end to this topic unless I make one for myself. So at this point I will fall silent on these matters which, without doubt, he[3] divined would be in the future just as they are now—he who first called them "hindrances." Now I want to pass on to you a very few more of our school's arguments pertaining to virtue, which we maintain suffices for the happy life.

[12] "That which is good makes men good. For in the art of music too, that which is good makes the musician. The fortuitous does not make a good man. Therefore, fortuitous things are not goods." The Peripatetics reply to this by saying that the initial premise is false. "Men do not necessarily become good by that which is good," they say. "In music, there is something good, like a flute, a string, or some instrument suited to the practice of music. Yet none of these makes the musician."

[13] Here we will respond: "You do not understand how we have positioned that which is good in music. For we do not say that it is

what instructs the musician, but what it creates; you come to the furnishings of the art, not to the art itself. If there is anything good in the art of music itself, it will surely make the musician."

[14] I want to make this even clearer now. The good in the art of music is spoken of in two ways: one, by which the work of the musician is aided, and the other, by which the art itself is aided. Instruments, pipes, organs, and strings pertain to the work, but not to the art itself. For the artist exists even without these; perhaps he cannot use the art without them. This is not equally twofold in man; for the good of man and of life are the same.

[15] "That which can happen to anyone most contemptible and most vile is not good. But wealth happens both to the pimp and to the trainer of gladiators. Therefore, they are not goods." "What you propose is false," they say, "for we see goods happening to the most humble in grammar, medicine, and the art of steering."

[16] But these arts do not profess greatness of soul; they do not rise to the heights nor do they despise the things that depend on chance. Virtue elevates man and places him above the things dear to mortals; it neither desires too much nor dreads the things that are called good or evil. Chelidon, one of Cleopatra's effeminate courtiers, possessed a grand estate. Recently, Natalis, a man of such a foul tongue and impure character (in whose mouth women would cleanse themselves), was the heir of many and had many heirs. What then? Did money make him impure or did he defile the money? Money falls into some men as a coin falls into the sewer.

[17] Virtue stands above such things. It is valued by its own standard. It judges none of these things, however they may come about, to be good. Medicine and navigation do not wipe out awe for such things for themselves and their own. One who is not a good man can nevertheless be a doctor, a helmsman, a grammarian - by Hercules, as much as a cook! Things come to you not as you would wish, but as you are.

[18] A treasury is worth as much as it holds; nay, it comes to be valued by what it holds. Who puts any value on a full purse except that which the amount of money stowed in it has effected? The same

thing happens to the possessors of great estates - their possessions and trappings are accessories to them.

Why, then, is the wise man great? Because he has a great soul. It is true, therefore, that what can happen to the most contemptible person is not a good.

[19] Therefore, I will never call pain a good; even a cicada or a flea possesses that. Nor will I deem the absence of pain and vexation a good - what creature is more idle than a worm? You ask what it is that produces a wise man? The same thing that produces a god. You must grant the wise man something divine, heavenly, magnificent. The good does not fall to every man's share, nor does it suffer any chance possessor.

[20] See how

Each clime what fruits and crops adorn,
Here golden corn, there luscious clusters born.
Elsewhere fruit-trees and herbs spontaneous grow,
Mark, how with saffron scents fair Tmolus glows!
What ivory India, frankincense Sheba sends!
While naked Chalybes produce their iron ore.

[21] Such products are apportioned to various regions so that human commerce might be mutually necessary, each having need to seek from the other. But the highest good has its own abode. It is not born where ivory is, nor where iron. Do you ask where the seat of the highest good is found? In the soul. Unless the soul is pure and holy, it cannot contain God.

[22] "Good does not spring from evil. But riches spring from greed. Therefore, riches are not a good." "It is not true," they say, "that good cannot be born from evil. For money comes from sacrilege and theft. So although sacrilege and theft are evil, they are only evil because they work more harm than good. For they produce gain, but with fear, anxiety, and torments of mind and body."

[23] Whoever says this must perforce admit that though sacrilege is an evil because it works much evil, yet it is also partly good because

it accomplishes some good. What can be more monstrous than this? And yet, we have altogether convinced mankind that sacrilege, theft, and adultery are to be regarded as among the goods. How many there are who do not blush at theft, how many who boast of having committed adultery! For petty sacrilege is punished, but sacrilege on a grand scale is honored with triumphal processions.

[24] Moreover, sacrilege, if it is wholly good in some respect, will also be honorable and will be called right conduct - for it is an action of our own choosing[4]. But no human being's mind can accept this conclusion.

Therefore, goods cannot spring from evil. For if, as you object, sacrilege is an evil for the single reason that it brings great harm, then if you but absolve sacrilege of its punishment and pledge it immunity, sacrilege will become wholly good. And yet the worst punishment for crime lies in the crime itself.

[25] You are mistaken, I say, if you put off those punishments to the executioner or the prison; they are punished immediately when they are committed, indeed, while they are being committed. Good does not arise from evil any more than a fig grows from an olive tree. Things born resemble their seed; good things cannot degenerate. Just as what is honorable does not arise from what is base, neither does good arise from evil. For honorable and good are one and the same.

[26] Some of our school respond to this as follows: "Let us suppose that money is good from whatever source it is obtained; nevertheless, money that comes from sacrilege is not therefore derived from sacrilege, even if it is obtained from sacrilege. Understand it this way: in the same urn there is both gold and a viper. If you take the gold from the urn, it is not, I say, because there is also a viper there that the urn gives me gold, but it gives gold even though it also contains a viper. In the same way, profit comes from sacrilege, not because sacrilege is shameful and criminal, but because it also involves profit. Just as in that urn the viper is an evil, not the gold that lies beside the viper, so in sacrilege the crime is an evil, not the profit."

[27] I disagree with them[5], for the cases are quite dissimilar. In the one instance I can take the gold without the viper, but in the other I

cannot make the profit without committing the sacrilege. The profit here is not placed beside the crime but is mixed up with it.

[28] "That which leads us into many evils while we are pursuing it is not a good. But while we are pursuing riches we fall into many evils; therefore, riches are not a good." "Your proposition," they say, "has two meanings, one: that we fall into many evils while we are seeking to obtain riches. But we also fall into many evils while we are seeking to obtain virtue. Someone seeking to advance his studies has suffered shipwreck, another has been captured.

[29] "The other meaning is this: that through which we fall into evils is not a good. It will not logically follow from this proposition that we fall into evils through riches or through pleasures; otherwise, if we fall into many evils through riches, riches are not only not a good, but they are an evil; but you say merely that they are not a good. Moreover," they say, "you concede that riches are of some use. You reckon them among the advantages of life; and yet by the same reasoning they will not even be an advantage, for through them many disadvantages come to us."

[30] To this, some reply: "You are mistaken to attribute disadvantages to wealth. Riches harm no one; a person is damaged either by their own folly or by another's wickedness, just as a sword kills no one by itself—it is merely the tool of the killer. Wealth does not harm you, even if you are harmed on account of your wealth."

[31] Posidonius, in my view, puts it better. He says that riches are the cause of evils, not because they actively do anything themselves, but because they spur on those who will act wrongly. For there is a difference between an efficient cause, which must do harm directly, and a precedent cause. Wealth provides this precedent cause—it puffs up the spirit, breeds arrogance, and draws envy, warping the mind so much that we take pleasure in money's reputation even when it will bring us harm.

[32] But all true goods ought to be free of fault. They are pure and do not corrupt or unsettle the mind. They elevate and expand it, yes, but without making it swell. Things that are truly good instill confidence, while wealth produces recklessness. Genuine goods grant

greatness of soul; riches lead to insolence—which is nothing more than a false appearance of greatness.

[33] "In that case," one objects, "riches are not only not a good, but are a positive evil." They would indeed be an evil if they harmed directly, if, as I said, they provided an efficient cause. But as it stands, they offer a precedent cause—and one that not only provokes the mind but actively attracts it. For they present a semblance of good that most find convincing, an illusion of truth.

[34] Virtue too has its precedent cause: it attracts envy. Many are resented for their wisdom, many for their justice. But virtue contains neither an efficient cause for envy nor a convincing semblance of one. On the contrary, the appearance virtue presents to the mind is one that rightly summons admiration and affection.

[35] Posidonius says we should put the question as follows: "Things that grant the mind neither greatness, nor confidence, nor freedom from care are not goods. But riches, good health, and their like accomplish none of these things. Therefore, they are not goods." He presses this line of questioning further, as follows: "Things that create insolence, conceit, and arrogance, rather than greatness of soul, confidence, and freedom from care, are evils. But we are driven to such vices by the gifts of fortune. Therefore, these are not goods."

[36] "By that reasoning," one retorts, "those things will not even qualify as advantages." The conditions for advantages differ from those for goods. An advantage is something that offers more utility than trouble. But a good must be unspoiled and entirely harmless. Something is not a good just because its benefits outweigh its drawbacks, but only if it is solely beneficial.

[37] Moreover, advantage pertains both to animals and imperfect humans and fools. Thus, it can be mixed with disadvantage, but it is called an advantage when judged by its greater part. The good pertains to the wise man alone; it must be inviolate.

[38] Take heart; only one knot remains for you, but it is a Herculean one: "Good does not arise from evil. Riches arise from many poverties; therefore, riches are not a good." Our school does not recognize this interrogation, but the Peripatetics both contrive it and

resolve it. Posidonius says this sophism, tossed around in all the dialecticians' schools, is refuted by Antipater thus: "Poverty is spoken of not through possession, but through subtraction or, as the ancients said, deprivation [Greek: kata stērēsin]. It speaks not of what one has, but of what one does not have. And so, nothing can be filled from many emptinesses; riches are made by many things, not many lacks. You understand poverty," he says, "differently than you ought. For poverty is not what possesses few things, but what does not possess many things; thus it is spoken of not from what it has, but from what it lacks."

[39] I could more easily express what I mean if there were a Latin word for anexistentia [Greek: anhuparxia]. Antipater assigns this meaning to poverty; I do not see what else poverty may be than the possession of little. We shall consider this another time, when we have ample leisure - what is the substance of riches and of poverty. But then, too, we shall consider whether it might be better to soften poverty, to pull down the brow of wealth, than to quibble about words as though the matter were already decided.

[40] Let us imagine we have been called to an assembly; a law is proposed to abolish riches. Are we to persuade or dissuade with these interrogations? With these, are we to bring it about that the Roman people should seek and praise poverty, the foundation and cause of their empire, but fear their own riches? That they should reflect how they found these among the vanquished, how ambition and largess and tumults burst into their most holy and temperate city from this source, how the spoils of nations are displayed too luxuriously, and what one people has snatched from all can more easily be snatched by all from one?

[41] It is better to persuade on this basis and to storm the emotions than to quibble. Let us speak more bravely if we can; if not, more openly. Farewell.

----

1. The manuscript tradition is divided here. One variant reads "velim" (I'm willing), the other "nolim" (I'm unwilling).
2. A quote from an unknown poet.

3. Presumably referring back to Cato.
4. Some scholars suggest an alternative reading: "it will be called honorable; for an honorable and right action is an action of our own choosing."
5. Some later manuscripts read "a quibus dissentio" here instead of simply "a quibus" found in earlier copies.

LETTER 88

THE PLACE OF LIBERAL STUDIES IN THE PURSUIT OF WISDOM

[1] You wish to know my thoughts on liberal studies. I do not respect them or count any study good that is undertaken for financial gain. Such studies are merely hired arts, useful only insofar as they prepare the intellect without occupying it for long. One should linger on them only as long as the mind is incapable of higher things - they are our prep work, not our life's work.

[2] You see why they are called "liberal" studies: because they are worthy of a free person. But there is only one study that is truly liberal, that which makes one free - namely, the pursuit of wisdom. It is lofty, steadfast, and magnanimous. The other so-called liberal arts are trivial and childish. Surely you cannot believe that there is any good in studies whose teachers you see to be the most disreputable and vile of men? We should not be learning such things - we should have learned them and moved on.

Some have questioned whether the liberal arts make one a good man. They do not even profess or aim at imparting such knowledge.

[3] The grammarian concerns himself with standards of speech and, if he wishes to go further afield, with histories - or at the outermost bounds of his domain, poetry. But which of these paves the way to virtue? Expounding on syllables, fussing over words, memorizing

stories and the rules and rhythms of verse - which of these rids one of fear, roots out desire, or reins in lust?

[4] The question is whether these arts teach virtue or not. If not, then they certainly do not even transmit it. If they do teach it, then they are philosophers. Do you want to know how far they are from taking their seat as teachers of virtue? Look how unlike each other are the things they study - and yet there would be a similarity if they were all teaching the same thing.

[5] Unless perhaps they would persuade you that Homer was a philosopher, using the very lines by which they argue that he was not. For at one moment they make him a Stoic, approving only of virtue, shunning pleasures, and not departing from morality even at the price of immortality. At another, they make him an Epicurean, praising the tranquility of a state at peace, and a life spent amidst feasts and song. Now they make him a Peripatetic, introducing three kinds of good; now an Academic, declaring all things uncertain. It is clear that none of these doctrines are in Homer, because they all are - for they are inconsistent with each other. Let us grant that Homer was a philosopher; evidently he became wise before he learned any poetry. Let us therefore learn the things that made Homer wise.

[6] To inquire which was older, Homer or Hesiod, is no more relevant than knowing why Hecuba, though younger than Helen, wore her years so badly. Really now, do you think it matters to investigate the respective ages of Achilles and Patroclus?

[7] You ask where Ulysses wandered, rather than taking pains to prevent our own constant wandering? There's no time to listen to whether he was tossed between Italy and Sicily, or beyond the world we know—for such an extensive wandering couldn't happen in such a confined space. The tempests of our own minds toss us daily, and our depravity drives us into all the ills of Ulysses. We're not lacking in beauty to entice the eyes, nor in enemies. On one side are wild monsters delighting in human blood; on another, the deceitful allurements of the ear; then shipwreck and all manner of adversities. Teach me this instead: how to love my country, my wife, my father; how to sail to these honorable ends, even after shipwreck.

[8] Why do you ask whether Penelope was chaste, or merely fooling her own time? Or if she suspected that man to be Ulysses before she knew? Teach me what chastity is, how great a good it is, and whether it resides in the body or the mind.

[9] I pass to the musician: you teach me how high and low notes harmonize, how a concord arises from the different tones of the strings. Accomplish rather that my mind be in harmony with itself, my resolutions not be discordant. You show me what modes are mournful; show me rather how not to utter a mournful note in adversity.

[10] The geometrician teaches me to measure estates, rather than teaching how to measure what suffices for a man. He teaches me to count and lends my fingers to avarice, rather than teaching that those calculations are irrelevant—that one whose vast holdings wear out the accountants is no happier. Indeed, how superfluous are the possessions of one who would be utterly miserable if compelled to tally up his own wealth!

[11] What good is it for me to know how to divide a plot of land, if I know not how to share with my brother? What benefit to precisely reckon the square feet of an acre, catching even what eludes the measuring rod, if a domineering neighbor saddens me by snatching a piece of my land? He teaches me how to lose nothing from my boundaries, but I wish to learn how to lose it all with cheer.

[12] "I am being driven out," he says, "from my paternal and ancestral lands." But tell me, who held that land before your grandfather? Can you work out whose it was, I won't even ask which man, but which people? You did not enter that estate as its owner, but as a tenant. And whose tenant are you? With good fortune, the heir's. Legal experts affirm that no public property can be acquired by use alone. This land you hold, that you call your own, belongs to the public—indeed, to all mankind.

[13] What an extraordinary skill you have! You know how to measure curved lines, to reduce any shape you encounter into a square. You chart the spaces between the stars—there is nothing that escapes your measurements. If you are such an expert, then measure

a man's soul. Tell me how great it is, or how small. You know what a straight line is, but how does this help you if you do not recognize what is straight in life?

[14] I come now to the one who boasts of his knowledge of heavenly bodies:

> *To what quarter cold Saturn's star withdraws,*
> *Through what celestial orbits Cyllenian fire wanders.[1]*

What good will this knowledge do? That I may worry when Saturn and Mars are in opposition, or when Mercury sets in the evening under Saturn's watchful gaze? Instead of learning this, why not learn that wherever those stars may be, they are propitious and unchangeable?

[15] The unbroken sequence of fate and its inescapable course governs all. The stars return through fixed stations and mark or move the outcomes of all things. But whether they cause whatever happens, how will understanding the immutable help you? Or if they merely signal events, what use is foreseeing what you cannot escape? Whether you know these things or not, [16] they will come to pass.

> *But if you note the swift sun and stars that follow*
> *In order, the morrow's hour will never deceive you,*
> *Nor will you be taken unawares by a cloudless night.*

Sufficient provision has been made to keep me safe from surprises.

[17] "Does the next hour not deceive me then? For what comes to the unknowing deceives." I may not know what will be, but I know what can be. From this knowledge, I will despair of nothing and anticipate everything. If some hardship is lessened, I consider it a blessing. The hour deceives me if it spares me, but not even then am I truly deceived. For just as I know anything can happen, I also know all will not necessarily occur. I undoubtedly look forward to favorable events, but I am prepared for the bad.

[18] In this matter, I must necessarily part ways with prescribed opinion. For I am not inclined to include painters among the liberal arts, any more than sculptors, marble-workers, or other ministers of luxury. I equally banish from these liberal studies wrestlers and the entirety of the oil-and-mud sciences. [Should I then also welcome perfumers, cooks, and others who lend their talents to our pleasures?][2] Tell me, what do those starving vomiters have to do with liberal pursuits, with their bodies fattened and their minds wasting away in torpor?

[19] Do we really believe that the following are liberal studies for our youth, when our ancestors exercised them in throwing spears, wielding wooden stakes, driving horses, and handling weapons? They taught their children nothing that could be learned lying down. But neither these nor those teach or nourish virtue. For what good is it to control a horse and temper its course with the bridle, only to be carried away by the most unbridled passions? What good is it to overcome many in wrestling or boxing, but be overcome by anger?

[20] "What then," you ask, "do liberal studies contribute nothing to us?" They are of great value for other purposes, but nothing for virtue. For even those common arts that rely on manual skill, while greatly assisting in life's basic needs, nevertheless do not pertain to virtue. "Why then do we educate our sons in the liberal arts?" Not because they can confer virtue, but because they prepare the mind for embracing virtue. Just as that elementary education which the ancients called "literature," whereby the basics are imparted to boys, does not teach the liberal arts but paves the way for their subsequent acquisition, so too the liberal arts do not lead the mind to virtue, but rather clear the path for it.

[21] Posidonius says there are four kinds of arts: the common and mean, the diversionary, the childish, and the liberal. The common arts are those of craftsmen, which rely on manual labor and are occupied with sustaining life; in them there is no pretense of seemliness or respectability.

[22] Diversionary arts are those that aim at the pleasure of the eyes and ears. Among these you may include engineers who devise

self-rising stages, platforms that grow silently to great heights, and other unexpected variations, either where things that were joined split apart, or where things that were separate come together of their own accord, or where things that protruded gradually subside into themselves. The eyes of the ignorant are struck by all such sudden effects because they do not know the causes.

[23] Childish arts, which have something in common with the liberal arts, are those the Greeks call "encyclical" and we call "liberal." But only those arts are truly liberal, or rather, to speak more precisely, free, which are concerned with virtue.

[24] "Just as," he says, "there is a natural part of philosophy, and a moral part, and a rational part, so too does this crowd of liberal arts claim a place for itself within philosophy. When one arrives at questions of nature, the testimony of geometry is relied upon; therefore geometry is a part of the very thing which it assists."

[25] Many things assist us and yet are not parts of us. Indeed, if they were parts, they would not assist. Food assists the body and yet is not a part of it. The service of geometry provides us something; thus it is necessary to philosophy, in the way that the carpenter is necessary to geometry itself. But the carpenter here is not a part of geometry, nor is geometry a part of philosophy.

[26] Furthermore, each has its own boundaries. The wise man seeks and knows the causes of natural things, the numbers and measures of which the geometer traces out and calculates. The wise man knows by what reason the heavenly bodies hold together, what force or nature they have; the mathematician grasps their courses and recourses and certain observations, through which they descend and rise and sometimes present the appearance of standing still, although it is not permitted for the heavenly bodies to stand still.

[27] The wise man will know what cause produces images in a mirror; that geometer can tell you how far the body ought to be from the image, and what shape of mirror renders what kind of images. The philosopher will prove the sun to be large; how large, the mathematician can say, who proceeds by a certain practice and training; but that he may proceed, certain principles must be granted to him.

However, an art is not independent which has a precarious foundation.

[28] Philosophy seeks nothing from another source, it erects its entire work from the ground up alone; mathematics, so to speak, is superficial, it builds on the work of others. It accepts first principles, by the benefit of which it arrives at further conclusions. If it were to proceed by itself to the truth, if it were able to grasp the nature of the entire universe, I would say it contributes greatly to our minds, which grow by the treatment of heavenly things and draw something from the heights. The mind is consummated by one thing, the immutable knowledge of good and evil; no other art, however, inquires about good and evil.

[29] He orders us to go around to each of the virtues individually. Courage despises the things that inspire fear; it looks down upon, challenges, and crushes the terrors that seek to subjugate our free-dom. Do liberal studies strengthen courage? Loyalty, the most sacred good in the human heart, is compelled by no necessity to deceive and is corrupted by no reward. "Burn me," it says, "flog me, slay me; I will not betray my trust, and the more aggressively torment tries to extract my secrets, the deeper I will hide them." Can liberal studies produce such resolution?

Temperance governs pleasures, hating and banishing some, rationing others and reducing them to a healthy measure, and never approaches any for their own sake. It knows that the best limit to our desires is to take not as much as you want, but as much as you should.

[30] Kindness forbids us to be arrogant towards our fellows and forbids greed. In words, deeds, and feelings, it shows itself courteous and agreeable to all. It considers no human misfortune to be foreign to itself. And it loves its own good most of all for this reason, that it will benefit someone else. Do liberal studies teach such character? No more than they teach simplicity, modesty and self-control, frugality and thrift, or mercy, which is as sparing of others' blood as of its own and knows that a person must not squander human life recklessly.

[31] "Since you say," the objection comes, "that virtue cannot be attained without liberal studies, how can you deny that they

contribute anything to virtue?" In the same way that we cannot attain virtue without food, and yet food has nothing to do with virtue. Wood contributes nothing to a ship, although a ship cannot be built except from wood. There is no reason, I say, for you to suppose that anything is made with the assistance of that without which it cannot be made.

[32] In fact, one could even argue that it is possible to attain wisdom without liberal studies; for although virtue must be learned, it is not learned through them.

Why should I think that one who does not know his letters will never become a wise man, when wisdom is not to be found in letters? Wisdom communicates the substance, not the words, and I rather think that the memory is more sure which relies on no external aids.

[33] Wisdom is a spacious and expansive thing. It needs an uncluttered place. One must learn about things divine and human, the past and the future, the ephemeral and the eternal - and about time. See how many questions arise about time alone: first, whether it is anything in itself; then, whether anything exists prior to time and without time; whether it began along with the universe, or whether, because there was something even before the universe, time also existed then.

[34] There are innumerable questions about the mind alone: where it comes from, what it is like, when it begins to exist, how long it exists; whether it passes from one being to another and changes dwelling places, cast into other forms of animals [transmigration of souls], or whether it serves no more than once and, when released, wanders the universe; whether it is corporeal or not; what it will do when it ceases to act through us, how it will use its freedom when it has escaped from this cage; whether it forgets its former state and only begins to know itself from the point when, withdrawn from the body, it has receded into the sublime.

[35] Whatever part of human or divine affairs you seize upon, you will be wearied by the immense abundance of things to be inquired into and learned. For these matters to have free lodging, so numerous and so great are they, the superfluous must be banished from the mind. Virtue will not confine herself in these straits; a great subject

requires wide space. Let all else be driven out, and let the entire breast be vacant for her.

[36] "But surely," one objects, "it is delightful to be acquainted with many arts." Let us retain only as much of them as is necessary. Do you regard a man as blameworthy who procures superfluous wares and makes a display in his house of costly objects, but not him who is engrossed with the useless furniture of learning? Desiring to know more than is sufficient is a form of intemperance.

[37] Besides, this pursuit of the liberal arts makes men troublesome, wordy, tactless, self-satisfied, and unwilling to learn the essentials because they have already learned the non-essentials. The grammarian Didymus wrote four thousand books. I should feel pity for him if he had merely read the same number of superfluous works. In these books he investigates Homer's birthplace, Aeneas' true mother, whether Anacreon was more of a rake or more of a drunkard, whether Sappho was a prostitute, and other questions the answers to which, if found, were forthwith to be forgotten.

[38] Go now and deny that life is long! But even when you come to our own countrymen, I can show you many works which ought to be cut down with the axe.

It is at the cost of vast amounts of time and of vexation to many ears that this tribute is won: "What a learned man!" Let us be content with the less pretentious tribute: "What a good man!"

[39] Is this what I come to? Must I unroll the annals of all nations to find out who first wrote poetry? Shall I reckon up--since I lack official lists--how many years lie between Orpheus and Homer? Shall I review the pointless criticisms of Aristarchus, with which he defaced the poetry of others, and wear out my life on syllables? Shall I thus cleave to the dust of geometry? Have I so far forgotten that wholesome precept: "Save time"? Must I know these things? And what may I choose not to know?

[40] Apion the grammarian, who traveled all throughout Greece under Gaius Caesar and was adopted into the name of Homer by all the cities, said that Homer, having completed both the Odyssey and the Iliad, added a beginning to his work in which he encompassed

the Trojan war. As proof of this, Apion offered that Homer had deliberately placed two letters in the first line indicating the number of his books.

[41] Someone who wishes to know many things must know trivialities such as these. But they do not consider how much time is robbed from them by ill health, public duties, private affairs, daily responsibilities, and sleep. Measure your lifespan; it does not have room for so many pursuits.

[42] I am speaking of the liberal arts; but philosophers too have much that is superfluous and strays from practical use! They too have stooped to quibbling over the parts of speech and the peculiarities of conjunctions and prepositions, encroaching on the grammarians and geometers. Whatever was superfluous in those other arts they have transferred to their own. The result is that they know how to speak more meticulously than to live.

[43] Listen to the great harm wrought by excessive hairsplitting and how inimical it is to truth. Protagoras says that one can argue equally well on either side of any question, including the question of whether one can argue on either side of any question. Nausiphanes holds that of the things that seem to exist, no one thing exists any more than it does not exist.

[44] Parmenides maintains that of the things that seem to be, nothing exists except the universe as a whole[3]. Zeno of Elea did away with all business by doing away with the one business, saying that nothing exists. The Pyrrhonists, Megarians, Eretrians[4], and Academics revolve around much the same position; they have introduced a new knowledge—that nothing can be known.

[45] Throw all of these into that superfluous crowd of liberal studies. The former impart knowledge that will be of no use to me; the latter steal away all hope of knowledge. It is better to know superfluous things than to know nothing. The one group does not light a torch by which the eyesight may be directed toward the truth, while the other gouges out my very eyes. If I believe Protagoras, there is nothing in nature except the dubious; if Nausiphanes, the only

certainty is that there is nothing certain; if Parmenides, nothing exists except the One; if Zeno, not even the One exists.

[46] What then are we? What are these things that surround us, sustain us? The whole of reality is either shadow or emptiness or illusion. I cannot easily say which angers me more—those who wanted us to know nothing, or those who have not even left us this consolation, to know that we know nothing. Farewell.

---

1. Refers to the planets Saturn and Mercury
2. The phrase in brackets is from a later manuscript tradition and its authenticity is disputed.
3. Alternative text: "Parmenides maintains that of the things that seem to be, nothing exists except the one."
4. Alternative text: "Cretans"

LETTER 89

THE PARTS AND SUBDIVISIONS OF PHILOSOPHY

[1] You desire something useful and necessary for one hastening towards wisdom: that philosophy be divided and its immense body arranged into distinct parts. For it is easier to come to an understanding of the whole by examining it piece by piece. If only all of philosophy could present itself to us just as the entire visage of the universe comes into view—surely it would be a sight most similar to the cosmos itself. It would certainly seize all mortals in admiration for it, leaving behind those things which we now, in our vast ignorance, believe to be great. But since this is impossible, we must behold philosophy in the same way that the mysteries of the universe are perceived.

[2] The mind of the wise person embraces philosophy's entire magnitude and surveys it no less swiftly than our vision takes in the heavens. But for us, who must penetrate the obscuring mists and whose sight fails even at a short distance, it is easier to have each component pointed out individually, as we are not yet able to comprehend the whole. Therefore, I will do as you require and divide philosophy into parts—but not fragments. For it is useful to partition it, but not to chop it up. To grasp the greatest things, like the smallest, is equally difficult.

[3] The populace is distributed into tribes, the army into centuries. Anything that has grown rather large is more easily recognized when separated into parts, which, as I have said, should be neither countless nor tiny. For an excessive number of divisions has the same disadvantage as no division at all; whatever is chopped up into dust is just as confusing as the undivided mass.

[4] So first, if you don't mind, I will explain the difference between wisdom and philosophy. Wisdom is the perfect good of the human mind; philosophy is the love and pursuit of wisdom. The latter strives for the destination that the former has reached. The origin of the word "philosophy" is clear, for the term itself confesses what it loves.

[5] Some have defined wisdom as the knowledge of things divine and human. Others describe it thus: "Wisdom is knowing the divine and human realms and the causes of each." This addition seems superfluous to me, because the causes of divine and human things are part of the divine domain. There have also been those who defined philosophy differently. Some called it the study of virtue; others, the study of correcting the mind; and by some it was termed the pursuit of right reason.

[6] It is generally agreed upon that there is some distinction between philosophy and wisdom. For it is impossible for that which is sought and that which seeks to be the same. Just as there is a great difference between greed and money, since greed covets while money is coveted, so too there is a difference between philosophy and wisdom. For wisdom is the effect and reward of philosophy; philosophy comes, but wisdom is the destination reached. Wisdom is what the Greeks call σοφίαν.

[7] The Romans also used to employ this word, just as they now use the word "philosophy." This is attested by the ancient comic poets[1] as well as the inscription on the tomb of Dossennus:

"Pause, stranger, and read the wisdom of Dossennus."

[8] Some of our Roman philosophers, although philosophy is the pursuit of virtue and wisdom the goal, nevertheless thought that the

two could not be separated. For there is no philosophy without virtue, nor virtue without philosophy. Philosophy is the pursuit of virtue, but it is virtue itself that is pursued; virtue, moreover, cannot exist without the pursuit of itself, nor can the pursuit of virtue exist without virtue itself. For it is not as with those who attempt to strike something at a distance, where the striker and the target are in different places. Nor is it like the roads that lead to cities, with the path to virtue lying outside it. The way to virtue is through virtue itself; philosophy and virtue are interconnected.

[9] The greatest and most numerous authorities have said that philosophy has three parts: ethics, physics, and logic. The first regulates the soul; the second investigates the nature of things; the third determines the precise meanings of words, their structure, and lines of argument, so that falsehood cannot creep in disguised as truth. There are some, however, who would divide philosophy into fewer parts, and others into more.

[10] Certain Peripatetics have added a fourth part, politics, because it requires a distinct discipline and is concerned with a different subject matter. Some have annexed to these parts economics, the science of managing one's household affairs. Others have even separated out the topic of types of life. But all of these additional topics will actually be found to be contained within ethics.

[11] The Epicureans believed that philosophy consisted of two parts: natural and moral philosophy; they discarded logic. But then, compelled by the subject matter itself to distinguish ambiguities and refute falsehoods masquerading under the guise of truth, they too introduced a topic that they call "judgment and rule" under another name—logic—but they consider it an accessory to the natural part.

[12] The Cyrenaics abolished natural philosophy along with logic and were content with moral precepts alone, but they too introduce in another way the very things they abolish. For they divide moral philosophy into five parts: one concerning things to be sought and avoided; the second, emotions; the third, actions; the fourth, causes; and the fifth, arguments. Causes belong to the natural part, arguments to the logical[2]. Aristo of Chios declared that not only were

natural and logical philosophy superfluous, but even contrary [to true philosophy].

[13] He also mutilated moral philosophy, the only part he had left, for he abolished the area containing advice, saying it belonged to the schoolmaster, not the philosopher—as if the wise man were anything other than a schoolmaster for the human race!

[14] So, since philosophy is threefold, let us begin by arranging its moral part. It has been decided to further divide this into three areas: the first being an examination that distributes to each his own and assesses the worth of each thing, which is most useful [for what is so necessary as assigning values to things?]; the second concerns impulse, and the third, actions[3]. For the first step is to judge the worth of each thing; the second, to conceive an ordered and tempered impulse towards them; the third, to make your impulse and action agree, so that you are consistent with yourself in all these matters.

[15] When any one of three elements is missing, it throws the others into disarray. What good is it to have all your values aligned if you are excessive in your impulses? What use is it to have restrained your passions and mastered your desires if in the very undertaking of affairs you are ignorant of timing, not knowing when, where and how each thing should be done? It is one thing to know the worth and value of matters, another to know the critical moments, and yet another to curb impulse and proceed to action—not rushing headlong. Life is in harmony with itself only when action does not fall short of impulse, and impulse arises from the worth of each endeavor and is accordingly more relaxed or more ardent, in proportion to the thing's deservingness of pursuit.

[16] The study of the natural world [in philosophy] is split in two: the corporeal and the incorporeal. Each is divided into its own stages, so to speak. The topic of physical objects is first divided into these: the things that produce, and the things produced from them. And the things produced are the elements. The topic of the elements themselves, as some believe, is singular; as others hold, it is divided into matter, the cause that moves all things, and the elements.

[17] It remains for me to divide the rational part of philosophy. All

discourse is either continuous or split between answerer and questioner. The latter is called dialectic, the former rhetoric. Rhetoric deals with words, meanings, and arrangement. Dialectic is divided into two parts: words and significations—that is, the things that are said and the terms in which they are said. There follows then an enormous subdivision of each. So at this point I will end and

Follow the topmost summits of the matter[4],

otherwise, if I should want to make parts of the parts, it will turn into a book of mere problems.

[18] These matters, Lucilius, best of men—I do not discourage you from reading about, as long as whatever you read you promptly apply to conduct.

Restrain those vices, rouse the apathetic parts in you, bind up the loose ends, subdue your obstinacy, harass your lusts and those of the crowd as much as you can, and to those who say "How long will it be the same old things?" reply: "I ought to be asking—'How long will you keep sinning in the same old ways?'"

[19] You want the cures to come before you stop the vices? But I will speak out all the more and, because you protest, I will persist. Medicine begins to work only when, in a diseased body, touch elicits pain. I will say things that do you good even against your will. Sometimes let an uncoddling voice come to you, and because you are unwilling to hear the truth individually, hear it in public.

[20] How far will you extend the boundaries of your possessions? A single owner finds too cramped the land that once held a nation. How far will you push your plowshares, not content to limit your estates even by provincial borders? Mighty rivers flow through private grounds, and vast waterways that form boundaries of great nations are yours from source to mouth. But even this is not enough unless your lands encircle the seas, unless your steward holds sway across the Adriatic, Ionian, and Aegean, unless islands, once homes of great leaders, are counted among your most trifling possessions. Spread your ownership as vastly as you wish; let an estate be what was once

called an empire. Claim as your own all you can, as long as more remains that belongs to others.

[21] Now I speak to you whose extravagance sprawls as widely as the greed of those others. To you I say: will there be no lake whose shores are not dominated by your mansion's towering façades? No river whose banks are not lined with your structures? Wherever hot springs bubble forth, there new palaces of excess will rise. Wherever the shore curves into a bay, you will lay foundations at once, unsatisfied with any land not shaped by your own hands as you drive back the sea. Though your dwellings gleam in every place—perched on mountaintops commanding vast vistas of land and sea, or reared up from the plain to mountainous heights—though you build abundantly and grandly, still you are but solitary, puny beings. How do all those chambers profit you? You can lie in but one. The places you are not, are not truly yours.

[22] To you I turn next, whose deep, insatiable gullet ransacks seas and lands, pursuing some creatures with hooks, others with snares, still others with nets of various kinds—all with great toil. No animals have peace, except when you grow weary of them. How measly the portions from those feasts, gathered by so many hands, that you sample with your pleasure-sated palates! How little of that dangerously captured game does the surfeited, queasy master taste! How little of those shellfish, imported from so far away, slips down that insatiable throat? Miserable ones, do you not realize that your hunger is vaster than your bellies?

[23] Speak these words to others so that, in speaking, you may hear them yourself. Write so that, in writing, you may read. Relate all things to character, to calming the frenzy of desire. Study not to know more, but to know better. Farewell.

---

1. The "togatae" were a genre of ancient Roman comedy that dealt with Roman subject matter, in contrast to the "palliatae" which were adaptations of Greek comedies.
2. B has "moral" here, but later manuscripts give "rational." Buecheler suggests a phrase may have dropped out, meaning "neither belongs to the 'moral.'"

3. Buecheler follows this order, but B gives "the second concerning actions, the third impulse."

4. A quote from Virgil's Georgics, Book 4, line 292

LETTER 90

THE GOLDEN AGE AND THE ORIGINS OF PHILOSOPHY

[1] Who can doubt, my dear Lucilius, that it is a gift of the immortal gods that we are alive, but a gift of philosophy that we live well? Thus we would surely consider ourselves even more indebted to philosophy than to the gods, insofar as a good life is a greater benefit than life itself - were it not that the gods themselves bestowed philosophy upon us. They gave knowledge of it to none, but the capability for it to all.

[2] For if they had made philosophy too a universal good, and if we were born wise, then wisdom would have lost what is best in it - that it does not fall to us by chance. As things are, what makes it precious and magnificent is precisely that it does not just come to us, that each person owes it to themselves, that it is not sought from another. What would you find to admire in philosophy, if it were a handout?

[3] Philosophy's sole task is to discover the truth about things divine and human. From philosophy, religion, dutifulness, justice, and the entire retinue of interconnected and unified virtues never depart. Philosophy taught us to worship the divine, to love the human, that sovereignty lies with the gods while fellowship links human beings. This fellowship remained inviolate for a time, before

greed tore society asunder, and became a cause of poverty even for those it made richest. For people ceased to possess all things the moment they desired all things for themselves.

[4] But those first humans, along with their descendants, followed uncorrupted nature. They had nature as both leader and law, entrusting themselves to the governance of one greater than they. For it is natural that the superior rules the inferior. Among herds of animals, either the largest in body or the fiercest in spirit takes the lead. The herd of bulls is led not by some inferior specimen, but by one that has surpassed the other males in bulk and sinew. The tallest elephant leads the elephant herd; among humans, the best is regarded as supreme. And so people would choose a ruler based on the spirit, and for this reason the happiness of nations was at its height when the more powerful could not be other than the one of higher moral character. For a person can safely have as much power as they want, if they believe they should only have power to do what is right.

[5] In that golden age, as it is called, Posidonius judges that the wise held sway. They restrained their hands and protected the weak from the strong, persuading and dissuading, pointing out what was beneficial and harmful. Their prudence ensured their people lacked nothing, their courage warded off dangers, and their kindness augmented[1] and adorned their subjects. Their duty was to command, not to reign. No one tested their might against those through whom they had gained power, and none had the inclination or cause for injury, as those who ruled well were well obeyed, and the king could threaten no greater punishment to the disobedient than banishment[2] from the realm.

[6] But as vices crept in and kingdoms turned to tyrannies, the need for laws arose, which the wise also established in the beginning. Solon, who founded Athens on equal rights, was among the seven renowned for wisdom. Had Lycurgus lived in the same era, he would have been the eighth addition to that sacred number. The laws of Zaleucus and Charondas are praised. They learned the principles they would establish for the then-flourishing Sicily and Greek Italy

not in the forum or the halls of advisors, but in the silent and holy retreat of Pythagoras.

[7] Thus far, I agree with Posidonius; however, I cannot concede that philosophy invented the arts used in daily life, nor attribute to it the glory of their creation. "Philosophy," he says, "taught men scattered and living in caves, hollowed rocks, or the trunks of hollow trees to construct shelters." But I judge philosophy no more devised these contrivances of roofs piled upon roofs and cities pressing upon cities than it did the fish ponds enclosed to shield gluttony from the dangers of storms, ensuring luxury had its harbors, where it could fatten distinct schools of fish, even while the sea raged most fiercely.

[8] What's that you say? Philosophy taught men to have locks and keys? What else was this but to give a signal to greed? Was it philosophy that suspended these threatening roofs at such great peril to the inhabitants? As if it were not enough to be sheltered by chance, finding some natural refuge without skill or difficulty. Believe me, that happy age existed before architects and [roof] decorators[3].

[9] These practices were born with the birth of luxury itself, when beams began to be cut into perfect squares, and a saw, guided by a steady hand, sliced through the marked lines on the wood.

> *"For in early times, they split the easily cleft wood with*
>   *wedges."*

For back then, they did not prepare ceilings to host banquets in dining rooms, nor were pine and fir trees transported in long processions of creaking wagons to be used for this purpose, just so that gilded and heavy coffers could hang from those ceilings. Instead, forked poles propped up their simple huts on both sides.

[10] With densely packed branches and heaped foliage arranged in a sloping manner, even the heaviest of rains would flow off. Under such roofs, they lived, but they lived securely. Thatched roofs sheltered free people, while beneath marble and gold dwells servitude.

On this point too, I disagree with Posidonius, who judges that the tools of craftsmen were devised by wise men.

[11] For by that logic, one might as well say that it was wise men who discovered

> *"How to catch wild beasts with snares, to deceive birds with*
> *birdlime,*
> *And to encircle great forests with dogs."*

For it was the cleverness of men, not their wisdom, that invented all such things.

[12] On this matter too I disagree, that it was wise men who discovered the metals of iron and copper, when the earth, scorched by forest fires, caused the veins of ore lying near the surface to melt and flow out[4]. Such things are discovered by men who are like those who prize them.

[13] Nor does the question of whether the hammer or the tongs came into use first seem to me as subtle as it does to Posidonius. Both were invented by someone of keen and sharp intellect, but not a great or lofty one, like anything else that must be sought by stooping the body and fixing the mind upon the ground.

The wise man lived simply, and why not? Even in our present age the wisest wish to be as unencumbered as possible.

[14] How, I ask you, can you consistently admire both Diogenes and Daedalus? Which of these seems wise to you? The one who invented the saw, or the one who, upon seeing a boy drink water from his cupped hands, immediately took out his cup from his bag and broke it, rebuking himself thus: "You fool, how long have I been burdened with such unnecessary baggage!" and then curled up to sleep in his barrel.

[15] Which man, I ask, would you deem wiser today—the one who devises a way to propel saffron-scented water to immense heights using hidden pipes, who fills or drains canals with a sudden gush, who so cleverly constructs a vaulted dining room that it presents a different appearance at each course, its ceiling changing as often as the dishes? Or the one who demonstrates to himself and others how nature demands of us nothing difficult or burdensome, how we can

live without marble cutters and engineers, clothe ourselves without importing silk[5], and possess everything necessary for our use if we are content with what the earth has placed on its surface? If humanity chose to heed this man, they would realize that cooks are as superfluous to them as soldiers.

[16] Those were wise men, or at least very like the wise, for whom the care of the body was a simple matter. The necessities are easily provided; it is luxury that requires labor and effort. Follow nature, and you will have no need of skilled craftsmen.

Nature did not want us to be preoccupied with such matters. She equipped us for whatever she compelled us to do. "But it is unbearably cold without clothing!" Well then, cannot the hides of wild beasts and other animals defend us amply from the cold? Do not many tribes cover their bodies with tree bark? Are not birds' feathers sewn together to make garments? Even today, do not a large portion of the Scythians clothe themselves in the pelts of foxes and mice, which are soft to the touch and impenetrable to winds?

[17] "But we need a thicker shade to ward off the heat of the summer sun." Well then, has not antiquity bequeathed to us many places which have receded into caverns, hollowed out by the ravages of time or some other chance[6]?

And have not people woven shelters of pliant branches with their own hands and smeared them with cheap mud, then covered the roof with straw and other woodland materials, thereby passing the winter untroubled, as the rains slip down the sloping sides[7]? Do not the tribes of the Syrtes, for whom no shelter is substantial enough to repel the excessive heat of the sun, dwell in dugouts, the parched earth itself their only protection[8]?

[18] Nature was not so hostile that she would allow all other creatures an easy life while man alone could not live without so many skills. She did not demand any of this from us; nothing had to be painstakingly sought out so that life might be prolonged. We were born into a world of plenty; it is we who have made everything difficult for ourselves, disdaining what is easy. Shelter, clothing, warmth for our bodies, food—things which are now a massive

undertaking—were readily available, free of charge and obtainable with little effort. For the measure of all things was according to necessity; it is we who have made them costly, we who have made them objects of wonder to be sought out with great and manifold skills.

[19] Nature suffices for what she demands. Luxury has deserted nature; each day it rouses itself and through so many ages continues to grow, abetting vices with ingenuity. At first, it began to lust after superfluities, then after things detrimental, and finally, it delivered the mind over to the body and commanded it to be a slave to the body's whims. All these skills with which the city is either kept in a whirl or in a constant din serve the body's business. Once everything was furnished to it as to a slave; now they are made ready for it as for a master. Hence we have workshops of weavers and carpenters; hence the perfumers' quarters; hence the soft, sensuous movements of the body they teach, and the soft and enervating songs. For that natural limit, which confined desires to necessities, has receded. Nowadays it is a sign of boorishness and poverty to want only as much as is enough.

[20] It is unbelievable, my dear Lucilius, how easily even great men are led from the truth by the charm of language. Take Posidonius, who in my opinion is one of those who have contributed the most to philosophy. While aiming to describe first how some threads are spun and others are drawn from soft, firm material, then how the loom stretches out the warp by means of hanging weights, how the woof is inserted and compacted by the batten, softening the firm texture compressed by the loom's cross threads[9], he asserted that even the art of weaving was invented by wise men—forgetting that an even more refined version was discovered later, in which:

The web is bound to the beam; the reed separates the threads of the warp;

> *The woof is inserted between them by the sharp shuttles,*
> *Which the broad teeth of the clattering comb compact*
>   *together.*[10]

What if he had happened to come upon the looms of our age, in which a garment is woven to conceal nothing, providing no assistance, I will not say to the body, but even to modesty?

[21] The sage then turns his attention to farmers, describing with equal eloquence the soil plowed by the blade and turned again, making the loosened earth more easily penetrable by roots. He speaks of scattered seeds and weeds pulled by hand, lest any wild, unwanted growth spring up to choke the crop. This work too, he claims, belongs to the wise, as if the tillers of fields even now do not discover many new methods to increase their yield.

[22] But not content with these arts, he consigns the sage to the mill. For he recounts how, imitating nature, the wise man first began to make bread. "The grain, taken into the mouth," he says, "is crushed by the clashing hardness of teeth, and whatever falls out is brought back to those same teeth by the tongue; then it is mixed with saliva to more easily slip down the lubricated throat. When it reaches the stomach, it is digested by the steady heat, and only then does it become part of the body."

[23] Following this example, someone placed a rough stone upon another, like unto teeth, one part stationary while awaiting the movement of the other; then by the friction of the two, the grains are broken and repeatedly worked until, ground down by frequent rubbing, they are reduced to fine flour. Then he moistened the meal with water, kneaded it with ceaseless handling, and shaped it into bread, which at first was baked by hot ashes and a glowing earthen pot, then by ovens gradually discovered and other methods whose heat could be regulated at will. He was not far from claiming that shoemaking, too, was invented by sages.

[24] Reason indeed contrived all these things, but not right reason. For they are the inventions of man, not the wise man, just as, by Hercules, are the ships with which we cross rivers and seas, sails fitted to catch the force of the winds, and rudders placed astern, which turn the vessel's course this way and that. The model was drawn from fish, which steer with their tails, and by its slight flexing to either side, direct their swift motion.

[25] "All these things," he says, "the wise man did indeed discover; but he deemed them too petty for him to deal with directly and entrusted them to his meaner assistants." No, they were thought out by none other than those who to this day oversee them. We know that certain inventions have only emerged in our own memory, such as the use of windows that transmit clear light through transparent panes, such as the vaulted ceilings of baths and the pipes let into walls to circulate heat that warms the room from bottom to top with even temperature. What need to mention the marble that makes temples and homes resplendent? The massive blocks of stone rounded into smooth columns with which we construct porticoes and spacious public halls? Or the shorthand symbols with which speech, however rapid, is taken down and the hand keeps pace with the quickness of the tongue? These are the inventions of the lowliest slaves;

[26] Wisdom sits on high; she does not train the hands, but is the mistress of the mind. Do you wish to know what she has found out, what she has accomplished? Not graceful bodily movements or various songs played on horn and flute, which shape the breath as it is inhaled or exhaled into a voice. She does not construct arms or walls or anything useful in war; rather, she favors peace and calls humankind to harmony.

[27] Wisdom, I say, is not a craftsman of tools for necessary uses. Why assign her such petty things? You see in her the architect of life. She holds the other arts, indeed, under her dominion. For those who serve life also serve the things that adorn life. But wisdom strains towards the blessed state, leads us to it, opens the way to it.

[28] She shows what evils exist and what evils seem to exist; she strips vanity from the mind. She bestows true greatness, but restrains that which is inflated, showy but empty. She does not allow us to be ignorant of the difference between grandeur and excess. She delivers knowledge of all nature and of her own. She declares what the gods are and of what sort, what the underworld is, what the household gods and guardian spirits are, what happens to souls elevated to the

second class of divinities, where they abide, what they do, what power they have, what they wish.

These are wisdom's initiations, through which not a local shrine but the vast temple of all the gods, the universe itself, is opened up. She has brought forth for minds to perceive the true images and faces of this temple. For the gaze is dull for such grand sights.

[29] Next, she returns to the beginnings of things and the eternal reason infused in the whole, and the force that shapes all seeds distinctly. Then she began to inquire about the soul - whence it came, where it is, how long it lasts, into how many parts it is divided. Then she turned her attention from corporeal to incorporeal things and examined truth and its proofs. After this, she looked into how ambiguities of language or meaning are discerned, for in both cases falsehoods are mixed with truths.

[30] The wise person, I say, did not withdraw from these liberal arts, as Posidonius thinks, but never approached them at all. For he would have judged nothing worthy of discovery that he would not judge worthy of constant use. He would not take up what should be set down.

[31] "Anacharsis," he says, "invented the potter's wheel, by whose revolution vessels are shaped." But then, because the potter's wheel is found in Homer, they prefer to believe the verses are spurious rather than the story. I contend that Anacharsis was not the originator of this invention, and if he was, he discovered it as a clever man, but not as a wise one. Just as the wise do many things as men, not as sages. Suppose the wise man to be the swiftest of men; he will outstrip all in running, by virtue of being swift, not wise. I would have liked to show Posidonius some glassblower who by his breath forms glass into manifold shapes which could scarcely be fashioned by the most skillful hand. These discoveries were made after we ceased to discover wisdom.

[32] "Democritus," he says, "is reported to have discovered the arch, that curving structure of stones gradually inclining toward each other, bound together by a keystone." I would say this is false; for

there must have been both bridges and gates before Democritus, and the tops of these are usually arched.

[33] Moreover, it has escaped you that this same Democritus discovered how ivory could be softened, how, by boiling, a pebble could be transformed into an emerald - a process still used to color stones that are useful in this way. Though the wise man discovered these things, he did not do so qua wise man; for he does many things which we see done just as well, or with more skill and dexterity, by the most unlearned.

[34] What, then, has the wise man found out and brought to light? First of all, truth and nature; and he has not followed these with slow-moving eyes, as other creatures do, which gaze sluggishly upon the divine. Next, the law of life, which he has applied to all things; and he has taught us not only to know the gods, but to follow them, and to receive the things that happen not as if they were mere accidents, but as if they were commands. He has forbidden us to give heed to false opinions, and has weighed the value of each thing by a true standard of judgment. He has condemned those pleasures with which remorse is intermingled, and has praised those goods which will always satisfy; and he has published the truth abroad that he is most happy who has no need of happiness, and that he is most powerful who has power over himself.

[35] I am not speaking of that philosophy which has placed the citizen outside his country and the gods outside the universe, which has bestowed virtue upon pleasure, but of that philosophy which counts nothing good except what is honorable - one which cannot be cajoled by the gifts either of man or of fortune, one whose value is that it cannot be bought for any value. That this philosophy existed in such a rude age, when the arts and crafts were still unknown and when useful things could only be learned by use - this I refuse to believe.

[36] Fortunate were those times, when the benefits of nature lay available for common use, before greed and luxury divided mortals and drove them to robbery instead of sharing. [Those men were not wise, even if they did what the wise ought to do.]

[37] Indeed, no one could admire any condition of the human race more, nor, if a god allowed him to fashion earthly things and give customs to nations, would he approve of anything other than what is recorded to have existed among those peoples, among whom

> *No farmers subjugated the fields,*
> *It was not even right to mark out or divide the plain with a*
> > *boundary;*
> *They sought everything for the common store, and the*
> > *earth itself*
> *Brought forth everything more freely with no one*
> > *demanding.*

[38] What race of men was happier than that one? They enjoyed nature's bounty in common; she sufficed to guard all, like a parent - this was the secure possession of public wealth. Why should I not call that the richest race of mortals, among whom you could not find a poor person?

Avarice burst in upon this excellently ordered condition and, wanting to sequester something and turn it to its own use, made everything another's and reduced itself from boundlessness to narrowness. Avarice introduced poverty and, by craving much, lost all.

[39] So now, though it tries to recover what it has lost, though it adds fields to fields, driving off a neighbor either by price or by force, though it expands country estates to the size of provinces and calls a long journey through one's own property a "possession" - no expansion of boundaries will lead us back to the point from which we have departed.

When we have done everything, we will have much; [but] we [once] had the whole.

[40] The earth itself was more fertile when untilled, and abundant for the use of peoples who did not ravage it. Whatever nature had brought forth, to find it was no less a pleasure than to point it out to another once found. None could either have too much or too little;

distribution was made in concord. The stronger had not yet laid hand on the weaker, the avaricious man had not yet hidden away what he might keep for himself, shutting out even the needy; one cared equally for another and for oneself.

[41] Weapons lay idle and hands unstained by human blood had turned all hatred against wild beasts. Those whom some dense grove had protected from the sun, who against the savagery of winter or rain were safe in meager shelter under the leaves, passed tranquil nights without a sigh. Anxiety keeps us tossing and turning in our purple sheets and prods us with the sharpest goads; but how soft a sleep the hard ground gave to those men!

[42] Ornate paneled ceilings did not overhang them. Rather, as they lay in the open, the stars glided by above and the heavens in their nightly revolution made for a wondrous spectacle, conducting their vast work in silence. The vistas of this most beautiful abode lay open to them by day just as much as by night. One could delight in observing the constellations as they set in one part of the sky and others as they rose from hiding in another.

[43] What joy it must have been to wander amidst such widely scattered wonders! But you, in contrast, tremble at every sound from the roof. If anything creaks, you flee in panic among your precious wall paintings. Their homes were not the size of cities. The spirit could roam free, a breeze blowing through the open spaces, light shade from a cliff or tree, translucent springs and brooks babbling along, not sullied by artificial works, pipes, or any forced channels, but running spontaneously. The meadows had a natural beauty, not contrived by art. Amidst all this stood a rustic dwelling, fashioned by the rough hand of a peasant. This was a home in tune with nature, a place one would be glad to live, fearing neither for it nor because of it. Nowadays, a large part of our fear stems from our very roofs.

[44] But although their life was outstanding and free from deceit, they were not wise—for in these later times, that word has taken on the highest sense. Yet I would not deny that they were men of lofty spirit, fresh from the gods, so to speak. For there is no doubt that the world, when it was not yet spent, produced better things. Just as their

character was stronger and more prepared for hardships, not everyone's talents were fully developed. Nature does not bestow virtue; becoming good is an art.

[45] Indeed, they did not search for gold, silver, or glittering gems in the deepest dregs of the earth. They even spared the dumb beasts. They were so far from killing their fellow man—not in anger or fear, but merely for the spectacle. Their clothing was not yet embroidered, gold was not yet woven, nor was it even mined.

[46] What, then, is the reason? It was ignorance of vice that kept them innocent. There is a great difference between choosing not to sin and not knowing how. They lacked justice, prudence, temperance, and courage. The rude life possessed certain qualities resembling all these virtues; but virtue does not enter a soul unless it has been schooled, taught, and guided to the heights by constant training. We are born for virtue but not with it, and even in the best of people, until you educate them, there is the material for virtue, not virtue itself. Farewell.

---

1. Alternative reading: managed
2. Alternative reading: that he would depart from the kingdom
3. The text here is uncertain. An alternative reading is: "Before architects. Those things..."
4. The text notes variant readings of "liquefactas" (melted) in later manuscripts vs. "liquefacta" in the earlier manuscript B.
5. some manuscripts read "servorum" (of slaves) instead of "sericorum" (of silk).
6. "multa dedit" is a correction by Madvig; the manuscripts have "abdidit". Buecheler suspects the whole clause may be corrupt, and H. Müller suggests "abdita dedit".
7. The original text includes a fragmentary note here which has been omitted from the translation: "quid ergo securi". G. Gemoll believes these words should be placed at the beginning of section 17
8. "stipula" is a correction by Hense and others, with the manuscript reading "despicula".

    Later manuscripts have "transiere" where the earliest manuscript B reads "transire".
9. Reading utrimque with later MSS for BA's utrumque.
10. From Ovid's Metamorphoses 6.55-58. Line 1: reading vincta with Ovid for iuncta in BA. Line 3: reading paviunt with Gruter for pariunt in BA.

LETTER 91

FORTUNE CAN DESTROY CITIES BUT NOT VIRTUE

[1] Our friend Liberalis is now in low spirits, having received news of the fire which has burned down the colony of Lugdunum[1]. This calamity would shock anyone, let alone a man who dearly loves his native city. The incident has driven him to examine his own mental fortitude, which he has no doubt exercised in preparation for misfortunes he imagined might occur. But I do not marvel that he was blindsided by this unexpected and nearly unheard of evil, as it is without precedent. Fire has assailed many cities, but completely destroyed none. For even when the enemy's hand launches flames upon the rooftops, the blaze often dies out in many places; and although it may rekindle itself repeatedly, rarely does it so voraciously consume everything that it leaves nothing for the sword. Seldom, too, has an earthquake been so violent and ruinous as to overthrow entire towns. Indeed, no conflagration has ever raged so uncontrollably that nothing remained for a second burning.

[2] Yet a single night has laid low all those glorious structures, each one of which could have made a single city famous. In a time of such profound peace, a catastrophe has occurred which would have been considered dreadful even in war. Who can believe it? While weapons lay quiet everywhere and security prevails throughout the

world, Lugdunum, the showpiece of Gaul, is missing - one must search for its site.

To all those publicly afflicted by Fortune, she has granted an anticipation of their impending suffering. No great entity has ever collapsed without some interval in its downfall. But here, only a night intervened between a mighty city and no city. In short, it took me longer to tell you of its destruction than it took for the city to perish.

[3] All these events have unsettled our Liberalis, whose spirit is usually steadfast and upright in the face of personal misfortunes. And not without reason is he shaken, for unexpected blows fall more heavily. The novelty of it adds weight to the disaster, and there is no mortal who does not grieve more over that which has also aroused his wonder.

[4] Therefore, we should anticipate everything. The mind must be sent forward in advance and ought to ponder not just the usual course of events, but all possible contingencies. For what is there that Fortune cannot drag down from the pinnacle of success when she desires? What does she not assail and shake all the more forcefully the more brilliantly it shines? What is formidable or difficult for her?

[5] Misfortune does not always assail us along a single path, nor even with its full force. At times, it turns our own hands against ourselves; at others, content with its own strength, it finds perils without an instigator. No time is exempt; even in the midst of pleasures, causes for pain arise. War surges forth in a time of peace, and the very aids to our security transform into sources of fear. Friend becomes foe, ally becomes enemy. The tranquility of summer is stirred into sudden tempests, fiercer than those of winter. We suffer hostilities without an enemy; and if other causes are lacking, excessive good fortune finds reasons for our ruin. Disease invades the most temperate, consumption the most robust, punishment the most innocent, and riots the most secluded. Chance selects some new misfortune by which to impose its strength upon us, as if we had forgotten its power.

[6] Whatever a long span of time has built up through many labors and much divine favor, a single day scatters and disperses. The

saying "a day brings on evil with haste" grants a long reprieve to hastening misfortunes—an hour, a moment is sufficient for the overthrow of empires. It would be some solace for our weakness and our affairs if all things perished as slowly as they are created; but as it is, growth is slow, destruction is rapid.

[7] Nothing, either private or public, is stable; the fates of both men and cities are tossed about. Amidst the calmest of times, terror arises, and evils burst forth from where they are least anticipated with no external disturbance causing them. Kingdoms that have withstood civil wars and foreign threats collapse with no push at all. How few are the states that have sustained lasting felicity!

Therefore, we must reflect upon all possibilities and fortify our minds against what may befall us.

[8] Contemplate exile, torture, disease, wars, and shipwrecks. Chance can snatch you from your homeland, your homeland from you; it can drive you into wastelands; this very place in which the crowd suffocates can become a solitude. Let the whole condition of human life be placed before your eyes, and let us anticipate in our minds not how often these things happen, but the utmost that can possibly happen, if we do not wish to be overwhelmed and stunned by misfortunes as if they were novel and unfamiliar. We must fully consider Fortune's power.

[9] How many times have the cities of Asia, how many times those of Achaea, fallen by a single quake? How many towns in Syria, how many in Macedonia, have been swallowed up? How often has this kind of destruction laid waste to Cyprus? How often has Paphos collapsed upon itself? The annihilation of whole cities is often reported to us, and yet we, to whom such reports are often delivered —what fraction of the whole of humankind are we?

Let us rise up, therefore, against the blows of Fortune, and whatever befalls us, let us recognize that it is not as great as rumor proclaims it to be.

[10] The opulent city, an ornament of the provinces in which it was both embedded and distinct, has burned, though perched on a single hill, and not a very broad one at that. Of all those cities which

you now hear styled great and famous, even the mere traces will be erased by time. Do you not see how, in Achaia, the foundations of the most celebrated cities have already crumbled, leaving no evidence that they ever even existed?

[11] Not only does what is made by human hands totter and fall; not only is what human skill and industry have erected overthrown by the passing days; even the peaks of mountains dissolve, entire regions subside, and lands once far from the sight of the sea are submerged by the waves. The raging force of subterranean fires has eaten away the hills through which they once blazed, reducing those lofty summits that were once the solace of mariners and watchtowers to lowly mounds. The very works of nature are assailed, and thus we ought to endure the destruction of cities with equanimity.

[12] All that stands is destined to fall. This fate awaits everything, whether internal forces and violent winds, bursting forth from their confinement, hurl off the weight that holds them down; or raging torrents, mightier in their hidden depths, shatter the obstructions before them; or the ferocity of flames rips apart the framework of the earth; or age, from which nothing is safe, slowly wears it down; or the oppressive atmosphere drives away populations and ruins abandoned places with decay. It would be tedious to recount all the ways of fate. But this one thing I know: all the works of mortals are doomed by mortality; we live amidst things destined to perish.

[13] These and similar consolations I offer to our friend Liberalis, who burns with an incredible love for his native city, which has perhaps been destroyed only to be raised up again better than before. Misfortune has often made room for greater prosperity. Many things have fallen only to rise again higher. Timagenes, an enemy to Rome's prosperity, used to say that the only sorrow he felt about the city's fires was his knowledge that better buildings would arise than those that had burned.

[14] In this city, too, it is likely that everyone will strive to restore grander and more secure structures than those lost. May they stand long and be founded under better auspices for a more extended age! For this colony is now in its hundredth year since its founding, an age

not extreme even for a man. Established by Plancus, it grew strong through its favorable location, though it has endured grave misfortunes within the span of a human lifetime.

[15] Therefore, let the mind be trained to understand and endure its lot, knowing that fortune leaves nothing untried. Against kingdoms, it has the same right as against kings; against cities, the same power as against men. None of this should provoke our indignation. We have entered a world in which these are the terms of life. Do you accept them? Obey. Do you not accept them? Depart, by whatever way you will. Be indignant only if some unfairness has been especially appointed for you. But if this necessity binds high and low alike, be reconciled to fate, by which all things are dissolved.

[16] We should not judge ourselves by our tombs and these monuments that line the roads in varying sizes. Ashes make all equal. We are born unequal, but we die equal. What I say about cities, I say also about their inhabitants: Ardea was captured just as Rome was. That founder of human law did not distinguish us by birth or the fame of our names, except while we live. But when the end of mortals is reached, he says, "Away with ambition! Let the same law apply to all that lies upon the earth." We are equal in our capacity to endure all things. No one is more frail than another, no one more certain of tomorrow.

[17] Alexander, king of the Macedonians, had begun to study geometry—unhappy man, to realize how little the earth was, of which he had seized but a fraction. Yes, I call him unhappy, because he should have understood the falseness of his title. For who can be "the Great" on so small a scale? The concepts being taught were subtle and required careful attention to learn—not what a madman could grasp, sending his thoughts across the ocean. "Teach me something easy," he said. To which his tutor replied, "These things are the same for all, equally difficult."

[18] Imagine Nature saying this: "Those things you complain about are the same for all. I can give no one anything easier, but whoever wishes will make them easier for himself." How? Through equanimity. You must experience pain, thirst, hunger, and old age—if

a longer stay among men shall be granted you—and sickness, loss, and death.

[19] However, you should not believe those who clamor around you; none of these things are evil, intolerable, or harsh. Their fear is born from consensus. In the same way you fear death, you fear infamy. Yet what is more foolish than a person who fears mere words? Our friend Demetrius is fond of saying that he regards the voices of the ignorant in the same way as he does the rumblings of the belly. "For what does it matter to me," he asks, "whether they sound from above or below[2]?"

[20] How insane it is to be afraid of being defamed by the infamous! Just as you have feared infamy without cause, so too do you fear those things that you would never fear unless rumor had commanded it. Would a good man suffer any harm when besmirched by unjust rumors?

[21] Let not even death harm us in this regard, though it too has a bad odor. None of those who accuse death have experienced it. Meanwhile, it is rash to condemn what you do not know. But this you do know: how useful death is to many, how it frees so many from torments, poverty, complaints, punishments, and weariness. We are not in anyone's power when death is in our own power. Farewell.

---

1. Modern-day Lyon
2. The Latin phrase "susum isti an deosum sonent" literally translates to "whether those [sounds] sound upward or downward." The intended meaning is whether the ignorant voices come from above (the mouth) or below (the belly).

LETTER 92

THE SUFFICIENCY OF VIRTUE
FOR A HAPPY LIFE

[1] I BELIEVE, LUCILIUS, YOU AND I WOULD AGREE THAT WHILE EXTERNAL things are acquired for the body, and the body is cherished for the sake of the soul, there are subservient parts within the soul itself through which we move and are nourished, bestowed upon us for the sake of the commanding faculty. In this commanding part, there is both something irrational and something rational. The former is subordinate to the latter, which alone is not referred to anything else but rather refers all things to itself. For even that divine reason which presides over all is subject to nothing, and our human reason is the same, being derived from the divine.

[2] If we are in accord on this point, it follows that we would also agree on the principle that the happy life depends on this one thing: the perfection of our reason. For reason alone does not succumb to the spirit, but stands firm against fortune, preserving us in calm security no matter the circumstances. And this alone is the one true good that can never be diminished. The man, I say, is blessed whom nothing makes lesser; he holds to the heights, relying on nothing except himself. For one who is sustained by any external support can fall. If it were otherwise, things outside our control would start to

greatly influence us. But what prudent person wants their constancy to fortune or to marvel at themselves for another's qualities?

[3] What is the happy life? It is peace of mind and lasting tranquility. This will be given by greatness of soul, by the steadfastness of a mind firmly grounded in good judgment. How is this state reached? By gaining a complete view of truth, by observing, in all that we do, an order, measure and propriety, by a will that is harmless and kind, focused on reason and never departing from it, inspiring love and wonder. To sum it up for you briefly, the wise man's soul should be such as befits a god.

[4] What more can one desire who possesses all that is honorable? For if dishonorable things can contribute anything to the best condition, then the happy life will reside in those things without which it cannot be honorable. And what is more shameful or foolish than to link the good of a rational soul with the irrational?

[5] Yet some judge that the highest good can be amplified because it is not quite complete when battling hostile fortune. Even Antipater, one of the great authorities of this school, says that he grants some small influence to external things, albeit very slight. But you see what manner of thing it is to not be content unless some tiny spark should shine upon the daylight. In the bright sunshine, what significance can a mere glimmer have?

[6] If you are not content with virtue alone, you will inevitably desire either tranquility, which the Greeks call *aochlēsia*, or pleasure. The former is acceptable to some degree, for the mind, when free from distress, has the leisure to contemplate the universe, undistracted from its study of nature. But pleasure, that latter aim, is fit only for beasts. Shall we add the irrational to the rational, the dishonorable to the honorable? Is the titillation of the body what leads to this [base] life? Why then hesitate to say that all is well with a man if his palate is satisfied?

[7] And this creature—I do not count him among men, let alone heroes—whose highest good consists of flavors, colors, and sounds? Let him be cast out from the preeminent position of living beings,

second only to the gods. Let him be lumped in with the mute animals that delight in fodder.

[8] The irrational part of the soul has two parts: one spirited, ambitious, uncontrolled, steeped in passions; the other low, languid, given over to pleasures. [The Epicureans] relinquished the former—unrestrained, yet superior, certainly braver and more worthy of a man. But they deemed the latter, the weak and abject part, necessary for the happy life.

[9] They bid reason to serve this part, and so they made the highest good of the noblest living creature something base and ignoble—a monstrous hybrid stitched together from ill-fitting parts. As our Virgil says of Scylla:

> *"Above, a human face and a maiden's lovely breast,*
> *Down to the waist; below, a monstrous body, a sea-dragon*
> *With dolphins' tails attached to a belly of wolves."*

Yet to this Scylla are joined wild beasts, terrible and swift. But from what freakish parts have they cobbled together their "wisdom"?

[10] Man's foremost art is virtue itself. But to this [the Epicureans] attach the useless, fluid flesh, fit only to be a receptacle for food, as Posidonius says. That divine virtue thus terminates in something slippery, with a lazy, decaying animal nature tacked on to its august and heavenly upper parts. The other condition, tranquility, offered no positive benefit to the mind, but at least removed impediments. Pleasure actively dissolves and saps all strength. What could be a more discordant amalgamation of elements? The most vigorous is lashed to the most torpid, the most severe to the most frivolous, the most sacred to the most profligate [even to the point of incest]. "What then?" he objects, "if sound health, tranquility and freedom from pain pose no obstacle to virtue, will you not seek them?"

[11] Why shouldn't I seek them? Not because they are good, but because they are in accordance with nature, and because I will choose them with good judgment. What then will be good about them? Just this one thing: that they are chosen well. For when I put

on appropriate clothing, when I walk as I should, when I dine as I ought, it is not the dinner or the walk or the clothing that is good, but my purpose in them - maintaining the appropriate measure in each thing that accords with reason.

[12] Let me add this as well: the choice of clean clothing is desirable for a person. For by nature, the human is a clean and refined creature. And so clean clothing is not good in itself, but rather the choice of clean clothing, because the good lies not in the thing but in the quality of the choice. Our actions are honorable, not the things that are done.

[13] What I have said about clothing, consider that I say the same about the body. For nature has also arrayed this around the soul as a kind of clothing; it is its covering. But who has ever judged a scabbard by the case? It is not the sheath that makes a sword good or bad. Therefore, I give you this same reply about the body too: if given the choice, I would indeed choose health and strength, but the goodness will lie in my judgment about them, not in the things themselves.

[14] "Indeed," says the objector, "the wise person is happy; yet he does not attain that highest good unless he is also equipped with the natural instruments. Thus, one who has virtue cannot be wretched, yet he is not supremely happy if he is deprived of natural goods such as health and soundness of limb."

[15] You grant what seems more unbelievable - that someone amidst the greatest and most constant pains is not wretched but is even happy. But you deny what is easier - that he is supremely happy. Yet if virtue has the power to keep someone from being wretched, it will more easily make him supremely happy. For less of an interval remains from happy to supremely happy than from wretched to happy. Or does the factor that has such strength that it can place one snatched from calamities among the happy, lack the ability to add what remains to make him supremely happy? Does it fail at the peak of the ascent?

[16] In life, there are both advantages and disadvantages, both of which lie outside ourselves. If a good man is not miserable, even if burdened by every disadvantage, how is he not most blessed if he

lacks some advantages? For just as he is not weighed down to wretchedness by a load of disadvantages, so he is not dragged from supreme blessedness by a lack of advantages. He is just as blessed without advantages as he is not miserable under disadvantages. Otherwise, his own good could be snatched away from him if it could be diminished.

[17] A little earlier, I was saying that a tiny flame adds nothing to the light of the sun, for whatever would shine without the sun is hidden by its brilliance. "But," one objects, "certain things block even the sun." Yet the sun remains whole[1] even among obstacles, and although something may lie between us and prevent our view of it, the sun is at work, speeding on its course. Whenever it shines out from amid the clouds, it is no smaller than when the sky is clear, nor is it any slower. For it makes a great difference whether something merely obstructs or actually impedes.

[18] In the same way, things that oppose virtue take nothing away from it; virtue is not lesser, but shines less brightly. To us, perhaps, virtue does not appear as resplendent and brilliant, but to itself, it remains the same and, like the sun behind clouds, deploys its power in obscurity. Therefore, calamities, losses, and injustices have the same effect on virtue as a mist has on the sun.

[19] There are those who say that the wise man, when his body is not prospering, is neither wretched nor blessed. But this view, too, is mistaken, for it equates the gifts of fortune with virtues and ascribes as much to things devoid of moral worth as to those possessing it. Yet what is fouler or more unworthy than to compare the venerable with the contemptible? For justice, piety, faith, fortitude, and prudence are venerable, while on the other hand, things that frequently abound more fully in the vilest individuals are vile, such as a sound leg, strong arms, teeth, and firm, robust muscles[2].

[20] Furthermore, if the wise man who is physically troubled is considered neither wretched nor blessed, but left in between[3], then his life will be neither desirable nor to be avoided. But what is so absurd as a wise man's life not being desirable? Or what is so beyond belief as the existence of a life that is neither to be sought nor

avoided? Moreover, if bodily adversities do not make one wretched, they allow one to be blessed. For circumstances that have no power to demote one to a worse state lack the ability to disturb the best state.

[21] "We recognize cold and hot," he says, "and tepid lies between them. In the same way, someone is happy, someone is miserable, and someone is neither happy nor miserable." I want to examine this analogy used against us. If I add more cold to the tepid, it will become cold. If I pour in more heat, it will eventually become hot. But for the person who is neither miserable nor happy, no matter how much I add to their miseries, they will not become miserable, as you say. Therefore, this analogy is flawed.

[22] Next, I present to you a person neither miserable nor happy. To them I add blindness—they do not become miserable. I add disability—they do not become miserable. I add constant, severe pains—they do not become miserable. One whom so many misfortunes do not shift into a wretched life, surely they do not dislodge them from a happy one either.

[23] If the sage cannot, as you claim, fall from happiness into misery, he cannot fall into non-happiness. For why would one who has begun to slip stop somewhere? What keeps him from tumbling to the bottom also holds him at the top. Why can the happy life not be cut short? It cannot even be reduced, and thus virtue on its own suffices for it.

[24] "What then?" he objects. "Is the sage who has lived longer, undisturbed by any pain, not happier than one who has always struggled with misfortune?" Answer me this: is the former any better or more honorable? If not, then he is not any happier either. One must live more rightly to live more happily; if one cannot do the former, he cannot do the latter. Virtue does not intensify, and thus neither does the happy life, which stems from virtue. For virtue is so great a good that it is unaffected by these minor additions—brevity of life, pain, and the body's various troubles. As for pleasure, it is unworthy of consideration.

[25] What is preeminent in virtue? Not needing the future, not counting one's days. In however small a span, it achieves eternal

goods. To us, this seems incredible and to exceed human nature. For we measure virtue's majesty by our own weakness, labeling it with the name of our vices. Yet is it not equally unbelievable for someone to say "I am happy" while in the height of torments? Such a cry has been heard in the very workshop of pleasure. "This day and that I deem most blessed," proclaimed Epicurus, while racked by the agony of blocked urine on one side and an ulcerated stomach incurable on the other.

[26] Why, then, should these things seem unbelievable among those who cultivate virtue, when they are also found among those ruled by pleasure? Even these degenerate and most base-minded individuals say that the wise man, in the midst of the greatest pains and calamities, will be neither miserable nor happy. And yet, this too is unbelievable—nay, more unbelievable still. For I do not see how virtue, once cast down from its lofty pinnacle, is not reduced to the lowest depths. It must either ensure happiness, or if driven from this, it will not prevent one from becoming miserable. That which stands cannot be overthrown; it must either conquer or be conquered.

[27] "To the immortal gods alone," they say, "belong virtue and the happy life; to us, mere shadows and semblances of such goods. We may draw near to them, but never fully attain them." Yet reason is common to both gods and men; in the former, it is fully developed, while in us, it is capable of full development.

[28] But it is our vices that lead us to despair; for that other, second-rate individual is inconstant in upholding the highest ideals, his judgment still wavers and is uncertain. He may long for the pleasures of sight and hearing, good health, a body not unpleasant to look upon, maintaining its natural condition, and furthermore, a rather lengthy span of life.

[29] Through virtue, one can lead a life without regret, but in the imperfect man, there is a certain potency of evil, for his mind is prone to wickedness. That apparent and vehement evil is absent[4]; he is not yet good, but is being molded for goodness. But whoever lacks something of goodness is evil. However, if one possesses virtue and a mind

at peace within the body, he equals the gods and, mindful of his origin, strives towards them.

[30] No one endeavors to ascend improperly to that place from which he has descended. Why, then, should you not believe that something divine exists within a being who is a part of God? This whole universe that encompasses us is both one and God; we are His partners and His limbs. Our soul is capable of great things and is carried to lofty heights if vices do not drag it down. Just as our bodies are formed to stand erect and gaze upon the heavens, so too is our soul—which can extend itself as far as it desires—shaped by the nature of existence to wish for equality with the gods. And if it uses its own strength and stretches into its proper space, it strives toward the greatest heights by no path but its own.

[31] Great was the labor to ascend to heaven, but now the way is found and the journey is made with boldness, contemptuous of all things. The soul pays no heed to wealth, deeming gold and silver most worthy of those shadowy depths in which they once lay, estimating them not by the glittering splendor that dazzles the eyes of the inexperienced, but by the ancient mire from which our greed separated and mined them.

The soul knows, I say, that true riches are situated elsewhere than where they are commonly piled up; it is the mind that must be filled, not the coffers.

[32] We may place the soul in dominion over all things and usher it into possession of the whole of nature, so that it might bound its own empire by the rising and setting sun, and like the gods, possess all things.

> *With its vast wealth, it may look down from on high upon*
> *the wealthy,*
> *none of whom takes as much pleasure in his own prosperity*
> *as he does anguish in another's.*

[33] When the soul has raised itself to these lofty heights, it regards the body too as but a necessary burden—not as something to

love, but rather to manage. Nor does it subject itself to that over which it is set. No one is free who is a slave to his body. For to pass over all the other masters which an excessive concern for the body inevitably finds, the body's own rule is capricious and demanding.

[34] Sometimes he departs this life with a tranquil mind, sometimes with an exultant leap, unconcerned about what will eventually become of what he leaves behind. But just as we pay no heed to trimmed hair and beard clippings, so too that divine soul, when departing from its human vessel, cares not whether fire consumes its former receptacle, stone entombs it, earth grinds it to dust, or wild beasts tear it asunder. No more does it consider such matters its concern than a newborn does the afterbirth. Let the birds scatter the abandoned corpse or "the carcass be prey for dogs of the sea"[5]—what is that to him, who is nothing?

[35] But even while he dwells among men, he has no fear of any postmortem threats from those who deem it too little to be feared only up to the moment of death. "I do not shrink," he says, "from the executioner's hook nor the revolting mutilation of my corpse, a gruesome sight for onlookers. I ask no one to perform my final rites; I entrust my remains to no one. Nature has seen to it that none shall go unburied. Time will lay to rest those cast out by cruelty." Maecenas put it eloquently:

"I care not for a tomb. Nature buries the abandoned."

You would think it the utterance of a man with his tunic belted high. For he had a noble and manly spirit, though prosperity sometimes loosened his moral belt. Farewell.

---

1. Alternative reading: "the sun itself is undiminished"
2. Alternative translation: "sinews"
3. Alternatively, "in the middle"
4. Some manuscripts include the phrase "from the good" after "absent."
5. A quote from Vergil.

LETTER 93

DEATH COMES TO ALL; LIVE
EACH DAY FULLY

[1] In your letter lamenting the death of the philosopher Metronax, you remarked that he could have and should have lived longer. I find myself missing the sense of fairness you demonstrate in every other matter and towards every other person, but which has abandoned you here, as it does everyone in this one area. I have known many who are fair-minded towards their fellow humans, but towards the gods, not a single one. We rail against Fate daily, demanding: "Why was this man snatched away in the midst of his journey? Why is that one not taken? Why does he draw out a old age burdensome to himself and others?"

[2] Tell me, which do you consider more equitable - that you obey Nature, or that Nature obey you? What does it matter how quickly you depart from where you must depart regardless? Our care should not be to live long, but to live fully. For living long requires Fate, but living fully requires a soul. Life is long if it is fulfilled; and it becomes fulfilled when the soul has rendered its own good unto itself and transferred authority over itself to itself.

[3] What benefit are eighty years idled away to any man? That one did not live, but merely lingered in life. He did not die late, but rather,

he was a long time dying. "He lived eighty years," you say. That depends on the day from which you start counting his death!

[4] "But," you object, "he expired in the bloom of life." Yet he fulfilled the duties of a good citizen, a good friend, a good son; he was not found wanting in any regard. His age may have been incomplete, but his life was complete. "He lived eighty years," you repeat. No, he existed for eighty years - unless perchance you say he lived in the same way trees are said to live.

I implore you, Lucilius, let us strive to make our lives not just long in duration, like precious objects, but heavy in weight and meaning. Let us measure life by activity, not by time. Do you want to know the difference between this vigorous soul who spurned Fortune, who fulfilled all the duties of human life and ascended to the highest good, and that other fellow who merely let many years pass him by? The former lives on even after death; the latter perished before he ever truly died.

[5] So let us praise and count as blessed the man who invested however little time he was allotted wisely and well. For he beheld the true light. He was not just one of the crowd, but truly lived and flourished. At times he enjoyed fair winds; at others, as often happens, the brilliant radiance of a mighty star burst forth amidst the clouds. Why do you ask how long he lived? He lives still! He has vaulted across to join our descendants and committed himself to memory.

[6] And yet I would not refuse the addition of more years to my life, though I will profess that nothing was lacking for my happiness, even if its span is cut short. For I have not shaped myself for that day which greedy hope had promised would be my last, but I have looked upon every day as if it could be my final one. Why do you ask me when I was born, whether I should still be counted among the young?

[7] I have my own measure. Just as a man can be perfect in a lesser stature of body, so too can life be perfect in a lesser span of time. Age is something external. How long I may exist is not for me to say; that I do exist, is my own doing. This is what you should expect of me - that

I not pass through my days as if through an obscure mist, but that I truly live my life, not merely endure it.

[8] Do you ask what is the fullest extent of life? To live until one attains wisdom. He who reaches it has attained not the longest end, but the greatest. Let him rejoice boldly and give thanks to the gods, and credit himself and the nature of things for what he has been. Rightly he will take credit, for he has given back a better life than he received. He has set forth the model of a good man, showing what kind and how great he could be. If anything had been added, it would have been more of the same.

[9] And yet, how long do we live on? We have enjoyed the understanding of all things. We know from what principles Nature raises herself aloft, how she orders the universe, by what cycles she brings back the year, how she has enclosed all that ever was and made herself her own end. We know that the stars course on by their own motion, that nothing is fixed but the earth, while all else runs on with unceasing speed. We know how the moon outstrips the sun, why, though slower, she leaves the swifter light behind; how she receives or loses her light, what cause intrudes the night, what brings back the day. To that place must we go, where we can gaze upon these things more closely. [10] "And with this hope," says our wise man, "I depart more boldly, because I judge the way open for me to my own gods. I have indeed deserved to be admitted among them, and already I have been with them in spirit, sending my mind to them as they sent theirs to me. But suppose that I am utterly annihilated, and that after death no part of man remains; I have a spirit just as lofty, even if I am to pass away into nothingness."

[11] "He did not live as many years as he could have." And yet a book of few pages can be praiseworthy and useful; you know how ponderous are the annals of Tanusius, and what men think of them. Some men's lives are long in the same way that Tanusius' annals are long.

[12] Do you consider the man who is slain on the final day of the games any more fortunate than the one who perishes in the middle of the spectacle? Do you believe that anyone is so foolishly enamored

with life that he would prefer to have his throat cut in the spoliarium[1] than in the arena itself? We do not precede one another by any great length of time. Death makes its way through us all; the slayer quickly catches up to the slain. It is the smallest of matters over which we are so exceedingly anxious. But what does it matter how long you evade that which you cannot escape in the end? Farewell.

---

1. The place where fallen gladiators were stripped of their armor

LETTER 94
THE ROLE AND VALUE OF PHILOSOPHICAL PRECEPTS

[1] SOME HAVE ACCEPTED ONLY THAT PART OF PHILOSOPHY WHICH GIVES precepts to each individual person, not considering man in general but advising how a husband should conduct himself toward his wife, how a father should educate his children, and how a master should govern his slaves. They relegate other areas as if wandering outside our practical needs, as though one could give advice about a part without first comprehending the sum of the whole of life.

[2] But Ariston the Stoic, on the contrary, regards this part as trivial, not penetrating into the heart but possessing old womanish[1] precepts. He says that the actual doctrines of philosophy and the establishment of the highest good are of the utmost benefit. Whoever has well understood and learned this dictates to himself what must be done in each case. Just as one learning to throw a javelin picks a target spot and trains his hand to direct his missiles, and when he has acquired this skill from instruction and practice, he uses it wherever he wishes - for he has learned to strike not just this or that target, but whatever he wants - so too one who has equipped himself for the whole of life does not need to be advised in parts, being skilled in the whole; for he knows how to live well overall, not just how to live with a wife or a son.

[3] But living well overall includes how he should live with wife and children.

[4] Cleanthes judges this part to be useful but feeble unless it flows from the universal principles, unless one has learned the very doctrines and main points of philosophy. This topic is therefore divided into two questions: whether it is useful or useless, and whether it alone can make a good man - that is, whether it is super-fluous[2] or renders all else superfluous.

[5] Those who consider this part superfluous say: "If something blocks and hinders the eyesight, it must be removed. With that obstacle present, he who gives precepts like 'you will walk thus, you will stretch out your hand to there' is wasting his efforts. In the same way, when something blinds the mind and obstructs the discernment of the order of our duties, it is futile to advise 'live thus with your father, thus with your wife.' For precepts will avail nothing as long as error is clouding the mind; but if that is dispelled, it will be clear what one owes to each duty. Otherwise, you are teaching a man what he should do if healthy, but not making him healthy."

[6] You instruct a poor man to act as if he were rich; but how can this be accomplished while his poverty remains? You are showing a starving man what to do as if he were well-fed. Instead, you must first remove the hunger that is lodged deep in his marrow. I tell you the same about all vices: the vices themselves must be eliminated, rather than advising what cannot be done while the vices persist. Unless you drive out the false opinions that plague us, neither the greedy man will listen to advice on how to use money, nor the timid man on how to despise dangers.

[7] You must make the greedy man understand that money is neither good nor evil; show him the most wretched of rich men. Make the timid man realize that the things we commonly dread are not as frightening as rumor portrays them, and that neither grief nor death are to be feared. [Death, which we all must face by nature's law, often brings great solace in that it comes to no one twice.] As a remedy for grief, you must instill a stubborn resolution of the mind, which lightens all suffering borne with defiance. The best quality of

pain is that if it is long it cannot be severe, and if it is severe it cannot be long. All things must be endured with fortitude that the immutable laws of the universe compel us to bear.

[8] When by these doctrines you have led a man to the contemplation of his true state, and he recognizes that the happy life depends not on pleasure but on living according to nature, when he has come to love virtue as man's sole good and to flee baseness as the only evil, and knows that all else—riches, office, health, strength, power—are neither good nor bad but lie in between, then he will not require an advisor for every action, proclaiming: "Walk thus, eat thus. This is appropriate for a man, that for a woman; this for a married man, that for a bachelor."

[9] For those who give such detailed advice cannot follow it themselves. It is the pedagogue advising the boy, the grandmother her grandson; the angriest of teachers lectures on the need to control anger. If you enter an elementary school, you will see that these maxims, pompously spouted by philosophers, are found in the primers of children.

[10] Will your precepts then be obvious or doubtful? The obvious do not require an advisor; the doubtful are not heeded on the advisor's word alone, so precepts are superfluous. Learn it thus: if your precepts are obscure or ambiguous, they must be supported by argument. But if you are going to prove them, your proofs are more effective and sufficient in themselves.

[11] Treat your friend this way, treat your fellow citizen this way, treat your associate this way. Why? Because it is just. The topic of justice teaches me all these things. There I find that fairness is to be sought for its own sake, that we are compelled to it not by fear nor hired to it by reward, that one is not just if anything in this virtue pleases him other than the virtue itself. When I have persuaded myself of this and absorbed it fully, how do those precepts benefit me, which instruct one already learned? Giving precepts to one who knows is superfluous; to one who does not know, it is insufficient. For he ought to hear not only what is instructed to him, but also why.

[12] Those who hold true opinions about good and evil—are the

precepts necessary for them, I ask, or not? One who does not hold them will not be helped by you at all; rumor running contrary to your admonitions has already possessed his ears. One who has an accurate judgment about what is to be sought and what is to be avoided knows what he must do, even if you are silent. Therefore that entire part of philosophy can be put aside.

[13] "There are two reasons why we go astray: either there is in the soul an evil contracted from wrong opinions, or, even if it is not occupied by falsehoods, it is inclined toward falsehoods and is quickly corrupted by the semblance of things, drawing it where it should not go. And so we ought either to treat the sick mind and free it from vices, or take preemptive measures for the mind when it is idle but inclined to worse things. The doctrines of philosophy accomplish both. Therefore, that sort of preceptive instruction accomplishes nothing."

[14] Besides, if we give precepts to individuals, the task is incomprehensible. For we ought to give some to the moneylender, others to the farmer, others to the merchant, others to one pursuing the friendships of kings, others to one who will love his equals, others to one who will love his inferiors.

[15] In marriage will you instruct how a man should live with a wife he married as a virgin, how with one who had experienced another's bed before marriage, how with a wealthy woman, how with one who brought no dowry? Or do you not think there is some difference between a barren woman and a fertile one, between an older woman and a young girl, between a mother and a stepmother? We cannot encompass all types, and yet each requires its own rules. But the laws of philosophy are concise and bind all cases.

[16] Add now that the precepts of wisdom ought to be finite and certain; if they cannot be limited, they are outside of wisdom; wisdom knows the boundaries of things.

"Therefore that preceptive part is to be put aside, because what it promises to a few, it cannot furnish to all. But wisdom holds all people."

[17] There is no difference between the insanity of the public and

that which is entrusted to physicians, except that the latter labors under a disease, the former under false opinions. One derives the causes of madness from ill health, the other is an unhealthy state of mind. If one were to give precepts to a madman as to how he ought to speak, how to walk, how to behave in public and in private, one would be more insane than the person one was advising. The black bile must be treated and the very cause of the madness removed. The same must be done in this other insanity of the mind; the disorder itself must be shaken off, otherwise the words of those advising will vanish into the void.

[18] These statements come from Aristo, to which we shall respond point by point. First, as to his assertion that if anything obstructs the eye and impedes vision, it ought to be removed. I admit that in this case, there is no need for precepts in order to see, but rather for a remedy by which the organ is cleansed and escapes the hindrance that impairs it. For we see by nature, and one who removes obstacles restores nature's function. But nature does not teach what is owed to each duty.

[19] Moreover, one whose suffusion [cataract] has been treated does not immediately regain sight, but can also restore it to others; one freed from wickedness also frees others. There is no need for encouragement, nor even for counsel, for the eye to perceive the properties of colors; it will distinguish white from black even without prompting. The mind, on the other hand, needs many precepts to discern what must be done in life. Nevertheless, the physician not only treats the ailing eyes but also advises them.

[20] "Do not," says he, "immediately expose your weak vision to bright light; proceed first from darkness to shadowy places, then venture further and gradually accustom yourself to endure clear light. Do not study directly after eating; do not task your eyes when they are swollen and inflamed; avoid the rush and force of cold wind striking your face," and other similar admonitions that are no less beneficial than medicines. Medicine supplements remedies with counsel.

[21] "Error," says Aristo, "is the cause of sin. Precepts do not remove

this from us nor overthrow false opinions about good and evil." I concede that precepts by themselves are not effective in uprooting a distorted mental conviction. But it does not follow that they are of no benefit, particularly when combined with other measures. First, they refresh the memory; secondly, what seemed rather confused when considered as a whole becomes clearer when divided into parts. Otherwise, by this logic, you might say that consolation and exhortation are also superfluous. But they are not superfluous; therefore, neither are admonitions.

[22] "It is foolish," he says, "to prescribe to a sick person how they ought to act as if they were well, when their health must first be restored, without which the precepts are useless." Yet do not the sick and the healthy have certain precepts in common which they should both be advised of? Such as not to eat food too greedily and to avoid overexertion. The poor and the rich have some precepts in common.

[23] "Cure avarice," he says, "and you will have no reason to admonish either the poor or the rich, if the desire of both has subsided." But is it not one thing to not covet money, and another to know how to use money? Even those who are not greedy do not understand the proper use of it, let alone the greedy who have no moderation. "Remove the errors," he says, "and precepts become superfluous." This is false. For suppose that avarice is slackened, that luxury is confined, that rashness has had reins put on it, that sluggishness has been spurred; even with vices removed, we must still learn what we ought to do and how we ought to do it.

[24] "Admonitions," he says, "will accomplish nothing when applied to serious faults." Medicine cannot conquer incurable diseases either, yet it is still employed, for some as a remedy, for others as relief. Not even the power of universal philosophy, though it summon all its strength for the purpose, will remove a chronic and ingrained plague of the soul. But that does not mean it heals nothing because it does not heal everything.

[25] "What good does it do," he asks, "to point out the obvious?" A great deal of good; for sometimes we know facts without paying attention to them. Admonition does not teach, but it engages the

attention, rouses us, and concentrates the memory, preventing us from slipping away. We often disregard what lies right before our eyes. Admonishing is a form of exhortation. The mind often tries to ignore even the obvious; therefore, the notoriety of the most notorious facts must be forced upon it. Here we must cite Calvus' jibe against Vatinius: "You all know that bribery took place, and everyone knows that you know it."

[26] You know that friendships should be scrupulously honored, but you do not do it. You know it is wrong for a man to demand chastity of his wife while he himself seduces other men's wives; you know that as the adulterer should have no dealings with her, neither should you yourself with a mistress - and yet you do not act accordingly. Therefore, your memory must be refreshed repeatedly; for the precepts should not just be stored away, but ready at hand. Any wholesome maxims need to be often agitated and often reflected upon, so that they may be not only familiar to us, but also prepared for use. And add now the fact that even obvious things tend to become more obvious through repetition.

[27] "If your precepts are doubtful," he objects, "you will have to add proofs; so the proofs, not the precepts, will be beneficial." But cannot the authority of the advisor carry weight even without proofs? It is much like how the legal opinions of jurists hold sway even when no reasoning is provided. Besides, the precepts themselves contain much force in their own right, especially if woven into verse or condensed into prose maxims, like those famous lines of Cato: "Buy not what you need, but what is necessary; what you do not need is dear even at a penny." Similar are those lines that resemble oracular responses: "Be thrifty with time" and "Know thyself."

[28] Surely you would not demand a reason if someone recited these verses to you:

> *The remedy for wrongs is to forget them.*
> *Fortune favors the bold; the sluggard hinders himself.*

Such sayings require no advocate; they touch our emotions and prove effective by virtue of nature exercising her power.

[29] The seeds of all honorable things are contained in the soul, and they are roused by admonition, just as a spark, fanned by a gentle breeze, develops its natural fire. Virtue is awakened when touched and stirred. Moreover, certain notions are indeed present in the mind, but not readily available; they begin to be at our disposal once verbalized. Certain ideas lie scattered about in different places, which the untrained mind is unable to pull together. Therefore they must be assembled and connected so that they have more potency and more effectively uplift the spirit.

[30] If precepts do not help at all, then all instruction should be abolished and we should be content with nature alone.

Those who say this fail to see that one person's intellect is nimble and upright, another's slow and dull, and certainly some are more naturally gifted than others. The power of the intellect is nourished and augmented by precepts, gaining new beliefs in addition to its inborn ones, and correcting those that are misguided.

[31] "If one does not have correct judgments," he objects, "how will admonitions help him, entangled as he is with faults?" In this way, obviously: that he may be freed from them. For his natural disposition has not been snuffed out, but obscured and suppressed. Even so, it still strives to rise again and struggles against its flaws. But once it has gained assistance and help from precepts, it waxes strong— unless, that is, chronic ruin has infected it and put it to death. For in that case, not even the teachings of philosophy, with all the force they can muster, will rebuild it. Really, what is the difference between the doctrines of philosophy and its precepts, except that the former are general and the latter specific? Both advise, but one does so comprehensively, the other in detail.

[32] "If someone," he says, "holds correct and honorable principles, it is superfluous to advise him." Not at all; for even the learned may know what they ought to do, but fail to fully grasp it. We are hindered from doing what is right not only by our emotions, but also by our inexperience in discerning what each situation demands. At times,

our mind is well-ordered but idle, untrained in finding the path of duty, which advice can reveal.

[33] "Banish," he says, "false opinions about good and evil, replace them with true ones, and advice will have nothing left to do." Undoubtedly, the mind is regulated by this method, but not by this alone. For although we may conclude through reasoning what is good and evil, precepts still play their part. Both prudence and justice consist of duties, and duties are arranged by precepts.

[34] Moreover, the very judgment of good and evil is strengthened by the performance of duties, to which precepts lead. The two are in agreement; precepts cannot come first without duties following. And duties follow their own order, which shows that precepts must come first[3].

[35] "Precepts," he says, "are infinite." This is false. For regarding the greatest and most necessary matters, they are not infinite. They have subtle differences, varying with times, places, and persons, but even for these, general precepts are given.

[36] "No one," he says, "treats insanity with precepts; therefore, neither should wickedness be so treated." The cases are different. For if you remove insanity, sanity returns; but if we banish false opinions, a clear understanding of what we must do does not immediately follow[4]. Even for that to follow, advice will reinforce correct judgment about good and evil. It is also false that precepts have no effect on the insane. For just as they are not sufficient alone, they aid in the cure. Both warning and chastisement restrain the insane—I speak now of those whose mind is disturbed but not destroyed.

[37] "Laws," he says, "do not make us do what we ought, and what are they but precepts mingled with threats?" First, laws do not persuade because they threaten, while precepts do not compel but entreat. Second, laws deter from crime, precepts exhort to duty. Add to this that laws also contribute to good morals, especially if they not only command but also teach[5].

[38] On this matter, I disagree with Posidonius, who says: "I disapprove of the fact that explanatory introductions have been added to Plato's laws. For a law should be brief, so that the uneducated may

more easily grasp it. It should be like a divinely uttered pronounce-ment; it should command, not argue. Nothing seems to me more pointless and absurd than a law with a prologue. Advise me, tell me what you want me to do; I'm not here to learn, but to obey." But do such prologues actually benefit anyone? You will notice that states with bad laws tend to have bad customs. "But laws don't benefit every-one," he objects.

[39] Well, neither does philosophy; but that doesn't make it useless and ineffective in shaping minds. Really though, isn't philos-ophy a law of life? But let's assume laws are not beneficial; it does not follow that advice is also useless. By that logic, you'd also have to deny the efficacy of consolation, dissuasion, encouragement, censure, and praise. All of these are forms of advice. It is through such means that one arrives at a perfected state of mind.

[40] Nothing instills honorable inclinations in the mind and recalls those who are wavering and prone to vice back to virtue more effectively than associating with good men. Gradually, their influence seeps into the heart and the power of their precepts is felt through frequent contact and conversation. Just encountering wise men is edifying, by Hercules, and one can profit from a great man even when he is silent.

[41] I could not easily tell you how this benefits you, though I understand that it has. "Certain tiny creatures," as Phaedon remarks, "when they sting are not even felt; so subtle and deceptive is their power to inflict harm. A swelling indicates the bite, but no wound can be seen on the swelling itself." The same will happen to you in the company of wise men: you will not realize how or when it benefits you, but you will realize that it has.

[42] "What's the point of all this?" you ask. Good precepts, if they are often with you, will benefit you just as much as good examples. Pythagoras says that a different mental attitude develops in those who enter a temple and view images of the gods up close while awaiting the utterance of an oracle.

[43] Moreover, who could deny that even the most inexperienced

are effectively struck by certain precepts? For instance, these very brief maxims that carry great weight:

> *Nothing in excess.*
> *A greedy mind is satisfied by no gain.*
> *Expect from another what you have done to another.*

We hear these sayings with a certain impact, and no one can doubt or question "Why?"; the truth itself compels us, even without reasoning.

[44] If reverence restrains the mind and curbs vices, why can admonition not accomplish the same? If reproof instills a sense of shame, why should admonition fail to do so, even if it employs bare precepts? Surely, the most effective and penetrating admonition is that which supports its precepts with reason, which adds why each action must be taken and what fruits await the one who acts and obeys the precepts. If progress is made through commands, it is also made through admonition; and indeed, progress is made through commands; therefore, it is also made through admonition.

[45] Virtue is divided into two parts: the contemplation of truth and action. Instruction imparts contemplation, while admonition guides action. Right action both exercises and demonstrates virtue. If one who persuades benefits the prospective doer, then one who admonishes will also benefit. Thus, if right action is necessary for virtue, and admonition reveals right actions, then admonition is necessary.

[46] Two things above all impart great strength to the mind: faith in truth and self-confidence. Admonition creates both[6]. For it is believed, and when it has been believed, the mind conceives great inspiration and is filled with confidence. Therefore, admonition is not superfluous.

Marcus Agrippa, a man of prodigious spirit and the only one of those whom the civil wars made famous and powerful to enjoy public success, used to say that he owed much to this maxim: "For by concord small things grow, by discord the greatest things fall apart." By this, he claimed to have become the best of brothers and friends.

[47] If such maxims, when intimately welcomed into the mind, mold it, why can this branch of philosophy, which consists of such maxims, not accomplish the same? Part of virtue consists of learning, part of training; you must both learn and confirm what you have learned by putting it into practice. If this is so, not only the teachings of wisdom are beneficial but also the precepts that constrain and banish our passions as if by edict.

[48] "Philosophy," they say, "is divided into these parts: knowledge and a state of mind. For one who has learned and grasped what must be done and avoided is not yet wise, unless his mind has been transformed by what he has learned. This third part of instructing derives from both knowledge and mindset. Thus it is superfluous for perfecting virtue, for which those two suffice."

[49] By that logic, then, consolation is also superfluous, for it too derives from both, as do encouragement, persuasion, and argumentation itself. For these also proceed from a well-ordered and strong state of mind. But although such things come from the best state of mind, the best state of mind comes from them; it creates them and is itself created from them.

[50] Moreover, what you speak of is the mark of one who is already a perfect man, having attained the pinnacle of human happiness. But reaching such heights is a slow journey. In the meantime, even those who are imperfect but making progress must be shown the way forward in conducting their affairs. Perhaps wisdom itself will provide this guidance even without prompting, for it has already led the mind to a state where it can only be moved towards what is right. Weaker intellects, however, require someone to lead the way, saying: "you shall avoid this, you shall do that."

[51] Furthermore, if one waits for the time when they will know the best course of action on their own, they will stumble along the way, and by stumbling, be hindered from reaching that point where they can be content with themselves. Therefore, one must be guided until they can begin to guide themselves. Children learn according to

instruction, their fingers held and guided by another's hand through the shapes of the letters, then they are ordered to imitate the examples set before them and mold their handwriting to match. In the same way, our mind is aided while it is learning according to instruction[7].

[52] These are the reasons why this part of philosophy is shown to be not superfluous.

The next question is whether it alone is sufficient to create a wise person. We will dedicate a separate discussion to this question. In the meantime, setting arguments aside, is it not apparent that we need some advocate to give us precepts that run counter to the precepts of the masses?

[53] No utterance reaches our ears without doing harm. Those who wish us well and those who curse us are both detrimental. For the imprecations of the latter instill false fears in us, while the affection of the former, by wishing us well, teaches us wrongly. It sends us towards far-off, uncertain, wandering goods, when we could draw happiness from within our own home.

[54] It is not permitted, I say, to travel a straight path. Parents pull us astray, as do servants. No one errs only for themselves, but spreads their madness to those nearest them and receives it in turn. And so the vices of the masses are present in individuals, because the masses bestowed those vices. While each person worsens their neighbor, they are made worse. They learned inferior ways, then taught them[8]. Thus is born that immense wickedness, a concentration in one place of each person's worst traits. Therefore, let us have some guardian to pluck at our ear from time to time, to drive away rumors and argue against the praising crowds.

[55] You are mistaken if you think that vices are born with us. They crept in later; they were foisted upon us. And so let frequent admonitions repel the opinions that din around us.

[56] Nature allies us with no vice; she produced us whole and free. She placed nothing in plain sight to entice our greed. Beneath our feet she cast gold and silver, and what we trample and crush underfoot are the very things for which we ourselves are trampled and

crushed. Nature lifted our faces toward the heavens, desiring that we who look up may behold all that she made magnificent and wondrous. The risings and settings, the swift revolution of the hastening world, revealing earthly realms by day and heavenly ones by night, the slow progressions of the stars—most sluggish if you compare them to the whole, yet swiftest if you ponder the vast distances they traverse with unceasing velocity—the eclipses of sun and moon in their mutual obstructions, and other marvels in succession, whether arising by fixed order or leaping forth from sudden causes, like the nighttime trails of fire, the flashes in the sky opening without any impact or sound, the columns and beams and various likenesses of flames. These things she arranged to pass above us;

[57] Yet gold and silver, and iron that never brings peace because of them—these she hid away, as if they were entrusted to us for ill. We have hauled into the light the causes of our own perils and the means of our undoing, wrenching them from earth's heavy mass. We have handed over to Fortune the evils that plague us, and we are not ashamed that what lay in the deepest earth is now held in the highest esteem among us. Do you wish to know how false a glitter has deceived your eyes?

[58] Nothing is fouler than these metals, nothing more obscure, so long as they lie sunken and enveloped in their own mire. And why not? They are extracted through the shadows of the longest tunnels. Nothing is more misshapen than they are while being formed and separated from their dregs. Look upon the very craftsmen through whose hands this barren and infernal type of earth is purified; you will see with how much soot they are smeared.

[59] And yet these things stain minds more than bodies, and there is more filth in the owner of them than in the laborer.

Therefore it is necessary to be admonished, to have some advocate of good sense and, amid such a din and tumult of falsehoods, to hear one voice at last. What will that voice be? Surely the one that whispers wholesome words into your ear, deafened by the great clamors of ambition, the voice that says:

[60] There is no reason for you to envy those whom the people

call great and fortunate; no reason for applause to shake your composed mental state and sanity; no reason for that purple-decked official under his rods to make you despise your own tranquility; no reason for you to judge the man for whom the way is cleared to be any happier than you, whom the attendant shoves off the path. If you wish to wield a command beneficial to yourself and burdensome to none, banish the vices.

[61] Many are found who would set cities ablaze, who would raze to the ground what has been impregnable for centuries and secure through generations. They would raise siege ramps level with citadels and batter walls built to wondrous heights with rams and engines. Many are those who would drive armies before them, press hard upon the backs of the enemy, and come to the great sea drenched in the blood of nations. But even these, in order to conquer the enemy, have been conquered by their own greed. No one resisted them as they advanced, but neither did they themselves resist their own ambition and cruelty. At the time when they seemed to drive others, they were being driven themselves.

[62] The madness of laying waste to foreign lands drove the unfortunate Alexander, sending him to the unknown. Can you believe him sane, he who began with the calamities of Greece, the very place where he was educated? He who snatched from each what was best for them, ordering Sparta to serve and Athens to be silent? Not content with the destruction of so many states, which Philip had either conquered or bribed, he overthrew others in other places and carried his arms around the entire world. His cruelty, like that of monstrous beasts that bite more than hunger demands, never ceased.

[63] He had already cast many kingdoms into one; already the Greeks and Persians feared the same man; already even nations free from Darius were accepting the yoke. Yet he pressed on beyond the Ocean and the sun, indignant at turning his victories away from the paths of Hercules and Liber, preparing to do violence to Nature herself. He did not wish to go, but he could not stand still, just like weights cast down a slope, whose going ends only when they lie flat.

[64] It was not foreign wars or domestic valor or reason that

persuaded Gnaeus Pompey, but a mad love of false greatness. Now he was off to Spain and the armies of Sertorius, now to round up the pirates and pacify the seas[9].

[65] These were the pretexts for perpetuating his power. What drew him to Africa, to the north, to Mithridates and Armenia and every corner of Asia? An endless desire for expansion, no doubt, since he seemed to himself alone too small. What drove C. Caesar alike to his own doom and that of the state? The pursuit of glory, ambition, and no limit to his wish to tower above the rest.

[66] He could not bear to see one before himself, though the republic bore two above itself. Tell me, when C. Marius—for he received one consulship but seized the rest—slaughtered the Teutones and Cimbri, when he pursued Jugurtha through the deserts of Africa, do you think he sought out so many perils at the prompting of virtue? Armies drove Marius, ambition drove Marius.

[67] These men, while disrupting everything around them, were themselves disrupted like whirlwinds that engulf what they snatch up, even as they themselves are spun about beforehand. And for this reason they attack with greater force, because they have no control over themselves. Thus, having inflicted harm on many, they also feel that same destructive power which injured others. Never believe that anyone can become happy through another's unhappiness.

[68] All these examples, forced upon our eyes and ears, must be unraveled. We must drain our hearts, so full of harmful talk. Virtue must be ushered into that occupied space to root out falsehoods and notions that please despite contravening truth. Virtue must separate us from the crowd, in which we place too much trust, and restore us to pure beliefs. For this is wisdom: to return to nature and be reinstated to that place from which popular delusion has driven us.

[69] Abandoning the advocates of madness and withdrawing far from that mutually noxious gathering is a large part of sanity. To recognize this truth, observe how differently each person lives for the public compared to himself. Solitude does not inherently teach innocence, nor do the countryside instruct in frugality. But when the

witness and spectator have departed, vices subside, as displaying and observing them is their very reward.

[70] Who dons purple that he would exhibit to no one? Who sets out a secret feast on golden platters? Who, reclining under some rustic tree's shade, unfurls the pageantry of his own extravagance alone? No one is luxurious for his own eyes, not even for a few intimates. A man displays the trappings of his vices in proportion to the size of his admiring crowd.

[71] So it is. An admirer and accomplice is the incitement to all our mad pursuits. You will stop our lusting if you make it impossible for us to show off. Ambition, luxury, and excess desire a stage. You will cure them if you conceal them.

[72] Therefore, if we are situated amid the clamor of cities, let an admonisher stand beside us. Against those who extol immense estates, let him praise the man rich with little, measuring wealth by its use. Against those exalting influence and power, let him esteem leisure devoted to literature and a mind turned from external things to its own concerns.

[73] Let him reveal that those acclaimed as fortunate by the masses tremble and stand astonished on their envied pinnacles, holding a far different opinion of themselves than others have of them. For what seems lofty to others is, to them, a precipice. So they are frightened and alarmed whenever they look down that sheer drop of their own elevation, pondering the vicissitudes of fate and the particularly precarious footing at such heights.

[74] In times of prosperity, they fear the very things they once pursued, and the greater their fortune, the heavier it weighs upon them. It is then that they praise the tranquility of a life of leisure and independence, growing to despise the glittering trappings of success and seeking to escape from their still-standing fortunes. Only then will you see them philosophizing out of fear[10] and offering sound advice to those burdened by misfortune. For as if good fortune and a good mind were contradictory, we tend to be wiser in adversity; prosperity robs us of our better judgment. Farewell.

---

1. The original Latin text has a textual issue here, with variant readings of "anilla," "anillam," or "atillam." This follows the emendation "anilia" proposed by Buecheler, meaning "old womanish."
2. The original Latin contains a textual error, reading "supervacmis." Here the correction "supervacuus" is adopted.
3. The later manuscripts have "ad inveniendam" (to find) instead of "adveniendam" found in BA.
4. Buecheler suggests "redit, at" (returns, but) instead of "redita est" (is returned) found in BA.
5. The later manuscripts have "quod" (because) instead of "quo" found in BA.
6. Pincianus, from an old manuscript, reads "utramque" (both) instead of "utraque" (each).
7. Some later manuscripts have "proposita" (set before) instead of "praeposita."
    Later manuscripts have "iuvatur" (is aided) instead of "iuvat" or "vivat."
8. Later manuscripts have "deinde" (then) instead of "dein."
9. Colligandos: Following Madvig's emendation instead of the original "colligendos."
10. Alternative reading: "dread."

LETTER 95

THE DECLINE OF MORALS
AND THE RISE OF VICE

[1] You ask me to present now what I had said should be postponed to its own day, and to write you whether that part of philosophy which the Greeks call paraenetic [advisory] and we call preceptive is sufficient for the perfection of wisdom. I know you will take it in good part if I refuse. All the more do I promise, and I do not allow the common saying to be lost: "Do not later ask for what you would be unwilling to get."

[2] For sometimes we earnestly seek that which we would refuse if someone offered it. Whether this is fickleness or subservience, it must be punished by the readiness with which we assent. We wish to seem to want many things, but we do not want them. A reciter brought a huge history, written in the tiniest script, folded up most tightly, and when a great part had been read, he said, "I will stop, if you wish." There were shouts of "Read on, read on," from those who wished him to be silent then and there. We often want one thing and pray for another, and we do not tell the truth even to the gods, but the gods either do not hear, or they take pity on us.

[3] I, dismissing pity, shall take my revenge, and shall hurl at you a huge letter, which if you read unwillingly, you may say: "I brought this on myself," and count yourself among those who are tormented by a

wife won with great effort, among those who are unhappily possessed of riches acquired by extreme sweat, among those who are tortured by honors sought by every art and work, and the rest who have attained their misfortunes. But to attack the subject itself, omitting the introduction, they say, "The happy life consists of right actions; precepts lead to right actions; therefore precepts suffice for the happy life."

[4] Precepts do not always lead to right actions, but only when the disposition is compliant; sometimes they are applied in vain, if wrong opinions beset the mind.

[5] Then even if people act rightly, they do not know that they are acting rightly. For no one, unless formed from the beginning and composed with reason in every way, can follow all the numbers [of virtue], so as to know when and to what extent and with whom and how and why he should act. One cannot attempt honorable things with the whole mind, nor even consistently or gladly, but will look back, will hesitate.

[6] "If," he says, "honorable action comes from precepts, precepts are abundantly sufficient for the happy life; but the former is true, therefore the latter also." To these we shall reply that honorable actions are done by precepts, but not by precepts alone.

[7] "If other arts," he says, "are content with precepts, wisdom will also be content, for it is the art of living. Yet the helmsman is made by the one who instructs: 'Move the rudder thus, lower the sails thus, use a following wind thus, resist a contrary wind thus, lay claim to a wind that is doubtful and shared.' Precepts shape other craftsmen as well; therefore, they will be able to do the same for this craftsman of living."

[8] All those arts are occupied with the instruments of life, not with the whole of life. Therefore, many things hinder and impede them from without - hopes, desires, fears. But this art, which has professed to be the art of life, cannot be forbidden by anything from exercising itself; for it scatters impediments and pierces through obstacles. Do you want to know how unlike the condition of the other arts is to this one? In those arts, it is more excusable to err willingly

than by accident; in this art, the greatest fault is to go astray of one's own accord.

[9] What I mean is this: a grammarian will not blush at a solecism if he has made it knowingly; he will blush if he has made it unknowingly. A doctor, if he does not understand that his patient is dying, sins more, as far as his art is concerned, than if he pretends not to understand. But in this art of living, the fault of those who err willingly is more shameful.

Now add the fact that most arts, indeed the most liberal of all arts, have their own decrees, not just precepts, as does medicine. Thus, there is one sect of Hippocrates, another of Asclepiades, another of Themison.

[10] Moreover, no contemplative art is without its own decrees, which the Greeks call dogmata. We may call them either decrees, decisions, or tenets - you will find them in geometry and astronomy. But philosophy is both contemplative and active; it observes and at the same time acts. For you are mistaken if you think that it promises only mundane activities; it aspires higher. "I scrutinize the whole universe," philosophy says, "and I do not confine myself to the company of mortals, content to persuade and dissuade you. Great matters summon me, situated above you:

[11]

> *For I will begin to discourse to you about the highest system*
> *of heaven and the gods,*
> *And I will reveal the origins of things;*
> *From where nature creates, increases and nourishes all*
> *things,*
> *And to where that same nature dissolves them when they*
> *perish,*

as Lucretius says. It follows, therefore, that since philosophy is contemplative, it has its own decrees.

[12] What then? No one will properly carry out their duties unless they have been taught the rational method by which they can fulfill

all the requirements of those duties in each circumstance. A person who has learned precepts only for the case at hand rather than for every situation will not observe these duties. Precepts given for particular scenarios are feeble in themselves and, so to speak, rootless. It is philosophical tenets that fortify us, that safeguard our peace and tranquility, that simultaneously encompass our entire life and the whole nature of things. This is the difference between the tenets of philosophy and mere precepts: the latter depend on the former, while the former are the cause of both the latter and of all things.

[13] "The ancient wisdom," they say, "prescribed nothing more than what to do and what to avoid, and people were much better then. After the advent of scholars, good people have disappeared. For that simple and open virtue has been converted into an obscure and clever kind of knowledge; we are taught to argue, not to live."

[14] No doubt, as you say, that ancient wisdom was especially crude at its birth, just like the other arts which grew more refined as they developed. But there was not yet even a need for painstaking remedies. Wickedness had not yet risen to such a height nor spread so widely. Simple remedies could counter simple vices; now, our defenses must be all the more laborious as the assaults we suffer are more violent.

[15] Medicine was once the knowledge of a few herbs that could stop bleeding wounds from flowing and allow them to heal. Then, little by little, it attained its present highly complex variety. No wonder it involved less trouble then, when bodies were still sturdy and strong, and food was simple, not corrupted by art and indulgence. But after food began to be sought not for alleviating hunger but for provoking it, and a thousand seasonings were devised to stimulate gluttony, what used to be nourishment for those in need became a burden to the stuffed.

[16] Hence the pallor, the trembling of wine-soaked sinews, the emaciation from indigestion (more pitiable than that from hunger), the uncertain footing of the staggering, the constant reeling as if in a state of drunkenness itself. Hence the seepage of fluid throughout the skin, the distended belly badly accustomed to taking in more than it

could hold, the suffusion of jaundiced bile, the discolored countenance, the decay of the body rotting from within, the fingers curved back with stiffening joints, the numbing or incessant trembling of the sinews that lie insensate.

[17] What shall I say of the dizziness of the head? Of the torments of the eyes and ears, the writhing pains of the brain inflamed, and all the internal ulcers that afflict the organs through which we purge ourselves? Consider, too, the innumerable varieties of fever, some raging with violent onset, others creeping with subtle infection, still others that come with shivering and grievous shaking of the limbs.

[18] Need I recount the other countless diseases, the punishments of luxury? Those who had not yet abandoned themselves to the allurements of vice were immune to these ills; they commanded themselves and attended to their own needs. They fortified their bodies with work and true toil, wearying themselves with running, hunting, or tilling the earth. Their hunger was sated by food that could please only those who craved it. Thus there was no need for the vast array of medical equipment, nor for so many lancets and salve-boxes. Health was simple, springing from simple causes; it is the many courses of the feast that have bred the many forms of sickness.

[19] See what a mass of things destined to pass through a single throat luxury mingles together, plunderer of sea and land! Inevitably, such disparate foods quarrel amongst themselves, are gulped down only to be ill-digested, each striving against the others. It is no wonder that inconstant and shifting disease arises from such discordant nourishment, or that the assembled elements, forced together from opposing parts of nature, seethe in turmoil. Thence come as many kinds of illness as there are modes of living.

[20] That greatest of physicians and founder of the medical art declared that women neither lose their hair nor suffer foot troubles, yet nowadays they are afflicted by baldness and gout alike. The nature of women has not changed, but has been overpowered; for in rivaling masculine indulgences, they have taken on the bodily afflictions of men as well.

[21] They keep watch no less through the night, they drink no less,

challenging men with perfumed oils and unmixed wine. Like men they expel by vomiting what they have swallowed with reluctant stomachs, retasting in reverse the entire contents of the banquet; like men they crunch on snow to soothe an inflamed gut. But in lust they do not even yield to males, born to be penetrated—may the gods and goddesses destroy them! So perverse a form of impudence have they devised, playing the man upon men. What wonder then, that the greatest of doctors and the most skilled observer of nature is found mistaken, when so many women are gouty and bald? They have thrown away the advantages of their sex along with its vices, and because they have cast off their womanhood, they are condemned to the diseases of men.

[22] The physicians of old were unaware of the practice of administering food more frequently and fortifying failing veins with wine. They did not know to let blood and alleviate prolonged sickness with baths and sweating. They were ignorant of the hidden power in binding the legs and arms to recall the vital force residing in the center to the extremities. There was no need to consider many kinds of remedies when the dangers were very few.

[23] But now, how far the evils of poor health have advanced! We are paying these as the interest on pleasures desired beyond all measure and right. You will not be surprised that diseases are innumerable—just count the cooks. All study has ceased, and the liberal arts professors preside over deserted corners without any attendance. In the schools of rhetoricians and philosophers there is utter solitude, yet how celebrated the kitchens are, what a crowd of youth bustles around the hearths of wastrels!

[24] I pass over the throngs of unfortunate boys who, after the banquets have ended, await other indignities of the bedchamber. I pass over the troops of male prostitutes, sorted by nations and colors so that all may have the same smoothness, the same youthful measure of first beard, the same style of hair, lest anyone with straighter locks be mingled with those of curly hair. I pass over the crowd of bakers, I pass over the table-servants by whom, at a given signal, they scurry to serve the meal. Good gods, how many men a

single belly keeps busy! [25] What? Do you think those mushrooms, a voluntary poison, do no secret work even if they have not proved immediately fatal?

What? Do you not think that summer snow draws a hardened hide over the liver? What? Those oysters, that most slothful flesh fattened on muck—do you reckon they bring on no sluggish heaviness? What? That fish sauce of our allies, the precious rottenness of vile fish—do you not believe it scorches the innards with its salty putrefaction? What? That pus-like food which is transferred almost directly from the fire into the mouth—do you judge it to be extinguished without harm in the very bowels? How foul and pestilent, then, are the belches, how great the antipathy exhaled from those reeking yesterday's debauch! You may be sure the feast is rotting, not digesting, once consumed.

[26] I remember there was once talk of a famous dish into which a hurrying cook-shop had crammed whatever is wont to lead the day-long feast among gourmands, hastening to its own loss. Mussels and sea-urchin roes and oysters cut round to the very Quick where they are eaten were separated at intervals by sea-urchins. Whole mullets, carved up and reconstructed without any bones, had been laid as a foundation underneath[1].

[27] We tire of individual dishes; flavors are jumbled together into one. What ought to happen in the belly now happens at the dinner table. I am waiting for them to serve food that has already been chewed. And how is this much worse than picking out morsels for a feast and having the cook do the work of the teeth? "It is most indulgent to luxuriate over each dish individually; let everything be served at once, blended into the same flavor. Why should I reach my hand out for one thing at a time? Let many dishes arrive together, let the adornments of multiple courses unite and cohere."

[28] Let those who chase after boasting and glory from such feasts know straightaway that these dishes are not for show, but for the private indulgence of the conscience. Let the usual carefully-arranged platters all be drenched with the same sauce. Let there be no difference: let oysters, sea urchins, mussels, and mullets all be piled

together in a jumbled, stewed mess." The vomit of a glutton would not be more confused.

[29] Just as these foods are hopelessly entangled, so too do they give rise not to isolated illnesses but to baffling, diverse, multiform diseases, against which even medicine has begun to arm itself with many treatments and precautions.

I say the same to you about philosophy. It was once simpler, among lesser transgressions that were curable with just a light touch. But against such a massive upheaval of morals, every remedy must be attempted. If only this plague could be vanquished once and for all!

[30] We are in a frenzy not just as individuals but as a society. We restrain acts of homicide and punish individual murders, but what of wars and the glorious atrocity of slaughtering entire peoples? Neither greed nor cruelty knows any limit. When such crimes are committed in secret by individuals, they are less harmful and grotesque. But cruelties are carried out by senatorial decrees and plebiscites, and what is forbidden in private is ordered by the state.

[31] Acts that would warrant capital punishment if committed in secret are praised when our leaders commit them openly. Are you not ashamed, O gentlest of races, to delight in one another's blood, to wage wars and pass them on to be waged by your children, when even mute beasts keep peace among themselves?

[32] Against a madness so powerful and widespread, philosophy has been forced to become more industrious, marshaling as much strength as was gained by the vices it aimed to combat.

It used to be a simple matter to chide those overindulging in wine and demanding fancier food; the spirit did not require great force to be led back to frugality, from which it had only slightly strayed.

[33] But now there is need for swift action and a master's skill; pleasure is sought from every quarter. No vice stays within its own bounds; extravagance plunges headlong into greed. We have forgotten all decency. Nothing is shameful if its price is right. Man, a sacred thing to his fellow man, is now slaughtered in play and jest. It was once considered wrong to train a person to inflict and receive

wounds, but now he is trotted out naked and defenseless, and a human death makes for a satisfying spectacle.

[34] In the face of such perversity of character, something stronger than usual is required to dispel these deep-rooted maladies. We must take action through decrees to utterly uproot the entrenched false beliefs. If we add to these decrees instruction, consolation, and encouragement, they may prove effective, but alone they are powerless.

[35] If we wish to hold people to their obligations and tear them away from the vices that grip them, they must learn what is evil and what is good. They must understand that everything except virtue changes its name, now becoming evil, now good. Just as the first bond of military service is reverence, love of the standards, and the disgrace of desertion—and then afterward all else is easily demanded and commanded of those bound by the oath—so it is with those whom you wish to guide to the blessed life. The first foundations must be laid, and virtue insinuated into their souls. Let them be held by a kind of superstitious awe of virtue; let them love it, wish to live with it, and refuse to live without it.

[36] "What then?" you ask. "Have not some become honorable without subtle instruction and made great progress by obeying bare precepts alone?" I admit this, but theirs was a felicitous nature that snatched up salvation in passing. For just as the immortal gods have learned no virtue, having been created with every quality and goodness being a part of their nature, so also certain among mankind, endowed with a marvelous character, arrive without lengthy instruction at those things which are usually taught, embracing honor as soon as they hear of it. Hence spring those minds so swift to seize virtue, either fertile of themselves or tilled by good habits. But for those who are dull, obtuse, or beset by evil customs, the rust upon their souls must be scoured away over time.

[37] But while proper teaching of philosophical doctrines more swiftly leads those inclined to goodness to the heights, it will also aid those who are weaker and extricate them from false opinions. You may see how necessary these doctrines are in this way: certain

notions have settled within us that make us lazy towards some things and reckless towards others. This audacity cannot be checked, nor that laziness roused, unless the causes—false admiration and false fear—are rooted out. As long as these possess us, you may say "You owe this to your father, this to your children, this to your friends, this to your guests," but greed will hold you back when you try. A man will know he must fight for his country, but fear will dissuade him. He will know he must toil for his friends to the last drop of sweat, but self-indulgence will forbid it. He will know that keeping a mistress is the gravest insult to a wife, but lust will drive him in the opposite direction.

[38] So it will be of no benefit to offer precepts unless you first remove the obstacles to those precepts, just as it does no good to place weapons in plain sight and bring them nearer to hand unless the hands are free to use them. For the mind to absorb the precepts we provide, it must first be set free.

[39] Suppose someone does what they ought; they will not do it consistently or evenly, for they will not know why they act as they do. Some of their actions will turn out right, whether by chance or through practice, but they will not hold in their grasp the rule by which to measure them, to trust that what they have done is right. One who is good merely by chance will not promise to remain so forever.

[40] Furthermore, precepts may perhaps lead you to do what you ought, but not in the way you ought; if they fail in this, they do not guide you to virtue. The person so advised will do what they should, I grant you, but that is not enough, since the merit lies not in the deed itself but in how it is done.

[41] What is more shameful than an extravagant feast that consumes a knight's annual income? What deserves the censor's reprimand more, if someone indulges himself and his appetites in this way, as those gluttons put it? Yet the most frugal of men have hosted inaugural feasts costing a million sesterces. The same act is disgraceful if done for gluttony, but escapes reproach if done for the sake of prestige—for then it is not luxury but a ritual expenditure.

[42] When an enormous mullet—but why do I not mention the weight as well, to provoke the appetite of certain folk? They said it was four and a half pounds—when this was sent to Tiberius Caesar, he ordered it to be taken to the market and sold, remarking, "My friends, may I be deceived in all things if either Apicius or P. Octavius does not buy that mullet." His speculation turned out better than expected: they bid against each other, Octavius won, and earned great glory among his peers for having purchased for five thousand sesterces a fish that Caesar had sold and that not even Apicius would buy. It was shameful for Octavius to pay so much, but not for the one who bought it to send to Tiberius, though I would criticize him too—he admired a thing he thought worthy of Caesar.

[43] Suppose one sits at a sick friend's bedside: we approve. But if he does it for the sake of an inheritance, he is a vulture awaiting a corpse. The same actions are either base or noble; what matters is why and how they are done. All deeds will be honorable if we devote ourselves to honor and judge it the only good in human affairs, along with what stems from it; all else is good only for a day.

[44] Therefore, we must instill a conviction that pertains to our whole life—this is what I call a "decree." As this conviction is, so will be our actions and thoughts; and as these are, so will be our life. Persuasion applied piecemeal is not enough for one arranging the whole.

[45] In his book titled "On Duties", Marcus Brutus gives many precepts to parents, children, and siblings; yet no one will follow these precepts as they ought, unless they have an end goal in mind. We must set before ourselves the highest good as our ultimate aim, towards which we strive and to which our every act and word should have regard. Just as sailors must direct their course by a fixed star, so too must we guide our lives by a clear purpose.

[46] An aimless life is a wayward one. Once a goal is deemed truly necessary, we must resolve to pursue it. You will concede, I think, that nothing is more disgraceful than hesitating, vacillating, and fearfully retracing one's steps. This fate will befall us in all matters unless we

rid ourselves of the doubts that distract our minds, hold us back, and prevent us from fully committing to the attempt.

[47] It is common to teach how the gods should be worshipped. Let us prohibit lighting lamps on the Sabbath, for the gods have no need of light, and even mortals take no pleasure in soot. Let us forbid morning salutations and sitting at the temple doors. Human ambition is gratified by such attentions, but one who knows God truly is the one who worships him. Let us ban bringing linens and bath scrapers to Jupiter, or holding a mirror before Juno. God seeks no servants - why should he? He himself attends to the human race; he is available to all people, everywhere.

[48] One may be instructed in the proper way to offer sacrifices and how to avoid burdensome superstitions, yet this will never suffice until one conceives in one's mind a fitting image of God - possessing all, bestowing all, doing good without reward. What reason have the gods for doing good[2]? It is their very nature.

[49] Anyone who thinks the gods are unwilling to do harm is mistaken; they are incapable of it. They can neither suffer injury nor inflict it, for harming and being harmed go hand in hand. That highest and most beautiful Nature has placed them beyond danger, but in so doing has ensured they are not a danger themselves.

[50] The first act of worshipping the gods is to believe in them; next, to acknowledge their majesty and their goodness, without which there can be no majesty. To know that they preside over the world, governing all things by their power; that they guide the fortunes of humankind, watching over us as a whole, though at times unconcerned with individuals[3]. They neither cause nor possess evil. It is true they chastise some, restrain some, and impose penalties on some, occasionally even punishing the innocent as an example. Would you win over the gods? Then be good. Whoever imitates them has worshipped them amply.

[51] Here is another question: how should we deal with our fellow humans? What principles should guide us? Should we spare human blood? What a low bar it is to merely not harm someone whom you ought

to actively help! It is hardly praiseworthy for a person to treat another person with basic decency. Shall we instruct people to lend a hand to the shipwrecked, point the way for the lost traveler, and share their bread with the hungry? When could I ever enumerate all the things one should do or avoid, when I can sum up the entire duty of human beings with this simple maxim: All that you see, all that is contained within the divine and human spheres, is one; we are but limbs of a great body.

[52] Nature brought us forth as kin, birthing us from the same source and for the same ends. She instilled in us mutual affection and made us compatible with one another. She established fairness and justice; by her decree, it is more wretched to cause harm than to suffer it. By her command, helping hands should always be at the ready.

[53] Let this verse be imprinted in your heart and often on your lips:

"I am human; nothing human is alien to me."

Let us hold our possessions in common; we are born for fellowship. Our society is very much like an arch of stones: it would collapse if they did not mutually support each other, and it is precisely this that sustains it.

[54] Having considered the gods and humanity, let us examine how we should make use of things. Our instructions will have been given in vain if we have not first grasped what opinion we ought to hold regarding every matter - poverty and riches, renown and disgrace, homeland and exile. Let us judge each thing on its own merits, setting popular opinion aside, and ask what it really is, not what it is called.

[55] Let us move on to the virtues. Some teacher will advise us to prize prudence highly, to embrace courage, and to cleave to justice even more closely than the other virtues, if possible. But this will accomplish nothing if we do not know what virtue is, whether it is singular or plural, separate or interconnected, whether possessing

one virtue means possessing them all, and how they differ from each other.

[56] A craftsman does not need to inquire into the origins or applications of his craft any more than a pantomime actor needs to philosophize about the art of dance; if these arts understand themselves, nothing more is required. For they do not pertain to life as a whole. But virtue entails knowledge of other matters as well as itself; we must learn about virtue itself in order to understand it.

[57] An action will not be right unless the will is right, for action stems from the will. In turn, the will will not be right unless the mind's attitude is right, for the will stems from this. Furthermore, the mind's attitude will not be at its best unless it has grasped the laws of life as a whole and determined how each thing should be judged, unless it has analyzed things back to the truth. Tranquility does not occur except for those who have attained an unchangeable and certain judgment; all others repeatedly fall and then are restored, and they fluctuate between the things they have abandoned and the things they seek.

[58] What is the cause of this wavering? It is that nothing is clear to those who rely on the most uncertain guide: popular opinion. If you wish to will the same things always, you should will what is true. One does not attain the truth without dogmas; they give coherence to life. Good and bad, honorable and disgraceful, just and unjust, pious and impious, the virtues and the practice of virtues, the possession of beneficial things, esteem and worth, health, strength, beauty, keen perception of the senses—all these require an assessor to determine how much each is to be valued at.

[59] For you are mistaken and believe certain things to be of greater value than they are—so mistaken that those things held in highest regard among us, namely riches, influence, power, ought to be valued at a mere sesterce [a small coin]. You will not realize this unless you have examined the actual standard by which these things are relatively assessed. Just as leaves cannot be green by themselves but require a branch to which they may cling and from which they

may draw sap, so too these precepts, if isolated, wither away; they want to be grafted onto a school of thought.

[60] Moreover, those who abolish dogmas fail to understand that dogmas are actually confirmed by the very act of their abolition. For what are they saying? That life is sufficiently unfolded by precepts, and that the dogmas of wisdom are superfluous. And yet this very claim they make is itself a dogma—just as much, by Hercules, as if I were now to say that we should abandon precepts as superfluous and employ only dogmas, directing our studies to them alone. By the very act of my denying that precepts should be focused on, I would be issuing a precept.

[61] Some matters in philosophy require admonishment, others demonstration—and a great deal of it, because they are abstruse and can scarcely be made clear with the utmost care and skill. If proofs are necessary, so too are dogmas which deduce the truth by arguments. Some things are self-evident, others obscure: self-evident are those grasped by the senses and those grasped by the memory; obscure are those beyond these. But reason is not satisfied by obvious things; its higher and nobler function is to deal with hidden things. Hidden things require proof, and proof cannot exist without dogmas. Therefore, dogmas are necessary.

[62] The same thing that produces common sense also perfects it —a firm conviction about certain matters. Without this conviction, if everything floats uncertainly in the mind, then foundational principles become necessary to provide an unwavering basis for judgment.

[63] When we advise someone to hold a friend in the same regard as oneself, or to remember that an enemy may become a friend, we are encouraging love in the first case and moderating hatred in the second, adding: "It is just and honorable." Our foundational principles encompass what is just and honorable; therefore, these principles are essential, for without them the former advice is impossible.

[64] But let us combine the two, for branches are useless without roots, and the roots are strengthened by what they have produced. No one can fail to know the utility of hands—they visibly assist us. But the heart by which the hands live, from which they take their power

and motion, is hidden away. I can say the same about precepts: they are overt, while the foundational decrees of wisdom reside in secret. Just as only the initiated know the holiest mysteries of sacred rites, so in philosophy, those arcane matters are revealed to those admitted and received into the sacred truth. But the precepts and other such things are known to the uninitiated as well.

[65] Posidonius judges as necessary not only precepts (for nothing prohibits us from using this word), but also persuasion, consolation, and exhortation. To these he adds the investigation of causes, aetiologian, which I see no reason we should not dare to say, since the grammarians, guardians of the Latin language, rightly call it so. He says a description of each virtue will also be useful—what Posidonius calls ethologian, some name characterismon—rendering the signs and marks of each virtue and vice, by which similar things may be distinguished from each other.

[66] This serves the same powerful function as instructing by precept. For one who instructs by precept says: "You will do these things if you wish to be temperate." One who describes says: "The temperate person is one who does these things and abstains from those." You ask the difference? One gives the precepts of virtue, the other its model. I confess these descriptions—and to use a word of the tax-collectors, these iconismos—are useful. Let us put forth things deserving praise; an imitator will be found.

[67] Do you think it useful to be given the signs by which you may recognize a noble steed, so you are not deceived in buying one, so you do not waste effort on a nag? How much more useful is it to know the marks of an excellent mind, which one may be allowed to copy in oneself from another.

[68]

> *"From birth, the foal of a noble steed strides boldly*
> *Through the fields, flexing his supple legs;*
> *He leads the way, braves threatening rivers,*
> *Ventures onto unknown bridges, undaunted*
> *By hollow noises. Proud is his arched neck,*

Keen his head, short his belly, plump his back.
His valiant chest ripples with muscle
Then, if distant arms clash, he cannot keep still,
Ears pricked, limbs trembling,
Huffing gathered fire from flared nostrils.

[69] While depicting something else entirely, our esteemed Virgil has painted a portrait of the brave man; indeed, I could ascribe no other likeness to such a great man. If I had to portray Marcus Cato—undaunted amidst the din of civil wars, first to march against armies already crossing the Alps, throwing himself into the fray of citizen against citizen—I would grant him no other countenance, no other bearing.

[70] Certainly no one could have stepped forth more boldly than the man who simultaneously stood against both Caesar and Pompey, provoking each faction as the rest fueled either Caesar's might or Pompey's. He demonstrated there was yet a third side—that of the Republic. For it is not enough to say of Cato: "By hollow noises undaunted." Of course not! He quailed not before real, imminent dangers—against ten legions, Gallic auxiliaries, barbarians intermixed with citizens, he released his unshackled voice and exhorted the Republic not to back down on liberty's behalf, but to try every recourse, falling into servitude with more dignity than walking into it.

[71] What vigor, what spirit in that man! What confidence amidst a cowering citizenry! He knows he is the one man whose status is not in question; for the issue is not whether Cato will be free, but whether he will live among the free. Hence his disdain for perils and swords. Marveling at the man's indomitable resolve, unshaken amidst the crumbling Republic, one longs to declare:

"His valiant chest ripples with muscle."

[72] It will be beneficial not merely to describe what sorts of men the virtuous tend to be, sketching out their form and features, but to recount and set forth what manner of men they truly were - to tell of

that final and most valiant wound of Cato, through which freedom sent forth its spirit[4]; to speak of the wisdom of Laelius and his rapport with his dear Scipio; to laud the exemplary deeds, both at home and abroad, of that other Cato; to extol those wooden couches of Tubero which, when laid out for a public feast, were covered with goatskins in place of blankets, and those earthenware vessels set out for banquets before the very shrine of Jupiter. What else was this but to consecrate poverty on the Capitol? Even if I had no other deed of his by which to count him among the Catos, would we think this too trifling a matter? That was a true censorship, not merely a dinner.

[73] Oh, how little do those who thirst for glory understand what it is or how it is to be sought! On that day, the Roman people beheld the household goods of many a man, but marveled at those of one alone. The gold and silver of all those others has been shattered and melted down a thousand times over, yet the earthenware of Tubero shall endure throughout the ages. Farewell.

---

1. The difficult Latin phrase "dissecti structique" is interpreted here, following scholar Buecheler, to mean the mullets were first cut up, deboned, and then restructured in the dish. Some manuscripts have the alternate reading "destructique" (and destroyed).
2. Some manuscripts read "benefit" rather than "beneficent".
3. Madvig suggests "incuriosi" (unconcerned) for "curiosi" (concerned).
4. Here "emisit" with Stephanus, as opposed to "amisit" in other manuscripts.

LETTER 96

EMBRACING THE
TRIBULATIONS OF LIFE

[1] AND YET HERE YOU ARE, INDIGNANT AND COMPLAINING, NOT realizing that in all of this there is no true evil, save for the very indignation and complaint! If you ask my opinion, I believe there is nothing wretched for a man except believing something in the nature of things to be wretched. I shall not tolerate myself on the day I cannot tolerate something.

I am unwell; it is part of my fate. My household has fallen ill, my investments have soured, my house is crumbling, losses and wounds and toils and fears assail me; such is life. This is too little; such is what ought to be. [2] These things are decided, not mere accidents. If you trust me, I now lay bare to you my inmost feelings; in the face of all that seems adverse and hard, I am thus disposed: I do not merely obey God, but agree with His will. I follow Him from my soul, not because I must. Nothing will ever befall me that I receive with sadness or a sour face. I will pay no tribute unwillingly. All these things to which we sigh and shudder, they are the tributes of life; of these, my Lucilius, hope not for exemption nor beg reprieve.

[3] The pain of your bladder has disquieted you, letters have arrived bearing unwelcome news, losses continue, I shall press the point, you have feared for your life. But tell me, did you not know that

you were wishing for these when wishing for old age? In a long life, all of this exists, just as on a long road there is dust and mud and rain. [4] "But I wished to live, yet be free of all discomforts!" Such an effeminate cry ill becomes a man. You will see how I receive this wish of yours; I make it with a great soul, not merely a good one - let neither gods nor goddesses allow Fortune to coddle you!

[5] Ask yourself, if some god granted you the choice, whether you would choose to live in the marketplace or the military camp. And yet to live, Lucilius, is to wage war. Thus those who are tossed about, who trek up and down through laborious and arduous paths and undergo the most dangerous expeditions, these are brave men, the vanguard of the camp; but those whom a stale and idle peace coddles while others toil, they are naught but turtle-doves, safe only to be insulted. Farewell.

LETTER 97

MORAL DECAY IS NOT
UNIQUE TO OUR TIMES

[1] You are mistaken, my dear Lucilius, if you think that extravagance, neglect of good morals, and other vices which each age has complained about are unique to our times. These faults belong to mankind, not to any particular era. No generation has been free from guilt. And if you start judging the morals of each age, it's shameful to admit that never has vice been more brazen than under Cato's watch.

[2] Can you believe that bribery was rampant in the very trial in which Publius Clodius[1] was accused of that act of adultery committed in secret with Caesar's wife, violating the sacred rites which are said to be performed on behalf of the people with all men sent away beyond the enclosure, so that even male animals in artwork are covered up? Yet money was indeed given to the judges and, what is even more disgraceful under our current conventions, sexual favors with upper-class wives and youths were exacted on top of that as part of the bribe.

[3] The acquittal was an even greater crime than the original offense. The adulterer on trial parceled out adulteries, and was only confident of his safety once he made the judges partners in his guilt. All this occurred in a trial in which Cato, of all people, had given testimony, if nothing else.

I will quote Cicero's own words, because it's almost too outrageous to believe:

[4] "He summoned them to him, made promises, pleaded on their behalf, and made payoffs. And then - O ye gods, what utter corruption! - giving certain judges access to upper-class women and youths for the night was the crowning bonus for some of them[2]."

[5] There's no point in carping about the price; the fringe benefits were worth even more. "Want to sleep with this man's wife? I'll give her to you. Want this rich woman here? I'll guarantee you a night with her. You're bound to commit adultery, unless you want to lose the case. That beauty you desire will come to you. I promise you a night with her and I won't delay; my word will be made good before the next court date." Arranging adulteries is even worse than committing them - it's outright pimping to respectable wives.

[6] These judges in the Clodius case had asked the Senate for protection, which would only be necessary if they were going to convict, and they got it. So after the defendant was acquitted, Catulus cleverly quipped to them: "Why did you request a guard from us? So no one would steal your money?" Yet amidst these shameful jokes, the adulterer got off scot-free before the trial, playing the pimp during it - wriggling out of a guilty verdict that he deserved even more than he managed to escape.

[7] Do you believe that any age was more corrupt in its morals than the one in which lust could be constrained neither by sacred rites nor by legal trials—the very legal inquiry, conducted under special decree of the Senate, in which more crime was committed than investigated? The question was whether anyone could be safe after committing adultery; it became clear that no one could be safe without it.

[8] This was a showdown between Pompey and Caesar, between Cicero and Cato—yes, that famous Cato whose mere presence, it's said, kept the people from demanding bawdy "Floral games" with stripping prostitutes. If you believe men were more upright in their judgments than in their spectating then, think again. Such things

have happened and will happen again; licentiousness in cities may subside for a time out of discipline and fear, but never of its own free will.

[9] So don't go imagining that we today have given free rein to lust while imposing minimal legal constraints. No, the young generation now is far more temperate than the one when a defendant would deny adultery before his judges while those same judges confessed it to him, when debauchery was committed for the very purpose of judging a case, when Clodius—as popular for his vices as he was guilty of them—held trysts during the actual pleading of his cause. Who could believe it? A man damned for a single adultery was acquitted thanks to his many others!

[10] Every age will produce its Clodiuses, but not every age its Catos. We have an easy downhill path to vice, because there's never a lack of guides or companions. The thing itself proceeds even without a guide or companion. The road leads not just downhill to vice but straight down a cliff. And what makes most people incorrigible is this: in every other art, practitioners are ashamed of their mistakes and annoyed at themselves for going astray. But in life, people delight in their moral errors.

[11] A helmsman takes no joy in wrecking his ship; a doctor isn't glad when he loses a patient; an advocate doesn't celebrate if his client is convicted through his own fault. But by contrast, everyone takes pleasure in his own misdeeds. That man revels in the adultery he was enticed into by its very difficulty. This one gloats over his fraud and theft, and doesn't dislike his crime until he dislikes the consequences. This perversity arises from bad habits.

[12] Otherwise, to assure you that even in the souls most wedded to evil there dwells an awareness of good and an understanding (though not an avoidance) of what is base: all people conceal their sins, and even when they succeed, they enjoy the fruits of those sins while denying the sins themselves. But a good conscience is willing to step forward and be recognized. Wickedness itself fears the darkness.

[13] I think Epicurus put it well: "It can befall a wrongdoer to

escape notice, but not to be sure of escaping notice." Or if you think this point can be better expressed another way: "Hiding does no good for sinners because even if they have the good luck to hide, they don't have the confidence of hiding." Exactly so: crimes can be safe from discovery but not safe from anxiety.

[14] If this is how it is explained, I do not consider it to be in conflict with our school of thought. Why? Because the first and greatest punishment for those who err is to have erred. No crime goes unpunished, even if fortune adorns it with its gifts and protects and vindicates it, since the punishment for wickedness lies in the wickedness itself. Nevertheless, these secondary punishments also oppress and pursue the criminal - to always fear, to be terrified, and to distrust one's own security.

So why would I free evil from this torment? Why not always leave it in suspense?

[15] Let us disagree with Epicurus when he says that nothing is just by nature and that crimes are to be avoided because fear cannot be avoided. But let us agree that evil deeds are scourged by conscience and that the greatest torment comes from the fact that a perpetual anxiety urges and lashes the evildoer, who can never trust the guarantors of their own security. For this very point, Epicurus, is proof that nature makes us shrink from crime, because even when safe, no one is free from fear[3]. Fortune may free many from punishment, but no one from fear.

[16] Why is this, unless it is because an aversion to that which nature has condemned is ingrained in us? This is why those in hiding never have confidence that they will remain hidden, because their conscience convicts them and reveals them to themselves. Moreover, it is characteristic of the guilty to tremble with fear. It would be a sorry state of affairs for us if many crimes escaped the law and its retribution and the punishments prescribed by law, were it not that those natural and grievous offences against Nature must pay the penalty in ready money, and that in place of suffering the punishment comes fear. Farewell.

---

1. Some editions give the praenomen as "Aulus" rather than "Publius".
2. Quoted from Cicero, Letters to Atticus 1.16.5, with "ye gods" added in the original Latin.
3. Another reading inserts "est" (is) here: "For this very point is, Epicurus, proof that..."

LETTER 98

CHERISHING THE PAST, ACCEPTING THE PRESENT

[1] Never believe that anyone who depends on good fortune for their happiness is truly happy. Those who find joy in external things stand on shaky ground; the happiness that entered from outside will surely depart. But the happiness that arises from within is faithful, firm, ever-growing, and accompanies us to the end. All those other things that the masses marvel at are only good for a day. You may ask, "What then? Can they not be useful and bring pleasure?" Who would deny it? But only if they depend on us, and not we on them.

[2] All the things that fortune gazes upon become fruitful and pleasant only if the one who possesses them also possesses himself and is not at the mercy of his possessions. For they err, Lucilius, who judge that fortune grants us anything good or bad; she merely provides the raw material for good and bad things, the beginnings of things that will turn out well or ill for us. For the mind is mightier than any fortune; it guides its affairs in either direction and is the cause of a happy or miserable life for itself.

[3] The bad man turns everything to evil, even those things that came with the appearance of being the best; the upright and honest man corrects the wrongs of fortune, softens hardships and difficulties by knowing how to endure, and accepts favorable circumstances with

thankfulness and modesty, and adverse events with steadfastness and courage. Even if he is prudent, even if he does everything with precise judgment, even if he attempts nothing beyond his strength, that perfect good which is placed beyond the reach of threats will not fall to his lot unless he is as sure about the uncertainties of life as he is about its certainties.

[4] Whether you choose to observe others (for it is easier to pass judgment on the affairs of others than on one's own) or yourself, putting aside all self-favoring, you will feel and admit this truth: that none of these things men desire and cherish are of use, unless you have armed yourself against the fickleness of chance and the storm of circumstance that follows upon them, unless, amidst individual losses, you say frequently and without complaint, "The gods have deemed otherwise."

[5] No, by heaven, let me seek a stronger and more just poem to brace your spirit, and say this whenever something turns out contrary to your expectations: "The gods know better." With this attitude, nothing will shake you. But such an attitude will be yours only if you have contemplated beforehand what the changeableness of human affairs can do, before you experience it; only if you possess your children, your spouse, and your property in such a way that you do not expect always to possess them, and only if you will not be more miserable if you cease to have them. The mind that is anxious about the future is miserable, wretched even before the miseries come, because it is worrying in order that the things in which it takes delight last to the very end.

[6] For such a mind will never be at peace and, in anticipation of the future, will lose the present things which it might have enjoyed. The grief over a lost possession is equal to the fear of losing it[1].

[7] I do not counsel you to be negligent, however. By all means, steer clear of what is to be feared. Whatever can be foreseen by planning, foresee it. Whatever may cause injury, contemplate it well in advance and avert it. In this very endeavor, confidence and a mind resolutely steeled to endure all things will serve you best. One who can bear fortune can also beware of her. Surely one who is not

perturbed when times are tranquil. Nothing is more wretched or foolish than to fear prematurely. What madness it is to anticipate one's troubles!

[8] In short, to succinctly capture my thoughts and describe for you those fretful folks who are a burden to themselves: they are as intemperate in the thick of their troubles as they are in anticipation of them. The person who grieves before it is necessary grieves more than is necessary. For it is the same lack of composure that prevents him from assessing grief and awaiting it. It is the same lack of self-restraint that conjures for itself a vision of perpetual felicity, that whatever befalls it is bound to grow, not merely endure. Forgetting this see-saw on which mortal affairs are tossed, such a one guarantees for himself alone the constancy of Fortune's favors.

[9] I think Metrodorus put it superbly in that letter of consolation to his sister when she lost her son, a boy of the finest character: "All that mortals possess is mortal." He is speaking of those goods to which people flock. For that true good does not perish; it is certain and everlasting - wisdom and virtue. This alone accrues to mortals as something immortal.

[10] But people are so unprincipled and oblivious of where they are headed, of how each individual day upsets them, that they marvel at losing anything when they are bound to lose everything in a single day. Whatever you are, you are inscribed as its owner; it is in your possession but it is not your own. For that which is infirm, nothing is firm; for that which is fragile, nothing is eternal and invincible. It is as inevitable to perish as to cause loss, and this very thought, if we comprehend it, is a comfort. With a level head, lose what is destined to perish.

[11] What solace, then, do we find in the face of these losses? This: to hold tight in memory the things lost and not allow their profit to vanish along with them. To have had is taken from us; to have had in the past, never. Exceedingly ungrateful is the person who, having lost something, ascribes no value to having received it. Chance robs us of the thing but leaves behind for us its use and fruit, which we have squandered in the unfairness of desire[2].

[12] Say to yourself: "Of these things that seem dreadful, not one is insuperable. Each one, many before us have already conquered: Mucius the fire, Regulus the cross, Socrates the poison, Rutilius exile, Cato death by the sword. Let us too overcome something."

[13] Once again, the things that entice the masses with their specious luster of prosperity have been scorned by many, time and time again. As a general, Fabricius rejected riches; as a censor, he stigmatized them. Tubero deemed poverty worthy both of himself and of the Capitol when, by using earthenware at a public banquet, he demonstrated that a man ought to be content with what the gods even now make use of. Sextius the Elder, though born to take up the reins of state, refused the broad stripe offered by the deified Julius, knowing that what can be given can also be taken away.

Let us too, then, do something spirited of our own accord; let us be counted among the exemplars. [14] Why have we grown faint? Why do we despair? Whatever could have been done can still be done, if only we cleanse our minds and follow nature. To stray from her path is to be enslaved to cravings, to fears, to the whims of chance. We may return to the true way; we may be restored to our proper state. Let us be restored, so that we may endure pain, however it attacks the body, and say to fortune: "You struggle against a man; seek one you can defeat."

[15] By these and similar discourses, the violence of that ulcer is assuaged - an ulcer which I certainly hope is soothed, and either healed or stabilized and left to age along with the patient himself[3]. But I am untroubled for his sake; it is our own loss we are concerned with, being robbed of such an extraordinary old man. For he is replete with life and desires nothing further for himself, but only for those who find him useful.

[16] It is an act of generosity that he lives on. Anyone else would have ended these torments by now, but he thinks it as disgraceful to flee death as to flee to death. "What then?" you ask, "If circumstances warrant, will he not take his leave?" Of course he will depart, if he can no longer benefit anyone. If all he does is minister to his pain, what reason has he to remain?

[17] This, my dear Lucilius, is what it means to study philosophy in practice and to train for reality: to note what resilience a wise man maintains against death and against pain when the former approaches and the latter weighs heavily. What ought to be done must be learned from one who does it. Thus far, it has merely been a matter of argument, whether it is possible for anyone to resist pain, or whether even great souls succumb when death draws near.

[18] What need is there for words? Let us confront the matter at hand: death does not make him braver in the face of pain, nor does pain make him braver in the face of death. He trusts in himself against both, neither enduring pain patiently in the hope of death nor willingly dying out of weariness with pain.

He bears the one and awaits the other. Farewell.

---

1. The Latin phrase "miseratio" was added by Buecheler.
2. The text is uncertain. Later manuscripts read "use" rather than "habit" here.
3. The testimony of an ancient grammarian, and the change of subject in the text, may indicate that a considerable passage is lost and that another letter begins here. Cf, the senex egregius of § 15.

LETTER 99

REMEMBRANCE WITHOUT BITTERNESS

[1] I AM SENDING YOU THE LETTER I WROTE TO MARULLUS WHEN HE lost his young son and was said to be taking it badly, in which I did not follow my usual custom. I did not think he should be handled gently, as he deserved reproach more than comfort. For when a man is stricken and bearing a great wound poorly, one must yield to him for a little while; let him satisfy his grief or at least pour out its first impulse. Those who have taken it upon themselves to mourn should be corrected immediately and taught that even some tears are foolish.

[2] "Are you expecting consolation? Receive a rebuke instead. You are bearing the death of your son too weakly; what would you do if you lost a friend? Your son of uncertain promise has passed away, a mere child; it is a small matter that is lost.

[3] We seek out reasons for grief and we even wish to complain about Fortune unfairly, as if she would not provide just causes for complaint. But by Hercules, you already seemed to me to have enough spirit even to face solid evils, let alone these shadows of evils at which men moan for form's sake. If you had lost a friend, which is the greatest of all losses, you should have made the effort to rejoice more because you had him than to mourn because you had lost him.

[4] "But most people do not reckon how much they have received,

how much they have enjoyed. This grief has this evil among others: it is not only useless, but ungrateful. So your efforts were wasted because you had such a friend? During so many years, in such close intimacy of life, in such familiar fellowship of studies, nothing was accomplished? Do you bury your friendship with your friend? And why do you grieve for having lost him, if having had him does not help you? Believe me, a great part of those we have loved, though chance has removed their persons, still abides with us. The past is ours, and there is nothing more secure for us than that which has been.

[5] We are ungrateful for past gains, because we hope for the future, as if the future—if only it comes—will not soon be in the past. A man limits his happiness too narrowly if he rejoices only in the present; both the future and the past serve for our delight—the one by anticipation, the other by memory—but the one is contingent and may not come to pass, while the other must have been. "What madness it is, therefore, to lose our grip on that which is the surest thing of all? Let us rest content with the pleasures we have quaffed already, if only, while we quaffed them, the soul was not perforated like a sieve, only to lose again whatever it had received."

[6] There are countless examples of people who have laid to rest young sons without shedding a tear, who have returned from the funeral pyre to the Senate chamber or to any other official duty, and at once engaged in something else. And rightly so; for in the first place, it is useless to grieve if you make no progress by grieving. In the second place, it is unfair to complain about what has happened to one man but is in store for all. Again, it is foolish to lament when there is so little difference between the lost and the loser. Hence, we should be more resigned in spirit, because we follow closely those whom we have lost.

[7] Consider the swiftness of rapidest time, ponder the brevity of this span through which we hasten at utmost speed. Observe this procession of humanity, all tending towards the same end, distinguished by the smallest of intervals, even where they seem greatest; he whom you think has perished has merely been sent ahead. What

could be more senseless than to weep for one who has preceded you, when you must travel the selfsame road?

Will anyone be shocked by an event which he knew could not but happen? Or if he did not think on death in the case of a fellow man, he has deceived himself. [8] Will any be shocked by an event which he declared impossible not to occur? Whoever complains that someone has died, complains that he was but a man. The same terms bind us all: he to whom it befalls to be born, remains to die.

[9] We are differentiated by mere intervals, equalized by our end. This stretch that lies between our first day and our last is shifting and uncertain: if you consider its vexations, even for a boy it seems long; if its speed, even for an old man it is but brief. Nothing is not slippery and treacherous and more unstable than the greatest storm. All things are tossed about and shift into their opposite at Fortune's behest; amid such turmoil of mortal affairs, nothing is assured for anyone save death. Yet of this do all complain, in this alone is no one deceived. "But he died in boyhood." I do not yet say that he is better off who quickly makes his exit from life; let us turn to him who has grown old.

[10] By how little does he surpass the infant! Envision the vastness of unending time, and grasp the whole; then compare this that we call a human lifetime with the infinite: you will see how scant is that for which we pray and which we seek to lengthen. Of this, how much do tears and worry occupy! [11] How much death before it comes, how much ill health, how much fear! How great a portion is held by years either raw or useless! Half of this time is spent in sleep. Add toils, griefs, dangers, and you will comprehend that even in the longest life the actual amount of living is smallest.

[12] But who will grant you that it does not fare better with one who is allowed a quick return, whose journey is finished before weariness sets in? Life is neither good nor evil; it is the scene of good and evil. Thus that child lost nothing save a hazardous gamble where loss was likelier. He might have turned out temperate and prudent, he might under your care have been moulded to nobler things; but (and this is a juster object of fear) he might have become like the many.

[13] Look at those young fellows whom luxury has cast forth from the noblest of houses into the arena; look at those who practice each other's lusts - and their own - in mutual degeneracy, not one of whose days passes without drunkenness or some signal scandal; it will be clear that there was more to fear than to hope for in their case. Therefore you should not seek out reasons for grief nor aggravate slight discomforts by taking offense.

[14] I do not urge you to strive and rise up; I do not judge you so poorly as to think you need to summon all your virtue against this trial. This is no true pain, but merely a sting; it is you who turn it into suffering. "Undoubtedly philosophy has made much progress, if you can bravely face the loss of a boy still better known to his nurse than to his father!"

[15] What then? Am I now advocating callousness, that even at the funeral itself your face should be rigid and your spirit not allowed even to contract in grief? Not at all. That would be inhumanity, not virtue, to behold the burials of your loved ones with the same eyes as you beheld them living, and to not be moved at the first severing of familiar ties. But suppose I were to forbid it; some feelings are beyond our control. Tears fall even when we try to hold them back, and when shed, they relieve the soul.

[16] What, then, is the answer? Let us allow the tears to fall, not command them; let them flow as freely as emotion expels them, not as custom demands. But let us add nothing to our genuine grief, nor augment it according to the example of others. Ostentatious sorrow exacts more than real sorrow; how few are sad merely for their own sake! They lament more loudly when heard, but when silent and alone, when they see certain people, they are roused again to fresh weeping. Then they lay violent hands upon their own heads [in a display of grief], which they could have done more freely with none to prevent it; then they pray for their own death; then they toss themselves from their couches. But without a spectator, their grief subsides.

[17] In this matter, as in others, we are plagued by this fault: we conform to the pattern of the masses, looking not to what is proper,

but to what is customary. We abandon nature and surrender ourselves to the people, who are never a good guide in anything, and in this matter, as in all others, are most inconsistent. If they see someone bearing his grief with fortitude, they call him impious and savage; if they see another collapsing and clinging to the corpse, they call him womanish and weak.

[18] Therefore, we must refer everything back to reason. But nothing is more foolish than to court a reputation for sadness and to sanction tears which, in my judgment, a wise man should sometimes permit to fall of their own accord, and sometimes allow to flow by their own force. I will explain the difference. When the first shock of bitter news strikes us, when we are holding the body that will soon pass from our embrace to the flames, then natural necessity wrings tears from us, and the impact of grief shakes the whole body and likewise compresses and expels the moisture that wells up in our eyes.

[19] These tears fall by a forcing-out, despite our resistance. But there are other tears to which we give free rein when we revisit memories of those we have lost. And there is a certain sweetness mingled with the sadness, when their pleasant conversations, their cheerful company, their dutiful affection come to mind. Then our eyes relax, as if in joy. The latter tears we indulge in; by the former we are overcome.

[20] Therefore, there is no reason for you to hold back tears or force them out for the sake of the circle of people standing and sitting around you. Tears should neither cease nor flow as disgracefully as when they are feigned; let them fall of their own accord. They can flow in a calm and composed manner. Often, without compromising the wise man's authority, tears have flowed with such moderation that they lacked neither humanity nor dignity. It is permissible, I say, to yield to nature while preserving one's dignity.

[21] I have seen venerable men at the funerals of their loved ones, on whose faces love shone forth, with all the trappings of mourning removed. There was nothing except what was given to true emotions. There is a certain grace even in grieving; the wise man must preserve

this, and just as in other things, there is a proper measure in tears as well. The joys and sorrows of the imprudent overflow.

[22] Accept what is necessary with equanimity. What has happened that is incredible or new? How many are even now arranging a funeral, how many are purchasing the necessities of life, how many mourn after your mourning! Whenever you consider that he was a boy, consider also that he was a human being, to whom nothing certain is promised, whom fortune does not necessarily guide to old age. When fortune sees fit, it dismisses us.

[23] Moreover, speak of him often and honor his memory as much as you can. It will return to you more frequently if it comes without bitterness, for no one willingly associates with sadness, much less with a sad person. If there were any conversations of his, any jokes, however small, that you heard with pleasure, repeat them often. Boldly affirm that he could have fulfilled the hopes you had conceived in your paternal heart.

[24] To forget one's loved ones, to bury their memory with their bodies, and to weep excessively is the mark of an inhuman heart. Birds and beasts love their own in this way, whose love is agitated and almost rabid, but completely extinguished when they are lost. This is not fitting for a wise man. Let him continue to remember, but cease to mourn.

[25] I by no means approve of what Metrodorus says: that there is a certain pleasure akin to sadness, and that one should seek this out in times of mourning. I have written out Metrodorus' very words below.

Μητροδώρου ἐπιστολῶν πρὸς τὴν ἀδελφήν. Ἔστιν γάρ τις ἡδονὴ λύπῃ συγγενής, ἣν χρὴ θηρεύειν κατὰ τοῦτον τὸν καιρόν.[1]

[26] I have no doubt how you will feel about those who seek pleasure amidst grief itself—no, who pursue it by means of grief, hunting for gratification even through their tears. These are the people who accuse us of excessive rigor, disparaging our precepts as harsh, because we say that sorrow must either not be admitted into the soul

at all or else be swiftly driven out. Tell me, which is more incredible or inhuman—to not feel grief at the loss of a friend, or to go fishing for pleasure in the midst of grief?

[27] Our teaching is honorable: once emotion has shed a few tears and foamed off, so to speak, the mind must not be surrendered to sorrow. But you say that pleasure should be blended with the sorrow itself? Is that how we console children, with a sweet treat? How we quiet an infant's crying, by dripping in milk? Not even at the moment when your son is on his funeral pyre or your friend breathing his last do you allow pleasure a reprieve. No, you want to titillate grief itself! Which is more honorable—to banish sorrow from the soul, or to grant admittance to pleasure even alongside sorrow? "Grant admittance," did I say? No, pleasure is actively pursued, and from grief itself, no less!

[28] "But," he objects, "there is a certain pleasure akin to sadness." We might be permitted to say that, but you certainly are not. You Epicureans recognize only one good, pleasure, and only one evil, pain. What kinship can there be between good and evil? But suppose there were—is now the ideal time to unearth it? Must we pry into sorrow itself, to see if it contains something delightful and pleasurable tucked within it?

[29] Certain remedies, though healthful to some parts of the body, are too foul and unseemly to apply to others. What helps elsewhere without damaging modesty becomes shameful when done to an intimate area. Are you not ashamed to doctor grief with pleasure? This wound must be treated with harsher medicine. Better to reflect that no sensation of evil can reach one who has perished; for if it reaches him, he has not perished.

[30] I say that nothing can harm a person who no longer exists; he still lives if he can be harmed. Do you imagine it's unpleasant for him because he doesn't exist, or because he still exists in some form? But torment cannot arise from non-existence, which has no sensation. Nor can it arise from continued existence, for he has escaped death's greatest disadvantage: ceasing to be.

[31] Let us also say this to the one who weeps and longs for

someone snatched away in early life: in terms of the brevity of existence, if you compare it to the universe as a whole, we are all on equal footing, young and old alike. For less comes to us from our entire lifetime than what anyone might call the smallest amount, since indeed the smallest amount is some part of a whole. This thing we call life is next to nothing, and yet, oh our madness, it is arranged to cover a wide span.

[32] I have written these words to you, not as though you should expect a remedy so late [for I am sure that you have already said to yourself whatever you will read], but so that I might rebuke that tiny delay during which you withdrew from yourself, and encourage you for the future to raise your spirits against fortune and foresee all its weapons, not as though they might come, but as though they will surely come. Farewell.

———————————————

1. Translates to: From Metrodorus' letters to his sister: 'For there is a certain pleasure akin to pain, which one must pursue at this time.'

LETTER 100

SUBSTANCE OVER ORNAMENTATION

[1] YOU WRITE THAT YOU HAVE READ WITH GREAT EAGERNESS THE BOOKS of Papirius Fabianus, which bear the title "Civilium", and that they did not meet your expectations. Forgetting that the discussion is about a philosopher, you then criticize his style of composition. Suppose what you say is true, and his words pour forth rather than being carefully arranged. There is a certain charm in this and an inherent grace in a discourse that slips along gently. For I think it makes a great difference whether the words fall by chance or flow deliberately. Consider now the immense contrast in what I am about to say: Fabianus seems to me not to pour forth his speech but to pour it out - so abundant is it, delivered without agitation yet not without speed.

[2] He openly confesses and declares that his speech is not labored over or long-tortured. But let us assume it is as you wish. He has put in order not his words, but his character; what he writes is intended for the soul, not for the ear.

[3] Besides, if he were speaking, you would not have had time to consider the parts, so much would the whole have swept you away. In general, things which please at first glance prove less satisfying when examined closely. But it also counts for much to have occupied the

eyes at first sight, even if careful contemplation will find something to criticize.

[4] If you ask me, he who snatches away our judgment is greater than he who deserves it. I know the latter is safer; I know he can more boldly promise himself a future. Anxious oratory ill becomes a philosopher. Where will he ever be brave and steadfast, where will he ever take a stand, who is afraid of words?

[5] Fabianus was not careless in his speech, but secure. You will find nothing sordid in it. The words are well-chosen, not far-fetched, nor inverted and placed contrary to their nature in the fashion of our times, yet they are brilliant, though taken from common speech. You have honorable and noble thoughts, not forced into epigrams but expressed with breadth. We shall see what has been insufficiently pruned, what insufficiently structured, what does not conform to this modern polish. When you have surveyed it all, you will see no empty subtleties.

[6] There may indeed be lacking variety of marbles, and pipes to conduct water through the chambers, and the cells of the poor, and other things which luxury, not content with simple adornment, jumbles together. As they say, the house is straight. Consider, too, that there is no agreement about style. Some want it adorned but austere; some take such delight in the unadorned that they purposely disarrange even what chance has smoothed out gracefully, and break off their sentences to avoid conforming to expectation.

[7] Read Cicero: his composition is uniform, bending its gait slowly and with an easy grace. Asinius Pollio's style, by contrast, is rugged and erratic, liable to leave you stranded when you least expect it. In short, all of Cicero's phrases come to a definite close, while Pollio's end abruptly, with a scant few exceptions that adhere to a fixed pattern and single model.

[8] You say, moreover, that you find everything in Fabianus's writings to be unassuming and lacking in loftiness—a fault of which I consider him free. His words are not lowly but tranquil, fashioned not for a degrading but for a level path suited for a calm and well-ordered soul. What his speech lacks is the fiery vigor and provocations you

seek, along with the sudden, piercing barbs of epigrams. But examine his work as a whole and see how well-groomed it is; it is respectable. His style does not currently possess dignity, but it shall grant it.

[9] Name someone you can rank above Fabianus. If you say Cicero, whose books pertaining to philosophy are nearly as numerous as Fabianus's, I will yield—but it is no mean feat to be lesser than the greatest. If you say Asinius Pollio, I will yield again, but let us reply: in a matter of such import, to be third in prominence is to be second only to two. Let us name Livy as well; for although he wrote dialogues that you could no more categorize as philosophy than history, he also penned volumes expressly dedicated to philosophy. I will grant him a place too. Consider, however, how many men are surpassed by one who is himself surpassed by three—and the three most eloquent, no less!

[10] But Fabianus does not excel in all aspects: his style, though elevated, is not bold; though copious, it is neither vehement nor torrential; though pure, it is not transparent. "One might wish," you say, "for sterner words against vice, for a more intrepid stance against dangers, a more arrogant defiance of fortune, a more scornful censure of ambition. I want to hear luxury rebuked, lust denounced, tyranny broken. Let there be some of the orator's sting, the tragedian's grandeur, the comedian's subtlety." You wish to confine him to petty matters, to mere words. But he has devoted himself to the grandeur of his subjects, drawing eloquence behind him like a shadow, though that is not his aim.

[11] Undoubtedly, not every detail will have been carefully considered, nor will every word stimulate and provoke deeper thought—this much I concede. Many ideas will be put forth without making an impact, and at times the discourse will drift along unproductively. But there will be an abundance of illuminating insights throughout, covering an immense scope without growing tedious. In the end, one thing above all will be made clear to you: that the author believed what he wrote. You will understand that his aim was for you to know what pleased him, not for him to please you. Everything in his work is directed toward personal

growth and the cultivation of a sound mind; popular acclaim is not the object.

[12] I have no doubt that his writings are of this character, even if my recollection of them is more impressionistic than precise. Their tenor lingers with me not because of any recent close study, but in broad strokes, as is typical of one's familiarity with something from long ago. When I attended his lectures, his words struck me as earnest and substantial—not artificially polished, but full of meaning. They seemed designed to uplift a youth of good character, to inspire imitation without a sense of the goal being unattainable—which, in my view, is the most effective form of encouragement. For the teacher who awakens a desire to emulate him, while removing hope of success, will dishearten his students. Still, he had an abundant verbal repertoire and a magnificent overall impact, without calling attention to the merits of isolated passages. Farewell.

LETTER 101

LIFE'S FLEETING AND
FRAGILE NATURE

[1] EACH DAY, EACH HOUR REVEALS HOW FLEETING OUR EXISTENCE IS, and some fresh evidence reminds us of our fragility, so quick to forget. Just when we contemplate the eternal, we are forced to confront our mortality.

You may wonder what prompts this solemn opening. Surely you knew Senecio Cornelius, that distinguished and dutiful Roman knight. From humble beginnings, he had advanced himself, and his path to further heights lay clear before him.

[2] After all, stature is easier to augment than to attain in the first place. Even wealth lingers longest around poverty, struggling to break free from its grip. Senecio was already verging on riches, propelled by the two most potent forces: the arts of acquisition and preservation. Either one alone could have made him wealthy.

[3] This exceedingly frugal man, as prudent with his health as with his estate, had seen me that morning as was our custom. He sat at the bedside of a gravely ill friend without prospect of recovery, remaining until nightfall. Then, after a cheerful dinner, he was seized by a sudden, violent illness—quinsy—that barely allowed his constricted throat to draw breath until dawn. Within the span of a

few hours, he departed—he who had just discharged all the duties of a hale and hearty man.

[4] Here was one who conducted business by land and sea, who had also dabbled in public life, leaving no potential source of profit unexplored. In the very midst of thriving enterprises, in the very surge of swelling wealth, he was snatched away.

> *Go now, Meliboeus, and dutifully plant your pear trees,*
> *arrange your vines in tidy rows.*

How foolish it is to map out a life when we are not even masters of the morrow! What madness to embark on distant hopes: "I will buy, I will build, I will lend, I will collect, I will hold office—and then, at long last, I will resign myself to a leisurely old age, weary and content."

[5] Believe me, all things—even for the fortunate—are uncertain. No one should promise themselves anything from the future. Even what we hold slips through our fingers, and chance cuts into the actual hour we are pressing to our hearts. Time marches on by fixed law, but through a haze of unknowing. What does it matter to me whether Nature's course is sure, when my own is unsure?

[6] We plan lengthy voyages and, after wandering foreign shores, a late return to our native land. We plan for military service and the plodding rewards of hard campaigns. We angle for governorships and the step-by-step promotion of our careers—all while death stands at our elbow. Because we never think of death except when it strikes another, instances of human frailty repeatedly rush upon us, grabbing our attention but never holding it longer than those moments of astonishment.

[7] What could be more foolish than to marvel at something happening on any given day, when it can happen on every day? A boundary has indeed been set for us, fixed in place by the inexorable necessity of the fates, but none of us knows how close we are to that boundary. So let us shape our minds as if we have reached the end. Let us defer nothing. Let us balance our ledgers with life each day.

[8] The greatest flaw in life is that it is always imperfect, that some part of it is always postponed. One who daily puts the finishing touch on their life has no need for time. But from this lack, fear is born, and a longing for the future that gnaws at the mind. Nothing is more wretched than the anxiety of what is to come - which way things will turn out, how much remains or what it will be like - the troubled mind is agitated by an inescapable dread.

[9] How shall we escape this tumult? In one way: if our life does not project into the future, if it is collected into itself. For one who is suspended in anticipation, the present is meaningless. But when whatever I owed to myself has been repaid, when the steadied mind knows there is no difference between a day and an age, whatever succession of days and events is to come, it looks down from on high and contemplates the sequence of times with much laughter. For what disturbance will the variability and fickleness of chance bring, if you are sure against uncertainties?

[10] So hurry, my dear Lucilius, to truly live, and count each day as a separate life. One who has prepared himself in this way, whose whole life has been complete each day, is secure; but for those living in hope, each coming moment slips away, and greed creeps in, and the fear of death - most wretched, and rendering all things wretched. Hence that most disgraceful vow of Maecenas, in which he does not refuse frailty and disfigurement, and finally the sharpened cross - so long as amidst these ills his life is prolonged:

[11]

> *"Make me weak in hand, lame in foot with a hip;*
> *Pile on a humped back, knock out my loose teeth;*
> *So long as life remains, it is well; sustain it for me,*
> *Even if I should sit on the piercing cross."*

[12] What was once considered the most wretched fate, if it befell a man, is now wished for and sought after as a reprieve from death, like a suppliant begging for his life. "You may cripple me," he says, "as long as breath remains in my broken and useless body. You may muti-

late me, as long as some extension of time is granted to this monstrous and twisted form. You may impale me and seat me upon a sharp cross." Is it worth it to press upon one's wound and hang stretched out on the gallows, just to postpone that which is the best part of misfortune - the end of suffering? Is it worth clinging to a soul only to prolong the agony?

[13] What should one wish for such a man, if not the mercy of the gods? What is the meaning of this effeminate and disgraceful verse? This bargaining born of the most senseless fear? This shameful begging for life? Do you think Virgil ever recited to a man like this:

"Is it truly so wretched to die?[1]"

He prays for the worst of evils, longing to be stretched out and made to endure what is most grievous to suffer. And for what reward? Merely a longer life. But what kind of life is it to die slowly, day after day?

[14] Can someone actually be found who is willing to waste away amidst tortures, to perish limb by limb, and to breathe out his life drop by drop rather than expiring all at once? Can someone be found who, forced upon that unhappy tree [the cross], already feeble, depraved, and with shoulders and chest crushed into a hideous swelling - a man for whom there were many reasons to die even before the cross - still desires to draw out a soul that will only be made to endure so many torments?

Deny now that it is a great blessing of nature that we must die. Many are prepared to bargain for even worse: to betray a friend in order to live longer, to deliver their own children to violation by their own hand, just so they might see the light of day, complicit in so many crimes. This mad desire for life must be shaken off, and we must learn that it makes no difference when we suffer that which must someday be suffered.

[15] What matters is how well you live, not how long; yet often living well means not living long. Farewell.

1. Virgil, Aeneid 12.646

LETTER 102

CONTEMPLATING THE IMMORTALITY OF THE SOUL

[1] JUST AS ONE WHO AWAKENS ANOTHER FROM A PLEASANT DREAM IS A bother—for they steal away the dreamer's pleasure, which, though false, still produces the effect of a true joy—your letter has done me an injustice in such a way. It has called me back when I had given myself over to fitting thoughts and was ready, if permitted, to go still further in my contemplations.

[2] I was taking delight in inquiring about, or rather, by heaven, in believing in the eternity of souls. I was gladly lending myself to the opinions of great men who promise this most pleasing prospect more than they prove it. I was giving myself over to such a grand hope. Already I was growing weary of myself, already I was scorning the remaining tatters of my feeble years, ready to pass over into that boundless expanse of time and take possession of all eternity. But suddenly I was startled awake by the arrival of your letter and I lost that beautiful dream. If I dismiss you, I shall resume it and buy it back.

[3] Your first letter asserts that I did not fully explain the whole question in which I was trying to prove the belief we [Stoics] hold— that the fame which comes after death is a good thing. You argue that

I did not resolve the objection raised against us: "No good," they say, "is made up of things that are separate. But this [posthumous fame] is made up of things that are separate."

[4] What you ask, my dear Lucilius, belongs to another area of the same question, and that is why I had postponed discussing not only this point but also some others related to it. For as you know, certain rational inquiries are mixed in with moral ones. And so I handled the straightforward part pertaining to morals: whether it is foolish and superfluous to be concerned for anything beyond one's final day; whether our goods perish with us and he who no longer exists has nothing; whether any fruit can be gathered or aimed for from something which, when it comes, we will not feel.

[5] All of these considerations deal with morals, and so they have been put in their proper place. But the arguments the logicians [Dialecticians] raise against this view needed to be separated out and therefore set aside. Now, since you demand it all, I will go through everything they say and then counter each point individually.

[6] Unless I say something first, the refutations will not be intelligible. What is it that I want to say beforehand? That some bodies are continuous, like a human being. Some are composite, like a ship or a house—in short, all things whose separate parts have been forced into one by some joint. Some are made of distinct parts whose members are still separate, like an army, a people, or a senate. For the individuals who make up such bodies cohere by law or duty, but are separate and distinct by nature. What else do I still want to say in advance?

[7] We believe that no good can consist of disparate elements. For one good should be contained and governed by one spirit; there should be one primary element of one good. If you ever desire this, it is proven on its own; meanwhile it had to be postulated, because our own weapons are hurled against us.

[8] "You say," he objects, "that no good consists of disparate elements? But that famous renown of good men is the favorable opinion of a second party. For just as fame is not the speech of one

person, nor infamy the low opinion of one, so renown is not having pleased one good person. Multiple distinguished and notable men must agree on this for it to be renown. But this is produced from the judgments of many, that is, of separate individuals; therefore it is not a good."

[9] "Renown," he says, "is praise bestowed upon a good man by good men; praise is speech, a voice signifying something; but a voice, even if it comes from good men, is not a good. For not everything a good man does is good. For he both applauds and hisses, but no one calls applause or hissing good, even if he admires and praises everything the man does, any more than one calls a sneeze or cough good. Therefore renown is not a good."

[10] "In sum, tell us whether it is the good of the praiser or the praised: if you say it is the good of the praised, you do as ridiculous a thing as if you were to claim that it is my good that someone else is healthy. But to praise the worthy is an honorable action; thus it is the good of the praiser, whose action it is, not of us who are praised. But this is what was in question."

[11] I will now respond to each point briefly. First, it is still in question whether there is any good consisting of disparate elements, and both sides have their opinions. Second, does renown require many votes of approval? It can be content with the judgment of even one good man; one good man judges us good.

[12] "What then?" he says. "Will fame also be one man's opinion and infamy one man's malicious talk? I understand glory too," he says, "to be more widely dispersed, for it requires the agreement of many." The case of these things is different from the former. Why? Because if one good man thinks well of me, I am in the same position as if all good men thought the same; for everyone, if they know me, will think the same. Their judgment is alike and the same, equally untainted by truth. They cannot disagree; so it is as though all think the same, because they cannot think otherwise.

[13] One person's opinion is not enough for [achieving] glory or fame." In that case [with glory], the judgment of one can hold the same weight as the judgment of all, because if everyone were asked

their view, it would be the same. But here [with fame] there are varying opinions of dissimilar people. You will find fickle affections, everything doubtful, trivial, suspicious. Do you think there can be one unified opinion of all? A single person does not have one unified opinion. Truth is pleasing to that person [seeking glory]; truth has one essence, one appearance. But among these people [seeking fame] there are falsehoods to which they assent. There is never consistency in falsehoods; they are changeable and at odds with each other.

[14] "But praise," one objects, "is nothing other than a voice, and a voice is not a good." When they say that renown is praise of the good offered by the good, they are referring not to the voice itself, but to the sentiment behind it. For even if a good man is silent, but judges someone worthy of praise, that person has been praised.

[15] Moreover, praise is one thing, a formal eulogy another; the latter requires a voice. Thus, no one speaks of a "funeral praise", but rather a "funeral oration", which is a duty that relies on a speech being given. When we say someone is worthy of praise, we are promising not kind words from people, but their considered judgments. Therefore, praise can come even from someone who is silent, who thinks well [of the praised] and praises a good man in his own mind.

[16] Next, as I said, praise refers to the mind, not to the words that have given voice to the conceived praise and disseminated it to the awareness of many. The one who judges that someone deserves praise is the one who praises. When our famous tragedian [Naevius] says it is magnificent "to be praised by a man who is praised", he means "praised by one worthy of praise." And when an equally ancient poet [Ennius] says "praise nourishes the arts", he is not talking about formal eulogy, which corrupts the arts. For nothing has corrupted eloquence and every other pursuit that panders to the ears as much as popular approval.

[17] Fame certainly requires a voice, but renown can occur even without a voice, content with [good] judgment. It is complete not only among those who are silent, but even among those who cry out against it. I will explain the difference between renown and glory:

glory consists of the judgments of many, renown of the good. "But," one objects, "to whom does renown, that is, praise offered to a good man by good men, belong as a good?"

[18] Is it the good of the praised or the praiser? Both, I say. It is my good, as the one being praised, for Nature has given birth to me as a lover of all, and I rejoice in having done good and am gladdened to have found grateful interpreters of my virtues. It is the good of many that they are grateful, but it is also my own good. For my mind is so disposed that I consider the good of others as my own, especially of those to whom I myself am the cause of their goodness.

[19] The good of those praising is that their act is born of virtue, and every action of virtue is good. This could not have happened to them if I were not such as I am. And so to be deservedly praised is the good of both - just as, by Hercules, it is the good of the one judging to have judged rightly, and the good of the one about whom the judgment was made. Do you doubt that justice is both the good of the one who has it, and the good of the one to whom it pays what is owed? To praise the deserving is justice. Therefore, it is the good of both.

[20] We have given more than enough reply to these quibblers. But it should not be our purpose to engage in clever arguments and to drag philosophy down from her majesty into these narrow confines. How much better it is to go by the open and straight path than to map out twisting routes for oneself which one must retrace with great trouble! For these disputations are nothing other than the sport of those who are skillfully trying to outwit each other.

[21] Speak rather of how natural it is for the mind to extend itself into the immeasurable. The human spirit is a great and noble thing; it suffers no limits to be set for it except those that are shared even with the gods. First, it does not accept a humble homeland - not Ephesus or Alexandria, or any land that is even now more populous with residents or more cheerful with buildings. Its homeland is whatever encircles the universe at the highest point, this entire vault within which lie the seas and lands, within which the air, separating human things from the divine, also unites them, in which so many celestial lights keep watch, each at its appointed task.

[22] Next, he refuses to allow himself to be constrained by a narrow lifespan: "All the years," he says, "are mine. No era is closed off to great minds; no period of time is impervious to thought. When that day comes which will separate this mixture of the divine and human, I will leave behind this body where I found it and willingly return myself to the gods. Even now I am not without them, but am detained in this heavy earthly prison."

[23] Through these delays of mortal time, we rehearse for that better and longer life. Just as a mother's womb holds us for ten months and prepares us not for itself, but for the place into which we seem to be delivered when ready to draw breath and survive in the open air, so too during this span that stretches from infancy to old age, we mature toward another birth. A different origin awaits us, a different state of affairs. We cannot yet endure heaven except at intervals; therefore, look forward fearlessly to that decisive hour: it is not the last for the soul, only for the body.

[24] Whatever lies around you, regard it as the baggage of a traveler's inn: you must move on.

[25] Nature strips you as bare when departing as when entering. You cannot take out more than you brought in; indeed, you must lay down a large part of what you brought with you into life. That outer layer enclosing you, your skin, will be stripped away; your flesh and coursing blood that flows throughout your body will be stripped away; your bones and sinews, the scaffolding of what is fluid and prone to collapse, will be stripped away.

[26] That day which you dread as your last is the birthday of eternity. Lay down your burden - why hesitate, as if you had not previously departed the body in which you were hidden? You linger, you struggle; at your birth too you were expelled with great effort from your mother's womb. You wail, you cry - but this very act of crying is a sign of the newborn, though then it was pardonable: you arrived inexperienced and ignorant of all things. From the warm soft refuge of your mother's innards, the freer air struck you; then the touch of rough hands offended you, and tender and knowing nothing, you were stunned amidst the unfamiliar.

[27] Now it should not feel strange to be separated from that of which you were previously a part; with evenness of mind, dismiss those limbs now superfluous and lay down that body you have long inhabited. It will be cut apart, buried, destroyed. Why grieve? So it usually happens: the integuments of the newborn always perish. Why cherish those things as if they were your own? They merely covered you. The day will come which will tear you away and lead you forth from the company of the foul and fetid womb.

[28] Now, as much as you can, withdraw yourself from pleasures, except those connected with necessities and serious pursuits. From this point on, set your mind to ponder something deeper and more sublime. One day, the secrets of nature will be revealed to you, this haze will be dispelled, and brilliant light will strike you from all sides.

Picture to yourself how magnificent that radiance must be, with so many stars blending their light together; no shadow will disturb the serenity. The entire expanse of the sky will shine with equal brilliance; day and night are but changes in the atmosphere of the lower realms. Then you will say that you lived in darkness, when you see the entirety of the light and behold it in its totality, which you now glimpse dimly through the narrowest channels of your eyes. And yet, you marvel at it from afar; what will the divine light seem to you when you see it in its proper place?

[29] This thought allows nothing sordid, nothing low, nothing cruel to settle in the mind. It proclaims the gods as witnesses of all things. It bids us to win their approval, to prepare ourselves for the future, and to set eternity before us. Whoever grasps this in their mind dreads no armies, is not terrified by the trumpet's blare, and is driven to fear by no threats.

[30] Why should one who hopes to die be afraid? Even one who judges the soul to remain only as long as it is held by the bonds of the body, scatters it abroad as soon as it is released, so that it may be of use even after death. For though the man himself has been snatched from sight, yet

"The hero's courage, the honor of his race,

Abide in memory[1]."

Reflect how much good examples profit us: you will recognize that the presence of great men is no less useful than their memory. Farewell.

---

1. Lines from Virgil's Aeneid (4.3-4)

LETTER 103

AVOIDING OFFENSE WHILE OFFERING KINDNESS

[1] WHY DO YOU FIXATE ON THOSE MISFORTUNES WHICH MAY BEFALL you, but also may not? I speak of fires, collapsing buildings, and other calamities that strike us without warning. Turn your attention instead to the dangers that stalk us daily, lying in wait to ensnare us. Accidents, though potentially severe, are relatively rare - a shipwreck, or an overturned carriage. But the threat that man poses to his fellow man is an everyday peril. Steel yourself against this; face it with vigilant eyes. There is no evil more common, more unrelenting, more enticing in its guise.

[2] A storm threatens before it rises; buildings creak before they crumble; smoke heralds a fire. But man's capacity for destruction strikes suddenly, and is cloaked all the more carefully the closer it draws near.

You are mistaken if you trust the faces of those you meet; they have human visages, but the souls of beasts. The one difference is that an animal's initial onslaught is its most dangerous; once you have passed by, they do not seek you out. For hunger or fear alone drive them to violence out of necessity. But man destroys man by choice.

[3] Yet even as you contemplate the peril that comes from man, reflect also on your duty as a human being. Be watchful of the one,

lest you be harmed; mindful of the other, lest you do harm. Rejoice in the good fortune of all, be moved by their troubles, and remember what kindness you owe and what behavior you must guard against.

[4] What do you gain by living in this way? Not that they will not wrong you, but that they will not deceive you. As much as you can, then, withdraw into philosophy. She will shelter you in her embrace; in her sanctuary you will be safe, or at least safer. Only those traveling the same road collide with one another. But philosophy herself you should not vaunt; to many, she has been the cause of peril when pursued with arrogance and defiance.

[5] Let philosophy strip away your faults, not disparage those of others. Let her not recoil from the ways of the public, nor make such a show of condemning whatever she does not do herself. One can be wise without ostentation, without arousing envy. Farewell.

LETTER 104

THE RESTORATIVE POWERS
OF COUNTRY LIFE

[1] I FLED TO MY VILLA IN NOMENTUM - BUT FROM WHAT DO YOU THINK? From the city? No, from a fever that was creeping up on me. It had already begun to take hold. The doctor said my veins were pulsing irregularly, erratically, disturbing their natural rhythm. So I immediately ordered my carriage to be readied. Though my dear Paulina tried to stop me, I persisted in departing, keeping in mind what my master Gallion always said. Once when he began to run a fever in Achaia, he boarded a ship at once, declaring that his illness was not of the body, but of the place.

[2] I told this to my Paulina, who looks after my health with loving devotion. For knowing that her very breath depends on mine, I am learning to take care of myself in order to preserve her. And though old age has made me more resilient in many ways, I forfeit this benefit when I remember that, in this old man, a youth also resides who must be spared. So, since I cannot persuade Paulina to love me with less fervor, she persuades me to cherish myself more diligently.

[3] For we must indulge honorable affections. And at times, even if circumstances weigh heavily upon us, we must call back the breath of life for the sake of our loved ones, holding it at the very threshold of departure, even through great anguish. A good person should live not

as long as they desire, but as long as they ought. One who does not value wife or friend enough to tarry longer in life, who would persist in dying, is a coward. Let the mind also impose this duty on itself: when the welfare of one's family demands it, a person must check the wish for death, if it has only just begun, and oblige themselves to live on for their sake.

[4] It takes a tremendous soul to return to life for another's cause - a noble act many great men have often done. But I also consider it the height of humane feeling to guard one's old age with extra care (the greatest reward of which is a more carefree self-governance and a bolder enjoyment of life), if you know that your continuing presence is a sweet, useful, and longed-for boon to any of your loved ones.

[5] Moreover, this realization bears no small joy and recompense. For what is more delightful than to be so cherished by a spouse that, because of her, you become even more precious to yourself? My Paulina, then, can credit to my account not only her own fears for me, but mine for her as well.

[6] You ask, then, how my plan of traveling turned out? As soon as I escaped the oppressive atmosphere of the city and that reek of smoking kitchens which, when in full swing, pour forth a ruinous mess of steam and soot, I perceived at once a change in my health. Can you imagine how my strength increased after I reached the vineyards? Set loose in pastureland, I fell upon my food. So I have recovered again, and that mental sluggishness and gloominess has not lingered in my hesitant body and anxious mind. I am beginning to study with all my energy.

[7] The place does not contribute much to this, unless the mind lends itself to itself, which will have solitude in the midst of busyness, if it so chooses. But the mind that picks out resorts and seeks leisure will find distractions everywhere. They say that when someone complained to Socrates that his travels had done him no good, he replied: "It serves you right! You were traveling in your own company."

[8] Oh, what a blessing it would be for some people to wander away from themselves! As it is, they obsess over themselves, worry themselves, corrupt themselves, and terrify themselves. What good

does it do to cross the sea and change cities? If you want to escape the things that weigh on you, you need to be not somewhere else, but someone else. Imagine you have arrived at Athens, imagine Rhodes; choose any state you fancy. What difference does it make what its customs are? You will bring your own along.

[9] You will judge wealth to be a good thing. Then poverty will torment you—a false poverty, which is most wretched. For no matter how much you possess, you will feel lacking by as much as you are surpassed, since someone else has more. You will judge public office to be a good thing. But you will be vexed that this man became consul, that man even became consul again. You will envy every time you read a name recorded more often in the annals. Such will be the madness of your ambition that no one will seem to come after you if anyone comes before you.

[10] You will judge death to be the worst evil, though there is nothing bad about it except what precedes it—the fear of it. Not only real dangers but imaginary ones will terrify you; you will be tormented constantly by phantoms. What good will it do you

> *to have escaped so many Greek cities*
> *And made your way safely through the midst of the foe?*

Peace itself will supply you with fears. Once a mind is alarmed, it will not even trust what is safe. When it has formed the habit of blind panic, it becomes helpless even in ensuring its own security[1]. For it does not avoid danger but runs from it, and we lay ourselves more open to dangers when we turn our backs.

[11] You will consider it a most grievous misfortune to lose someone you love. Yet this is no more sensible than weeping because leaves fall from beautiful trees that adorn your home. Whatever gives you delight, look upon it just as you would the flowers in springtime. Enjoy them while they bloom, for chance will strike them down, each in its own day. But just as the loss of leaves is easy to bear because they grow back, so too the loss of those you love and consider life's joys can be repaired, even if they do not return in the same form.

[12] "But they will not be the same!" you protest. And you will not be the same either. Every day, every hour changes you, although this change is more apparent in others since it does not happen openly to you. Some are taken away from us, while we ourselves are secretly stolen away. You will ponder none of this nor apply remedies to these wounds. Instead, you will sow the seeds of anxiety by hoping for some things and despairing of others. If you are wise, blend the two together. Neither hope without despair, nor despair without hope.

[13] What good has travel itself ever done anyone? It has not moderated their pleasures, reined in their desires, suppressed their anger, or broken the uncontrolled impulses of love. In short, it has not removed any evils from the mind. It has not provided sound judgment or dispelled error, but like a child marveling at the unfamiliar, it has detained them for a short while with the novelty of their surroundings.

[14] But the inconstancy of a sick mind is provoked and rendered more unstable and fickle by the very act of travel. And so people eagerly abandon the places they sought with utmost desire, flitting away like birds and departing more swiftly than they came.

[15] Travel will acquaint you with foreign peoples, reveal new shapes of mountains, expanses of unfamiliar plains, valleys watered by ever-flowing streams, and the nature of some great river—whether it swells in summer like the Nile, or vanishes from sight like the Tigris, which runs an underground course before re-emerging at full size, or winds in frequent twists and turns like the Maeander, plaything of the poets, often approaching its own bed before curving away again. But for all that, travel will make no one better or saner.

[16] We must spend our time in study, learning from the authors of wisdom. We must learn what has been discovered and seek out what remains to be found. Only in this way can the mind be delivered from wretched slavery into freedom. As long as you remain ignorant of what to avoid and what to seek out, what is necessary and what is superfluous, what is right and what is wrong—your journeys will not be travel but mere wandering.

[17] That constant traveling of yours will bring you no relief, for you journey weighed down by your afflictions, and your ills follow close behind you. If only they really did follow behind - then at least they would be further away! But as it is, you carry them with you, not lead them along. And so they press upon you everywhere, burning you with the same pains no matter the place. [The cure must be sought in the mind of the sick man, not in his surroundings.]

[18] If someone breaks his leg or dislocates a joint, he doesn't board a carriage or ship, but calls for a doctor to set the fractured limb and put the dislocated part back in its place. What then? Do you believe that a mind broken and wrenched in so many places can be healed by a mere change of scenery? That malady is too grave to be cured by a bit of travel.

[19] Journeying does not make one a physician or an orator; no art is learned simply by being in a particular place.

What's that you say? Can wisdom, the greatest art of all, be picked up along the road? Believe me, there is no journey that can transport you beyond desires, beyond anger, beyond fears. If there were, all humanity would surge there en masse. As long as you carry with you the causes of your ills, those woes will continue to harass and plague you as you wander over land and sea.

[20] Do you marvel that flight does not help you? You flee along with the very things you're trying to escape. Therefore, you must first improve yourself, cast off your burdens, and constrain your unruly desires within healthy limits. Root out all iniquity from your soul. If you wish your travels to be delightful, first heal your traveling companion - yourself. Avarice will cling to you as long as you consort with greedy misers; arrogance will stick with you as long as you keep company with the proud; and cruelty will never leave you if you lodge in the quarters of a torturer. The fellowship of adulterers will inflame your lusts.

[21] If you wish to shed your vices, you must withdraw far from the examples of vice. The greedy man, the seducer, the cruel tyrant, the cheat - all would do you great harm if they were close by you, but in fact they reside within you.

Seek out better company: live with the Catos, with Laelius, with Tubero. And if you find it beneficial to consort also with the Greeks, spend your time with Socrates and Zeno. The one will teach you how to die if it becomes necessary; the other, how to die before it's necessary. Live with Chrysippus and Posidonius: they will impart to you knowledge of things human and divine; they will bid you to be not just a clever speaker tossing out words to delight your listeners, but to steel your mind and stand tall against fortune's threats.

[22] For truly, in this turbulent, storm-tossed life, there is but one haven: to scorn what may come, to stand firm and ready to receive fortune's arrows with unyielding breast, neither cowering nor turning away.

[23] Nature has produced us to be magnanimous, and just as she has given to certain animals a wild spirit, to some a cunning one, and to others a timid one, so to us she has given a glorious and lofty spirit, seeking to live in the most honorable way, not the safest. This spirit is most similar to the universe, which it follows and emulates as far as mortal steps allow. It puts itself forward, believing itself to be praised and observed. It is the master of all things and stands above all things.

[24] Therefore, it should not submit itself to anything, nor should anything seem difficult or capable of bending a man of such spirit. "Forms terrible to behold, and death and labors" - indeed, these are not at all terrible if one can gaze upon them with clear eyes and pierce the darkness. Many things held as terrors in the night, the day turns into objects of laughter. Our excellent Vergil did not say "forms terrible to behold, and death and labors" are terrible in reality, but in appearance - that is, they seem terrible, but are not. I ask, what in these things is as formidable as rumor has spread?

[25] Why, I beg you, Lucilius, should a man fear labor, or a mortal fear death? I often encounter those who think that what they cannot do is impossible, and who say that we speak of things greater than human nature can bear.

[26] But how much better do I think of them! They too can do these things, but they do not wish to. Finally, whom have these things

ever failed when attempting them? To whom have they not appeared easier in the doing? It is not because they are difficult that we do not dare, but because we do not dare that they are difficult.

[27] If, however, you desire an example, take Socrates, that most persevering old man, tossed about through all hardships, yet unconquered by poverty (which domestic burdens made heavier for him) and by labors (which he endured even in military service). By these things he was exercised at home, whether we recall his wife, wild in her ways and impudent in speech, or his unruly children who resembled their mother more than their father. If you consider it rightly, he was either in war, or under a tyranny, or in a freedom more cruel than wars and tyrannies. For twenty-seven years the fight went on; after the end of hostilities, the city was given over for punishment to thirty tyrants, most of whom were his enemies.

[28] The latest charges against Socrates were framed in the gravest terms: he was accused of violating religious rites and corrupting the youth, leading them to disrespect the gods, their fathers, and the state. After this came prison and poison. Yet none of it disturbed Socrates' spirit, not even enough to change his expression. O what singular and amazing praise! To the very end, no one saw Socrates become either more cheerful or more sad. He remained constant amid such inconstancy of fortune.

Do you want another example?

[29] Consider this more recent Marcus Cato, with whom fortune dealt even more hostilely and persistently. Though it opposed him in every place, and finally even in death, fortune nonetheless showed that a brave man can live against its will and die against its will. Cato spent his entire life either bearing arms in civil wars or wearing the toga [as a politician] in a state already conceiving civil war. You could say that he, no less than Socrates, devoted himself as a slave to freedom—unless perhaps you think that Gnaeus Pompey, Caesar, and Crassus were allies of liberty.

[30] No one saw Cato change, though the state changed so often: he showed himself the same in every condition—as praetor, when repulsed, during prosecution, in his province, in the assembly, with

the army, and at his death. Indeed, during that crisis of the state, when on one side stood Caesar supported by ten fiercely combative legions and the backing of all foreign nations, and on the other Gnaeus Pompey, alone sufficient against all, while some inclined to Caesar and others to Pompey, only Cato carved out another party for the Republic.

[31] If you want to picture that period in your mind, you will see on one side the common people and all the masses roused for revolution; on the other the aristocrats and equestrian order, whatever was hallowed and chosen in the state; and left in the middle, the Republic and Cato.

You will marvel, I tell you, when you recognize

"The son of Atreus, Priam, and Achilles fierce to both."

[32] For Cato condemns and disarms both sides. This is his judgment of each: he says if Caesar wins he will die, if Pompey he will go into exile. What had he to fear, who had determined for himself what would befall him whether his side conquered or was conquered—terms that could have been dictated by the angriest of enemies? And so he perished by his own decree. You see that men can endure hardship: [...]

[33] He led his army on foot through the middle of Africa's deserts, proving that thirst can be endured. On parched hills, dragging the remains of a defeated army without any baggage train, he bore a lack of water while wearing full armor, and whenever there was a chance for water, he drank last. This shows that dishonor and disgrace can be disregarded. On the very same day he was rejected, he played ball in the comitium², demonstrating that the power of one's superiors need not be feared. He provoked both Pompey and Caesar at the same time, neither of whom dared offend the other except to win the other's favor. This reveals that both death and exile can be scorned—he sentenced himself to exile and to death, and in the meantime, to war.

[34] We can therefore have a spirit so resolute against such things,

if only we are willing to withdraw our necks from the yoke. But first of all, pleasures must be rejected; they weaken and effeminate us, and to attain them requires much from Fortune. Next, riches must be spurned—they are the wages of slavery. Gold, silver, and whatever else burdens blessed houses should be abandoned; freedom cannot be had for free. If you value freedom highly, then all else must be valued little. Farewell.

---

1. Some manuscripts read "you become," rather than "it becomes."
2. The comitium was an open space in the Roman Forum where public assemblies were held.

LETTER 105

THE MERITS OF OBSCURITY
AND MODERATION

[1] I WILL TELL YOU WHAT PRECAUTIONS TO TAKE IN ORDER TO LIVE MORE securely. However, I suggest that you listen to these precepts as if I were advising you on how to maintain good health at your villa in Ardea.

Consider what motivates a person to bring about the destruction of another: you will find hope, envy, hatred, fear, and contempt.

[2] Of all these, contempt is by far the lightest, such that many have hidden in it as a remedy. Without a doubt, a person violates one whom he holds in contempt, but he passes over him; no one persistently or diligently harms a person who is despised. Even one lying prostrate on the battlefield is passed by while the fight rages with those still standing.

[3] You will avoid the hope of the wicked if you possess nothing that might provoke alien and improper desire, if you own nothing of notable value. For even small things are coveted if they are remarkable or rare. You will escape envy if you do not thrust yourself before the eyes of others, if you do not boast of your blessings, if you know how to rejoice in your heart.

[4] Hatred either arises from offense—this you will avoid by

provoking no one—or it is unwarranted, from which common sense will protect you. This has proven dangerous for many; some have incurred hatred without even an enemy. As for not being feared, both moderation in fortune and gentleness of character will ensure this for you; let men know that you are one whom they can offend without danger. Let your reconciliation be both easy and certain. Yet to be feared is as troublesome at home as abroad, by slaves as much as by free men. No one lacks sufficient strength to cause harm. Add now the fact that he who is feared also fears; no one has been able to be both fearsome and secure.

[5] Contempt remains, the extent of which is in the power of the one who has brought it upon himself—he who is despised because he wished it, not because he deserved it. The disadvantage of this is dispelled by both worthy arts and the friendships of those who are powerful in the presence of some powerful person—connections to whom it will be expedient to attach yourself without becoming entangled, lest the remedy cost more than the danger.

[6] Yet nothing will benefit you as much as keeping quiet and conversing minimally with others, but maximally with yourself. There is a certain sweetness of conversation that creeps in, coaxes, and draws out secrets just like drunkenness or love. No one will keep silent about what he has heard. No one will speak only as much as he has heard. He who did not keep silent about the subject matter will not conceal the source. Each person has someone whom he trusts as much as he himself is trusted. While he may guard his own garrulousness and be content with one pair of ears, he will create a crowd if what was just recently a secret becomes rumor.

[7] A great portion of security comes from doing no wrong. Those who lack self-control lead confused and troubled lives; they fear in equal measure to the harm they inflict, and find no moment of respite. They tremble with the deed done, paralyzed; their conscience allows them no peace, compelling constant self-examination. Whoever awaits punishment, suffers it; whoever deserves it, awaits it.

[8] A guilty conscience may at times provide a measure of safety, but never security; for even if undiscovered, it imagines the constant

possibility of discovery. The mind is unsettled even in sleep, and whenever another's crime is mentioned, it turns to its own. The wicked deed seems insufficiently blotted out, inadequately concealed. The criminal may fortuitously evade detection for a time, but never the dread of it. Farewell.

LETTER 106

WHETHER GOOD IS CORPOREAL

[1] MY REPLY TO YOUR LETTERS HAS BEEN RATHER DELAYED - NOT because I am entangled in a thicket of pressing business. Never let that excuse reach your ears, for I am at leisure, as are all who wish to be. Our activities do not pursue us - rather, we embrace them, imagining busyness to be proof of our prosperity. So what, then, was the reason I did not write back immediately? The very topic you were inquiring about fits into the context of the work I am composing.

[2] As you know, I aim to encapsulate the entirety of moral philosophy and elucidate every question pertaining to it. Thus I wavered between putting you off until this subject's proper place arrived in due course, or pronouncing judgment for you out of sequence. It seemed the kinder choice not to keep you waiting, having journeyed so far [in your philosophical studies].

[3] Therefore, I will extract this matter too from that connected series of thoughts, and if there are any other points of this nature, I will send them to you unprompted, without your needing to ask.

What sort of points, you wonder? Those which are more pleasurable than profitable to know - like the question you pose: is the good a corporeal entity?

[4] The good activates, for it is profitable. That which activates is a

corporeal entity. The good stirs the soul and, in a sense, molds and contains it - the distinctive qualities of body. The goods of the body are corporeal; therefore, so too are those of the soul.

[5] For the soul is also a corporeal entity. The good of a human being must necessarily be corporeal, since a human is corporeal in nature. I speak falsely unless you believe that the factors said to sustain and safeguard or restore one's soundness of body are also corporeal. Therefore the good of a human, too, is corporeal. I do not imagine you will question whether the emotions are corporeal - so that I may reinforce another point you did not ask about - unless you doubt that they transform our countenance, furrow our brow, brighten our expression, summon a blush, or drain the color from our faces. Well? Do you believe that such visible imprints upon the body can be stamped by anything other than a corporeal entity?

[6] If the emotions are corporeal, so too are the sicknesses of the soul, like greed, cruelty, vices which have become ingrained and reached a state beyond correction. Therefore, wickedness and all its forms - spite, envy, arrogance. Therefore, the virtues as well: firstly because they are the opposites of the vices, and secondly because they will exhibit for you the same telltale signs [of corporeality].

[7] Do you not see how fortitude gives vigor to the eyes? How much focus prudence provides? How much modesty and tranquility reverence bestows? What serenity joy brings? What sternness severity imparts? What relaxation gentleness offers? It is the body, therefore, that changes the color and condition of the body, exercising its dominion over it.

All the virtues I have mentioned are good, as is everything that comes from them. Is there any doubt that something which can be touched is a body?

[8] "For nothing can touch or be touched except a body," as Lucretius says. All those things I mentioned would not change the body unless they touched it; therefore, they are bodies.

[9] Even now, that which has such power to impel, compel, restrain, and inhibit[1] is a body. What then? Does fear not restrain? Does boldness not impel? Does fortitude not send forth and give

impetus? Does moderation not rein in and recall? Does joy not uplift? Does sadness not weigh down?

[10] In short, whatever we do, we act under the command of either vice or virtue. That which commands the body is a body, and that which exerts force on the body is a body. The good of the body is corporeal, and the good of a person is also the good of the body; therefore, it is corporeal[2].

[11] Since I have indulged you as you wished, I will now tell myself what I see you are going to say: we are playing with pawns [engaging in trivial pursuits]. Subtlety is wasted on superfluous matters; these things do not make one good, but learned. The path to wisdom is more open, or rather, it is simpler to use letters [education] for a good mind, but we, as with other things, lavish ourselves excessively on philosophy itself.

[12] We suffer from intemperance in all things, including letters; we learn not for life, but for school. Farewell.

---

1. Some manuscripts read "iubeat" (command) instead of "inhibeat" (inhibit).
2. Some manuscripts add "res est" (is a thing) after "corporalis".

LETTER 107
ACCEPTING EVENTS WITH EQUANIMITY

[1] Where has your wisdom gone? Your keen discernment? Your magnanimity? You are now vexed by trifles? Your servants saw your preoccupations as an opportunity to flee. If friends deceived you—for let them keep the label our misjudgment has bestowed upon them, lest their shame be diminished—you would find something lacking in all your affairs. But as it stands, you are only lacking those who were wasting your time and believed you a burden to others.

[2] None of this is unusual or unexpected. To be offended by such things is as absurd as complaining about being splashed in public or soiled by mud. Life is like visiting the baths, facing a crowd, or taking a journey: some things will be thrown at you[1], others will befall you by chance. Living is not for the faint of heart. You have set out on a long road, and you are bound to slip, crash, fall, grow weary, and cry out, "O death!"—that is, to tell a falsehood. In one place you will leave a companion behind; in another, you will bury one; in another, you will live in fear. This arduous journey must be traveled amid such tribulations.

[3] Do you wish to die? Let the mind be prepared for all things; let it know it has come to a place where the thunder of Jove's lightning is heard, where

Grief and vengeful cares have made their beds,
Where pale diseases dwell, and sad old age.

Amid such company must life be spent. These ills you cannot escape, but you can scorn them—and scorn them you will if you often reflect on what is to come and take the sting out of future afflictions.

[4] Everyone approaches more bravely a state for which they have long prepared, standing firm even against hardships if they have previously rehearsed facing them. In contrast, the unprepared are terrified by even the most trivial of troubles. We must strive to ensure nothing takes us by surprise. And because all new things are more grievous, constant reflection will see to it that you are a novice to no misfortune.

[5] "My slaves have abandoned me." Others have been robbed, accused, killed, betrayed, trampled, targeted by poison or slander—whatever you might say, it has happened to many. Next come the host of various missiles aimed our way. Some have already struck us; some are still in flight, arriving imminently; some destined for others merely graze us in passing.

[6] Let us not be surprised by any of those things we were born for, which no one should complain about since they are the same for all. When I say they are the same, I mean that even what someone avoids, they had the potential to suffer. True justice is not that which all have experienced, but that which is decreed for all. Let us impose fairness on our minds and pay the taxes of our mortality without complaint.

[7] Winter brings cold weather: we must feel the chill. Summer returns with heat: we must swelter. The inclement weather assails our health: we must fall ill. In some places we will encounter wild beasts and humans more dangerous than any beast. Water will snatch one thing, fire another. We cannot change this condition of the world, but what we can do is take on a great spirit, worthy of a good person, so we may bravely endure chance events and live in harmony with Nature.

[8] For Nature, as you see, tempers her reign with changes; clear skies follow cloudy ones; the seas are thrown into disorder after a period of calm; the winds take their turn; day follows night; one part of the heavens rises while another sets. Eternity is made up of opposites.

[9] Our mind must adapt itself to this law; let it follow along and obey. Let it believe that whatever happens was bound to happen and not try to reproach Nature. The best course is to endure what you cannot change, and to follow the God under whose guidance all things come about, without complaining. It is a poor soldier who follows his commander with groans.

[10] So let us receive our orders energetically and cheerfully, and not desert[2] this most beautiful course of work, into which all our sufferings are woven.

And let us address Jupiter, by whose steering[3] this vast edifice is guided, in the way our esteemed Cleanthes addresses him in most eloquent verses, which I may be permitted to render into our language, following the example of Cicero, a man of the greatest eloquence. If they please you, you will appreciate them; if not, you will know that in this I have followed Cicero's precedent:

[11]

> *Lead me, O Master of the soaring sky,*
> *Where'er you will; I follow without pause.*
> *Alert I stand. Should I resist, I still*
> *Must follow grieving, suffer what I could*
> *Have done with noble spirit. Fate conducts*
> *The willing soul, but drags the unwilling on.*

[12] Let us live this way, let us speak this way; let Fate find us ready and alert. Here is the great soul—one that has entrusted itself to Fate. In contrast, the petty, degenerate soul fights against it, criticizes the order of the universe, and would rather reform the gods than itself. Farewell.

———————————

1. Lipsius' correction; the original text reads "intermittentur" (will be interrupted).
2. Some later manuscripts read "not desert"; the earliest manuscripts have "not fail".
3. Some later manuscripts read "by whose steering"; the earliest manuscripts have "by whose dwelling".

LETTER 108
TRUE PHILOSOPHERS TRANSFORM LIVES

[1] THE MATTER YOU INQUIRE ABOUT IS ONE OF THOSE THINGS WHICH are only worth knowing for the sake of knowing. But since it does pertain, and you are in haste, not wanting to wait for the books I am now arranging that will contain the whole department of moral philosophy, I will explain it at once. First, however, I will write about how this eagerness for learning, which I see burns fiercely in you, should be managed, lest it impede itself.

[2] Things are not to be gathered at random, nor should the whole be greedily invaded at once; the whole will be reached through the parts. The burden must be adapted to one's strength, and no more should be occupied than what one can adequately handle. You are to draw not as much as you wish, but as much as you can hold. Simply have a good mind; you will grasp as much as you desire. The more the mind receives, the more it expands itself.

[3] I remember Attalus giving us these precepts when we besieged his school, arriving first and leaving last, and even summoning him to discussions when he was out walking—he was not only available to his students but met them halfway. "The same purpose," he said, "should belong to both teacher and learner: the one should wish to be useful, the other to make progress."

[4] Whoever comes to a philosopher should daily carry away with them some good—they should return home either sounder or more open to being healed. And return they will, for such is the power of philosophy: it helps not only the diligent but even those who simply associate with it. Those who come into the sun, even if not for that purpose, will be colored [tanned]. Those who have sat in a perfume shop and lingered a little too long carry the fragrance of the place with them. And those who have been in a philosopher's company must necessarily draw from it something that would benefit them even if they were inattentive—pay attention to what I say: inattentive, not resistant.

[5] "What then? Do we not know certain people who have sat many years with a philosopher and have not even taken on their color?" Of course I know them—the most persistent and diligent folks, whom I call not disciples of the philosophers but merely tenants.

[6] Some people come to hear the philosophers not to learn, but as we are drawn to the theater for pleasure, to delight our ears with oratory, voice, or stories. You will see that a great number of these listeners treat the philosopher's lecture hall as a resort for their leisure. They do not attend with the aim of shedding their vices or receiving some rule of life by which to test their character, but to enjoy a pleasurable listening experience. Some, however, even come equipped with writing tablets, not to take down the subject matter, but only the words, which they repeat with as little profit to others as they hear them without benefit to themselves. Certain listeners are stirred by impressive-sounding remarks and grow excited, assuming the enthusiasm of the speakers in their expressions and spirits, not unlike the way half-men [eunuchs] tend to become frenzied and ecstatic at the sound of the Phrygian flute player.

[7] It is the beauty of the subject matter that transports and spurs them, not the empty clang of words. If some vigorous argument is made against death, or a defiant statement against Fortune, the audience is immediately delighted to put into practice what they hear. They are moved by the words and become what they are urged to be,

if only that mental attitude persists, if the masses—who dissuade from virtue—do not immediately obstruct that noble impulse. Few are those who have been able to carry home the state of mind which they had conceived.

[8] It is easy to rouse a listener to a desire for what is right; for Nature has laid the foundations and planted the seeds of virtue in us all. We are born for all these same things; when a stimulus is applied, then those noble qualities of the soul are awakened and activated, as it were. Do you not see how the theaters resound whenever any sayings are spoken that we recognize as true and collectively testify to be valid?

[9]

"The poor lack much; the greedy man lacks everything.
To none is the miser kind, to himself he is most cruel."

At these verses, even the most sordid miser applauds and rejoices to hear his own sins reviled. How much more, then, do you think this happens when such things are spoken by a philosopher, when beneficial precepts are interspersed with poetic verses, which thus even more effectively send those same ideas home into the minds of the ignorant? [10] "For," as Cleanthes used to say, "just as our breath produces a louder sound when a trumpet forces it through the narrow straits of a long pipe to pour it out through the wider opening at the end, so the constraints of poetic meter make our thoughts more resonant and clear." The selfsame ideas are heard more casually and make less impact when expressed in prose; but when rhythm is added and noble thoughts are condensed into poetic feet, those identical ideas are launched forth as if hurled by a more powerful arm.

[11] Much is said about the contempt for money, and the longest of speeches teach that men should consider their wealth to reside in their spirit, not their patrimony. A man is truly rich when he has adapted himself to his poverty and made himself wealthy with little. Yet the mind is struck more deeply when such ideas are expressed in verse:

> *The mortal who desires the least is the one who lacks the*
> *   least.*
> *He who is able to wish for only what suffices already has*
> *   what he wants.*

[12] When we hear these and similar sentiments, we are led to confess the truth. Those for whom nothing is enough admire these words, applaud them, and proclaim their hatred for money. When you see them thus affected, urge on, press the point, and drive it home, leaving behind ambiguities, syllogisms, quibbles and all other displays of ineffectual cleverness. Inveigh against greed, inveigh against luxury. When you see you have made progress and moved the minds of your hearers, bear down more forcefully. It is scarcely credible how much good such speech can do, aimed at providing a remedy and wholly directed to the good of the listeners. For tender minds are most easily won over to a love of what is honorable and right, and truth lays her hand on those still teachable and only slightly corrupted, if she finds a worthy advocate.

[13] Indeed, when I used to hear Attalus declaiming against vice, error, and the evils of life, I often felt pity for humankind and believed him to be sublime and superior to human limitations. He would say that he himself was a king, but to me he seemed more than a king, for he presumed to pass judgment on kings themselves.

[14] Moreover, when he began to commend poverty and demonstrate how anything exceeding our basic needs is a superfluous and burdensome weight, I often felt the urge to walk out of his school a poor man. When he started to mock our pleasures, to praise a chaste body, a sober table, and a mind pure not only from illicit pleasures but even from superfluous ones, I felt the desire to restrict my gluttony and appetite.

[15] Some of these teachings have stuck with me, Lucilius, for I had approached it all with great enthusiasm. Later, when I returned to city life, I retained a few of these good beginnings. Thus, for my whole life, I have renounced oysters and mushrooms. For they are not really food, but temptations that coax the sated to eat more—most

welcomed by those who stuff themselves beyond capacity, as these morsels go down easily and come back up just as readily.

[16] Likewise, I abstain from perfume for life, since the best odor for the body is none at all. So too I keep my stomach free of wine. I shun the bath for life, believing it useless and even effeminate to stew the body and drain it with sweating. Other indulgences I tossed aside have crept back, yet in such a way that I maintain moderation in the things I resumed—a moderation bordering on abstinence and perhaps even more difficult. For some things are more easily cut off completely than used temperately.

[17] Since I have begun to explain to you the greater enthusiasm with which I approached philosophy as a young man than I proceed with now as an old one, I will not be ashamed to confess the love that Pythagoras instilled in me. Sotion used to tell me why Pythagoras had abstained from animal flesh, and why Sextius did so later on. They each had different reasons, but both were admirable.

[18] Sextius believed that man had sufficient nourishment without resorting to blood, and that a habit of cruelty is formed whenever butchery is practiced for pleasure. He added that we should limit the materials of luxury, arguing that a variety of foods, especially those foreign to our bodies, are contrary to good health.

[19] Pythagoras, on the other hand, maintained that there is a relationship between all living beings, and a mutual exchange of souls passing into different forms. If you believe him, no soul perishes or even pauses except for a brief moment when it is being poured into another body. We shall see through what cycles of time and after traversing how many dwelling places the soul returns into a human being. Meanwhile, Pythagoras struck fear of crime and parricide into people, since they might unknowingly assault the soul of a parent and violate it with sword or tooth if a related spirit happened to be dwelling in that creature.

[20] When Sotion had explained these ideas and bolstered them with arguments, he would say: "You do not believe that souls are assigned to different bodies, that what we call death is merely a migration? You do not believe that the soul of a man, preserved in

these cattle, beasts, or creatures submerged in water, once lodged there? You do not believe that nothing in this world truly perishes, but only changes its abode? And that not only heavenly bodies revolve in fixed circuits, but animals too alternate in their paths, with souls being driven through an endless cycle? Great men have put faith in these notions."

[21] "Therefore, withhold your judgment for now, but keep an open mind. If these doctrines are true, abstaining from animal flesh is a mark of innocence; if false, it is frugality. What harm does this credulity do to you? I am merely depriving you of the food of lions and vultures."

[22] Stirred by these arguments, I began to abstain from animal flesh, and by the end of a year, the habit was not only easy for me but pleasant. I believed my mind to be more active, though I would not claim so with certainty today. You ask how I came to abandon the practice? My youth coincided with the early reign of Tiberius Caesar. At that time, foreign rites were being expelled, but abstinence from certain animals was being proposed as evidence of superstition. So at my father's urging, who feared not prosecution but hated philosophy, I returned to my previous habits. Nor did he have much difficulty in persuading me to begin dining more lavishly.

[23] Attalus used to praise a mattress that resists the body; even as an old man, I use one in which no impression can be left. I mention this to show you how enthusiastically new recruits are driven towards the best things, if only someone encourages and inspires them.

But errors are made partly by teachers who instruct us how to argue, not how to live, and partly by students who bring to their teachers an aim of cultivating their wits, not their souls. Thus what was once philosophy has become mere philology.

[24] It matters greatly with what purpose you approach each endeavor. The man who pores over Virgil to become a grammarian does not read that glorious line in the proper spirit: "Time flies never to return." We must wake up! Unless we make haste, we will be left behind. The swift day drives us on, and we are carried away unaware.

We arrange everything for the future while dawdling on the edge of the abyss.

But the grammarian merely observes how often, in speaking of time's swift passage, Virgil uses the verb "flies":

Life's finest days are the first to flee from wretched mortals;
Diseases and sad old age creep in, then toil and the
    harshness
Of unrelenting death sweeps us away.

[25] The man who has a philosophical outlook draws a different lesson from these same lines. "Virgil," he remarks, "never says that our days pass, but that they flee - the most rapid form of movement. The best days are the first to be snatched away. Why then do we not hurry ourselves along so we can match the speed of this swiftest of all things? The best in life flies by; inferior things rush in to replace it."

[26] Just as the purest liquid flows out first from a bottle, with the dregs and sediment settling to the bottom, so in our human life, the best comes at the beginning. [Do we allow others to drain off the finest portion so we can keep the lees for ourselves?] Let this thought sink into your soul and be valued like an oracle's pronouncement:

Life's finest days are the first to flee from wretched mortals.

[27] Why the finest days? Because what remains is uncertain. Why the finest days? Because when young we can learn; our faculties are pliant and easily directed to better paths. This is the time suited for work, for driving our talents through studies, for training our bodies through exercise. What's left is more sluggish, languid, closer to the end.

So let us put our whole hearts into this endeavor. Ignoring all distractions, let us labor towards this one aim: lest we fail to realize, until it's too late, the swift passage of that most fleeting thing - time - which we are powerless to hold back. Let us treat each day that dawns as the best, and make it our own.

[28] We must seize what flees from us. The one who reads that poem with the eyes of a grammarian does not consider this: that each day is best because diseases creep in, old age weighs heavy, and while still thinking of youth, it looms overhead. But he says that Virgil always mentions diseases and old age together, and by Hercules, not undeservedly so. For old age is an incurable disease.

[29] Moreover, he says, Virgil has imposed this epithet on old age, calling it sad:

Diseases and sad old age creep in.

In another place he says:

Pale diseases and sad old age dwell there.

It is no wonder that from the same material each person gathers what is suitable to their own pursuits; in the same meadow, the ox seeks grass, the dog a hare, the stork a lizard.

[30] When someone takes up Cicero's book on the Republic, a philologist looks for one thing, a grammarian another, and one devoted to philosophy yet another; each directs their attention differently. The philosopher marvels that so much could be said against justice. When the philologist approaches this same reading, he takes note of this: that there are two Roman kings, one of whom has no father, the other no mother. For there is doubt about the mother of Servius, while Ancus, the grandson of Numa, is said to have no father.

[31] He also notes that the one whom we call dictator and read to be so named in histories, was called by the ancients the master of the people. Even today this is extant in the augural books, and it is evidence that he who is named by that one is the master of the horse. He equally notes that Romulus perished in an eclipse of the sun; that appeal to the people existed even from the time of the kings; that this is so in the pontifical books and certain others think so, as does Fenestella.

[32] When a grammarian explicates the same books, he first records in his commentary that the word "expressa" [explicit] is really used by Cicero, that is "re ipsa" [in fact], and no less "sepse" [himself], that is "se ipse" [he himself]. Then he transitions to those things which the custom of the age has changed, as when Cicero says: "since we have been called back from the very chalk by its interruption." What we now call chalk in the circus, the ancients called calx. Then he collects verses of Ennius and especially those about

[33] In his writings about Africanus, Ennius states:

> *"For him, no citizen nor enemy*
> *Could offer a reward worthy of his deeds[1]."*

From this, he claims to understand that among the ancients, "ops" signified not only aid but also effort. For Ennius says[2] that no one, whether citizen or enemy, could give Scipio[3] a reward worthy of his effort. Then he thinks himself fortunate because he has found a model for Virgil's lines:

[34] "Over whom the mighty gate of heaven thunders." This, he claims, Virgil snatched from Ennius, who snatched it from Homer. For in Cicero's very work On the Republic there is this epigram of Ennius:

> *"If it is right for anyone to ascend to the regions of the*
> *heavens,*
> *For me alone the greatest gate of heaven lies open."*

[35] But lest I too, while pursuing another task, lapse into mere philology or grammar, let me offer this reminder: the lectures and readings of the philosophers should be applied to the goal of a happy life, not so that we may chase after ancient or contrived words, inappropriate metaphors and figures of speech, but so that we may learn beneficial precepts, magnificent sayings, and spirited words, which may soon be translated into action. Let us learn them in such a way that what were once mere words become deeds.

[36] I judge that no one deserves worse of all mortals than those who have learned philosophy as if it were some venal craft, who live differently than they teach one ought to live. For they carry around themselves as examples of a useless discipline, guilty of every vice they attack.

[37] No instructor of that sort can benefit me any more than a seasick helmsman can in a storm. The rudder must be gripped as the surge sweeps over, the struggle is with the sea itself, the sails must be wrested from the wind—how can a dazed, vomiting captain aid me? By how much greater a tempest do you think life is tossed about than any raft? There is no time for talk, but for taking the helm.

[38] All that they say, all that they spout to the listening crowd, is borrowed. Plato said it, Zeno said it, Chrysippus and Posidonius said it, as did a mighty throng of Stoics, so many and of such stature. How can they prove it to be their own? I will show you: let them do what they have talked about.

[39] Since I have now said what I wished to convey to you, I will satisfy your desire and transcribe in full in another letter what you requested, lest you approach a thorny subject that requires alert and curious ears when already weary. Farewell.

---

1. The original has "quibit" (will be able) according to Pincianus, while the manuscripts BA have "quivult" (wishes).
2. Vahlen and Haase have "ait enim Ennius" (for Ennius says), while manuscripts BA have the corrupted "ait operaenim ineius".
3. Pincianus corrects to the dative "Scipioni"; manuscripts BA have the accusative "Scipionem".

LETTER 109

FRIENDSHIP'S ROLE IN THE PHILOSOPHIC LIFE

[1] You wish to know whether a wise man can be of help to another wise man. We say that the wise man is complete, having attained the highest good. How then, you ask, can anyone be of help to one who possesses the supreme good?

Wise men do benefit each other, for they exercise their virtues and keep their wisdom sharp through interaction. Each one desires someone with whom to share ideas and inquire into the truth.

[2] Skilled wrestlers hone each other through practice; musicians inspire one another by playing in harmony. In the same way, the wise man needs to engage his virtues actively. As he stimulates his own mind, so too is he stimulated by another sage.

[3] What good, then, will one wise man do for another? He will spur on his motivation, point out opportunities for honorable actions. Beyond this, he will share some of his own insights—teaching what he has discovered. For there will always be more for even a sage to find, fresh paths for his mind to eagerly explore.

[4] The wicked harm one another, making each other worse by provoking anger, validating sadness, and encouraging indulgence. And the struggles of the wicked are greatest when vices intermingle

and wickedness converges. Following this logic, a good man will therefore benefit a fellow good man. "How so?" you ask.

[5] He will bring him joy, bolster his confidence. In witnessing each other's tranquility, the happiness of both will grow. Moreover, he will impart knowledge of certain things—for not even a sage knows everything. But even if he did, a fresh perspective could devise shorter paths and point out easier ways to navigate the whole undertaking.

[6] So a wise man is of aid to a wise man, not merely through his own strength, but through the strength of the one he assists. The wise can surely manage on their own if need be; nevertheless, even one who is running strong is helped by a cheering voice. "But the wise man serves himself, not the other sage. Realize this: strip away his own power, and he will accomplish nothing."

[7] By that logic, you might as well say there is no sweetness in honey. For the one who should perceive it has a tongue and palate so ill-adapted to that taste that such a flavor either makes no impression or is found offensive. There are those who, from some defect of constitution, find honey bitter. Both parties must be in proper condition for one to be of help and the other to be receptive to that beneficial influence.

[8] "If it is superfluous," he argues, "to add heat to the highest degree of warmth, then it is also superfluous that something benefits one who has been brought to the highest degree of good. Does the farmer, equipped with every tool, seek further equipment from another? Does the fully armed soldier, ready to rush into battle, desire additional weapons? Therefore, neither does the wise man, for he is sufficiently equipped and armed for life."

[9] To this I reply: even one who has attained the highest degree of warmth still requires added heat to maintain that summit. "But," he objects, "the heat itself preserves its own intensity." Firstly, there is a great difference between the cases you compare; for heat is singular, while benefiting takes various forms. Moreover, heat is not assisted by the addition of more heat in order to stay hot; but the wise man cannot maintain his mental disposition unless he has admitted some friends similar to himself, with whom he may share his virtues.

[10] Consider also that there exists a friendship between all virtues. Therefore, he benefits who loves the virtues of someone equal to himself and inspires a reciprocal love. Like attracts like, especially when the things are honorable and know how to esteem and be esteemed.

[11] Furthermore, no one except the wise man can skillfully influence the mind of the wise, just as only a human can rationally move another human. Therefore, just as reason is needed to influence reason, so in order for perfect reason to be moved, there is need of perfect reason.

[12] Those who bestow upon us the intermediary goods—money, favor, security, and other things dear or necessary for the uses of life—are also said to benefit us. In these matters, even the foolish man will be said to benefit the wise. But to truly benefit is to move the soul in accordance with nature by its own virtue, so as to move the soul of the one benefited. This cannot happen without the good of the one conferring the benefit as well. For it is inevitable that in exercising the virtue of another, he exercises his own.

[13] But even setting aside those things which are either the highest goods or the means of attaining them, wise men can still benefit each other. For discovering a wise man is in itself a desirable thing for another wise man, because all good is dear to the good by nature, and each one is drawn to the good just as he is to himself.

[14] It's necessary, for the sake of this argument, that I transition from this question to another. The question is whether a wise man should engage in deliberation, or whether he should call on someone for advice. This is something he must do when it comes to these civil, domestic, and—so to speak—mortal affairs. In these matters, he needs the advice of others in the same way he needs a doctor, a helmsman, an advocate or someone to arrange a lawsuit. Therefore, at times, one wise man will benefit another wise man, for he will offer counsel. But even in those grand and divine matters, as we said, by jointly reflecting on what is honorable and by mingling their minds and thoughts together, they will be useful to each other.

[15] Moreover, it's in accordance with nature both to embrace

friends and to take delight in the growth of one's friends as if it were one's own. For if we don't do this, not even virtue will remain with us, since virtue grows strong by exercising perception. Virtue urges us to make good use of the present, to make provision for the future, to deliberate and to apply the mind. One who has taken a partner for himself will apply and develop his mind more easily.

Therefore, he will seek either a perfect man or one who is progressing and close to being perfect. That perfect man will be beneficial if he assists their joint deliberation with wisdom.

[16] People say that one sees more clearly into another's business [than into one's own]. This fault comes upon those who are blinded by self-love and whose fear knocks out of them the clear view of expediency in times of peril. A wise man, being more secure and free from fear, will begin to gain in wisdom. But nonetheless there are certain things that even wise men see more carefully in another than in themselves. Besides, the wise man will offer to another wise man that most pleasant and honorable thing: "to will the same thing and reject the same thing." He will lead this outstanding work under an equal yoke.

[17] I have completed the task you demanded, although it was part of the regular sequence of subjects that I cover in my volumes on moral philosophy. Consider what I'm in the habit of saying to you frequently—that in these matters we are doing nothing other than exercising our mental acuity. For I return to this point so often: How does this thing help me? Make me braver now, more just, more self-controlled. There's no time yet for mental exercise; I still need a doctor.

[18] Why do you demand useless knowledge from me? You have made grand promises; go on, fulfill them. You said I would be unterrified even if swords flashed around me, even if a blade touched my throat. You said I would be untroubled even if fires blazed around me, even if a sudden whirlwind swept away my whole ship over the entire sea. Guarantee me this—that I despise pleasure and glory. Later you will teach me how to untie knots, to parse ambiguities, to see through obscurities. For now, teach me what is necessary. Farewell.

LETTER 110

EMERGING FROM LIFE'S WOMB INTO ETERNITY

[1] From my estate in Nomentum, I send you greetings and bid you keep a sound mind - that is, may you have all the gods favorably disposed to you. One who has propitiated themselves has the gods appeased and favoring them. Set aside for now the belief held by some, that each of us is given a god as a guardian - not of the highest rank, but one of a lower grade, from the number that Ovid calls "plebeian gods." However, in setting this notion aside, I wish you to remember that our ancestors, who followed Stoicism, believed that to each person a Genius and a Juno were assigned.

[2] Later, we shall see whether the gods have so much free time that they can manage the affairs of private individuals. In the meantime, know this: whether we have been assigned guardian spirits or have been neglected and left to fortune, you can invoke nothing more severe upon anyone than to wish that they may have the gods angry with them. But there is no reason why you should wish, upon anyone you think deserving of punishment, that they have hostile gods. They already do, I assert, even if they appear to prosper under divine favor.

[3] Apply your diligence here and examine closely the true nature of our circumstances, not what they are called. You will realize that more misfortunes happen to us than befall us. How often has what

was called a calamity actually been the cause and beginning of happiness? How frequently has a situation greeted with much rejoicing set the stage for a plunge into danger, elevating someone already eminent to an even higher place from which their fall, when it inevitably comes, is all the more devastating?

[4] But the act of falling itself contains nothing evil if you consider the end, beyond which nature casts no one down. The boundary of all things is near - yes, both the point from which the fortunate are ejected and that from which the unfortunate are released. It is we who prolong both conditions, drawing them out with long-reaching hope and fear. If you are wise, though, measure all human affairs by the human lot. Simultaneously limit both your joys and your fears, for it is not worthwhile to rejoice at length lest you end up fearing at length.

[5] But why do I present this as a confined evil? There is no reason you should fear anything. These things that disturb us and leave us stunned are empty. None of us have shaken out the truth, but we have handed down fear from one to another. No one has dared to approach what perturbs them and examine the nature and merit of their dread. And so false and hollow things still retain credibility, because they are not exposed.

[6] Let us consider it worth our while to look at them intently. It will quickly become clear how brief, how uncertain, how harmless the things we fear really are. The turmoil in our minds is just like how it seemed to Lucretius:

> *"For just as children tremble and fear everything in blinding*
> *darkness,*
> *so we in the light sometimes fear things."*

What then? Are we not more foolish than any child, fearing things in the light?

[7] But Lucretius, it is false to say that we do not fear in the light; we have made everything around us darkness. We see nothing, neither what may harm us nor what may benefit us; we stumble

through life never stopping or treading more carefully because of it. You see, however, how mad it is to rush forth in the dark. But by Hercules, we act in such a way that we must be called back from even further, and although we do not know where we are being carried, we still persist quickly toward that place we are aiming for.

[8] But if we are willing, it can become light. There is only one way this can happen: if someone accepts this knowledge of human and divine things through learning, if he does not just sprinkle himself with it but stains himself with it, if he ponders the same things over again, although he knows them, and frequently brings them back to himself, if he seeks out what things are good, what things are bad, which things have been falsely given this name, if he seeks out what is honorable and what is disgraceful, and what is providence.

[9] The keenness of the human mind is not limited to these things; it desires to look ahead and beyond this world, to where it is being carried, from where it arose, toward what end such rapid movement of events is hastening. We have dragged the mind down from this divine contemplation into sordid and lowly things, so that it might serve greed, so that having abandoned the world and its boundaries and the masters overturning everything, it might dig through the earth and seek what evil it might unearth from it, not content with what is offered.

[10] Whatever was going to be good for us, god and our parent placed very close at hand; he did not wait for us to search it out and gave it freely. Harmful things he buried deeply. We can complain about nothing except ourselves; those things by which we were going to perish, with Nature unwilling and hiding them, we have brought forth. We have surrendered our mind to pleasure, the indulgence of which is the beginning of all evils, we have handed it over to ambition and fame, and to all other equally vain and empty things.

[11] So what do I now encourage you to do? Nothing new—for new remedies are not sought for new evils—but this first of all: that you consider with yourself what is necessary, what is superfluous.

Necessary things will meet you everywhere; superfluous things must be sought always and with your whole mind.

[12] Now, do not heap excessive praise upon yourself if you have scorned gilded couches and jewel-encrusted furnishings. For what virtue is there in disdaining the superfluous? True self-admiration is warranted when you spurn even necessities. It is no great feat to live without royal pomp, to forgo boars by the thousand, flamingo tongues, and other monstrosities of a jaded luxury that, having tired of whole creatures, selects choice morsels. I will admire you then if you refuse even moldy bread, if you convince yourself that grass, when necessary, sprouts for man and not just beast, if you know tree-tops can fill a belly which we stuff with such expensive rarities as if it would preserve what it devours. The stomach should be filled without fuss. For what does it matter what it receives, since whatever it takes in will be lost?

[13] You delight in the delicacies procured from land and sea, some more pleasing if rushed fresh to table, others if long fed and fattened until they ooze and strain against their pens. You relish the aroma cleverly coaxed out in their preparation. Yet, by Hercules, once these painstakingly gathered and exotically seasoned dishes slide down your throat, one identical ugliness will greet them all. Would you scorn the pleasures of the palate? Consider the end result.

[14] I recall Attalus declaring to an awestruck audience: "For long the trappings of wealth deceived me. I marveled whenever their glint caught my eye from one spot or another. I assumed what lay hidden matched the lustre of what was on display. But at one lavish event, I beheld all the riches of Rome wrought in gold, silver, and materials surpassing both in value: exquisite hues and raiment sourced beyond our borders and even past enemy lands. On one side stood radiant troops of slave-boys in splendid attire; on the other, women. The imperial fortune had released its full store of wonders for review.

[15] 'What is this,' I asked, 'but a provocation of man's unbidden desires? What is the meaning of this pageant of lucre? Have we gathered to study greed?' Yet, by Hercules, I departed with less avarice than when I arrived. I scorned riches not because they were superflu-

ous, but petty. Did you note how swiftly that procession, for all its stately grandeur, passed by in mere hours?

[16] This fleeting folly consumes our whole lives, though it cannot fill a single day!" He added this insight too: to the owners, these luxuries seemed as pointless as they did to the spectators.

[17] And so I say this to myself, whenever such things dazzle my eyes, whenever I come across an impressive house, a well-dressed retinue of servants, a litter carried by handsome attendants: Why are you in awe? Why are you amazed? It is all just a show. These things are displayed, not truly possessed, and while they please, they pass away.

[18] Turn your attention instead to true riches. Learn to be content with little and cry out with great and courageous voice: "We have water, we have porridge, let us challenge Jupiter himself to a contest of happiness![1]" Let us do so, I implore you, even if those things are lacking. It is shameful to stake a happy life on gold and silver, and equally shameful to stake it on water and porridge.

[19] "What then shall I do, if I do not have those things?" You ask what is the remedy for poverty? Hunger puts an end to hunger; besides, what difference does it make whether the things that compel you to be a slave are great or small? What does it matter how little it is that fortune can deny you?

[20] Even this very water and porridge are subject to another's whim. But he is free not who is under fortune's control in small ways, but he who is entirely beyond its reach. That's right: you must desire nothing if you wish to challenge Jupiter who desires nothing.

These were the words of Attalus to us; if you are willing to reflect on them often, you will strive to be happy, not merely to appear so - and to appear so to yourself, not to others. Farewell.

---

1. Some later manuscripts read "facility" instead of "happiness" here.

LETTER 111

FACING THE TRUTH OF OUR CIRCUMSTANCES

[1] YOU ASKED ME WHAT THE LATIN TERM IS FOR "SOPHISMS." MANY have tried to coin a name for them, but none has stuck - evidently because the concept itself was not accepted by us Romans and was not in use, so the name for it was also resisted. However, the most fitting term seems to me to be the one Cicero used: he calls them "cavillationes" [quibbles or verbal tricks].

[2] Whoever surrenders himself to these quibbles indeed weaves together cunning little questions, but makes no progress toward life, becoming neither braver, more temperate, nor loftier. But one who has practiced philosophy as a remedy for himself becomes mighty in spirit, full of confidence, insurmountable, and greater than those who approach him.

[3] It's just like what happens with great mountains, whose loftiness appears less to those gazing from afar; but when you have drawn near, then it becomes clear how high the peaks really are. Such, my dear Lucilius, is the true philosopher, concerned with realities, not artifices. He stands on high, worthy of admiration, truly eminent. He does not rise up on his tiptoes or walk about on his toes like those who use deceit to enhance their stature, wishing to seem taller than they are. He is content with his own grandeur.

[4] And why should he not be content to have grown to a height where Fortune cannot reach with her hands? He is thus above mortal affairs and equal to himself in every condition of life, whether his course proceeds favorably or he is tossed about and travels through adversities and difficulties. Those quibbles I was speaking of a little while ago cannot produce this steadfastness. The mind may amuse itself with them, but it makes no progress, and they drag philosophy down from her heights to the flat ground.

[5] I would not forbid you to engage in those verbal tricks sometimes, but only when you wish to do nothing at all. Yet they have this worst feature: they create a sort of self-satisfaction and hold the mind spellbound by the appearance of subtlety, delaying it when the mass of matters calls, when a whole lifetime barely suffices to learn this one thing - to despise life. "What then? To rule it?" you ask. That is the second task; for no one has ruled life well unless he has first despised it. Farewell.

LETTER 112

A VISION OF THE WISE MAN'S SPLENDID SOUL

[1] By Hercules, I sincerely wish that your friend could be shaped and instructed as you desire. But he is caught in a very difficult state—or rather, a most troublesome one: he is undisciplined and has been broken by bad and long-standing habits. Let me give you an example from my own craft to illustrate.

[2] Not every vine submits to grafting. If it is old and withered, or weak and slender, it will either fail to take the shoot, or will not nourish it and unite it to itself, transforming it to its own character and nature. So it is our practice to cut it off above ground, so that if it does not take, we may try our luck a second time by grafting it again below ground.

[3] This friend you write of and commend to me lacks strength; he has indulged in vices. He has simultaneously withered and hardened. He cannot absorb reason nor nourish it. "But," you say, "he himself desires to reform." Don't believe it. I'm not accusing him of lying to you; he just thinks he desires it. Excess has ruined his moral taste. He'll quickly relapse and reconcile with his old ways.

[4] "But he claims to be disgusted with his life," you argue. I won't deny that. For who isn't disgusted? People both love and hate their

vices at the same time. We can only pass judgment on him, then, once he has proven to us that excess is now hateful to him. As of now, they are on bad terms, but not yet divorced. Farewell.

LETTER 113

THE MIND'S GRASP OF ITS OWN CONSTITUTION

[1] You wish me to write to you my thoughts regarding the question much debated by our school: whether justice, courage, prudence, and the other virtues are living beings. Through such subtle arguments, my dearest Lucilius, we have reached the point where we appear to exercise our intellects on useless things and waste our leisure on debates that will yield no profit. Nevertheless, I shall do as you desire and explain what our school thinks on the matter. But I confess to being of a different opinion: I believe there are some things that befit a man wearing Greek sandals and a philosopher's cloak. Therefore, I shall relate what moved the ancients, or what the ancients discussed,

[2] It is agreed that the mind is a living being, since it enables us to be living beings, and living beings have derived their name from it. Virtue, moreover, is nothing else than the mind in a certain disposition; therefore it is a living being. Furthermore, virtue acts; but nothing can act without impulse, and impulse belongs only to a living being. Therefore, if virtue has impulse, and impulse belongs only to a living being, then virtue is a living being. "If virtue is a living being," they say, "then virtue itself possesses virtue."

[3] And why should it not possess itself? Just as the wise man does

everything through virtue, so virtue acts through itself. "It follows, then," they say, "that all the arts are living beings, and so are all our thoughts and conceptions of the mind. It follows that many thousands of living beings dwell in the compass of our chest, and that each of us is, or carries around within us, many living beings."

Do you ask what can be said in reply to this? Each of those things will be a living being; but they will not be many living beings. Why? I will explain, if you grant me your subtle attention and focus.

[4] Each living being should have its own individual substance; but all those things [the virtues, arts, thoughts] have one mind in common; therefore they can each be individual entities, but they cannot be many entities. I am both a living being and a man, but you will not say that we are two separate beings. Why? Because we would need to be distinct from each other. What I mean is this: for two to exist, they must be separable. Whatever is multiple within a unity falls under a single nature; therefore it is one thing.

[5] My mind is a living being, and I am a living being, yet we are not two. Why? Because my mind is a part of me. A thing will be counted by itself only when it stands by itself. But when it is a mere member of another, it cannot be regarded as a separate entity. Why? I will tell you: because that which is distinct must be its own, with its own properties, complete in itself, and within its own boundaries.

[6] I declared that I held a different opinion. For if this premise is accepted, not only will the virtues be considered living creatures, but so too will the opposing vices and emotions, such as anger, fear, grief, and suspicion. This idea will proceed to absurd lengths; every opinion and every thought will be a living creature. This is in no way acceptable. For not everything that comes from a human is itself human.

[7] "What is justice?" he asks. A certain disposition of the soul. "Therefore, if the soul is a living creature, so is justice." By no means. For justice is a state and a kind of power of the soul; the same soul transforms itself into various shapes, but it does not become a different living creature as many times as it does something different. Nor is that which is done by the soul a living creature.

[8] If[1] justice is a living creature, if courage is, if the other virtues are, do they then cease to be living creatures, only to begin again later, or are they always such? Virtues cannot cease to be. Therefore, many living creatures—innumerable ones, in fact—reside in this soul of ours.

[9] "They are not many," he objects, "because they are bound together as one and are parts and limbs of one being." You are thus picturing for us a soul like the Hydra, having many heads each of which fights on its own, harms on its own. And yet none of those heads is a living creature, but rather the head of a living creature— the Hydra itself, however, is one living creature. No one has called the lion or serpent in the Chimaera a living creature; these were parts of it, and parts are not living creatures themselves. What reason do you have to conclude that justice is a living creature?

[10] "It acts," he says, "and benefits. That which acts and benefits has impulse; that which has impulse[2] is a living creature." This would be true, if it had its own impulse; but it does not have its own impulse[3], only that of the soul.

[11] Every living creature, until it dies, remains what it began as; a human, until death, is human, a horse remains a horse, a dog a dog. They cannot transition into something else. Justice, a certain disposition of the soul, is a living creature. Let us accept this; then courage too is a living creature, a certain disposition of the soul. But which soul? The same one that was just now justice? It is bound to the prior creature; it is not permitted to transition into another creature. It must persevere in the state in which it first began to exist.

[12] Moreover, one soul cannot belong to two living creatures, much less to many. If justice, courage, temperance, and the other virtues are living creatures, how will they share one soul? They must each have their own, or else they are not living creatures.

[13] One body cannot belong to multiple living creatures. They themselves admit this. What is the body of justice? "The soul." What then? What is the body of courage? "The same soul." But one body cannot belong to two living creatures.

[14] "But," they say, "the same soul takes on the disposition of

justice, of courage, and of temperance." This could happen if, at the time it was justice, it was not courage, and at the time it was courage, it was not temperance. But in reality, all the virtues exist simultaneously. So how can they each be living creatures, when there is only one soul, which cannot constitute more than one living creature?

[15] Finally, no living creature is part of another living creature. But justice is a part of the soul; therefore, it is not a living creature. I seem to be wasting effort on a matter already conceded; this notion deserves more indignation than debate. No living creature is identical to another. Survey the bodies of all creatures: each has its own coloring, its own shape and size.

[16] Among other reasons for which the genius of the divine craftsman is marvelous, I also reckon this: that amid such an abundance of things, he never produced the exact same thing twice. Even those that seem similar, when compared, are different. He made so many kinds of leaves, each marked with its own distinctive features. So many animals, and no two are matched in size; there is always some difference. He took pains to ensure that things that were distinct would also be dissimilar and unequal. Yet you say that all the virtues are equal. Therefore, they are not living creatures.

[17] Every animal acts on its own accord. Virtue, however, does nothing on its own, but rather acts together with man. All animals are either rational, like humans and gods, or irrational, like wild beasts and cattle[4]. The virtues are certainly rational; yet they are neither humans nor gods; therefore, they are not animals.

[18] Every rational animal does nothing unless it is first provoked by the appearance of something, then feels an impulse, and finally gives assent to confirm this impulse. Let me explain what assent is. Suppose I ought to take a walk: I only actually walk when I have told myself this and approved this opinion of mine. Suppose I ought to sit down: only then do I sit down. This assent is not present in virtue.

[19] Consider prudence, for instance. How will it assent to the notion "I ought to walk"? Its nature does not allow for this. For prudence looks out for the one whose quality it is, not for itself.

Indeed, it can neither walk nor sit. Therefore, it does not have assent, and is not a rational animal. If virtue is an animal, it is a rational one.

[20] But it is not rational; therefore, it is not an animal either. If virtue is an animal, and virtue is good, then is not every good thing an animal? It is. Our philosophers admit this.

To save one's father is good, to give an opinion prudently in the Senate is good, and to decree justly is good. Therefore, both saving one's father is an animal and giving an opinion prudently is an animal. This line of reasoning has gone so far that you can't hold back laughter: to be silent prudently is good, to dine frugally is good[5]; so both being silent and dining are animals.

[21] By Hercules, I won't stop amusing myself and playing games with these subtle absurdities! If justice and courage are animals, they are certainly terrestrial ones. Every terrestrial animal gets cold, hungry and thirsty. Therefore, justice gets cold, courage gets hungry, and clemency gets thirsty.

[22] Furthermore, shall I not ask them what shape these animals have? That of a human, a horse, or a wild beast? If they grant them a rounded shape like they give to god, I will ask whether greed, extravagance and madness are equally round. For they too are animals. If they make these round as well, I will still ask: is prudent walking an animal? They must confess, and then say that walking is an animal, and indeed a round one!

[23] But don't think that I am the first of our school to speak unorthodoxly—this is my own opinion: there is disagreement between Cleanthes and his disciple Chrysippus about what constitutes walking. Cleanthes says it is breath extending from the commanding faculty to the feet, while Chrysippus holds that it is the commanding faculty itself. Why then should each person not claim the right to form their own opinion, following Chrysippus' example, and mock all those "animals"—more than the world itself can contain?

[24] "The virtues," he objects, "are not many animals, and yet they are animals. For just as someone can be both a poet and an orator while still being one person, so too are these virtues animals—but

not many of them. The mind is the same thing as a just, prudent and brave mind, relating in a certain way to the individual virtues."

[25] With the dispute set aside, we agree. For the time being, I do concede that the mind is an animal—though I will examine later what opinion I hold on the matter. But I deny that its actions are animals. Otherwise, all words and verses would be animals too. If prudent speech is a good, and every good is an animal, then speech is an animal. A prudent verse is a good, and every good is an animal; therefore, a verse is an animal. And so, "I sing of arms and the man" is an animal—which they cannot call rounded, since it has six feet!

[26] "By Hercules," you say, "what we're doing right now is completely frivolous." I burst with laughter when I imagine a solecism, a barbarism, or a syllogism as an animal, assigning them appropriate appearances like a painter. Are we arguing about this with furrowed brows and wrinkled foreheads? I cannot say here what Caelius did: "O wretched nonsense!" It is ridiculous. Why then don't we deal with something more useful and beneficial, seeking how we can attain the virtues, and what path may lead us to them?

[27] Teach me not whether courage is an animal, but that no animal is happy without courage—unless it has steeled itself against misfortunes and mastered through practice all adversities before encountering them. What is courage? An impregnable fortress for human frailty. Whoever surrounds themselves with it endures secure in this siege of life, relying on their own strength and weapons.

[28] Here I wish to relate to you a sentiment from our friend Posidonius: "Never think that you are safe from Fortune's weapons; fight with your own. Fortune does not arm against herself; and so men equipped against their foes are unarmed against Fortune herself."

[29] Alexander laid waste to and routed the Persians, the Hyrcanians, the Indians, and whatever nations extend all the way to the Ocean in the East. But Alexander himself, at one moment grieving a slain friend, the next pining for a lost one, would lie in the darkness, now lamenting his crime, now his longing—the conqueror of so many kings and peoples succumbing to anger and sorrow. For he had

made it his aim to have power over all things except his own emotions.

[30] Oh, how great are the delusions that grip men who desire to extend their right of dominion across the seas and judge themselves most blessed if they occupy many provinces with their soldiery and join new ones to the old. They know not what that true kingship is, that great dominion equal to the gods' own.

[31] To rule oneself is the greatest empire. Let justice teach me how sacred a thing it is, looking to another's good, seeking nothing for itself but its own practice. Let it have nothing to do with ambition and fame; let it be content with itself.

Above all, let each person persuade himself of this: I must be just without reward. That is too little; let him further persuade himself of this: May it be my delight to expend myself willingly on this most noble virtue. Let all thought be turned as far as possible from private advantage. It matters not how many know of your fairness; something greater resides in being just[6]. Affix this further point in your mind which I mentioned a little while ago: it is of no concern how many are acquainted with your uprightness.

[32] The person who wishes their virtue to be publicized labors not for virtue but for glory. Do you not wish to be just without glory? But, by Hercules, often you will have to be just even with infamy. And then, if you are wise, let ill repute honestly acquired be your delight. Farewell.

---

1. The word "if" before "justice" and "courage" was added by Muretus.
2. The words "that which has impulse" were added by later manuscripts; they are missing in the earliest sources.
3. Again, the words "its own [impulse] it does not have" are missing in the earliest manuscripts.
4. Some later manuscripts add "aut pecora" here, which is omitted in manuscripts B and A.
5. Some later manuscripts add "bene" here, which is omitted in B and A.
6. Alternative translation: "in justice".

LETTER 114

SPEECH AS A MIRROR OF THE SOUL

[1] You ask why, at certain times, a corrupted style of speech emerged, and how tastes became inclined towards particular faults, so that at one time a pompous mode of expression was in vogue, and at another, a clipped and singsong style. Why at one period were bold ideas that overstepped the bounds of credibility admired, and at another, abrupt and enigmatic sentences that hinted at more than met the ear? Why was there an age that exploited figures of speech without restraint? As the common saying goes, one you've often heard which has passed into a proverb among the Greeks: a person's speech mirrors their life.

[2] Just as each individual's way of speaking resembles their way of acting, the style of public discourse sometimes imitates public morals, if the discipline of the state has broken down and given itself over to indulgence. Luxuriant speech is proof of public extravagance, at least when it is not just in one or two people, but is accepted and gains approval.

[3] The mind cannot have one complexion and the soul another. If the soul is sound - composed, serious, and temperate - the intellect too is dry and sober. When the soul is tainted, the intellect also

catches the infection. Don't you see that if the spirit has grown feeble, the limbs drag and the feet move sluggishly? If the spirit is unmanly and soft, that softness is apparent in the very gait? If it is vigorous and fierce, the stride quickens? If it is mad or, what resembles madness, angry, the body's movements are disordered, and there is a rush, not a step. How much more do you think this affects the intellect, which is entirely interwoven with the soul, molded by it, obedient to it, taking its law from it?

[4] How Maecenas lived is too well known to need retelling now - how he walked, how spoiled he was, how he longed to show himself off, how unwilling he was to conceal his vices. Well then, is not his speech just as loose-belted as he was? Are his words not as dandified as his dress, his retinue, his house, his wife? He would have been a man of great intellect had he followed a straighter path, had he not shrunk from making himself understood, had he not been so loose in his writing too. You will see, therefore, that his eloquence was that of a drunken man - twisting, wandering, unrestrained.

[5] What could be more disgraceful than "a river and woods with leaf-crowned banks?" See how "they plow the channel with boats and, with the waters churned up, dam back the gardens." What's this? If someone "curls a woman's hair, bills and coos, begins to sigh so that the tyrants of the grove may be honored by weary necks." "An irremediable faction pokes around at feasts, makes attempts on homes with a flagon, and spends its hope on death." "A genius scarce attends his own festival. The mother or wife clothes the slender wax tapers and the crackling mill of the hearth."

[6] When you read this, does it not immediately occur to you that this is the man who always walked about the city in loose tunics? For even when he was acting on behalf of the absent Caesar, it was customary to ask for the countersign from one so loosely attired. This is the man who appeared in the courts, on the rostra, in every public assembly dressed in such a way that his head was covered with a cloak, with both ears sticking out, just as is customary for the impersonators of runaway slaves in mimes. This is the man whose retinue in public, at the very height of the civil wars when the city was in a

state of anxiety and armed, consisted of two eunuchs - who were, however, more men than he was himself. This is the man who took a thousand wives, although he only ever had one. These words, so shamefully constructed, so carelessly tossed out, so unconventionally arranged, show that his character too was no less novel, perverse, and unparalleled.

[7] He is accorded the highest praise for his gentleness; he refrained from the sword, abstained from bloodshed, and displayed his power through nothing else but license. Yet he corrupted this very claim to praise by these monstrosities in his style of speaking.

[8] For it is evident that he was soft, not gentle. His circumlocutions in composition, his inverted words, his strange ideas (which are often grand, to be sure, but which lose their energy in the telling) make it clear to anyone. His head was turned by excessive good fortune, a failing that is sometimes one of character, sometimes one of circumstance.

[9] When prosperity has spread luxury far and wide, attention to the body becomes more careful at first. Next, people take pains with their furnishings. Then effort is expended on their very houses, so that they expand into the spaciousness of the countryside, so that the walls gleam with marbles imported from across the seas, so that the ceilings are adorned with gold, so that the sheen of the floors matches that of the paneling. Next, the lavishness is transferred to banquets, and there they seek commendation through novelty and changes in the customary order, so that the dishes that commonly end the meal are served first, so that the fare given to guests on arrival is offered to them as they depart.

[10] When the mind becomes accustomed to disdaining the conventional and regards the usual as beneath it, it seeks novelty even in oratory. It revives archaic, obsolete words and coins new, unfamiliar ones. It takes frequent, audacious metaphors--a recently popular trend--as a sign of refinement.

[11] Some cut their thoughts short, hoping to win favor by leaving the listener hanging and intrigued. Some drag them out and belabor the point. While anyone attempting great things must approach the

precipice of error without falling in, some are enamored with the flaw itself. Thus, wherever you see corrupt speech being applauded, there you can be sure morals too have strayed from the proper course.

Just as the extravagance of banquets and clothing points to a diseased society, so too does verbal licentiousness, if widespread, reveal that the minds from which the words spring have likewise sunk low.

[12] You should not be surprised that such depravities are embraced, and not only by the uncouth masses but by the educated elite as well. For they are distinguished by their togas, not their judgments. Even more shocking is that not only stylistic vices, but vices themselves are praised. This has always been so; no talent has found favor without indulgence. Name any man of great renown and I will tell you what his age excused in him and knowingly overlooked. I will give you many whose faults did them no harm, and some who profited from them. I will name men of the highest repute, held up as paragons, who would be utterly canceled if you set them straight, so intertwined are their virtues and vices.

[13] Moreover, oratory has no fixed rules. Convention, which never remains constant, transforms it. Many borrow words from a different era, speaking like the Twelve Tables[1]. For them, even the Gracchi, Crassus, and Curio are too polished and modern; they revert all the way back to Appius and Coruncanius[2]. Others, in their desire for only the well-worn and familiar, sink into squalor.

[14] Both are corrupted, albeit in different ways - just as surely as wanting to use only fancy, sonorous, poetic words and shunning the necessary and commonplace. The one pampers himself more than is right, the other neglects himself unduly. The former depilates his legs, the latter won't even pluck his armpits!

[15] Let us now turn to the topic of literary composition. How many types of faults shall I describe to you in this regard? Some authors favor a rugged and harsh style; they deliberately disrupt the flow if anything too smooth slips in. They dislike writing to have an even structure, believing that a vigorous and powerful style is one that jars the ear with its unevenness. The compositions of others have

no structure at all, but are mere melodic arrangements, to such an extent that it is soothing and glides along softly.

[16] What shall I say of the style in which words are drawn out and, long awaited, scarcely arrive at the closing cadence? Or of that slow-moving rhythm at the end of sentences, like that of Cicero, sinking to a soft finish and conforming to his established manner and cadence? The fault lies not only in the type of thoughts expressed, if they are either petty and childish, or reckless and more daring than modesty allows; or if they are florid and excessively sweet; or if they lead to no meaningful end and, without conveying anything of substance, are merely pleasing to the ear.

[17] These faults are initiated by some dominant figure who sets the current fashion in eloquence; the rest then imitate him and pass the style from one to another. Thus when Sallust was in vogue, truncated sentences, words falling away sooner than expected, and an obscure brevity were cultivated as a stylistic fad. Lucius Arruntius, a man of uncommon restraint who wrote histories of the Punic War, was an imitator of Sallust and inclined to that style. In Sallust occurs the phrase "he made an army with silver" [that is, he procured it with money]. Arruntius became enamored of this expression and inserted it on every page. In one place he says: "they made flight for our men." In another place: "Hiero, king of the Syracusans, made war." And in yet another place: "the reports of which made the Panhormitans surrender to the Romans." I wished to give you a sampling; the entire book is woven with these expressions. What was rare in Sallust becomes frequent and almost continuous in Arruntius - and not without reason; for the former stumbled upon these expressions, while the latter sought them out deliberately. You see, then, the consequence when someone's flaw is taken as a model.

[19] Sallust said "with waters wintering." Arruntius, in the first book of his Punic War, says "suddenly the weather wintered." Elsewhere, when he wishes to say that the year was cold, he says: "the entire year wintered." And in another place: "then he sent sixty lightly-burdened transports, in addition to the soldiers and necessary sailors, though the North wind wintered." He does not cease to stuff

this word in at every opportunity. In a certain place, Sallust says: "during the civil wars he sought renown for fairness and virtue." Arruntius could not restrain himself from writing, right in his first book, that "immense renowns" [famas] circulated about Regulus.

[20] Therefore, these and similar vices, which imitation has stamped upon someone, are not indicators of extravagance or a corrupted mind; for one's affects should be distinctive and arise from within, and it is from these that you should judge a person's true disposition. The speech of an irascible man is irascible, that of an agitated man is too hasty and rash, and that of an effeminate man is soft and fluid.

[21] You see those men who pluck out or thin their beards, who closely crop and shave their lips while leaving the rest of their hair to grow long, who wear cloaks of shocking colors and togas of translucent fabric, who refuse to do anything that might escape notice - they provoke and call attention to themselves, desiring to be criticized so long as they are seen. Such is the style of Maecenas and all the others who go astray not by chance, but knowingly and willingly.

[22] This springs from a great sickness of the mind. Just as in drunkenness the tongue does not stagger until the mind has yielded to the weight and is weakened or betrayed, what else is that manner of speech but a kind of intoxication that troubles no one unless the mind falters? Therefore, let the mind be treated, for from it flow perceptions, words, comportment, countenance, and gait. When the mind is sound and strong, the speech too is robust, courageous, and manly; but if the mind has been overthrown, everything else crumbles with it.

[23]

> *"When the king is safe, all have a single purpose;*
> *When he is lost, they break faith."*

Our mind is our king. While it remains safe, all else stays true to its duty - they obey and submit. But when the mind wavers even a little, they hesitate. And when the mind has succumbed to pleasure, its arts and acts also languish, and every effort stems from weakness and irresolution.

[24] Since I have employed this analogy, I will continue with it: our mind is now a king, now a tyrant. It is a king when it takes heed of what is honorable, caring for the body entrusted to it and commanding nothing base or sordid. But when the mind is impotent, lustful, and self-indulgent, it adopts the loathsome and dread title of tyrant. Then uncontrolled passions beset it and press upon it - at first they rejoice, as a populace is apt to revel in profligate largess, grasping at what it cannot consume.

[25] But when the disease eats away more and more at the mind's strength, and decadence sinks into marrow and sinew, then the tyrant, rejoicing at the sight of those whom it has rendered useless by excessive greed, takes the afflictions of others as its own pleasures - it becomes a procurer and celebrant of the lusts whose enjoyment it has snatched away by gorging itself. The tyrant finds no delight in its abundance of pleasures, but is embittered that it cannot pass every delicacy down its gullet and belly, that it does not wallow with a whole horde of male and female prostitutes, and grieves that a great part of its happiness, being shut out by the body's limitations, lies idle.

[26] Tell me, my dear Lucilius, is it not utter madness that none of us considers that he is mortal, that none of us acknowledges his own frailty? No, our greater insanity is this: none of us realizes that he is but one man! Behold our kitchens and the cooks scurrying amidst the multitude of fires; do you suppose they toil for a single belly, to which food is furnished with such tumult? Behold our cellars, bursting with the vintage of countless ages; do you imagine there is but one belly, for which so many consulships and regions lock away their wines? Look at the lands turned by plough in so many places, the thousands of farmers tilling and digging; can you believe it is for one belly that crops are sown in Sicily and in Africa alike?

[27] We would be far more sensible, and our desires more moderate, if each man were to take stock of himself, were to measure his own bodily needs, and realize how little he can consume, and for how

short a time. Yet nothing will benefit you more in acquiring temperance in all things than to ponder often the brevity and uncertainty of life; whatever you do, look to death. Farewell.

---

1. The earliest Roman legal code.
2. Orators of the 3rd century BC

LETTER 115

AVOIDING PREOCCUPATION WITH SUPERFICIALITIES

[1] My dear Lucilius, I do not wish for you to be excessively preoccupied with mere words and composition. There are greater matters that demand your care. Ask what you should write, not how; and write not merely for the sake of writing, but so that you may feel what you have written, and make it your own, as if sealing it upon your heart. Whenever you see a speech that is overly refined and polished, know that the mind behind it is no less entangled in trifles.

[2] Those with true greatness speak with more ease and surety; their every word carries more confidence than artifice. You know those dandified youths, sleek of beard and coiffure, looking as if they stepped straight out of a bandbox. From them you can hope for nothing robust, nothing of substance. Speech is the mirror of the soul: if it is overembellished, painted and contrived, it reveals a character that is likewise lacking in sincerity, containing some element of fragility. Ornateness is not the adornment of a man.

[3] O, if only we could glimpse the soul of a good man, what a beautiful countenance would we behold! How holy, how magnificent its placid radiance, illuminated on one side by justice, on the other by fortitude, its light blended with temperance and prudence! And to these would be added the luster of frugality, continence, forbearance,

generosity, and that rarest of human virtues—humanity itself. Foresight joined with refined judgment, and towering above all, magnanimity—ye gods, what grace and gravitas these would lend! What authority, wedded to charm! None could call it lovable without in the same breath naming it worthy of reverence.

[4] Should one behold this face, more lofty and resplendent than is customarily glimpsed among mortals, would one not pause as if encountering the divine, and inwardly pray for the privilege of such a vision? Then, drawn forth by the beckoning benevolence of that gaze, one would adore and entreat it. And having long contemplated a presence so far surpassing the ordinary measure beheld among us, with an aspect gentle and yet ablaze with vibrant fire, one would at last, with awe and trembling, utter that line of our own Virgil:

[5]

> *O maiden, by what name shall I address you? For your*
> *countenance is not that of a mortal, nor has your voice*
> *a human ring.*

> *Bless us, and lighten whatever toils are ours.*

And lighten them it shall, if we are minded to reverence it. Yet this is a reverence paid not by slaughtering fattened bulls, nor by hanging up offerings of gold and silver, nor by pouring coins into temple coffers, but by the devotion of a pure and upright will.

[6] No one, I tell you, could fail to burn with love for virtue if only we were blessed with the ability to gaze upon her. But as it is, many obstructions cloud our vision, either striking our eyes with an overwhelming glare or cloaking virtue in shadows. Yet if we wish to free our mind's eye from these hindrances, much as certain medications are used to sharpen and purge our physical sight, we would be able to perceive virtue even when she is shrouded by the body, beset by poverty, or veiled in humility and ignominy. We would discern, I say, her beauty even through the tattered robes that conceal her.

[7] By the same token, we would just as clearly perceive wicked-

ness and the rot of a soul mired in misery, even when obscured by the blinding shimmer of abundant riches, or when the false glitter of high offices and grand powers dazzles the beholder on every side.

[8] Only then will we understand how utterly contemptible are the things we so admire, much like little children who treasure any old toy, prizing a cheap trinket bought for a few coppers above even their parents and siblings. What difference is there between us and them, as Aristo says, except that we go mad over paintings and statues, the costly playthings of fools? They take delight in smooth pebbles found on the seashore, flecked with a bit of color. We marvel at enormous slabs of stone, quarried from the sands of Egypt or the wilds of Africa, that adorn some portico or spacious banquet hall big enough to hold a crowd[1].

[9] We admire walls veneered with thin sheets of marble, knowing full well the cheapness they conceal. We deceive our own eyes, and when we overlay our ceilings with gold, do we not simply delight in a lie? For we are well aware of the unlovely timbers that lurk beneath that gold.

This flimsy façade of ornamentation is plastered over more than just our walls and ceilings. All those people you see strutting about with their heads held high—their prosperity is a mere gilded surface. Look closer and you will see the mass of wickedness that lies beneath that thin veneer of dignity.

[10] Money itself—the very thing that keeps so many magistrates and judges so preoccupied, the very maker of magistrates and judges —ever since it began to be held in high esteem, true esteem for all else has withered. We have become mere merchants, bought and sold in turn, asking not what a thing truly is but what its price might be. For a fee we are righteous; for a fee, unrighteous. We pursue virtue so long as it promises some reward, ready to shift to the opposite if vice should offer a higher return.

[11] Our parents instilled in us this reverence for gold and silver, and this lust, seeping into our tender minds, rooted deeply and grew up along with us. Then the masses, though they agree on little else, unite in this: This they venerate, this they wish for their loved ones.

When they seek to show gratitude, they consecrate this as the greatest of mortal goods. Alas, to such a state have we brought our values that poverty is now a curse and a disgrace—despised by the rich and loathed by the poor.

[12] Furthermore, the verses of poets fan the flames of our passions, extolling riches as life's singular glory and adornment. It seems the immortal gods can give nothing better, can possess nothing greater.

[13]

> *The Sun's palace stood lofty with towering columns,*
> *Resplendent, glittering with gold.*

Behold his chariot as well:

> *Golden was the axle, golden the pole, golden the wheel's*
> *Curving rim, the array of spokes silver.*

Indeed, the era they wish to portray as the best, they dub the "Golden Age."

[14] Even among the Greek tragedians, there is no shortage of those who would exchange innocence, well-being, and good repute for profit.

> *Let them call me the basest of men, so long as*
> *They call me rich. We all ask if a man is wealthy, none if he*
>   *is good.*
> *They inquire not why or whence, but only what you*
>   *possess.*
> *Everywhere, each man was valued only as much as he had.*
> *Do you ask what possessions would shame us? None at all.*
> *Either to live rich or die poor is my wish.*
> *He dies well, whosoever dies while making a profit.*
> *Money, that immense boon to humankind,*
> *With which no pleasure of a mother or fawning*

Child can compare, not even a parent revered for his merits;
If something so sweet sparkles in the countenance of Venus,
Rightly does she stir the loves of gods and men.

[15] When these final verses were pronounced in a tragedy of Euripides, the entire populace rose up in a single outburst to expel both the actor and the play, until Euripides himself leapt into their midst, imploring them to wait and witness the end the admirer of gold would meet. In that drama, Bellerophon paid the penalty, which each man pays in his own life.

[16] For no avarice comes without punishment, though it itself be punishment enough. Oh, what tears, what toils it exacts! How wretched it yearns to be, how wretched it is to attain its desires! Add to that the daily anxieties that torment each person in proportion to his possessions. Money is held with greater torment than it is acquired. How they groan over losses, which loom large when they occur and seem larger still! In the end, though Fortune may deprive them of nothing, whatever is not gained is a loss.

[17] "But," people say, "they call that man happy and rich, and wish to possess as much as he has." I admit it. What then? Do you think any are in a worse state than those who have both misery and envy? If only those who long for riches would confer with the rich! If only those seeking honors would consult the ambitious who have attained the pinnacle of status and prestige! Surely they would alter their prayers, even as the others take on new desires, having condemned their former ones. For there is no one whose happiness, even if it comes swiftly, quite satisfies him. They complain about their decisions and their advancements, forever preferring what they left behind.

[18] This, then, is what the study of philosophy promises to bestow upon you, and in my view there is nothing greater: you will never have cause to be dissatisfied with yourself. The path to this unshakable happiness, which no storm can assail, is not paved with cleverly arranged words or a gently flowing style of oratory. Let your words proceed as they will, so long as your soul maintains its equilib-

rium, its grandeur, and its freedom from the tyranny of others' opinions—so long as you take pleasure in the very things that displease the crowd, measuring your progress by your conduct in life and considering your knowledge sufficient to the degree that you curb your desires and banish your fears. Farewell.

---

1. The text mentions "monilia" (necklaces or trinkets) bought by children, which Erasmus emended from the manuscripts' "mobilia" or "mobiba."

LETTER 116

REASON'S RULE OVER THE PASSIONATE MIND

[1] THE QUESTION HAS OFTEN BEEN POSED WHETHER IT IS BETTER TO have moderate emotions or none at all. Our school seeks to banish the emotions, while the Peripatetics aim to temper them. I myself fail to see how any ailment can be either healthy or beneficial in moderation. Do not fear; I shall not deprive you of anything you wish not to have refused. I will show myself agreeable and indulgent regarding those things to which you cleave, and which you consider necessary, useful, or pleasing in life; I will simply remove their destructive qualities. For when I forbid you to crave, I will still permit you to desire, so that you may act just as boldly as before, but with greater discernment, and so that you may better appreciate pleasures themselves. Why should those pleasures not reach you more fully if you command them, rather than serve them as a slave?

[2] "But," you protest, "it is natural to be tormented by longing for a friend; grant the right to tears that fall for so just a cause. It is natural to be affected by the opinions of others and saddened by their misfortunes; so why not allow me this fear of ill repute, honorable as it is?" There is no vice that lacks some defense; none that does not start with a modest and plausible case for itself, but then spreads more

widely. You will not succeed in halting a vice once you have permitted it to begin.

[3] Every passion is feeble at the outset. Later it rouses itself and gathers strength as it advances; it is more easily excluded than driven out. Who can deny that all the passions flow, as it were, from a certain natural source? Nature has entrusted us with care for ourselves, but when we indulge this care excessively, it becomes a vice. Nature has intermingled pleasure with necessary things—not so that we should seek pleasure for itself, but so that the addition of pleasure may render those things without which we cannot live more agreeable to us. Pleasure is luxury if sought for its own sake.

Therefore, let us resist the passions at their inception, for, as I have said, it is easier to deny them admittance than to control them once admitted. "Allow some measure of grief," you say, "and some measure of fear." But that "some measure" tends to extend itself further and does not stop where you wish.

[4] The wise have the ability to safely govern themselves, and they will check their tears and pleasures at will. For us, though, since it is not easy to retreat, it is best not to advance at all.

[5] Panaetius, it seems to me, responded with great elegance when a young man asked whether a wise man should fall in love. "As for the wise man," he said, "we shall see. But you and I, who are still far from being wise, should not entrust ourselves to a thing so disordered, so uncontrollable, enslaved to another, and contemptible to itself. For if it does not spurn our advances, we are provoked by its acquiescence; if it rejects them, we are inflamed by its disdain. The ease of love is as harmful as its difficulty—with ease we are captured, with difficulty we contend. Therefore, conscious of our own weakness, let us be still. Let us not entrust our feeble spirit to wine, nor to beauty, nor to flattery, nor to any other sweetly alluring things."

[6] What Panaetius said in reply to the question about love, I say about all the passions. As much as we can, let us retreat from slippery ground; even on dry land we stand with little strength.

[7] Here you will confront me with that common protest against the Stoics: "Your promises are too grandiose, your precepts too harsh.

We are mere mortals, we cannot deny ourselves everything. We will feel pain, but only a little; we will desire, but in moderation; we will anger, but we will be appeased." Do you know why we cannot do these things?

[8] Because we do not believe we can. No, I swear, the truth is something else: it is because we love our vices that we defend them, and we would rather make excuses for them than shake them off. Nature has given man enough strength, if only we use it, if we gather our powers and rouse them all for our own benefit, certainly not against ourselves. Unwillingness is the problem; inability is the pretext. Farewell.

LETTER 117

STOIC PRINCIPLES ON VIRTUE AND PLEASURE

[1] You will cause me a great deal of trouble, my dear Lucilius, and while you remain unaware, you will drive me into a major quarrel and annoyance by posing such petty questions to me - questions in which I can neither dissent from our school without losing favor, nor consent to them without sacrificing my conscience. You ask whether the Stoic belief is true, that wisdom is good, but the act of being wise is not good. Allow me first to explain what the Stoics believe; then I will dare to pronounce my own opinion.

[2] Our school holds that what is good is corporeal, because whatever is good produces an effect, and whatever produces an effect is a body. What is good benefits us. But for something to benefit us, it must actively do something; and if it acts, it is a body. The Stoics say that wisdom is good; it follows that they must also declare wisdom to be corporeal.

[3] However, they do not think that the act of being wise falls under the same category. It is incorporeal and incidental to something else, namely wisdom. Therefore, being wise neither acts nor benefits. "What then?" you say, "Do we not proclaim that it is good to be wise?" We do, but only with reference to that on which it depends, namely wisdom itself.

[4] Before I begin to withdraw and take my stand on the other side, hear how this is answered by others. "In that way," they say, "living happily is not good either." Like it or not, they must reply that the happy life is indeed good, but living happily is not good.

[5] Here is another objection raised against the Stoics: "You wish to be wise. Therefore, being wise is a thing worth seeking. If it is worth seeking, it is good." Our school is forced to twist their words and insert an extra syllable which our ordinary language does not permit. If you will allow me, I will add it. "That which is good," they say, "is worth seeking; but that which befalls us when we have attained the good is worth taking. It is not sought as a good, but it comes as an extra to the good we seek."

[6] I do not share this view. I judge that the Stoics sink to this level of argument because they are already bound by their initial premise and are not permitted to change their formula. We tend to concede much to the presumptions of mankind, and to us, the fact that something seems true to everyone is evidence for its truth. Among other reasons, we infer that the gods exist because a belief in gods is ingrained in everyone, and there is no nation anywhere so far beyond the reach of laws and moral codes that it does not believe in some gods. When we discuss the immortality of the soul, the consensus of humankind - either fearing or worshipping the spirits of the underworld - carries considerable weight with us. I make use of this widespread persuasion: you will find no one who does not think both that wisdom is good and that being wise is good.

[7] I will not do what the vanquished usually do and appeal to the people. Let us begin to fight with our own weapons.

Does what happens to a thing exist outside of that to which it happens, or within that to which it happens? If it is within the thing to which it happens, then it is just as much a body as that to which it happens. For nothing can happen without touch, and what touches is a body. If it is outside, then after it has happened, it departs. What departs has motion, and what has motion is a body. You hope I will say that running is not the same as a course, being hot is not the same as heat, shining is not the same as light. I concede these are different things, but not of a different kind.

[8] If health is indifferent, then being healthy is also indifferent. If beauty is indifferent, then being beautiful is indifferent. If justice is good, then being just is good. If baseness is bad, then being base is bad—just as surely, by Hercules, as if inflammation of the eyes is bad, having inflamed eyes is also bad. That you may know this, neither can exist without the other. One who is wise is a wise person; a wise person is wise. It cannot be doubted that the quality of the one is the quality of the other, to such an extent that to some the two seem to be one and the same.

[9] But I would gladly inquire: since all things are either bad or good or indifferent, in which category is being wise? They deny it is a good; it is certainly not a bad; it follows that it is intermediate. But we call intermediate and indifferent that which can happen to the bad as much as to the good, like money, beauty, or noble birth. Being wise can only happen to the good; therefore it is not indifferent. Yet it is also not a bad, because it cannot happen to the bad; therefore it is a good. What only the good possess is a good. Only the good possess being wise; therefore it is a good.

[10] "It is an attribute of wisdom", he says. This thing you call being wise, does it create wisdom or is it affected by it? Either way, it is a body. For both that which is made and that which makes are bodies; if it is a body, it is a good. It lacked only one thing to keep it from being a good, the fact that it was incorporeal.

[11] The Peripatetics believe there is no difference between wisdom and being wise, since each of them includes the other. For do you think anyone is wise except one who possesses wisdom? Do you think anyone who is wise does not possess wisdom?

[12] The ancient dialecticians make a distinction here, and the Stoics have adopted their division. I will explain its nature. To own a field is one thing; the field itself is quite another, as you'll no doubt agree, since owning a field relates to the owner, not to the field itself. Similarly, wisdom is one thing, and being wise is another. I think you'll concede that there are two elements involved here: that which

is possessed, and the one who possesses it. Wisdom is possessed, while the wise person is the possessor. Wisdom itself is a perfected mind, or a mind brought to its highest and best state, for it is the art of life. And what is being wise? I cannot call it simply "a perfected mind," but rather that which befalls one who has a perfected mind. So the one is a good mind, while the other is, so to speak, the possession of a good mind.

[13] "There are," they say, "natural bodies, like a man or a horse. There then follow certain declarative movements of the mind relating to those bodies. These have a distinct quality, separate from the bodies themselves, as when I see Cato walking. Perception reports this, and the mind believes it. What I see, the object to which I direct my eyes and attention, is a body. But when I then say 'Cato is walking,' it is not a body that I am speaking of now," they claim, "but rather a certain declaration about a body, which some call an 'utterance,' others a 'proposition,' and still others a 'statement.'" So when we say "wisdom," we conceive of something bodily, but when we say "he is wise," we are speaking about a body. But there is a vast difference between speaking of the person directly and speaking about him.

[14] Let's assume for now that these are two separate things—for I am not yet declaring my own view—what's to stop one of them from being distinct and yet still good? I was saying a moment ago that a field is one thing and owning a field another, was I not? Of course, for the owner has one nature, and that which is owned another. The latter is land, the former a person. But in our present case, both elements—the possessor of wisdom and wisdom itself—are of the same nature.

[15] Moreover, in the previous example, that which is possessed is distinct from the one possessing it, while here both the possession and the possessor reside in the same individual. A field is possessed by legal right, wisdom by nature. The field can be alienated and handed over to another, but wisdom never departs from its owner. So you really have no basis for comparing things that are dissimilar.

I had begun to say that those two things could be distinct and yet both be good, just as wisdom and the wise person are two separate things, yet you concede that both are good. Just as there is no contradiction in both wisdom being good and the possessor of wisdom being good, there is likewise no contradiction in wisdom being good and the possession of wisdom—that is, being wise—being good.

[16] This is what I wish to be wise in - so that I may have wisdom. What then? Is that not a good, without which even wisdom is not good? You certainly say that wisdom, if given without the ability to use it, is not to be accepted. What is the use of wisdom? To be wise. This is what is most precious in wisdom; if you take it away, wisdom becomes superfluous. If tortures are evil, then to be tortured is evil - to such a degree that tortures would not be evil if you removed their consequence. Wisdom is the condition of a perfected mind, and to be wise is the function of a perfected mind. How can the functioning of wisdom not be good, when wisdom itself is not good without that function?

[17] I ask you, is wisdom desirable? You admit it is. I ask, is the use of wisdom desirable? You admit it is, for you say you would not accept wisdom if you were forbidden to use it. What is desirable is good. To be wise is the function of wisdom, just as to speak eloquently is the function of eloquence, and to see is the function of the eyes. Therefore, to be wise is the function of wisdom, and the function of wisdom is desirable; therefore, to be wise is desirable. If it is desirable, it is good.

[18] I have long condemned myself for imitating those whom I accuse, and for expending words on what is obvious. For who can doubt that if heat is an evil, then to be hot is also an evil? If cold is an evil, then to be cold is an evil? If life is a good, then to live is also a good? All these things are around wisdom, not within it. But it is within wisdom itself that we must dwell.

[19] Even if we wish to digress a bit, wisdom has ample and spacious retreats. We can inquire into the nature of the gods, the sustenance of the stars, the varied motions of the constellations - whether our own motions are moved by theirs, whether the impulse for all bodies and souls comes from there, and whether even those things we call chance are in fact constrained by fixed laws, with

nothing in this universe occurring suddenly or without order. These matters are now far from the shaping of morals, but they uplift the mind and raise it to the magnitude of the very things it contemplates. The other matters I was speaking of a little while ago diminish and depress the mind and, contrary to what you think, do not sharpen it but rather wear it down.

[20] I implore you, are we wasting on a matter that is perhaps false and certainly useless the attention owed to greater and better things? How will it benefit me to know whether wisdom is one thing and being wise another? How will it benefit me to know that the former is good, but the latter is not? [So be it then.] I will act rashly and take a chance on this wish: may wisdom be yours, and being wise be mine. We will be equals.

[21] Show me instead the path I must take to reach those goals you describe. Tell me what I should avoid and what I should seek, the pursuits that will strengthen my wavering spirit, how I may repel those assaults that strike and shake me from all sides, how I can stand firm against such a multitude of misfortunes, how I can repel the calamities that have broken in upon me and those into which I myself have broken in. Teach me how to bear hardship without groaning, and good fortune without another's envy, and how to not simply await that final, inevitable end but to take flight of my own accord when I see fit.

[22] To my mind, nothing seems more disgraceful than wishing for death. For if you wish to live, why do you pray for death? Or if you do not wish to live, why ask the gods for what they granted you at birth? That you will die someday has been determined without your consent, but that you may die when you please is within your power. The former is a necessity, the latter a choice.

[23] I recently read, I swear, the most disgraceful opening by an eloquent man: "Thus," he said, "may I die as soon as possible." Foolish fellow, you wish for what is already yours! "May I die as soon as possible." Perhaps in uttering those words you have already grown old. What else detains you? No one holds you back; depart by whatever way you fancy. Choose any part of nature you wish and bid it grant

you egress. Are not water, earth, air the very elements that govern this world? They are the stuff of life but also the paths to death.

[24] "May I die as soon as possible"—what do you mean by "as soon as possible"? What day do you set for it? It can happen sooner than you wish. Such words betray a feeble mind, grasping for pity with dramatic abjurations. The man who wishes for death does not truly want to die. Ask the gods for life and health; if it is your pleasure to die, this alone is death's blessing—that you cease to wish at all.

[25] It is these matters, my dear Lucilius, that we must ponder and study. This is wisdom, this is sagacity—not to bandy about empty subtleties in trivial debates. Fortune has placed before you so many questions that you have not yet resolved, and here you are, quibbling! How foolish it is to practice drills when the signal for battle has already sounded. Set aside these toy weapons; the arms of decision are called for now. Tell me, by what reasoning can I keep my spirit free of sadness and dread? How can I shed the burden of these hidden desires? Let us take action!

[26] You say "Wisdom is a good, but the process of becoming wise is not a good." By such logic we are denied the opportunity to grow in wisdom, and this entire pursuit is mocked as an exercise in futility. But what would you say, I ask you, if you knew that people also debate whether future wisdom is in fact good? For what doubt is there, pray tell, that empty grain stores do not yet feel the harvest to come? That a child, in his tender strength, has no inkling of the youth that awaits him? Meanwhile, the promise of health on the horizon offers no aid to the sick man, any more than a runner straining in fierce competition is refreshed by thoughts of the leisure that will be his many months hence.

[27] Who does not know that the very fact that something lies in the future means it is not yet good? For what is truly good is unquestionably beneficial. And unless a thing is present, it cannot benefit. If it does not benefit, it is not good; but if it does benefit, then it already exists. I will one day be wise; and this will be a good when it comes to pass, but in the meantime, it is not. Something must first exist before it can be judged as being of any particular quality.

[28] How, I beg you, can that which does not yet exist already be deemed good? What more compelling proof could you want that a thing does not yet exist than my telling you it is yet to come? It is evident that what approaches has not yet arrived. Spring is on its way; I know now it is winter. Summer will follow; I know summer is not here. The surest evidence I have that something is not yet present is that it is still to come.

[29] I hope to be wise, but for now I am not wise. If I possessed that goodness already, I would be free of this flaw. The day will come when I shall be wise; from this you may deduce that I am not yet so. I cannot simultaneously dwell in that blessed state and this flawed one; the two cannot coexist, for good and bad do not abide together in the same place.

[30] Let us move swiftly past these over-clever trivialities and hurry on to matters that may actually offer us some aid. No man who anxiously sends for a midwife to attend his daughter in labor bothers to read through the proclamation detailing the order of the games. No one rushing to douse the flames engulfing his house pauses to study the chessboard and ponder how to free a trapped piece.

[31] But by Hercules, messengers assail you from all sides with news of your house on fire, your children in danger, your homeland under siege, your possessions being pillaged. Add to that shipwrecks, earthquakes, and whatever other calamities one might dread. Beset by such concerns, do you still make time for diversions that merely amuse the mind? Do you really want to split hairs debating the difference between wisdom and the process of becoming wise, tangling and untangling these knots, with catastrophe looming over your head?

[32] Nature has not granted us such an abundant and generous allotment of time that we can afford to squander any of it. Consider how much is lost even by the most careful among us: ill health robs us of some hours, family matters others; essential business and public duties consume yet more; and sleep divides our very lives with us.

From this time already so narrow, fleeting, and fast carrying us away, what good does it do to consign the greater part to waste?

[33] Moreover, the mind grows accustomed to amusing rather than healing itself, making a pastime of philosophy when it should be a remedy. Between wisdom and being wise I know not the difference; but I know it makes no difference to me whether I know such things or remain ignorant of them. Tell me: once I have learned the difference between wisdom and being wise, will I then be wise? Why then do you detain me among the vocabulary of wisdom rather than its works? Make me braver, more secure, fortune's equal, her superior.

And her superior I can be, if I direct all that I learn to that end. Farewell.

LETTER 118

REASON AS JUDGE OF GOOD AND EVIL

[1] YOU DEMAND MORE FREQUENT LETTERS FROM ME. LET'S COMPARE accounts; you will be insolvent. It was agreed that you would write first, and I would reply. But I won't be difficult; I know you're good for the credit. So I will give in advance and not do what Cicero, that most eloquent man, bids Atticus do—to write down "whatever comes into his head, even if he has nothing to say."

[2] There can never be a lack of something for me to write about, even setting aside all those things that fill Cicero's letters: which candidate is struggling; who is fighting with outside help and who with their own strength; who seeks the consulship relying on Caesar, who on Pompey, who on their wallet; how stingy the moneylender Caecilius is, from whom relatives can't extract a penny at less than 12% interest.

It's better to deal with one's own troubles than those of others, to scrutinize oneself and see how many things one is a candidate for, yet fails to vote for.

[3] This, my dear Lucilius, is outstanding, secure and free—to seek nothing and to bypass Fortune's entire election. How delightful do you think it is, when the tribes are summoned and the candidates are on tenterhooks in their temples, one promising money, another

canvassing through an agent, another wearing out their hands with the kisses of those to whom, once elected, they will refuse their hand to touch—to stand there at leisure, watching these dealerships, neither buying nor selling anything?

[4] How much greater is the joy of one who looks with unconcern not on the elections for praetorships or consulships, but on those great contests where some seek annual honors, others permanent power, others fortunate outcomes in war and triumphs, others riches, marriages and children, others their own safety and that of their family! What greatness of spirit it is to seek nothing, to entreat no one, and to say: "Fortune, I have no business with you. I do not give you access to me. I know that Catos are rejected by you and Vatiniuses elevated. I ask for nothing." This is how to make one's fortune private.

[5] So we can write such things to each other and endlessly plow this never-exhausted field, observing so many thousands of restless people who, in order to obtain something pernicious, strive through hardships toward misery and seek things they will soon have to flee or even loathe.

[6] For who has ever had enough once they attained what seemed excessive to them when they desired it? Happiness is not greedy, as people think, but petty; that's why it satisfies no one. You think those things are lofty because you lie far beneath them; but to one who has reached them, they are low. I'm lying if he doesn't still seek to climb; what you think is the summit is but a step.

[7] Ignorance of the truth afflicts everyone badly; deceived by rumors, they are carried away as if towards good things, then upon attaining them, they see that they are bad, empty, or less than what they had hoped for, having suffered much. The majority marvel at deceptions from a distance, and commonly mistake goods for great things.

[8] To prevent this from happening to us as well, let us inquire what the good is. There have been various interpretations of it; different people have expressed it differently. Some define it thus: "The good is what attracts the mind, what calls it to itself." To this it is

immediately objected: What if it does attract, but to destruction? You know how many evils are alluring. But the true and the likely differ from each other; that which is good is connected with the true, for nothing is good unless it is true. But what invites to itself and entices is likely; it kidnaps, disturbs, and draws us in.

[9] Some have defined it thus: "The good is what moves the desire for itself, or what moves the impulse of a mind extending towards it." And to this the same objection is raised; for many things move the mind's impulse, which are sought to the seeker's detriment. Better are those who have defined it thus: "The good is what moves the mind's impulse towards itself according to nature, and is worth seeking only when it begins to be worth desiring." Now it is also honorable, for this is perfectly worth seeking.

[10] The very topic reminds me to say what the difference is between the good and the honorable. They have something mixed together and inseparable: there can be no good unless there is something honorable in it, and the honorable is certainly good. What then is the difference between the two? The honorable is the perfect good, by which the happy life is completed, by contact with which other things also become good.

[11] What I'm saying is this: there are certain things that are neither good nor bad, such as military service, a political mission, jurisdiction. When these have been administered honorably, they begin to be good and cross over from the doubtful into the good. The good becomes so by association with the honorable, the honorable is good through itself. The good flows from the honorable, the honorable comes from itself. What is good could have been bad; what is honorable could not be anything but good.

[12] Some have offered this definition: "The good is that which is according to nature." Heed my words carefully—that which is good is according to nature, but not everything which is according to nature is necessarily good. Many things may indeed align with nature, yet they are so trivial that it would be unfitting to label them as good. For they are minor, contemptible things. No good, however small, should be despised; for as long as it remains paltry, it is not yet good. When it

begins to be good, it ceases to be insignificant. How, then, do we recognize the good? If it is perfectly in accordance with nature.

[13] "You admit," one may say, "that what is good is according to nature; this is its essential property. Yet you also admit that there are other things which, though according to nature, are not good. How, then, can the former be good, while the latter are not? How does it attain a different quality, when the principal characteristic—being in accordance with nature—is common to both?"

[14] The distinction lies in magnitude itself. It is hardly a novel concept that certain things, through growth, undergo transformation. An infant, upon reaching puberty, takes on a different character—the former being irrational, the latter rational. In some cases, an increase in scale leads not merely to an expansion, but to an alteration in kind.

[15] One might argue, "That which becomes greater does not become something else. Whether you fill a flask or a cask with wine, it makes no difference; in both cases, the essential quality of the wine remains the same. A small amount of honey does not differ in taste from a large quantity[1]." But these are faulty comparisons, for in those instances, the quality[2] remains constant despite an increase in quantity.

[16] Some things, when amplified, persist in their own genus and maintain their original properties. Yet there are others which, after numerous increments, are finally transformed by the last addition, impressing upon them a new and different condition from their former state. A single stone creates an arch—the stone that wedges the slanting sides and binds them together by its intervention[3]. Why does the final addition produce the greatest effect, even though it is small in itself? Because it does not merely augment; it completes.

[17] Certain things, in the course of their progression, shed their previous form and transition into a new one. When the mind has contemplated something for a long time and, in tracing its magnitude, grows weary, it begins to call it infinite. This becomes something far different than it was when it seemed merely great, but limited. In the same way, we might conceive of something as difficult to cut through; yet as this difficulty increases, we come to regard it as

impossible to cut. Thus we progress from that which is moved with toil and strain to that which is immovable. By this same logic, a thing may start out as being in accordance with nature, but through its own magnitude, it is carried over into another property and rendered good. Farewell.

---

1. Later manuscripts read "et magnum" (and a large quantity), while earlier manuscripts BA omit this phrase.
2. Later manuscripts have "qualitas" (quality), whereas earlier manuscripts BA read "aequalitas" (equality).
3. Later manuscripts have "cuneavit" (wedged), while earlier manuscripts BA read "cenavit" (dined).

LETTER 119

MINIMALISM AS THE
HIGHEST WEALTH

[1] WHENEVER I DISCOVER SOMETHING WORTHWHILE, MY FRIEND Lucilius, I do not wait for you to say "Share it with me." I tell myself straightaway. You ask what it is that I have discovered? Open wide the folds of your cloak, for it is pure profit that I offer. I will teach you how you can become rich with utmost speed. How eagerly you wish to hear it! And rightly so, for I will lead you to immense riches by the shortest of paths. Yet you will still need a lender; to do business you must contract a debt—but I would not have you borrow through a middle-man nor have brokers advertising your name about town.

[2] I will provide you with a ready lender, the famous one from Cato's circle[1]—from him you will borrow. However small the loan, it will suffice if we seek from ourselves whatever else is lacking. For it makes no difference, my dear Lucilius, whether you lack desires or possess means. The sum total is the same in either case: you will not be tormented. Nor do I counsel you to deny anything to Nature—she is stubborn and cannot be overcome; she demands her due—but simply to know that anything beyond Nature is precarious, not necessary.

[3] I am hungry; I must eat. Whether the bread is common or the finest wheat matters not to Nature; she wishes the belly to be not

delighted but filled. I am thirsty; whether the water I drink comes from the nearest lake or is chilled with heaps of snow to be cooled by another's chill[2], it matters not to Nature. She bids only that the thirst be quenched; whether the cup be of gold, crystal, murra, or earthenware from Tibur, or simply the hollow of my hand, it is irrelevant.

[4] Look to the end purpose of all things and you will dispense with superfluities. Hunger summons me; let my hand reach out for what is nearest at hand; hunger itself makes appealing whatever I grasp first.

[5] A starving man despises nothing. You ask what it was, then, that delighted me? I think it a splendid saying: "The wise man is the keenest seeker of the riches of nature." "You present me," you say, "with an empty platter. What is the meaning of this? I had already arranged my money-bags. I was surveying the seas into which I might venture on business, the public revenues I might farm, the merchandise I might import. That is deception, to teach poverty after promising riches." Then do you consider a man poor, to whom nothing is lacking? "By the blessing," you reply, "of his own character and his own endurance, not of Fortune." Do you then not consider him rich for the very reason that his riches cannot cease to be his? Which would you prefer—to have much or to have enough?

[6] The one who has much desires even more—which is proof that he does not yet have enough; the one who has enough has attained what the rich man never does—an end to desire. Or do you think these things are not riches because no one has ever been proscribed on their account? Because on their account, no son has ever slipped his father poison, no wife her husband? Because they are safe in wartime? Because they bring leisure in peacetime? Because it is neither dangerous to possess them nor troublesome to manage them?

[7] "But he who merely does not shiver, hunger, or thirst has too little," you say. Jupiter himself has no more. What suffices is never too little, and what does not suffice is never too much. Alexander was a poor man after [conquering] Darius and the Indians. Am I mistaken? He seeks something to make his own, explores unknown seas, sends

new fleets into the ocean, and bursts through the very barriers of the world, so to speak. What is enough for nature is not enough for man.

[8] There has been found one who desires something after having everything—so blind are our minds and so prone are we to forget our beginnings once we've advanced. The man who was just recently the disputed lord of an unknown corner of the earth, upon reaching the world's edge, was saddened to return through what was now his own domain.

[9] Money has made no one rich; on the contrary, it has only struck each with a greater desire for itself. Do you ask what is the cause of this? He who has more begins to be able to have even more. In sum, you may drag out into the open any of those whose names are counted along with Crassus and Licinius. Let him present his census and reckon together whatever he has and whatever he hopes for. That man, believe me, is poor; or if you don't believe me, he can be.

[10] But this man here who has aligned himself with what nature demands is not only beyond the sensation of poverty but beyond its fear. But so that you may know how difficult it is to constrain one's affairs to nature's measure: this very man we are speaking of, whom you call poor, actually has something superfluous.

[11] But riches blind the public and draw attention to themselves if a large sum is carried out from some house, if much gold is overlaid on its very roof, if the household slaves are choice in their persons or spectacular in their dress. The prosperity of all those things is outward-facing; that man whom we have removed from both the public and from fortune is inwardly happy.

[12] As for those whom a false notion of wealth has possessed - poverty in disguise - they have their riches as we are said to "have" a fever, when really the fever has us. We commonly say the opposite, that "the fever has him in its grip." In the same way we should say, "riches have him in their grip." So there is nothing I would rather urge upon you than this advice, which no one takes to heart enough: measure all things by natural desires, which can be satisfied for free or at little cost. Just refrain from mixing vices with your desires.

[13] You ask, what sort of table, what kind of silver plate, with what uniform and nimble servants should food be served? Nature desires nothing beyond the food itself.

> *When thirst burns your throat, do you seek out cups of*
> *   gold?*
> *When hungry, do you turn your nose up at everything but*
> *peacock and turbot?*

[14] Hunger has no ambition; it is content to end, caring little how it gets there. These are the torments of unhappy luxury, which seeks how to be hungry even after fullness, how to stuff the belly rather than fill it, how to rekindle thirst after that first satisfying drink. Horace put it splendidly in denying that it matters to thirst from what cup the water is served or by how elegant a hand. For if you judge it relevant how well-coiffed the servant boy is or how translucent the goblet he offers you, then you are not really thirsty.

[15] Among her other gifts, nature has granted us this paramount blessing: she has divested necessity of squeamishness. It is superfluities that allow for picking and choosing - this is not quite proper, that not sufficiently praised, this offends my eyes. The founder of the universe who prescribed the rules of living for us intended that we be safe, not that we be spoiled. Everything conducive to our preservation is prepared and readily available; all the materials of indulgence are amassed with effort and anxiety.

[16] Let us therefore make use of this gift of nature, counting it among the greatest, and consider that she deserves our gratitude on no account more than this: that whatever is demanded by necessity is received without disdain. Farewell.

---

1. Cato the Elder (234-149 BCE)
2. Wealthy Romans chilled drinks with snow brought from the mountains.

LETTER 120
KNOWLEDGE OF GOOD AND EVIL THINGS

[1] Your letter roamed through several little questions, my dear Lucilius, but settled on one and desired it to be addressed: How did the knowledge of good and honorable things come to us? These two are separate for some, but for us they are merely distinct.

[2] Let me explain what I mean. Some think that the good is that which is useful; and so they apply the term to riches, horses, wine, and shoes. So cheapened is their conception of good, descending into such base things! They think the honorable is that which aligns with the rationale of right duty, such as dutifully caring for an elderly father, helping a friend in poverty, courageously going on a military campaign, or delivering a prudent and restrained opinion. We make these two things one and the same.

[3] Nothing is good except that which is honorable, and what is honorable is certainly good. I consider it superfluous to add what the difference is between them, since I have often said it before. This one thing I will say: we hold that nothing which someone can use badly is good to us. And you see how many use badly their wealth, noble birth, or strength.

So now I return to that about which you desired me to speak: how the first notion of good and honorable things came to us.

[4] Nature could not teach us this; she gave us the seeds of knowledge, but not knowledge itself. Some say we stumbled upon the awareness of virtue by mere chance - which is unbelievable, that the appearance of virtue occurred to someone accidentally! It seems to us that observation, comparing things that have often occurred, has collected this knowledge. By analogy our intellect judges both the honorable and the good. Since the Latin grammarians have granted this word citizenship, I do not think it should be condemned, but rather restored to its proper place. I will therefore use it not just as accepted but as customary.

[5] What is this analogy, you ask? I will tell you. We knew of bodily health; from this we conceived that there is also some health of the soul. We knew of bodily strength; from this we gathered that there is also strength of soul. Certain kind deeds, certain humane deeds, certain brave deeds had astounded us; we began to marvel at these as though they were perfect. But beneath them lurked many vices, which the visible appearance and splendor of some striking deed concealed; these we overlooked. Nature bids us to amplify what is praiseworthy, and everyone has exaggerated glory beyond the truth. From these things, therefore, we derived the semblance of immense good.

[6] When King Pyrrhus offered Fabricius gold, he rejected it, judging the ability to scorn a king's wealth to be greater than a kingdom itself. And when Pyrrhus's own physician promised to give the king poison, this same Fabricius warned Pyrrhus to beware of the plot. A soul unwilling to be conquered by gold was equally unwilling to conquer by poison. We marvel at this great man, whom neither promises from a king nor promises against a king could sway—a man steadfast in his good example, innocent in war (which is most difficult), who believed that certain acts were impermissible even against enemies. In the depth of the poverty he had made his glory, he shunned riches no differently than poison. "Live, Pyrrhus," he said, "by my good deed, and rejoice that Fabricius cannot be corrupted—a fact you had bemoaned until now."

[7] Horatius Cocles stood alone and blocked the narrow bridge.

He ordered his retreat cut off behind him, so long as the enemy's path was also cut off, and he resisted their onslaught until the beams, torn away, cracked and collapsed with a mighty roar. After looking back and sensing that his country was safe from danger through his own peril, he said, "If anyone wishes to follow, let him come this way." And he threw himself headlong, no less intent, in that swift stream, on emerging armed than on emerging unharmed. Retaining the glory of his victorious arms, he returned as safely as if he had crossed by the bridge.

[8] Such deeds reveal to us an image of virtue. I will add something that may perhaps seem wondrous: evil things have sometimes offered the appearance of moral goodness, and from the opposite direction the best quality has shone forth[1]. For as you know, Lucilius, vices border close upon virtues, and even in the corrupt and base there is a resemblance to rectitude. Thus the prodigal falsely imitates the generous, though there is the greatest difference between knowing how to give and not knowing how to save. Many, I say, do not give but toss away: I do not call a man generous who is angry with his own money. Negligence imitates easygoingness, rashness imitates bravery.

[9] This resemblance compels us to pay heed and to distinguish things that are related in appearance but greatly divergent in substance. And while we observe those whom some outstanding deed has made remarkable, we note who has done something with a noble spirit and great élan, but only once. We have seen one man brave in war but timid in the forum, bearing poverty with spirit but disgrace with servility. We praise the deed; we despise the man.

[10] We have seen a man who is generous to his friends, temperate towards his enemies, and who manages both public and private affairs with integrity and conscientiousness. He possesses unwavering patience in the face of adversity and prudence in taking necessary actions. When giving is called for, his hand is bountiful; when toil is required, he is persistent and steadfast, his mind uplifting his body above fatigue. Moreover, he is always consistent and true to himself in every action, good not only by conscious choice but by long habit. He

has reached the point where he is not only able to do right, but is unable to do anything but right. We recognize in him the embodiment of perfect virtue.

[11] We have divided virtue into its constituent parts: curbing desires, restraining fears, planning for the future, giving each their due. We have thus encompassed temperance, courage, prudence, and justice, assigning to each its proper function. How then did we come to understand virtue? Its inherent order, beauty, constancy, and the harmony of all its actions among themselves, its greatness towering above all else—these revealed it to us. From this, we grasped the nature of the blessed life, flowing onward with a favorable current, completely under its own control.

[12] But how did we arrive at this realization? I will explain. That perfect man, who has attained true virtue, never cursed Fortune or met misfortunes with sadness, believing himself to be a citizen and soldier of the universe, submitting to hardships as if under orders. Whatever happened to him, he did not spurn it as evil or a misfortune befallen him by chance, but as if assigned to him as his duty. "This, whatever it may be," he says, "is my lot. It is rough and difficult, so let me strive all the more earnestly to overcome it."

[13] The greatness of his spirit was undeniable—a man who never bemoaned adversities or bemoaned his fate. He made many realize his worth, shining forth like a light in the darkness, drawing the minds of all to himself by his calm and gentle manner, poised and equanimous in human and divine affairs alike.

[14] His mind was perfect, cultivated to its highest potential, inferior to nothing except the mind of God, from which a portion flows down even into the mortal breast. The mind is never more divine than when contemplating its own mortality, recognizing that man is born to fulfill his life, and that this body is not a permanent home, but a fleeting abode—an inn to be left behind when we become burdensome guests.

[15] The greatest proof, my dear Lucilius, of a soul emanating from loftier regions, is when it deems base and confining these material things in which it finds itself ensnared, and does not fear to

depart. For such a soul knows to where it will go, remembering from whence it came. Do we not see how many discomforts harass us, how poorly suited to us is this body of ours?

[16] We complain now of the head, now of the stomach, now of the chest and throat. At times our nerves torment us, at other times it's our feet; sometimes it's diarrhea, sometimes a running nose; now we have too much blood, now too little. We are assailed and driven out from every side—such is the lot of those who live in a borrowed dwelling.

[17] Yet despite being allotted a body so frail, we nevertheless set our sights on eternity. However long a human lifespan can extend, that is how much we try to grasp with our ambitions, never content with any amount of money or power. What could be more brazen, more foolish than this? Nothing suffices for those destined to die— no, for those already dying. For each day we stand closer to the end, and every hour presses us onward to that inescapable plunge. See the depth of blindness our mind suffers!

[18] What I speak of as future is happening as we speak, and much of it has already come to pass—namely, the part we have already lived. But we are mistaken to fear the final day, when each day contributes equally to our death. It is not the last step, where we collapse, that causes our weariness—it merely announces it. The final day reaches death, but every day draws us nearer. Death slowly whittles us down rather than snatching us suddenly.

Therefore, a great soul, aware of its higher nature, makes sure to conduct itself in its appointed station with honor and diligence. But it judges none of its outward trappings as its own, using them only as borrowed property, like a traveler passing through in haste.

[19] Whenever we see someone of such steadfastness, how can we not be struck by this uncommon nobility of character? Especially if, as I said, they demonstrate that their greatness is genuine through their consistency. A truly steady course persists; falsehood does not endure. Some alternate between being a Vatinius and a Cato[2]. One moment Curius is not strict enough for them, Fabricius not poor enough, Tubero not sufficiently frugal and content with simplicity;

the next they outdo Licinus in wealth, Apicius in feasts, and Maecenas in luxurious delights.

[20] The greatest proof of a troubled mind is vacillation, an incessant wavering between the pretense of virtues and the love of vices. Someone

> *often had two hundred slaves,*
> *Often only ten; at times speaking grandly of kings and*
>   *tetrarchs,*
> *Then saying "Let me have a three-legged table,*
> *A pinch of plain salt, and a cloak, however coarse,*
> *That can keep out the cold"; you could have given a million*
> *To this frugal man, content with little,*
> *And in five days he'd have nothing left.*

[21] The men Horatius Flaccus describes are just like this: never the same, not even similar to themselves, wandering so far astray into contradictions. Did I say "many men"? It's close to being all of them. There's no one who doesn't change his mind and his desires daily. One moment he wants to have a wife, the next a mistress; now he wants to be a king, now he strives to be the most obsequious of servants; one day he puffs himself up to the point of arousing envy, the next he hunkers down and shrinks lower than those who truly lie in the dust; sometimes he lavishes his money, other times he snatches it back.

[22] This is the surest proof of a foolish mind: it's one man one moment and another the next, and—what I judge to be the height of disgrace—it's inconsistent with itself. Consider it a great thing to play the part of a single man. But no one except the wise man plays one role; the rest of us are multifaceted. Now we seem to you frugal and serious, now prodigal and vain. We continually change masks, assuming the opposite of the one we've just removed. Therefore, demand this of yourself: that you maintain to the end the character you've resolved to present. Make it so you can be praised—or at the very least, recognized. About someone you saw yesterday, it could

rightly be asked, "Who is this?" Such is the extent of the change. Farewell.

---

1. According to Buecheler's emendation, following the text of the Codex Ottobonianus. The Codex Velzianus reads "emicuit," and BA have "nituit."
2. Vatinius was a despised sycophant; Cato was a paragon of moral excellence.

LETTER 121

THE IMPORTANCE OF LIVING
BY REASON

[1] I can see that you will take issue, my dear Lucilius, when I explain to you today's little question on which we have spent quite some time. For you will cry out again, "What does this have to do with ethics?" But cry out all you want, while I first confront you with others with whom you may dispute - Posidonius and Archidemus - they will accept the case. Then I will say: not everything that is moral makes for good morals.

[2] Some things pertain to nourishing a person, others to training them, others to clothing them, others to instructing them, and others to delighting them. Yet all things pertain to a person, even if not all things make them better. Morals touch upon different aspects in different ways: some correct and regulate them, while others examine their nature and origin.

[3] When I ask why nature brought forth man, why she preferred him to all other animals, do you think I have abandoned morals far behind? That is false. For how will you know what morals you should have, unless you find what is best for man, unless you examine his nature? Only then will you understand what you must do and what you must avoid, when you have learned what you owe to your nature.

[4] "I," you say, "wish to learn how to desire less, fear less. Shake off

superstition from me. Teach me that this thing called happiness is light and empty, and that a single syllable is very easily added to it." I will satisfy your desire, and I will encourage virtues and flog vices. Although someone may judge me too excessive and unrestrained in this regard, I will not stop pursuing wickedness, restraining the most savage passions, repressing pleasures that lead to pain, and protesting against prayers. Why not? When we have prayed for the greatest evils, and whatever we say in greeting has arisen from congratulation.

[5] Meanwhile, permit me to examine those matters that seem a little more remote. We were asking whether all animals have an awareness of their own constitution. That they do is especially apparent from the fact that they move their limbs aptly and readily, as if trained for this purpose. Every creature has agility in its own parts. A craftsman wields his tools with ease; a ship's captain skillfully turns the rudder; a painter swiftly marks out the colors, which he has placed in great variety before him for rendering a likeness, and passes easily in appearance and touch between the wax and his work. In the same way, an animal is mobile in every use of itself.

[6] We often marvel at the skill of expert dancers, whose hands are prepared to express every meaning and emotion, and whose gestures match the swiftness of the words. What art accomplishes for them, nature does for animals. They move their limbs with ease, never hesitating in the use of their own bodies. Newborn creatures do this immediately—they emerge with this innate knowledge, born fully trained.

[7] "The reason," one might object, "that animals aptly move their parts is because they would feel pain if they moved otherwise. As you say, they are compelled by fear, not volition, to move correctly." But this is false. Necessity-driven actions are slow; agility belongs to the spontaneously moving. Far from being driven to this by fear of pain, they strive for natural movement even when pain hinders them.

[8] So an infant, practicing standing and growing accustomed to bearing his own weight, falls as soon as he begins testing his strength, and rises again after each tearful tumble, until through pain he has trained himself for what nature demands. Some animals with harder

backs contort themselves and stretch out their feet at odd angles until they are repositioned. The overturned tortoise feels no torment, yet it is restless with longing for its natural state and does not cease its struggle until it stands upon its feet.

[9] Therefore, all creatures have an awareness of their own constitution [constitutio], and from this comes their agile command of their limbs. We have no greater proof that they come into life with this knowledge than the fact that no animal is clumsy in the use of itself.

[10] "A constitution," one objects, "is, as you say, the mind's principal state in relation to the body. How can an infant grasp this complex and subtle concept that even you struggle to articulate? All animals would need to be born logicians to understand this definition that confounds even most toga-clad men!" The objection would be valid if I claimed that animals understand the definition of a constitution, rather than the constitution itself.

[11] Nature is more easily understood than explained. And so that infant does not know what a constitution is, but he knows his own constitution. He does not know what an animal is, but he senses that he is an animal.

[12] Moreover, every creature understands its own constitution in a rough, general, and obscure way. We too know that we have a mind, but what the mind is, where it resides, what its nature or origin might be—this we do not know. Whatever our mind's perception of itself, however ignorant we may be of its nature and seat, so it is with all animals and their perception of their own constitution. For they must necessarily feel that through which they feel other things; they must have a sense of that which they obey and by which they are governed.

[13] There is not one among us who does not understand that there is something which sets its own impulses in motion, though what that may be, we do not know. One knows that there is an endeavor within oneself, but what it is or whence it comes, one does not know. Thus even infants and animals have a sense of their ruling part, though it is not sufficiently clear or distinct.

[14] "You say," one objects, "that every animal is first endeared to its own constitution, but that man's constitution is rational, and there-

fore man is endeared to himself not as an animal, but as a rational being. For man cherishes himself in that part wherein he is human. How then can an infant be endeared to a rational constitution when it is not yet rational?" Each age has its own constitution—one for the infant, another for the boy, another for the old man. They are all endeared to the constitution wherein they find themselves.

[15] The infant is toothless—to this constitution it is endeared. The teeth emerge—to this constitution it is endeared. For the plant too, which will grow into a crop of grain, has one constitution when it is tender and scarcely peeping above the furrow, another when it has grown strong and stands upon a stalk that is soft but able to bear its weight, and yet another when it yellows, ripens for the harvest, and its ear has hardened. Whatever constitution it has attained, it defends and settles into it.

[16] The age of an infant is different from that of a boy, which differs from that of a young man and an old man; yet I, who have been infant, boy, and young man, am still the same person. Thus, although one's constitution may change from one stage to another, the attachment to one's own constitution remains the same. For nature commends to me not my boyhood, youth, or old age, but myself. Therefore, the infant is endeared to the constitution which is his at the moment, not to that which will be his in youth. For even if some greater development awaits him in which he will change, nevertheless that wherein he is born is also according to nature.

[17] An animal first feels an attachment to itself, for there must be a point of reference to which all other things relate. I seek pleasure—for whom? For myself. Therefore, I am taking care of myself. I shrink from pain—on behalf of whom? Myself. Therefore, I am taking care of myself. If I do everything for the sake of my own care, then my care is prior to everything else. This care is inherent in all animals; it is not grafted on, but inborn.

[18] Nature brings forth her offspring, she does not cast them away. And because the surest protection comes from closeness, each creature is entrusted to itself. Thus, as I said in earlier letters, even delicate animals, newly emerged from their mother's womb or egg,

instinctively know what is harmful and avoid deadly threats. Vulnerable to predatory birds, they even recoil from the shadow of those flying overhead.

No animal enters life without a fear of death.

[19] "How," you ask, "can a newborn animal understand what is wholesome or deadly?" The first question is whether it understands, not how it understands. That they possess understanding is evident from the fact that they would do no more if they did understand. Why does a hen not flee from a peacock or a goose, but does from a hawk, so much smaller and not even known to her? Why do chicks fear a cat but not a dog? Clearly, they possess an innate knowledge of what can harm them, not gathered from experience; for they are cautious before they can have experience[1].

[20] Furthermore, lest you think this happens by chance, they neither fear things other than what they should, nor do they ever forget this vigilance and care; their avoidance of danger is instinctive. Moreover, they do not become more timid by living longer.

From this it is quite clear that they do not come to this through practice, but by an inborn love of self-preservation. Learning through experience is slow and variable; whatever nature imparts is equal in all and immediate.

[21] If, however, you insist, I will tell you how every animal tries to understand dangers. It senses that it is made of flesh; so it perceives what can cut its flesh, what can burn it, what can crush it, which animals are armed to injure; their appearance is drawn as hostile and inimical. These perceptions are interconnected; for each creature is at once endeared to its own welfare and seeks what helps it, while dreading what may harm it. Natural impulses toward the useful, natural aversions from the contrary; this happens without any thought dictating it, without judgment, wherever nature has given instruction.

[22] Do you not see what subtlety bees have for constructing their homes, what harmonious division of labor in their work? Do you not see how the spider's weaving is unchanging to any mortal, how much work it is to arrange the threads, some extended straight as a founda-

tion, others running round in a dense spiral through which smaller creatures, for whose destruction the web is spun, may be entangled and held as if in a net?

[23] This art is born, not learned. Thus, no animal is more skilled than another. You will see the spider's webs alike, the openings in the honeycomb's angles all the same. What art teaches is uncertain and uneven; what nature distributes comes in equal measure. Nature has imparted nothing more than the protection of oneself and the skill for it, and for that reason, they begin to learn and to live at the same time.

[24] It is no wonder that these things are born with that without which they would be born in vain. Nature has bestowed this first tool for survival, a attachment and affection for oneself. They could not be safe unless they wished to be. Yet this alone would not have profited them, but without it, nothing else would have profited. In no creature will you detect a cheapening of self, not even neglect. Even in the silent and brutish, though they are numb in other ways, there is an ingenuity for living. You will see that those which are useless to others do not fail themselves. Farewell.

---

1. Some manuscripts have variations like "experiri cavent" or "experts cavent" here, but "experisci cavent" seems to make the most sense in context.

LETTER 122

THE DANGER OF FOLLOWING CORRUPT EXAMPLES

[1] THE DAY ALREADY FEELS THE DAMAGE, HAVING SHRUNK BACK A BIT, yet there is still an ample span of time if one rises, so to speak, along with the very day. A person is more dutiful and virtuous who awaits the first light and greets the dawn; shameful is the one who lies half-asleep when the sun is high, whose wakefulness begins at midday -- and for many even this is pre-dawn.

[2] There are those who have utterly confused the duties of day and night, not opening their heavy, hungover eyes from yesterday until night begins to fall again. The condition of such people is said to be like those who nature, as Virgil says, has placed on the opposite side of the world from our abodes:

> *"And where the rising Sun first breathes on us with panting*
> *steeds,*
> *For them the late and reddening Evening Star kindles its*
> *tardy light."*

The life of these people, though not their location, is contrary to all others. There are some in the same city who are antipodes[1], who, as Marcus Cato remarks, have never seen the sun either rise or set.

[3] Do you think that those who do not know when to live know how to live? And do these people, who have entombed themselves while still alive, fear death? They are as ill-omened as night-owls. Although they may spend their darkness in wine and perfume, although they may draw out the entire period of their misdirected wakefulness with feasts carved into many courses, they are not partying but conducting their own funeral rites. Truly the rituals for the dead are held during the daytime.

Yet, by Hercules, no day is long for the active person. Let us extend our life; the business and proof of life is action. Let the night be curtailed and some of it transferred into day.

[4] Birds that are obtained for feasts are kept in the dark so they may easily grow fat through inactivity; similarly, a swollen, lazy corpulence invades the body of those lying idle without any exercise, and a proud but inert bulk grows beneath the surface. But the bodies of those who have devoted themselves to darkness appear hideous. Indeed their color is more suspect than those suffering from disease -- languid and sickly pale, their flesh is cadaverous even while alive. Yet I would call this the least of their ills. How much more darkness is in their minds! One is dazed in self-stupor, another is blinded, envying the unsighted. Who ever had eyes for the purpose of darkness?

[5] You ask how this mental depravity comes about of turning from the day and shifting one's whole life into the night? All vices fight against nature, all abandon the proper order. This is the aim of indulgence -- to delight in perversity, and not only to depart from what is right but to go as far away as possible, and then even to stand in exact opposition.

[6] Do you not think that those who drink while fasting, who pour wine into empty veins and pass out drunk at the dinner table, are living contrary to nature? Yet this is a common vice among young men who cultivate their strength, drinking amid naked bodies almost at the very threshold of the bath, or rather sweating out the wine they have consumed in frequent, boiling drafts. To drink after lunch or dinner is ordinary; this is what rustic heads of households do, igno-

rant of true pleasure. The wine that delights is that which does not float atop food, which penetrates freely to the nerves; the intoxication that pleases is that which enters a void.

[7] Do you not think that those who exchange clothing with women are living contrary to nature? Are not those who strive for boyhood to shine at an unnatural time living contrary to nature? What could be crueler or more wretched? Will he never be a man, having long endured being used like one? When his degrading sex ought to have rescued him, will not even age deliver him?

[8] Are not those who crave roses in winter, using the warmth of heated water and apt changes of temperature to coax forth the springtime lily in the dead of winter, living contrary to nature[2]? Do not those who plant orchards atop lofty towers, whose forests sway on the roofs and gables of houses, the roots springing from where the wanton treetops thrust themselves, live contrary to nature? Do not those who lay the foundations of their hot baths in the sea, who think they are not bathing luxuriously unless the heated pools are pounded by waves and storm, live contrary to nature?

[9] Having set out to desire all things contrary to nature's habit, they ultimately completely unlearn her. "It is daylight: time to sleep. It is time to rest: now let us exercise, now let us go out, now let us eat lunch. Soon the light approaches closer; it is time for dinner. We mustn't do what the masses do. It is a sordid thing to live the common, well-trodden path. Let the public have the day; let morning be made our own, special to us."

[10] Truly, such people are no different to me than the deceased. For how little do they differ from a funeral, and a bitter one at that, who live by torchlight and candlelight? We recall that many lived this life once, among them Acilius Buta, a praetorian to whom, after he had squandered a vast inheritance, Tiberius remarked upon his confessing his poverty, "You have woken up too late."

[11] Julius Montanus, a tolerable poet known to Tiberius more for his friendship than his talents, was reciting a poem. He had an excessive fondness for describing sunrises and sunsets. When someone complained that Montanus had spent the whole day reciting and

declared that no one should attend his performances, Pinarius Natta quipped, "I can never show greater generosity. I am prepared to listen to him from sunrise to sunset!"

[12] Montanus recited these lines:

> *"Now Phoebus begins to cast his burning rays,*
> *The blushing day begins to spread, the mournful swallow*
> *Prepares to bring food back to her chirping nest*
> *And starts to serve it, dividing it with her gentle beak."*

At this, Varus, a Roman knight and hanger-on of Marcus Vinicius who secured invitations to fine dinners by the sharpness of his tongue, cried out: "Buta is beginning to fall asleep!" Then, when Montanus continued reciting:

[13]

> *"Now the shepherds have corralled their herds in the stalls,*
> *Now sluggish night begins to cast her silent spell upon the*
> > *drowsy lands..."*

The same Varus interjected, "What's that you say? Night already? I must go pay my respects to Buta!" There was nothing more notorious than Buta's lifestyle, completely inverted from the norm, which many others practiced in those days as well.

[14] Some live this way not because they find the night hours inherently more pleasant, but because the usual routine brings them no joy. The light of day weighs heavily on a guilty conscience, and to a mind consumed by lust or disdain, sunlight that costs nothing seems dreary compared to expensive nocturnal pleasures. Moreover, profligates wish their lives to be the talk of the town while they live, thinking their efforts wasted if no one speaks of them. They can scarcely stand it when their exploits fail to become common gossip.

Many squander their fortunes on feasts and mistresses. But in a city with so much going on, run-of-the-mill depravity attracts no notice. To make a name for yourself among that crowd, your extravagance must be outrageous, not merely self-indulgent.

[15] I once heard Albinovanus Pedo, a most elegant storyteller, relate how he lived above the house of Sextus Papinius, one of those creatures of the night. "Around the third hour of the night," he said, "I hear the crack of whips. I ask what he's doing; they say he's going over accounts. Around the sixth hour, I hear an uproar; I ask what's happening; they say he's exercising his voice. Around the eighth hour, I wonder what the sound of wheels means; they say he's going for a ride."

[16] As daylight approaches, there is much scurrying about - servants are summoned, storeroom-keepers and cooks create a commotion. I inquire as to the reason for this bustle and am informed that he had called for mead, having just exited the bath. "This was most unusual for him," they said, "for he lived very frugally, consuming nothing except the night itself. Therefore, some may call him miserly and sordid, but you," they remarked, "would more aptly dub him a 'lamp-miser[3].'"

[17] You should not marvel at discovering such a vast array of particular vices; they are diverse, with countless manifestations, and their categories cannot be fully grasped. The pursuit of virtue is straightforward, while the ways of vice are manifold, capable of endless variations. The same applies to human character - those who follow nature's path are easygoing, relaxed, with only minor differences among them. But the corrupt are twisted in countless ways, at odds with everyone else and even themselves.

[18] Yet the principal cause of this affliction, in my view, is a disgust with ordinary life. Just as they seek to distinguish themselves from others through their dress, the refinement of their dining, or the elegance of their carriages, so too do they wish to stand apart in how they allot their time. They refuse to transgress in typical ways, finding the reward of infamy in common sins. This is what all those who live life "backwards," so to speak, are seeking.

[19] Therefore, Lucilius, we must hold fast to the path prescribed by nature and never deviate from it. For those who follow her lead, all

things are easy and unimpeded, but for those who struggle against her, life is no different than rowing against the current. Farewell.

---

1. Literally "opposite-footed", referring to those on the exact opposite side of the earth.
2. An alternate reading: "brumalium" (of the winter solstice) instead of "bruma lilium" (winter lily).
3. A play on words, suggesting he "spends" or "consumes" the night by staying up late working or studying, just as a lamp consumes oil.

LETTER 123
THE VALUE OF AUSTERE AND PRINCIPLED LIVING

[1] I ARRIVED AT MY VILLA IN ALBANUM LATE AT NIGHT, EXHAUSTED more by the inconvenience of the journey than its length. I have nothing prepared except myself. And so, I rest my weary body on my couch, considering the delay of my cook and baker a blessing. I reflect on how nothing is burdensome if you accept it with ease, and nothing is cause for indignation unless you make it so by indignation.

[2] "My baker has no bread," you say, but my steward does, as do my chamberlain and tenant farmer. "The bread is poor," you protest. Just wait: hunger will make it good. Even the softest, finest bread will seem delectable when you are famished. Therefore, one should not eat until hunger commands it. I will wait, then, and not eat until I either have good bread or have ceased to be particular.

[3] It is necessary to accustom oneself to little: many difficulties of place and time will confront even the wealthy and those equipped for pleasure, preventing them from having whatever they want. No one can have everything they desire, but they can refuse to want what they do not have, and cheerfully make use of what is offered. A well-disciplined and hardship-tolerant stomach is a considerable part of liberty.

[4] It is impossible to estimate the pleasure I derive from the fact

that my weariness is becoming accustomed to itself; I seek no masseurs, no baths, no other remedy than time. For what toil has contracted, rest removes. This dinner, however modest, will be more delightful than an inaugural banquet.

[5] I have suddenly put my mind to a sort of test, for this is simpler and truer. When one has prepared oneself and commanded patience, one's true strength of character is not so apparent as when it is revealed impromptu. The surest proofs are those given on the spot, if one looks upon troubles not merely with calmness, but with serenity; if one does not fly into a rage or quarrel; if one supplies what ought to be given by not desiring it, and reflects that one is accustomed to lack nothing.

[6] We do not realize how many things are superfluous until we begin to lack them; for we use them not because we ought, but because we have them. How many things we acquire because others have acquired them, because most people have them! Among the causes of our ills is that we live by example, not by reason; we are not ordered by rationality, but led astray by custom.

If few did these things, we would refuse to imitate them, but when more start to do so, we follow along as if it were more respectable because it is more frequent. Error holds the place of reason among us once it has become widespread.

[7] Nowadays, everyone travels with such an entourage that a cavalry of Numidians rides ahead and a troop of runners precedes the main party. It's considered shameful not to have anyone to shove approaching people out of the way or to kick up a great cloud of dust to announce the arrival of an important person. Everyone now has mules to carry their crystal and agate vessels and goblets engraved by the hands of great artists. It's thought disgraceful for you to have luggage that can be jostled without risk of damage. The slaves of these travelers ride along with their anointed faces, lest sun or cold injure their delicate skin. It's held to be beneath one's dignity not to have in your retinue a single boy whose healthy complexion doesn't require cosmetics.

[8] You must avoid the conversation of all such people. These are

the ones who pass vices from one to another and transmit them wherever they go. The worst sort seemed to be those who peddle words, but some peddle vices. Their talk is deeply harmful; for even if it doesn't instantly convince, it leaves seeds in the mind and follows us even when we have left their company, destined to spring up into evil later on.

[9] Just as those who have heard music carry the melody and sweetness of the songs in their ears, which hinders their thoughts and won't allow them to concentrate on serious matters, so the words of flatterers and those who praise what is wrong linger longer than the time it takes to hear them. It's not easy to shake a pleasing sound from one's mind; it pursues us, endures, and comes back after an interval. Therefore we should close our ears against evil talk, right from the start. Once they have gained entry and been admitted, they grow bolder.

[10] From this, people progress to saying: "Virtue, philosophy, and justice are just the rattling of empty words. The only happiness lies in doing well for yourself in life. To exist, to drink, to enjoy your inheritance—this is living, this is remembering that you are mortal. The days flow past and irretrievable life hastens by. Why hesitate to be wise? What good does it do to impose frugality on an age that can't always welcome pleasures—in the meantime, while it can, while there is a demand? Anticipate death, and let whatever it will snatch away perish now as far as you are concerned[1]. You have no mistress, no boy to make your mistress jealous. You go out sober every day. You dine as if you had to submit your account book to your father. That's not living, but acting as an extra in someone else's life."

[11] What madness it is to arrange the affairs of your heir while denying yourself everything, so that a large inheritance may turn a friend into an enemy. For the more he receives from you, the more he will rejoice at your death[2]. Do not value at a penny those gloomy and disdainful critics of another's life, those enemies of their own, those public school-masters, and do not hesitate to prefer a good life to a good reputation.

[12] These voices must be shunned just as Ulysses refused to sail

past those [the Sirens] unless he was bound. They have the same power; they lead away from country, from parents, from friends, from virtues, and they dash a wretched life upon the rocks, unless there is a shameful hope. How much better it is to follow the straight path and to bring oneself to the point where only what is honorable is pleasing to you.

[13] We will be able to achieve this if we know that there are two kinds of things, those which either attract or repel us. Riches, pleasures, beauty, ambition, and other alluring and smiling things attract us; toil, death, pain, ignominy, and a more austere life repel us. We ought, therefore, to train ourselves neither to fear these nor to desire those. Let us fight against the current and withdraw from the attractions; let us rouse ourselves to face the repellents.

[14] Do you not see how different the bearing is of those descending and those ascending? Those who go downward throw their bodies backward; those who climb a steep place lean forward. For if you are descending, Lucilius, it is a vice to give your weight to the forward part; if you are ascending, it is a vice to draw it backward. It is a descent into pleasures; into hardships and difficulties we must climb; in the former case, let us throw our bodies forward; in the latter, let us check them.

[15] Do you think that I am now saying that only those are dangerous to our ears who praise pleasure and implant the fear of pain, formidable things in themselves? I think that those also harm us who, under the guise of the Stoic sect, urge us to vices. For this is what they boast: only the wise man and the learned are lovers. "He alone has wisdom for this art; the wise man is also most skilled in drinking and feasting. Let us inquire up to what age young men are to be loved."

[16] Allow these principles to be given to the Greek custom[3]. Let us direct our ears rather to the following precepts: "No one becomes good by chance. Virtue must be learned. Pleasure is a lowly and petty thing, held in no esteem, common even to mute animals, to which the smallest and most contemptible creatures flock. Glory is a vain and fleeting thing, more fickle than the wind. Poverty is an evil to none

but those who resist it. Death is not an evil; why do you ask? It alone is the equitable law of humankind. Superstition is the error of a mind gone mad; it fears those it should love; it violates those it worships. For what difference does it make whether you deny the gods or defame them?"

[17] These things must be learned, nay, thoroughly learned by heart; philosophy should not be suggesting excuses for vice. A sick person has no hope of recovery if their doctor is urging them toward intemperance[4]. Farewell.

---

1. The sense seems to be to "spend now before death takes it.
2. Some later manuscripts read "tua morte" (at your death) instead of "tuamor" found in the earliest manuscripts.
3. The text of this sentence is uncertain in the manuscripts.
4. The text is uncertain here. The translation follows an emendation by Muretus.

LETTER 124

REASON AS THE KEY TO HUMAN EXCELLENCE

[1] I could recount to you many precepts of the ancients, if you did not shy away from such things and think it tiresome to examine subtle points. But you do not shy away, nor does any degree of subtlety deter you. It is not in keeping with your refined tastes to pursue only weighty matters with complete confidence[1]. What I appreciate is that you apply everything toward some edifying purpose and become annoyed only when hair-splitting leads nowhere. Which is not what I will strive to do now. The question is: is the good apprehended by feeling or by understanding? Connected with this is the idea that it does not exist in mute animals and infants.

[2] Those who place pleasure as the supreme good judge it to be perceptible by the senses, while we on the contrary deem the good to be intelligible, placing it in the mind. If the senses judged the good, we would reject no pleasure—for none fails to entice, none fails to delight—and on the other hand, we would willingly undergo no pain, for pain offends the senses.

[3] Moreover, those who are too fond of pleasure and those who fear pain above all else would not deserve reproach. Yet we condemn gluttons and the lustful, and we despise those who will dare nothing manly for fear of pain. But what sin are they committing, if they are

obeying the senses—that is, the judges of good and evil? For you have entrusted the senses with control over what to seek and what to avoid.

[4] But reason, of course, has been put in charge of this matter. Reason determines the happy life, virtue, morality—and likewise good and evil. Among pleasure-seekers, the basest part is allowed to give verdict on the higher, so that the senses, dull and sluggish faculties, slower in humans than other animals, pronounce on the good.

[5] What if one wished to distinguish minute objects not by sight but by touch? No other sense is finer or more precise than sight for discerning good and evil. You see the magnitude of their ignorance of truth, and how they have flung lofty and divine ideals into the dirt—those who rely on touch to judge the greatest good and evil. "But," they object, "just as every branch of knowledge and skill must begin with something plainly apparent and graspable by the senses, from which it may arise and grow, so too the happy life derives its foundation and starting point from things manifest and subject to sense-perception."

[6] "Indeed," I reply, "you Epicureans say that the happy life takes its start from manifest things."

[7] We say that things in accordance with nature are blessed. What is in accordance with nature is immediately and plainly apparent, just as what is whole. I do not call what is in accordance with nature, what befalls one from birth, good, but the beginning of good. You assign the highest good, pleasure, to infancy, so that the newborn begins there, where the perfected human arrives.

[8] You put the treetop in place of the root. If someone said that the infant, lying hidden in the mother's womb, still of uncertain sex[2], tender and imperfect and unformed, is already in some good, he would clearly seem to err. And yet how little difference is there between one who has just received life, and one who is a hidden burden of the maternal innards? Both are equally mature with respect to the understanding of good and evil, and the infant is no more capable of good than a tree or some mute animal.

Why then is good not present in tree and mute animal? Because neither has reason. For this cause it is not present in the infant either, for it too lacks reason; it will arrive at good when you have arrived at reason. There is some non-rational animal, there is some not-yet-rational, there is rational but imperfect; in none of these is good, reason brings that with itself.

[9] What then is the difference between those I have listed? In that which is non-rational, there will never be good. In that which is not yet rational, good cannot be present at that time. To be present in that which is rational but imperfect, good now can be, but is not.

[10] Thus I say, Lucilius: good is found not in any chance body, not at any chance age, and it is as far from infancy as last is from first, as perfect is from beginning. Therefore it is not in the tender, newly coalescing little body either. Why would it not be? No more than in the seed.

[11] If you said this, we recognize some good of tree and of seedling; this is not in the first leaf, which, sent forth, just then breaks the soil. There is some good of wheat; this is not yet in the milky grass nor when the soft ear emerges with its husk, but when summer and due maturity have ripened the grain. Just as all nature does not bring forth its own good unless perfected, so the good of a human is not in the human unless reason is perfected in him[3].

[12] But what is this good? I will tell you: a free mind, upright, subjecting other things to itself, itself subject to nothing. Infancy does not admit of this good; childhood does not hope for it; youth hopes wrongly for it. Old age is well off if it attains this good after long, focused study. If this is the good, it is also intelligible.

[13] "But," you say, "you have stated there is some good of trees, some of grass; therefore there can also be some good of infants." True good cannot in any way exist in mute animals, much less trees. That which is good in them is called good precariously. "What is it?" you ask. That which is according to the nature of each. Good can in no way fall to a mute animal; it belongs to a more blessed and better nature. Good does not exist where there is no place for reason.

[14] There are four natures: of the tree, the animal, man, and god. The latter two, which are rational, have the same nature, but differ in

that one is immortal and the other mortal. Therefore, the good of one, namely god, is perfected by nature; the other, man, by care. The rest are perfect only in their own nature, not truly perfect, lacking reason.

For that alone is perfect which is perfect according to universal nature, and universal nature is rational. Other things can be perfect in their own kind.

[15] In that which cannot contain a happy life, neither can that exist by which a happy life is produced. A happy life is produced by goods; therefore, good does not exist in a mute animal.

[16] A mute animal grasps present things by sense. It remembers past things when something occurs to remind the senses, like a horse remembers a road when brought back to its beginning. In the stable, truly, it has no memory of the road, however often trodden. But the third part of time, the future, does not pertain to mute animals.

[17] How, then, can the nature of those things seem perfect, which do not have the use of perfect time? For time consists of three parts: past, present, future. To animals is given only that which is heaviest in the course, the present. Memory of the past is rare and never recalled except by the occurrence of present things.

[18] Therefore, the good of a perfect nature cannot exist in an imperfect one. If such a nature possesses this good, then so do planted crops. I do not deny that dumb animals have great and excited impulses toward things that seem according to nature, but these impulses are disordered and turbulent. However, good is never disorderly or turbulent.

[19] "What then?" you ask. "Do dumb animals move in a disturbed and disordered way?" I would say that they move disturbedly and disorderly if their nature could comprehend order; as it is, they move according to their own nature. For that is disturbed which can at some time also be not disturbed; that is troubled which can be untroubled. No creature has a vice unless it can also have a virtue; such motion comes to dumb animals from their nature.

[20] But not to detain you too long, there will be some good in a dumb animal, there will be some virtue, there will be something

perfect—but not good absolutely, nor virtue, nor perfection. For these belong to rational beings alone, to whom it is given to know the why, how much, and how. Thus good exists in nothing except that in which reason exists.

[21] You ask what the point of this disputation is now, and how it will profit your mind? I say: it both exercises the mind and sharpens it, and in any case keeps it occupied with an honorable pursuit. But it also benefits by delaying those hastening toward depravity. Moreover, I say this: in no way can I benefit you more than by revealing to you your own good, by separating you from dumb animals, by placing you with God.

[22] Why, I ask, do you nourish and exercise the powers of the body? Nature has granted greater bodily powers to cattle and wild beasts. Why cultivate beauty? When you have done everything, you will be surpassed in comeliness by the dumb animals. Why arrange your hair with immense diligence? Though you spread it out like the Parthians, or bind it up like the Germans, or, as the Scythians do, let it fly loose, a thicker mane will toss on any horse, a more beautiful one will bristle on a lion's neck. When you have prepared yourself for speed, you will not be the equal of even a puny rabbit. Will you not, abandoning those things in which you must be surpassed while striving for what belongs to others, return to your own good?

[23] What, then, is this good? It is a mind that is perfected and pure, one that emulates the divine, rising above the merely human, placing nothing of its own outside itself. You are a rational being. So what is the good within you? Perfect reason. Do you summon reason to its ultimate end, nurturing its growth to the greatest extent possible? Judge yourself blessed when all your joy is born from reason, when you have faced what men dread, crave, or cherish, and found nothing—I do not say that you'd rather have, but that you'd even want.

[24] I will give you a brief formula by which to measure yourself, by which you may sense that you have become perfected: You will come to your own when you understand that those who are acclaimed as fortunate are actually most wretched. Farewell.

1. The precise meaning of "secure" is uncertain, with manuscript variants including "sicuti" and "sicut." The translation follows the emendation proposed by Buecheler.
2. The Erasmus edition has "incerti" (uncertain) here, while other manuscripts have "incepti" (begun).
3. Some later manuscripts add "illi" (in him) here, while earlier ones omit it.